TRIBAL PEOPLES AND DEVELOPMENT ISSUES

A Global Overview

Edited by

John H. Bodley
Washington State University

Mayfield Publishing Company
Mountain View, California

Library of Congress Cataloging in Publication Data

Tribal peoples and development issues [edited by] John H. Bodley.
    p.   cm.
  Bibliography: p.
  ISBN 0-87484-786-9
  1. Ethnicity. 2. Native races. 3. Acculturation. 4. Economic development. I. Bodley, John H.
GN495.6.T74 1987
305.8—dc 19   87-12508
                                                    CIP

Manufactured in the United States of America

10 9 8 7 6 5 4 3 2

Mayfield Publishing Company
1240 Villa Street
Mountain View, CA 94041

Sponsoring editor: Janet M. Beatty   Manuscript editor: Kathleen Engelberg   Typesetting: Text set in 10/12 Electra by TCSystems Printing and binding: Maple-Vail, 50# Decision Opaque Cover: An 1867 engraving titled "Conflict Between H.M.S. Cormorant and the Savages of Formosa." Courtesy of North Wind Picture Archives. Design by Cynthia Bassett

PREFACE

This book focuses on "tribals," sometimes called "indigenous peoples," "nations," or the "Fourth World." Before the intrusion of more powerful societies, these peoples lived in self-sufficient, small-scale, and unstratified societies. Only a few decades ago, many of these peoples were totally independent of state control, and, of course, a few remain autonomous. In fact, according to some estimates, 200 million tribals still exist. They clearly lead a very different way of life from that of urban residents of industrial societies or of the rural peasantry of the so-called "Third World" into which the tribals are rapidly being absorbed.

I use the term "tribal" reluctantly because of its imprecision. Technically, "tribal" refers to a nonhierarchical political organization that disappears the moment a tribe is conquered by a state; the tribes that national governments create for administrative purposes are not independent tribes in the original sense. The term "tribal," however, is well established and does highlight the distinctive cultural features of these societies that come under special pressure in the development context. While "tribal" may have negative connotations in some quarters, it should be obvious that I use it with no such implication. Alternative labels such as indigenous or Fourth World are also imprecise, and their use in this context is not as widely recognized.

Because development typically brings social disorganization, a decline in quality of life, and resource depletion in the tribal territory, tribals offer a major challenge to planners. Basic issues include the following: What is the quality of life of tribal cultures before development? How and why do development changes take place? What is the impact of development? What is the responsibility of national and international policy-makers toward tribals?

The debate is an old one, and its complex issues have not been resolved. It involves anthropologists, government administrators, missionaries, businesspeople, conservationists, and a variety of other scientists and explorers who have encountered tribal peoples. For the most part this anthology concentrates on the views and policies of nontribals toward tribals. I have included few examples of the directly expressed views of tribal peoples themselves, because my primary focus centers on the understandings that policymakers work with when they formulate policy. Their understandings, of course, often include assumptions about the wishes of tribals. The problem of how tribals express their views is addressed in part 7 under the topic "Human Rights and Political Struggle."

This book offers a broad cross section of published and previously unpublished case studies, policy positions, assessments, and recommendations. Many items are taken from conference papers and nonanthropological periodicals. I have drawn materials from throughout the world and from writings dating back to the mid–nineteenth century. More than half of the items, however, originally appeared within the past decade, and nearly a third date from the past five years. A wide range of tribal cultures is included, but most cases are drawn from the tribals of Amazonia, the Arctic, Australia, Melanesia, southern and southeastern Asia, and southern and eastern Africa.

This compilation neither documents the disastrous consequences of industrial expansion for tribal peoples, nor focuses primarily on culture change theory. It does include case studies that detail adverse impacts of development. My purpose is not to arouse outrage, however, nor to campaign for a particular policy approach, but rather to provide an overview of the issues and the diverse viewpoints that have been part of the policy debate. I see this as a source book of opinions, policies, and issues.

This collection is intended to complement my earlier work, *Victims of Progress*, which presents a broad overview of the interaction between tribals and civilization since 1820, particularly emphasizing the colonial period. *Victims* demonstrates that expanding industrial civilization destroys tribal cultures. Many contemporary tribal development issues receive relatively light coverage in *Victims*, although the second edition includes chapters on tribal political movements and nonnative support organizations. Anyone interested in examining closely related source materials that significantly extend the issues introduced in *Victims* will find *Tribal Peoples and Development Issues* especially useful. Of course either book will stand alone, but the two could easily be used simultaneously, because I have carefully avoided overlapping case studies. This book will be valuable for both graduate and undergraduate courses in culture change, economic development, contemporary problems, and in ethnographic survey courses or introductory anthropology courses that introduce these issues.

Most closely related to this book are probably the collections edited by Edward Spicer (1957) *Human Problems in Technological Change*, Paul Bohannan and Fred Plog (1967) *Beyond the Frontier*, and Ivan Brady and Barry Isaac (1975) *A Reader in Culture Change*. Yet no previous compilation has contained such a broad overview of the specific issues of tribals and development. Two recent collections, *Native Power*, edited by Jens Brosted (1985), and *Indigenous Peoples and the Nation-State*, edited by Noel Dyck (1985), also contain relevant contemporary case studies from a variety of perspectives. These issues certainly have critical implications for the peoples most directly involved, but they also hold general significance for students of anthropology. Tribal cultures still constitute the acknowledged core subject matter of anthropology.

ACKNOWLEDGMENTS

This collection grew out of my reading list for a graduate seminar, "Tribal Peoples and Development," which I taught in the spring of 1985 at Washington State University. Development of the course was supported in part by a grant from the International Program Development Office of Washington State University, which provided funds for graduate research assistant Tom Lamar, who worked on the early library phase of the project.

Many reviewers contributed thoughtful comments to this book, and I'd like to thank the following: James N. Anderson, University of California, Berkeley; Ruth M. Krulfeld, The George Washington University; Robert Lawless, University of Florida; Margarita B. Melville, Chicano Studies, University of California, Berkeley; Richard H. Moore, The Ohio State University; Paul Shankman, University of Colorado, Boulder; and George D. Westermark, Santa Clara University.

I attempted to contact the authors of the papers to get their approval, biographical information, or special comments. However, I was unable to contact several authors, and in such instances, the copyright holder gave approval independently of the author. Some authors may therefore be unaware that their material has been reprinted here, and I ask their indulgence.

To maximize the number of papers that could be included, I abridged many selections to focus more sharply on development issues, and in some cases, plates, tables, graphs, and maps were deleted at my discretion. In these cases, a reader may be rewarded by consulting the original source and examining the selection in its larger context. I have attempted to represent each selection fairly, and I am fully responsible for any misunderstanding that may result in the final product. Finally, I extend my gratitude to all those authors and publishers who have assisted me in this project.

John H. Bodley

CONTENTS

Part Seven
Human Rights and Political Struggle,   249

Part Eight
Parks, Conservation, and Tribals,   299

Introduction

Tribal Peoples and Development

The contemporary issue of tribal peoples and economic development can best be viewed in a broad historical context. The Neolithic world of 10,000 years ago was occupied by some 75 million people, organized into perhaps 150,000 tribal nations. These nations were politically autonomous, decentralized, and economically self-sufficient; they were small-scale communal societies with distinctive ways of life dependent on local ecosystems. The basic features of tribal nations were completely different from those of modern nation-states. These differences go far beyond the mere facts of "ethnicity," and they reflect a high degree of local autonomy. Particularly significant is the social equality found in tribal societies and the absence of leadership hierarchies and favored access by special classes to natural resources. Tribal nations were self-regulating systems that provided maximum independence in decision making at the lowest levels of society.

The archaeological record suggests that tribal nations were relatively secure adaptations that effectively satisfied basic human needs. The selections in part I address the specific issue of how well traditional tribal cultures work, even among ethnographically known modern groups. This is a particularly important issue because development changes are supposed to improve people's lives. In many parts of the world archaeological sequences reveal millenia of continuous occupation by tribal societies with only minor shifts in subsistence, which reflect fluctuation in the environment. There was, however, a steady, often barely perceptible trend toward intensification of subsistence effort and increased population density. This long-term trend culminated in dramatic changes in the Neolithic world some 6000 years ago when the first tribal nations became nation-states.

1

The new nation-states represented evolutionary "progress." They were larger, politically centralized, class-based societies with expansionist tendencies. It is not clear that states were an improvement in terms of satisfaction of human needs, because social hierarchy often meant that social benefits were inequitably distributed. States were also inherently unstable. Their appearance suddenly made the world unsafe for tribal nations. As states expanded in search of new resources, threatened tribes either became states in order to preserve their nationality or were absorbed or extinguished and their surviving populations converted into peasants. The early states spread slowly until the beginning of the industrial era, at which time they controlled nearly half the globe. Development progress over the past 200 years has seen hundreds of tribes extinguished along with millions of tribal peoples.

Today only a handful of independent tribal nations exist, and several million recent descendants of former tribal nations remain as culturally distinct colonized peoples who still aspire to autonomy. They are commonly called "indigenous peoples" because they are the original inhabitants of their territories. However, we lack precise terminology that takes into account the differing histories, cultures, political statuses, and aspirations of these diverse peoples. The state often designates conquered tribal nations as "tribes" for administrative purposes, but they become "peasants" when dependency and integration are complete and they remain on the land. When they move to urban areas, they are often called "ethnic minorities."

Historically, when states began to assume effective control over the territory of tribal nations and to extract resources from it for state interests, tribal nations found it difficult to sustain their original adaptive systems. They suffered demographic upheavals, resource depletion, internal inequality and conflict, and increased pathologies. They were often locked into grossly inequitable and discriminatory economic relationships with the dominant state society, and they were reduced to insecurity and poverty. This pattern of disruption and impoverishment continues to be the dominant outcome of modern development programs directed at tribal peoples. Indeed, this is one of the major dilemmas of development. Many of the selections that follow document this pattern and discuss possible ways of improving the situation.

Today there are some 200 million people who are members of recently conquered or still autonomous tribal nations. Of course, states permit few of these "indigenous peoples" to maintain their decentralized, communal adaptations, but much of the original self-sufficient pattern remains. Today's indigenous people continue to assert their autonomy, and their existence represents a major challenge to state policy makers both because independent tribal nations were so successful, yet so different from states, and because their autonomy claims are basically just.

THE INTEGRATION POLICY

Throughout this century people of good will have advocated a development policy of integrating tribal people into the dominant state society and economy as ethnic minorities while attempting to minimize the human costs incurred in the process. Ideally, this would mean preserving the "best" features of the traditional culture and eliminating those features that might be considered obstacles to economic progress. Integration has been the predominant solution to the challenge posed by the existence of indigenous peoples when direct extermination or blatant exploitation were acknowledged to be inhumane and inefficient. Various forms of development aid, education, protective legislation, and health and welfare programs have been implemented to achieve successful minority status for tribal peoples. Clearly, such efforts have had many positive results and have eased much pain; it is not surprising that integration policies continue to dominate the development field. However, when integration is pursued without a clear understanding of the original features of the indigenous community that contributed to its well-being, serious harm can easily be done. A major problem with development policies promoting integration is that their aim is usually to benefit individuals, often at the expense of the community. When development undermines a community's ability to defend and manage its own resources, or when it is imposed by outsiders, genuine benefits can hardly be expected.

For their part indigenous peoples have consistently resisted integration programs, realizing that they are a further threat to their independent existence. It can be assumed that people only surrender political autonomy under duress. Furthermore, the material benefits actually derived from this kind of development have seldom outweighed the costs. Given the apparent shortcomings of integration approaches to development, it is appropriate to examine the basic assumptions underlying them. These assumptions appear to include at least the following:

1. The way of life of indigenous peoples is materially inadequate.
2. Integration will improve their quality of life.
3. Interest in new technology on the part of indigenous peoples reflects a desire for integration.
4. Progress is inevitable.

Although all of these assumptions may be valid in certain respects, they are also very shortsighted, and when they go unchallenged there is little basis for dramatically different policy alternatives. Let us consider the first assumption. It is apparent that indigenous peoples themselves do not find their way of life materially inadequate when they are still in control of their undepleted natural resources. Poverty is a product of the state, created by class systems that impose relative deprivation and cause resource depletion.

These processes are endemic in modern states but conspicuously absent or minimal in tribal nations.

The assumption that integration into state society will improve the quality of life for indigenous peoples requires that they are indeed "successfully" integrated somewhere above the lowest levels of society. In reality very few indigenous peoples can hope for such "success." Integration into the impoverished classes is likely to result in a significant decline in quality of life, and this is clearly reflected in health and nutrition.

The fact that indigenous peoples universally come to desire industrially manufactured goods such as knives, guns, and metal pots is invariably interpreted as both proof of the inadequacy of their way of life and a vote for integration into the dominant society. Although it is certainly true that new technologies are often seen as advantageous, when indigenous peoples are still in control of their lives and territories, they select imported items that enhance their original adaptation. Some items, such as guns, may even be used to discourage outside intrusion. Of course the process of acquiring imports and actually using them may set in motion detrimental changes, but such results are rarely foreseen.

The argument that progress is inevitable actually represents the belief that there can be no place in today's world for independent tribal nations. It rests on all the preceding ethnocentric assumptions and implies a sort of Darwinian notion of "survival of the fittest." This view certainly reflects recent historical trends, but it ignores the fact that indigenous peoples have only rarely surrendered their autonomy voluntarily. "Progress" has been forced on them because expanding states required the resources they controlled. Such expansion clearly must have limits, and limits must be a matter of state policy. Ultimately, even states will be forced to acknowledge the value of careful resource management for genuine, sustained yield production. Ironically, the resources now controlled by indigenous communities are there only because they have been managed carefully by self-sufficient communal economies. Integration designed to exploit those resources for outside interests undermines local management and in the long run also threatens the resources. To argue that this is an inevitable process is both arrogant and shortsighted; it can also be a self-fulfilling prophecy that effectively blocks significant policy changes.

SELF-DETERMINATION

Perhaps the most significant new element confronting contemporary development planners is the directly expressed political demand of indigenous peoples themselves to retain their autonomy and to control their own future development. Tribal autonomy movements in Africa, the Philippines, India, North America, Central America, Indonesia, and Australia are discussed in parts VI and VII. These are clearly a major force for change and a genuine expression of the will of tribal peoples. In response, some countries have already begun to modify the standard integration approach to reflect the possibility of "self-determination" by tribal peoples. This new approach represents a growing recognition that indigenous peoples have been systematically denied their basic human rights to occupy their traditional lands and to enjoy their own way of life. According to this view, tribal peoples have been politically oppressed and economically exploited as virtual "internal colonies" within the countries that claim control over them. Ideally, self-determination would put tribal peoples in charge of their internal affairs and territorial resources again. Even though this sort of self-determination has a clear basis in international law and human rights resolutions and is clearly in line with the wishes of indigenous people, states have difficulty relinquishing power of any sort to subgroups. Where self-determination has been adopted as official policy, it is granted within a very narrow framework defined by the state. Even so, this is clearly a significant new policy direction and raises a whole series of new issues. Many of these questions are explored in the last three parts of this collection.

Complete self-determination for indigenous people would involve full ownership of their traditional territory as well as political control within it. They would be free to manage their resources as they saw fit. They could bar entrance to undesirable outsiders and block the extraction of resources or the intrusion of dams and highways. They would also be free to maintain a self-sufficient, communal socioeconomic system according to their own cultural traditions and social control mechanisms.

Achieving any degree of self-determination, particularly where control over valuable resources may be involved, is clearly an uphill struggle for indigenous peoples; it may also involve serious risks. Indigenous peoples may have little real political or economic power available to them, and they are likely to be at a distinct disadvantage in any struggle with the state for recognition of their rights. The need for political mobilization extending far beyond the traditional experience or capability of the society may encourage indigenous groups to form alliances with outside groups who may have their own agendas. Furthermore, political mobilization may in itself be incompatible with a decentralized, communal way of life. In spite of these obvious difficulties, the costs of integration policies and the potential rewards of self-determination are so high that where there is any possibility of success, indigenous peoples invariably choose it over integration.

The routes to self-determination for indigenous peoples are diverse. For example, those few groups who have not yet surrendered their autonomy, such as the Yanomami of Amazonia, might simply have their present independent status officially sanctioned, without ever going through a political mobilization self-defense process. For such special groups biosphere reserves, which are designed to preserve entire ecosystems, might be appropriate mechanisms. Other groups might require the restoration of lost territory and the creation of unique political structures, such as special provinces, to safeguard their interests.

Any suggestion that indigenous communities be allowed to either maintain or regain their distinctive self-sufficient, communal pattern may be met with a variety of misleading and irrelevant criticisms. For example, critics may misrepresent self-determination as a "human zoo" approach, falsely assuming that it is based on naive assumptions such as the following:

Indigenous peoples are noble savages.

Culture is or should be static.

Indigenous peoples must be isolated.

Cultures are entities to be protected.

It can then easily be argued that there are no noble savages, no static cultures, and no isolated peoples and that culture itself is merely an abstraction. Furthermore, it might be argued, self-determination is politically unrealistic idealism. Of course, the real issue is whether communities will have the right to control their own lives within their own territories. It just happens that the way of life of indigenous people may be both very different and very successful. Whether indigenous peoples are noble savages, how much they change, how isolated they may be, and whether their way of life is protected are issues for them to decide in their own way.

Some official agencies have already adopted the language of self-determination but unfortunately not the substance. For example, the World Bank advocates official support for self-determination and "cultural autonomy" for indigenous peoples. However, it does not envision that indigenous peoples will actually be able to control their own resources; it sees them instead as successfully integrated ethnic minorities. Others argue piously that it is wrong to allow a few people to maintain "inefficient" subsistence economies that lock up resources that might be used more profitably by the impoverished majority. This is of course the very heart of the issue, and it focuses attention on the real problem, which lies within the nation-state itself. Inequitable and imbalanced growth in the nation-state generates frontier expansion and converts the territory of indigenous peoples into internal colonies open for exploitation. Culture change is indeed required if indigenous peoples are to cease being victims of progress, but it is the state itself and its policies that must change.

In conclusion, I argue that the long-established policy of integration fails to deal adequately with the real issues of indigenous peoples as victims of progress. Rather than integration, genuine self-determination should be promoted as the most just, humane, and intelligent policy. There is certainly a basis for hope, even though we know that historically indigenous peoples have been exterminated and/or absorbed by expanding states. This has been a global process, and it has been official state policy. However, neither the policies nor the victims have always been passive. The victims have often resisted, and in this century we have seen policies toward indigenous peoples move steadily, from conquest to the extension of humane treatment, to an emphasis on integration, to the preservation of ethnic identity, to a gradual recognition that self-determination may be a legitimate human right of indigenous communities.

We have thus come almost full circle to a point at which some states may be prepared to permit the existence of independent indigenous nations. Such a self-determination approach must surely be the most ideal and humane policy. Although integration policies remain the dominant approach throughout the world, over the past decade the whole question of the status of indigenous people has been undergoing intensive reassessment. Full acceptance of self-determination policies is hampered by numerous conceptual and practical issues, but these issues are now being examined. As a contribution to this reassessment process, this collection of readings systematically reviews the historic pattern of interaction between tribal peoples and state societies and examines the dominant trends in state policy toward indigenous peoples throughout the world during this century.

I

Quality of Tribal Life

It makes little sense to talk about development issues and tribal peoples without a clear concept of what tribal peoples and their cultures are in fact like. The stated objective of most development projects is to improve quality of life, but ironically, as selections in later parts demonstrate, quite the opposite usually happens. Development, as it is typically promoted, lowers the quality of life of tribal peoples and quite literally impoverishes them. Why this is so should be a major concern for development planners. Resolving this dilemma requires an understanding of the specific features of tribal life that might be affected by development changes before the changes occur and an understanding of the actual quality of life prior to intervention by outsiders.

There is of course tremendous diversity among the groups treated here as "tribal," yet they do share a variety of features before the loss of their political and economic independence that results from the intrusion of state governments. In the tradition of Robert Redfield, I find it useful to treat tribal cultures as an ideal type representing a maximum contrast to nation-state cultures. This is an oversimplification, but it does help us understand the impact of development. In this brief introduction to part I, I will consider only some of the most obvious demographic, social, economic, and ecological features that relate to development issues.

Demographically, tribal populations are small-scale and low density. It is not unusual for the total population to number only 500 people with a density of only half a person per square kilometer. This means that the population may be occupying a considerable amount of territory that will appear to interested outsiders to be underutilized and there will be few people on hand to defend it. In spite of the global trend toward gradually increasing population density, local tribal groups often exhibit remarkable population stability; indeed, many specific cultural practices that serve as stabilizing mechanisms have been identified. Development intervention tends to disturb prior balances by first elevating mortality and then eliminating fertility controls, so that populations may either disappear or dramatically increase.

Tribal social systems normally lack social classes, although some, such as Pacific island chiefdoms, may be highly ranked. The crucial point for development issues is that tribal societies are basically communally organized, kin-based systems in which people are differentiated by age, sex, and personal characteristics, not primarily by ownership of property or by productive resources. Tribal pastoralists, however, who subsist on herds of domestic livestock, may distinguish more "wealthy" individuals and show some characteristics of incipient social classes. Typically, land in a tribal society is communally owned, and all individuals have access to the natural resources needed to support a family. Goods move on the basis of reciprocal exchanges in the absence of markets and true money. Production and consumption decisions are usually made at the household level, and local communities are largely self-sufficient, although regional systems for exchanging people and materials may be very important. It follows that tribal communities are highly dependent on local ecosystems and renewable resources. Tribals typically increase ecosystem productivity through a variety of management practices.

This kind of socioeconomic system obviously has a long record of satisfying human needs in a very egalitarian way that provides great security. Development programs tend to threaten all of these key socioeconomic features, without understanding or appreciating them. Development means participation in market economies that assume private ownership of key resources and great differences in wealth. The development of natural resources for export in order to generate individual wealth becomes the rationale for action under the development program, but this is in total contrast to the rationale of the tribal system. The two systems are fundamentally incompatible from the start; it is virtually certain that if outside interests decree the kind of development changes that occur, the results will be very destructive.

The first selection in this part is Redfield's classic treatment of the features of tribal cultures, or "folk societies," as he calls them, that distinguish them as ideal types from urban civilizations. In the second selection Sahlins focuses on the material conditions of hunting cultures, arguing that they are doing very well. Finally, Jelliffe reports that the Hadza, a specific group of hunter-gatherers, proved to be in excellent health. One might even conclude that affluent and healthy tribal societies are already "developed" according to the standard criteria that development planners employ.

1   The Folk Society

ROBERT REDFIELD

University of Chicago anthropologist Robert Redfield (1897–1958) was one of the founders of the anthropological study of "acculturation," or contemporary culture change in rural communities. Redfield is well known for his fieldwork in Mexico, which included extensive field studies of the Nahuatl village of Tepoztlan in Morelos in 1926–27 and the Maya village of Chan Kom in Yucatan in the 1930s. In 1948 he restudied Chan Kom to assess development-related changes. Redfield's paper is a classic attempt to define the characteristics of tribal cultures, which he calls "folk societies," in contrast to urban civilization. In his introduction, which is not included in this abridged selection, Redfield emphasizes that he is constructing an "ideal type" based on features drawn from many "folk societies" and representing logical opposites to corresponding features of urban societies. In the process he identifies most of the key features of tribals that are in fact critical to an understanding of development issues. Tribals are small, relatively isolated, homogeneous, integrated, nonliterate, self-sufficient systems. Each tribal system is "a little world off by itself." Peasants by contrast are dependent on cities and are moving along a continuum of increasing dependency. In Redfield's terms development would be the process by which tribal peoples (the folk), loose their unique features and become dependent peasants.

The folk society is a small society. There are no more people in it than can come to know each other well, and they remain in long association with each other. Among the Western Shoshone the individual parental family was the group which went about, apart from other families, collecting food; a group of families would assemble and so remain for a few weeks, from time to time, to hunt together; during the winter months such a group of families would form a single camp.[1] Such a temporary village included perhaps a hundred people. The hunting or food-collecting bands considered by Steward, representing many parts of the world, contained, in most cases, only a few score people.[2] A Southwestern Pueblo contained no more than a few thousand persons.

The folk society is an isolated society. Probably there is no real society whose members are in complete ignorance of the existence of people other than themselves; the Andamanese, although their islands were avoided by navigators for centuries, knew of outsiders and occasionally came in contact

Reprinted from *American Journal of Sociology* 52, no. 4 (1947): 295–98, by permission of the University of Chicago Press.

with Malay or Chinese visitors.[3] Nevertheless, the folk societies we know are made up of people who have little communication with outsiders, and we may conceive of the ideal folk society as composed of persons having communication with no outsider.

This isolation is one half of a whole of which the other half is intimate communication among the members of the society. A group of recent castaways is a small and isolated society, but it is not a folk society; and if the castaways have come from different ships and different societies, there will have been no previous intimate communication among them, and the society will not be composed of people who are much alike.

May the isolation of the folk society be identified with the physical immobility of its members? In building this ideal type, we may conceive of the members of the society as remaining always within the small territory they occupy. There are some primitive peoples who have dwelt from time immemorial in the same small valley, and who rarely leave it.[4] Certain of the Pueblos of the American Southwest have been occupied by the same people or their descendants for many generations. On the other hand, some of the food-collecting peoples, such as the Shoshone Indians and certain aborigines of Australia, move about within a territory of very considerable extent; and there are Asiatic folk groups that make regular seasonal migrations hundreds of miles in extent.

It is possible to conceive of the members of such a society as moving about physically without communicating with members of other groups than their own. Each of the Indian villages of the midwest highlands of Guatemala is a folk society distinguishable by its customs and even by the physical type of its members from neighboring villages, yet the people are great travelers, and in the case of one of the most distinct communities, Chichicastenango, most of the men travel far and spend much of their time away from home.[5] This does not result, however, in much intimate communication between those traveling villagers and other peoples. The gipsies have moved about among the various peoples of the earth for generations, and yet they retain many of the characteristics of a folk society.

Through books the civilized people communicate with the minds of other people and other times, and an aspect of the isolation of the folk society is the absence of books. The folk communicate only by word of mouth; therefore the communication upon which understanding is built is only that which takes place among neighbors, within the little society itself. The folk has no access to the thought and experience of the past, whether of other peoples or of their own ancestors, such as books provide. Therefore, oral tradition has no check or competitor. Knowledge of what has gone before reaches no further back than memory and speech between old and young can make it go; behind "the time of our grandfathers" all is legendary and vague. With no form of belief established by written record, there can be no historical sense, such as civilized people have, no theology, and no basis for science in recorded experiment. The only form of accumulation of experience, except the tools and other enduring articles of manufacture, is the increase of wisdom which comes as the individual lives longer; therefore the old, knowing more than the young can know until they too have lived that long, have prestige and authority.

The people who make up a folk society are much alike. Having lived in long intimacy with one another, and with no others, they have come to form a single biological type. The somatic homogeneity of local, inbred populations has been noted and studied. Since the people communicate with one another and with no others, one man's learned ways of doing and thinking are the same as another's. Another way of putting this is to say that in the ideal folk society, what one man knows and believes is the same as what all men know and believe. Habits are the same as customs. In real fact, of course, the differences among individuals in a primitive group and the different chances of experience prevent this ideal state of things from coming about. Nevertheless, it is near enough to the truth for the student of a real folk society to report it fairly well by learning what goes on in the minds of a few of its members, and a primitive group has been presented, although sketchily, as learned about from a single member. The similarity among the members is found also as one generation is compared with its successor. Old people find young people doing, as they grow up, what the old people did at the same age, and what they have come to think right and proper. This is another way of saying that in such a society there is little change.

The members of the folk society have a strong sense of belonging together. The group which an outsider might recognize as composed of similar persons different from members of other groups is also the group of people who see their own resemblances and feel correspondingly united. Communicating intimately with each other, each has a strong claim on the sympathies of the others. Moreover against such knowledge as they have of societies other than their own, they emphasize their own mutual likeness and value themselves as compared with others. They say of themselves "we" as against all others, who are "they."[6]

Thus we may characterize the folk society as small, isolated, nonliterate, and homogeneous, with a strong sense of group solidarity. Are we not soon to acknowledge the simplicity of the technology of the ideal folk society? Something should certainly be said about the tools and tool-making of this generalized primitive group, but it is not easy to assign a meaning to "simple," in connection with technology which will do justice to the facts as known from the real folk societies. The preciseness with which each tool, in a large number of such tools, meets its needs in the case of the Eskimo, for example, makes one hesitate to use the word "simple." Some negative statements appear to be safe: secondary and tertiary tools—tools to make tools— are relatively few as compared with primary tools; there is no making of artifacts by multiple, rapid, machine manufacture; there is little or no use of natural power.

There is not much division of labor in the folk society: what one person does is what another does. In the ideal folk society all the tools and ways of production are shared by everybody. The "everybody" must mean "every adult man" or "every adult woman," for the obvious exception to the homogeneity of the folk society lies in the differences between what men do and know and what women do and know. These differences are clear and unexceptional (as compared with our modern urban society where they are less so). "Within the local group there is no such thing as a division of labor save as between the sexes," writes Radcliffe-Brown about the Andaman Islanders. " . . . Every man is expected to be able to hunt pig, to harpoon turtle and to catch fish, and also to cut a canoe, to make bows and arrows and all the other objects that are made by men."[7] So all men share the same interests and have, in general, the same experience of life.

We may conceive, also, of the ideal folk society as a group economically independent of all others: the people produce what they consume and consume what they produce. Few, if any, real societies are completely in this situation; some Eskimo groups perhaps most closely approach it. Although each little Andamanese band could get along without getting anything from any other, exchange of goods occurred between bands by a sort of periodic gift-giving.

The foregoing characterizations amount, roughly, to saying that the folk society is a little world off by itself, a world in which the recurrent problems of life are met by all its members in much the same way. This statement, while correct enough, fails to emphasize an important, perhaps the important, aspect of the folk society. The ways in which the members of the society meet the recurrent problems of life are conventionalized ways; they are the results of long intercommunication within the group in the face of these problems; and these conventionalized ways have become interrelated within one another so that they constitute a coherent and self-consistent system. Such a system is what we mean in saying that the folk society is characterized by "a culture." A culture is an organization or integration of conventional understandings. It is, as well, the acts and the objects, in so far as they represent the type characteristic of that society, which express and maintain these understandings. In the folk society this integrated whole, this system, provides for all the recurrent needs of the individual from birth to death and of the society through the seasons and the years. The society is to be described, and distinguished from others, largely by presenting this system. . . .

NOTES

1. Julian Steward, *Basin-Plateau Aboriginal Sociopolitical Groups* (Smithsonian Institution, Bureau of American Ethnology, Bull. 120 [Washington: Government Printing Office, 1938]), pp. 230–34.

2. Julian Steward, "Economic and Social Basis of Primitive Bands," *Essays in Anthropology Presented to A. L. Kroeber* (Berkeley: University of California Press, 1936), pp. 341–42.

3. A. R. Radcliffe-Brown. *The Andaman Islanders* (Cambridge: At the University Press, 1933), pp. 6–9.

4. A. L. Kroeber, *Handbook of Indians of California* (Smithsonian Institution, Bureau of American Ethnology, Bull. 78 [Washington: Government Printing Office, 1925]), p. 13.

5. Robert Redfield, "Primitive Merchants of Guatemala," *Quarterly Journal of Inter-American Relations*, I, No. 4, 42–56.

6. W. G. Sumner, *Folkways* (Boston: Ginn & Co., 1907), pp. 13–15.

7. Radcliffe-Brown, *op. cit.*, p. 42.

2 Notes on the Original Affluent Society

MARSHALL SAHLINS

The popular view of life in a tribal society with a subsistence economy has always been that it was terribly difficult and unpleasant. This assumption was well established in anthropology for many years, and it still underlies the thinking of many development planners. Even evolutionary anthropologists assumed that technological progress was driven by material necessity and retarded by ignorance. The simpler the economy, the more precarious the existence. The possibility that simple hunter-gatherers, organized in bands, might actually enjoy a good life was officially recognized by anthropologists at the "Man the Hunter" symposium held in Chicago in 1965. This conference brought together 75 researchers from around the world, including many who had conducted fieldwork among hunter-gatherers. A variety of dramatic new perspectives on hunting and gathering emerged from the conference papers and the discussion. The paper presented by Marshall Sahlins proposing that simple hunter-gatherer bands represented the original "affluent society" has become a classic. Sahlins reverses conventional wisdom and proposes that evolution has been downhill in terms of human welfare. An expanded version of this argument appears as the first chapter of Sahlins' book *Stone Age Economics*, published in 1972.

Recent critics of the "affluent society" theory emphasize that this view is an oversimplification based on a biased sample and tends to ignore the fact that shortages did occur at times. It is also clear that not all hunter-gatherer societies fit this model. However, the basic argument is valid.

Marshall Sahlins, "Notes on the Original Affluent Society," in *Man the Hunter*, ed. Richard Lee and Irven DeVore (New York: Aldine Publishing Co., 1968), 85–89. Copyright © 1968 by Wenner-Gren Foundation for Anthropological Research, Inc.

Sahlins is a prominent American anthropologist and the author of numerous books and articles. His primary fieldwork was in Fiji. He received his Ph.D. from Columbia University in 1954 and taught at the University of Michigan from 1957 to 1974. He has been at the University of Chicago since 1974.

I should like to pick a point that is embedded in Colin Turnbull's discussion, implied in Suttles', elaborated in Lee's, and given ultimate explanation I think in Washburn's comments, particularly his suggestion that a 20–30 per cent use of productive capacity may prove quite adaptive over the long run. What I want to talk about is, as it were, the inner meaning of running below capacity, the consequences for the quality of hunting-gathering economical life.

If economics is the dismal science, the study of hunting-gathering economies must be its most advanced branch. Almost totally committed to the argument that life was hard in the Paleolithic, our textbooks compete to convey a sense of impending doom, leaving the student to wonder not only how hunters managed to make a living, but whether, after all, this was living? The specter of starvation stalks the stalker in these pages. His technical incompetence is said to enjoin continuous work just to survive, leaving him without respite from the food quest and without the leisure to "build culture." Even so, for his efforts he pulls the lowest grades in thermodynamics—less energy harnessed per capita per year than any other mode of production. And in treatises on economic development, he is condemned to play the role of bad example, the so-called "subsistence economy."

It will be extremely difficult to correct this traditional wisdom. Perhaps then we should phrase the necessary revisions in the most shocking terms possible: that this was, when you come to think of it, the original affluent society. By common understanding an affluent society is one in which all the people's wants are easily satisfied; and though we are pleased to consider this happy condition the unique achievement of industrial civilization, a better case can be made for hunters and gatherers, even many of the marginal ones spared to ethnography. For wants are "easily satisfied," either by producing much or desiring little, and there are, accordingly, two possible roads to affluence. The Galbraithean course makes assumptions peculiarly appropriate to market economies, that man's wants are great, not to say infinite, whereas his means are limited, although improvable. Thus the gap between means and ends can eventually be narrowed by industrial productivity, at least to the extent that "urgent" goods became abundant. But there is also a Zen solution to scarcity and affluence, beginning from premises opposite from our own, that human material ends are few and finite and technical means unchanging but on the whole adequate. Adopting the Zen strategy, a people can enjoy an unparalleled material plenty, though perhaps only a low standard of living. That I think describes the hunters.[1]

The traditional dismal view of the hunter's fix is pre-anthropological. It goes back to the time Adam Smith was writing, and maybe to a time before anyone was writing. But anthropology, especially evolutionary anthropology, found it congenial, even necessary theoretically, to adopt the same tone of reproach. Archeologists and ethnologists had become Neolithic revolutionaries, and in their enthusiasm for the revolution found serious shortcomings in the Old (Stone Age) Regime. Scholars extolled a Neolithic Great Leap Forward. Some spoke of a changeover from human effort to domesticated energy sources, as if people had been liberated by a new labor-saving device, although in fact the basic power resources remained exactly the same, plants and animals, the development occurring rather in techniques of appropriation (i.e., domestication. Moreover, archeological research was beginning to suggest that the decisive gains came in stability of settlement and gross economic product, rather than productivity of labor).

But evolutionary theory is not entirely to blame. The larger economic context in which it operates, "as if by an invisible hand," promotes the same dim conclusions about the hunting life. Scarcity is the peculiar obsession of a business economy, the calculable condition of all who participate in it. The market makes freely available a dazzling array of products all these "good things" within a man's reach—but never his grasp, for one never has enough to buy everything. To exist in a market economy is to live out a double tragedy, beginning in inadequacy and ending in deprivation. All economic activity starts from a position of shortage: whether as producer, consumer, or seller of labor, one's resources are insufficient to the possible uses and satisfactions. So one comes to a conclusion—"you pays your money and you takes your choice." But then, every acquisition is simultaneously a deprivation, for every purchase of something is a denial of something else that could have been had instead. (The point is that if you buy one kind of automobile, say a Plymouth fastback, you cannot also have a Ford Mustang—and I judge from the TV commercials that the deprivation involved is more than material.) Inadequacy is the judgment decreed by our economy, and thus the axiom of our economics: the application of scarce means against alternate ends. We stand sentenced to life at hard labor. It is from this anxious vantage that we look back on the hunter. But if modern man, with all his technical advantages, still hasn't got the wherewithal, what chance has this naked savage with his puny bow and arrow? Having equipped the hunter with bourgeois impulses and Paleolithic tools, we judge his situation hopeless in advance.

Scarcity is not an intrinsic property of technical means. It is a relation between means and ends. We might entertain the empirical possibility that hunters are in business for their health, a finite objective, and bow and arrow are adequate to that end. A fair case can be made that hunters often work much less than we do, and rather than a grind the food quest is intermittent, leisure is abundant, and there is more sleep in the daytime per capita than in any other conditions of society. (Perhaps certain traditional formulae are better inverted: the amount of work per capita increases with the evolution of culture and the amount of leisure per capita decreases.) Moreover, hunters seem neither harassed nor anxious. A certain confidence, at least in many cases, attends their economic attitudes and decisions. The way they dispose of food on hand, for example—as if they had it made.

This is the case even among many present marginal hunters—who hardly constitute a fair test of Paleolithic economy but something of a supreme test. Considering the poverty in which hunter and gatherers live in theory, it comes as a surprise that Bushmen who live in the Kalahari enjoy "a kind of material plenty" (Marshall, 1961, p. 243). Marshall is speaking of non-subsistence production; in this context her explication seems applicable beyond the Bushmen. She draws attention to the technical simplicity of the non-subsistence sector: the simple and readily available raw materials, skills, and tools. But most important, wants are restricted: a few people are happy to consider few things their good fortune. The restraint is imposed by nomadism. Of the hunter, it is truly said that this wealth is a burden (at least for his wife). Goods and mobility are therefore soon brought into contradiction, and to take liberties with a line of Lattimore's, the pure nomad remains a poor nomad. It is only consistent with their mobility, as many accounts directly say, that among hunters needs are limited, avarice inhibited, and—Warner (1937 [1958], p. 137) makes this very clear for the Murngin—portability is a main value in the economic scheme of things.

A similar case of affluence without abundance can be made for the subsistence sector. McCarthy and McArthur's time-motion study in Arnhem Land (1960) indicates the food quest is episodic and discontinuous, and per capita commitment to it averages less than four hours a day (see accompanying Figs. 1 and 2). The amount of daytime sleep and rest is unconscionable: clearly, the aborigines fail to "build culture" not from lack of time but from idle hands. McCarthy and McArthur also suggest that the people are working under capacity—they might have easily procured more food; that they are able to support unproductive adults—who may, however, do some craft work; and that getting food was not strenuous or exhausting. The Arnhem Land study, made under artificial conditions and based only on short-run observations, is plainly inconclusive in itself. Nevertheless, the Arnhem Land data are echoed in reports of other Australians and other hunters. Two famous explorers of the earlier nineteenth century made estimates of the same magnitude for the aborigines' subsistence activities: two to four hours a day (Eyre, 1845, 2, pp. 252, 255; Grey, 1841, 2, pp. 261–63). Slash-and-burn agriculture, incidentally, may be more labor-intensive: Conklin, for example, figures that 1,200 man hours per adult per year are given among the Hanunóo simply to agriculture (Conklin, 1957, p. 151: this figure excludes other food-connected activities, whereas the Australian data include time spent in the preparation of food as well as its acquisition). The Arnhem Landers' punctuation of steady work with sustained idleness is also widely attested in Australia and beyond. In Lee's paper he reported that

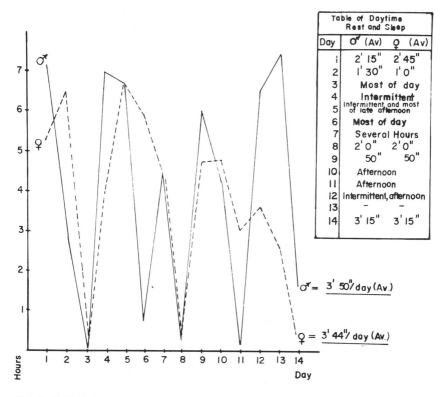

FIGURE 1
Hours per day in food-connected activities: Fish Creek Group
Source: Constructed from McCarthy and McArthur, 1960, p. 190.

productive members of !Kung Bushman camps spend two to three days per week in subsistence. We have heard similar comments in other papers at the symposium. Hadza women were said to work two hours per day on the average in gathering food, and one concludes from James Woodburn's excellent film that Hadza men are much more preoccupied with games of chance than with chances of game.

In addition, evidence on hunter-gatherers' economic attitudes and decisions should be brought to bear. Harassment is not implied in the descriptions of their nonchalant movements from camp to camp, nor indeed is the familiar condemnations of their laziness. A certain issue is posed by exasperated comments on the prodigality of hunters, their inclination to make a feast of everything on hand; as if, one Jesuit said of the Montagnais, "the game they were to hunt was shut up in a stable" (Le Jeune's *Relation* of 1634, in Kenton, 1927, 1, p. 182). "Not the slightest thought of, or care for, what the morrow may bring forth," wrote Spencer and Gillen (1899, p. 53).

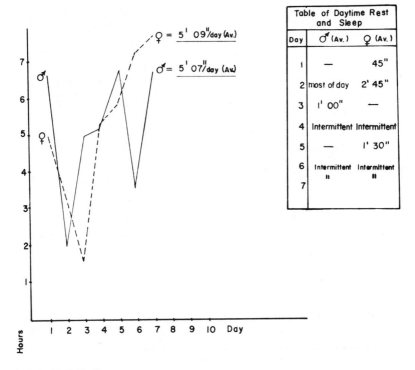

FIGURE 2

Hours per day in food-connected activities: Hemple Bay Group

Source: Constructed from McCarthy and McArthur, 1960, p. 191.

Two interpretations of this supposed lack of foresight are possible: either they are fools, or they are not worried—that is, as far as they are concerned, the morrow will bring more of the same. Rather than anxiety, it would seem the hunters have a confidence born of affluence, of a condition in which all the people's wants (such as they are) are generally easily satisfied. This confidence does not desert them during hardship. It can carry them laughing through periods that would try even a Jesuit's soul, and worry him so that—as the Indians warn—he could become sick:

> I saw them [the Montagnais] in their hardships and their labors, suffer with cheerfulness. . . . I found myself, with them, threatened with great suffering; they said to me, "We shall be sometimes two days, sometimes three, without eating, for lack of food; take courage, *Chihine*, let thy soul be strong to endure suffering and hardship; keep thyself from being sad, otherwise thou will be sick; see how we do not cease to laugh, although we have little to eat" (Le Jeune's *Relation* of 1634, in Kenton, 1927, 1, p. 129).

Again on another occasion Le Jeune's host said to him: "Do not let thyself be cast down, take courage; when the snow comes, we shall eat" (Le Jeune's *Relation* of 1634, in Kenton, 1927, 1, p. 171). Which is something like the philosophy of the Penan of Borneo: "If there is no food today there will be tomorrow"—expressing, according to Needham, "a confidence in the capacity of the environment to support them, and in their own ability to extract their livelihood from it" (1954, p. 230).

NOTE

1. I realize that the Netsilik Eskimo as described by Balikci constitute an exception in point. I shall not speak to this case here, but second Richard Lee's explanation (or disposition) of it.

REFERENCES

CONKLIN, HAROLD C.
> 1957. *Hanunóo Agriculture: a report on an integral system of shifting cultivation in the Philippines*, vol. 2. Rome: Food and Agriculture Organization of the United Nations.

EYRE, EDWARD JOHN.
> 1845. *Journals of expeditions of discovery into Central Australia and overland from Adelaide to King George's Sound, in the years 1840–1*. London: T. and W. Boone.

GREY, GEORGE.
> 1841. *Journals of two expeditions of discovery in north-western and western Australia, during the years 1837, '38, and '39*. London: T. and W. Boone.

KENTON, EDNA (Ed.).
> 1927. The Indians of North America. In *The Jesuit relations and allied documents: travels and explorations of the Jesuit missionaries in New France, 1610–1791*. New York: Harcourt Brace. (First published Burrows, 1896.)

McCARTHY, FREDERICK D., and MARGARET McARTHUR.
> 1960. The food quest and the time factor in aboriginal economic life. In Charles P. Mountford (Ed.), *Records of the American-Australian scientific expedition to Arnhem Land, vol. 2: anthropology and nutrition*. Melbourne: Melbourne University Press.

MARSHALL, LORNA K.
> 1961. Sharing, talking and giving: relief of social tensions among !Kung Bushmen. *Africa*, 31: 231–49.

NEEDHAM, RODNEY.
> 1954. Siriono and Penan: a test of some hypotheses. *Southwestern Journal of Anthropology*, 10(3): 228–32.

SPENCER, BALDWIN, and F. J. GILLEN.
> 1899. *The native tribes of central Australia*. London: Macmillan.

WARNER, WILLIAM LLOYD.
> 1937. *A black civilization: a study of an Australian tribe*. New York: Harper.

3 The Children of the Hadza Hunters

D. B. JELLIFFE,

J. WOODBURN,

F. J. BENNETT,

and

E. F. P. JELLIFFE

D. B. Jelliffe is a prominent pediatrician at the School of Public Health, University of California at Los Angeles. The Hadza, as described more fully by anthropologist James Woodburn (1968), are a prime example of an "original affluent" hunter-gatherer society, one in which basic subsistence requirements could be satisfied with as little as two hours of labor a day per adult and no seasonal shortage could be found. This article presents the results of a preliminary medical survey conducted in 1960. The findings provide strong confirmation of the basic view that even the simplest tribal cultures, under traditional conditions, can do an excellent job of meeting basic human needs. In the Hadza case the children were found not only to be quite healthy but to be healthier than native children living in urban poverty. Later medical surveys, conducted in 1966 and 1967 with much larger samples, yielded similar results.

The Hadza, or Watindiga, who number only about 800 in all, inhabit the extensive area of tsetse-infested savannah bush adjacent to Lake Eyasi in northern Tanganyika (Fig. 1). They are an isolated, somewhat short-statured, click-speaking group, and their origin and their relationship to other click-speaking people, such as the Kung Bushmen of South West Africa[1] and to the original cave painters of East Africa, are matters of speculation.

MODE OF LIFE

These people do not keep domestic animals of any sort and only one small peripheral group has adopted agriculture after intermarriage with the neigh-

Reprinted from *Journal of Pediatrics* 60, no. 6 (1962): 907–13, by permission of C. V. Mosby Company and the senior author. Copyright © 1962 C. V. Mosby Company.

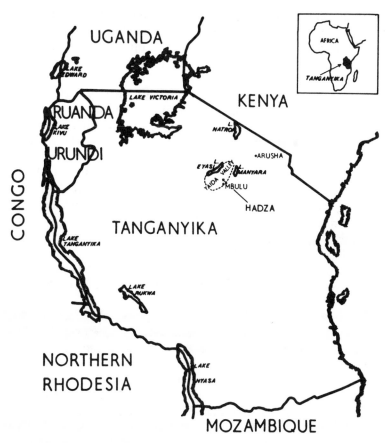

FIGURE 1
Map showing Hadza area of northern Tanganyika

boring Isanzu tribe. The women are food gatherers who search with digging sticks for yamlike roots and gather a wide variety of wild fruits and berries. The men collect wild honey, but are principally hunters, using exceptionally powerful bows and arrows coated with plant poisons (adenium and strophanthus), which are shot into the animal's abdomen if possible. Game killed by lion and other predators, its presence shown from afar by circling vultures, is also eaten—often in a state of putrefaction.

The Hadza, partly on account of their nomadic hunting life and their unique and difficult language, have made very little contact with other tribes except for exchanging honey, skins, and giraffe tails with the neighboring Mbulu for clothing, beads, gourds, pots, knives, tobacco, hashish (*Cannabis indica*), and metal for arrowheads. This contact is in fact accelerating due to the clearing of trees as part of a government tsetse eradication scheme, and the subsequent movement into Hadza country of cattle-owning people at present excluded by tsetse-borne animal trypanosomiasis. Yet another link with neighbors is due to dependence on the Isanzu for medicines and medical treatment, for previously there was no contact with European medicine.

Mobility is the essence of the Hadza way of life, since proper exploitation of the environment for food and water demands constant moves, especially in wet weather when animals no longer have to frequent a limited number of water holes. Property is minimal, so that a man might own bows, arrows, a knife, an axe, a stone pipe, a skin shoulder bag, beads, clothing being worn, and objects of ritual importance: a plume of ostrich feathers, and a decorated gourd for fat; whereas a woman would own the skins she wears, a sleeping skin, water gourds, perhaps a cooking pot, and the ritual objects of a gourd for fat and a decorated walking stick.

Housing is of 4 types: very small roughly constructed temporary grass huts, overhanging rock caves, hollowed-out dense bushes, or completely open rocky hilltops. The type varies with the season and the locality, providing, where necessary, some protection from either rain, wind, or wild animals.

The Hadza usually are to be found in camps occupied by 1 to 15 families. These camps are unstable units and may last from 1 week to 1 month and are of constantly changing composition. In a camp each elementary family has its own hut or sleeping area—the small children snuggling down at night against their parents. Young unmarried women share a space; visitors and young men usually sleep outside altogether. The basic core of a camp is usually a group of matrilineally related women and their husbands and children. When the local food supply is exhausted, the camp moves, and, if necessary, the very sick and dying are left to the hyenas and vultures. In this society there is no exogamy so that there is probably considerable genetic inbreeding, but this is counterbalanced by the degree of natural selection of the fittest, which the environment and society impose.

The scattered groups of families are brought together by 3 communal activities: a nocturnal dance which emphasizes the kinship relations, gambling (for men), and the ritual communal eating, exclusively by the men, of certain parts of large animals. This meat, known as *epeme*, usually consists of the more delectable fatty portions, such as the omentum or udders, and it is believed that if eaten by the hunter alone or by a woman it would give rise to illness.[2]

Child Rearing and Marriage

At birth, the cord is cut with a knife, tied with a thread of animal tendon or tree fiber, and dressed with a mixture of soot and fat. Camp is never moved when a child has been born until after the cord has sloughed off.

Children learn the essential skills of their parents at a very early age so that it is not uncommon for a boy of 10 to be able to shoot enough birds and

uxorious - dotingly fond or submissive
proscription - to forbid
The Children of the Hadza Hunters   25

small game to feed himself and for such a child to leave his parents and join another band.

Marriage also takes place early, sometimes to a partner of a different age group, for example, a young man of 18 to an old widow or a girl of 13 to a much older man. This arrangement, however, is satisfactory, as with uxori-local marriage the girl continues to stay with and receive help from her mother while her husband pays for her with the meat he shoots; whereas in the other case the young man goes to live with a mature and capable woman who can cook for him.

Diet

Food, including meat and yams, is mostly barbecued, and only older women are permitted to have cooking pots in which they boil meat. Wild fruits and berries are eaten raw—seeds and all in great quantities so that the stools have a unique appearance. The wide variety of edible indigenous fruits and berries, unfamiliar to the Western observer, is emphasized by Carr's[3] listing from Rhodesia.

The diet of the 2 sexes differs greatly as much of the food is eaten as soon as it is obtained—the men eating on the spot small animals or carrion. As all over the world, although most available foods (including baboon, vulture, and hyena) are eaten, a few items are not taken, for example termites, blood, and tortoises.

Change is being introduced already into the Hadza diet in the form of maize meal, which is being obtained in increasing amounts from the intrusive camps of laborers clearing edges of tree-covered savannah as a part of government-planned tsetse eradication. No form of alcoholic drink is prepared or bartered from the neighbors, although hashish and tobacco are smoked to the point of intoxication by means of straight, cigar-shaped, home-carved stone pipes.

Infant Feeding

Permissive breast feeding is the mainstay of infant feeding. This is prolonged until another pregnancy, and family spacing is ensured by a proscription of intercourse for many months after childbirth. Eventual cessation of breast feeding may be enforced by painting the breasts with various bitter herbal concoctions.

Rendered soft fat, as from the zebra, and bone marrow, both raw and cooked, are introduced in the early months followed by a thin gruellike mixture made of the uncooked powder, or the ground seeds, of the baobab fruit (*Adansonia digitata*) mixed with water. (Carr has drawn attention to the high ascorbic acid content—about 350 mg. per 100 Gm.—of the powder found in the ripe baobab pod.[3,4]) Honey will also be given.

When the infant has 2 to 4 teeth, prechewed meat will be fed by the mother, and by the age of about 18 months the full adult range of foods will be consumed.

SURVEY METHOD

The survey was intended to assess the child health situation among the Hadza with special reference to the more important tropical pediatric problems, including protein-calorie malnutrition of early childhood[5] and parasitic infestations. It also forms part of a larger over-all plan in progress to study patterns of child health in the different ecologic settings which East Africa provides in such profusion as to constitute almost a natural laboratory of child rearing techniques.

Because of their nomadic life in this large area of completely roadless bush, the initial problem was of contacting sufficient mobile encampments to permit examination of an adequate sample of children, and this was only possible because one of the writers (J. W.) had lived with the Hadza for the previous 2 years and had mastered their language and gained their confidence. At each camp an initial period was spent in reassurance and establishing rapport by the use of the classical gifts of beads, tobacco, bangles, and matches. Following this, all children up to about 11 years of age were examined clinically, following a check-off schedule of certain more obvious predefined physical signs and syndromes, which has been described elsewhere.[6,7]

A thick blood film was taken and stained with Giemsa for malaria parasites. A small sample of stool was removed with an anal glass tube and then preserved in 10 per cent formol saline and examined later. Infants and toddlers were weighed with a portable spring scale.

RESULTS

In all, 62 children (37 male and 25 female) were examined. Five were infants under 1 year of age, 23 were in the "preschool age group," and 34 were "school-age" children.

Nutritional Syndromes

The clinical nutritional status of all the children was good by tropical standards: in particular, the syndromes of kwashiorkor and nutritional marasmus, rickets, infantile scurvy, and vitamin B deficiency syndromes were not seen.

Nutritional Indicators

No edema, hypochromotrichia, angular stomatitis, follicular hyperkeratosis, or pellagra rash was seen. However, Bitot's spots were found in 13 per cent of "preschool age" children and in 17.3 per cent of older children.

The short stature of the adults made it apparent that standards of weight from the other ethnic groups would not apply, and this fact together with the small numbers involved and extreme uncertainty about ages have led us to omit the weights. Nevertheless, there were no obviously clinically underweight children and poor musculature was not seen. In addition, there was no clinical evidence of anemia.

Parasites

Malaria In children of all age groups, only 3 had an enlarged spleen, giving a spleen rate of 6.4 per cent. Of the blood films taken from all children, 11 were positive for *Plasmodium falciparum* malaria, 4 for *Pl. malariae*, and 2 for both infections at the same time. The over-all parasite rate was 27 per cent.

Intestinal parasites 56 stools were examined and Taenia ova were found in 4 and Giardia cysts in 3.

Miscellaneous Findings

Thirty per cent of the children had conjunctivitis; one had corneal scarring. All age groups were involved equally.

Thirteen children had their incisors markedly worn down, presumably from gnawing meat and bones. Only 2 had caries, while 2 showed obvious dental fluorosis, which was also noticed in adults. Two thirds of the children examined had medicinal incisions indicating past indigenous treatments— the commonest sites being the chest, the abdomen, and the face.

The following miscellaneous conditions were also noted: purulent nasal discharge, 6; umbilical hernia, 2; miliaria rubra, 2; skin sores, 2; otitis media, 1; and scalp ringworm, 1.

DISCUSSION

Although the number of children seen may seem small, it probably represents roughly a 25 per cent sample of the whole Hadza child population, and, as such, it gives an indication of the disease pattern at one particular season of the year. Although this tribe lives a life which most people would regard as extremely primitive, the striking feature on closer acquaintance is the remarkable adjustment that they have achieved with their environment. They have as yet built up none of the additional hazards which urbanizing communities in Africa[8] and elsewhere have of housing and crowding together of unrelated people, overrefined foodstuffs, bottle feeding,[9] ill-fitting clothing, ill-kept latrines, and insect-breeding water receptacles.

The main findings were the good health of the children in general, at least at the time of the survey, which was carried out during the dry season. In particular, the absence of obvious malnutrition and anemia were probably related to both the absence of such intestinal helminths as the hookworm and roundworm and the excellent infant feeding pattern, based on prolonged breast feeding and the introduction of animal protein in the second 6 months of life in the shape of bone marrow and prechewed meat. (In addition, during a 2-year period living with the Hadza, no case of kwashiorkor was seen. J. W.) The absence of hypochromotrichia was in striking contrast to the children of the much more sophisticated Baganda, who are reared largely on carbohydrate foods.[10]

The high incidence of conjunctivitis (30 per cent) may be related to the dusty environment, lack of water during the dry season, and to the constant smoke from the cooking fires. Similarly, the Bitot's spots found in these children may also represent the end result of chronic conjunctival irritation and trauma rather than reflecting any inadequacy of vitamin A intake.[11]

These children showed a comparatively low degree of malarial infection as compared with many tropical African communities. Even more striking was the absence of *Ascaris lumbricoides* and *Ancylostoma duodenale*, probably in part related to their mobile nomadic existence which results in little opportunity for heavy fecal contamination of the domestic environment. Tapeworm infections would be expected in a meat-eating group such as the Hadza whose principal method of cooking is lightly barbecuing on the hot ashes. However, the actual intermediate host is uncertain, warthog being the most likely.

The dental condition of Hadza children showed the worn incisors and low incidence of caries (4 per cent) expected with a diet composed of tough, fibrous vegetables and meat, containing no overmilled flour or sugar of any sort. Two children showed advanced dental fluorosis, as did numerous adults, presumably indicating a high fluoride content in water in the drinking pools used.

It is of interest that a field study carried out by Bronte-Stewart and colleagues[12] among the ecologically similar Kung Bushmen of Southwest Africa showed very similar findings in relation to good general nutrition, eye infection, and worn teeth.

The Hadza people of northern Tanganyka are one of the few remaining groups in the world dependent upon hunting and food gathering. Their mode of life, and particularly their methods of infant feeding, probably represent the way Man has existed for the major part of his existence prior to the historically recent development of agriculture, domestication of animals and commercial city dwelling. The future of the Hadza people, and of their children, is ominous. Government-sponsored policy, aimed at benefiting the country as a whole, is to extend tsetse fly control into this area by the progressive clearing of trees. This enables the more numerous surrounding tribes to move in with their cattle, but will ultimately reduce the land available to the Hadza to less than is essential for their widely wandering, hunting, and food gathering activities. It seems, then, as if the Hadza mode of life will change in the next decade, probably in the direction of cultivation. If this occurs, it is probable that the development of static, insanitary villages with mainly carbohydrate crops may tend to result in less healthy children than at present.

Our thanks are due Mr. M. B. Ronaldson, District Commissioner, and Dr. W. Thurston, District Medical Officer, Mbulu, for their most valuable assistance.

NOTES

1. Bronte-Stewart, B., Budtz-Olsen, O. E., Hickley, J. M., and Brock, J. F.: The Health and Nutritional Status of the Kung Bushmen of South-West Africa, South African J. Lab. & Clin. Med. 6: 187, 1960.

2. Woodburn, J.: Hadza Conceptions of Health and Disease (unpublished data).

3. Carr, W. R.: Notes on Some Southern Rhodesian Indigenous Fruits, With Particular Reference to Their Ascorbic Acid Content, Food Res. 22: 590, 1957.

4. Carr, W. R.: The Baobab Tree: a Good Source of Ascorbic Acid, Central African M. J. 4: 372, 1958.

5. Jelliffe, D. B.: Protein-Calorie Malnutrition in Tropical Preschool Children, J. PEDIATRICS 52: 227, 1959.

6. Jelliffe, D. B., Bennett, F. J., Stroud, C. E., Novotny, M. E., Karrach, H. A., Musoke, L. K., and Jelliffe, E. F. P.: Field Survey of the Health of Bachiga Children in the Kayonza District of Kigezi, Am. J. Trop. Med. 10: 435, 1961.

7. Jelliffe, D. B., Jelliffe, E. F. P., Garcia, L., and De Barrios, G.: The Children of the San Blas Indians. J. PEDIAT. 59: 271, 1961.

8. Kahn, E.: Pediatrics in an Industrialized Part of Africa, J. PEDIAT. 58: 277, 1961.

9. Jelliffe, D. B.: Culture, Social Change and Infant Feeding, Am. J. Clin. Nutrition (in press).

10. Jelliffe, D. B., Bennett, F. J., Welbourn, H. F., and Jelliffe, E. F. P.: The Health of Baganda Children (in press).

11. Darby, W. J., McGanity, W. J., McLaren, D. S., Phaton, D., Alemo, A. Z., and Medhen, A. K.: Bitôt's Spots and Vitamin A Deficiency. Pub. Health Rep. 75: 738, 1960.

12. Bronte-Stewart, *op. cit.*

II

First Contacts: The Loss of Autonomy

Perhaps the most important event in the development process for tribal peoples is the first sustained contact with "civilized" outsiders. This event often leads directly to economic dependency and the loss of political autonomy. These changes in turn are virtual prerequisites for further economic development. It is important to stress here that "contact" per se is not the issue; what really counts is the loss of autonomy that follows certain kinds of contact. Governments are rarely willing to tolerate the presence of politically sovereign tribes within their national boundaries. They usually move quickly to halt internal tribal conflict as well as armed resistance by tribal peoples to outside intrusion, even though these two forms of tribal political action may be critical to the successful maintenance and self-defense of tribal culture and the immediate welfare of the tribal population. When a tribal people can no longer expel outside intruders or use force to regulate its internal affairs, it can no longer be considered independent.

Other indications of loss of autonomy include the introduction of formal schooling and national court systems, the appointment of state-sanctioned political leaders, compulsory military service, and the payment of taxes. The loss of autonomy may directly undermine the previously high quality of life of traditional tribal society and set in motion changes that indirectly lead to further impoverishment. Hundreds of thousands of tribal people have lost their independence during this century, and only a few thousand have not yet surrendered. How this important first development event is viewed by policy makers relates directly to how all later development policy is conceived. For example, the element of political and economic conquest is easily ignored by planners, and it may sometimes be mistakenly assumed that tribals welcome the opportunity to develop. Tribal desires to direct their own development process may easily be disregarded by officials, and conquered tribals may themselves overlook the possibility of self-determination in development. The fact that tribal societies are often dramatically transformed in negative ways by "pacification" may also be ignored by development planners who prescribe further changes to compensate for problems created by government control itself.

The following selections examine a variety of twentieth-century first contact cases, ranging from relatively isolated groups such as the Copper Eskimo (Stefansson) and the Indians of the Brazilian Amazon (Ribeiro) to regional intertribal systems of thousands of people such as those in New Guinea in the 1930s (Murray). The specific issues examined in these cases are, How and why did contact occur? What were the conditions of tribal life at the time? What elements either attracted or repelled tribals from further contacts?

Tribal peoples invariably meet outsiders for the first time with feelings of great ambiguity. Fear, indifference, belligerence, and awe are often intermixed in the cases that follow. Some tribals obviously welcome contact as a chance to end internal conflicts and to gain valuable trade goods. Others fear a loss of their freedom. The element of physical resistance to outside intervention is obvious in the examples from New Guinea and the Amazon. The interest in acquiring metal tools is a striking element only in the Eskimo and Amazon examples.

4 Lessons in Living from the Stone Age

VILHJALMUR STEFANSSON

There are very few modern accounts of fully self-sufficient tribal peoples and even fewer accounts that explicitly evaluate the tribal way of life in comparison with our own. Vilhjalmur Stefansson is uniquely qualified to write such an analysis. He is one of the greatest modern explorers of the Arctic and has probably spent longer with traditional Eskimo peoples than any other trained observer. Stefansson studied anthropology and comparative religion at Harvard from 1903 to 1906. When he met the Copper Eskimo in 1910, he was already familiar with Eskimo culture and had adopted their methods of travel and of living off the land. At that time field anthropologists were burdened with bulky expeditions and seldom deliberately adopted native ways. Such "participant observation" was not yet an official field technique.

It is significant that in 1910 the Copper Eskimo still constituted a fully functioning autonomous cultural system. Stefansson found them to be quite healthy and happy, and he inferred that this was the result of their cooperative political economy, or what he called "communistic anarchy," based on the "golden rule." Their satisfactory way of life was not due to their simple technology, however, and unlike Sahlins, Stefansson does not suggest that they were an affluent society—they were merely healthy and happy in ways that we are not. Stefansson also shows clearly how their health and contentment began to break down as they became involved with the industrial economy. The intrusion of the industrial economy in Alaska is further described in part VI by Reinhard.

Slightly less embarrassing than owning to a philosophy of life is confessing that you have some idea, though vague and changing, as to what constitutes the good life. My ideas of it come chiefly from a comparison between civilization and primitive culture.

I feel that when Shaw intentionally speculates in his *Back to Methuselah* on the good life in coming millenniums he describes unintentionally the lives of some groups of our ancestors during millenniums of the remote past. For Shaw pictures the nearly ideal condition of the future in a way that has little relation to civilization as we find it about us to-day but which is reminiscent of a great deal that we call the lowest savagery.

So far as my picture of the good life is derived from experience, I get it mainly from people of the Stone Age with whom I lived in the Coronation

Gulf district of northern Canada. Or, rather, I get from comparing ten years among savages with forty years in civilization the feeling that a better life need not be a chimera—that we have had it in the past and may attain it again in the future.

It is only those who know the savage at first hand who really believe his way better than ours. Nor does the savage convert everyone who sees him. He has a chance to make converts only when there are many of him and few of us, so that we are compelled to adopt his life and to live it through years, not as visitors or patrons but as self-supporting members of the community.

Occasionally, however, it is given to comparative outsiders to see the light. There are few more complete outsiders, as a group, than missionaries; for they go to teach and not to learn. But even among them you find understanding now and then. David Livingstone for Tropical Africa, Hudson Stuck for Arctic Alaska, were great admirers of the unspoiled savage. These and a few other missionaries join the majority of scientific travelers in proclaiming that the less savages are civilized the finer people they are.

My party of one white and three "Americanized" western Eskimos reached the Stone Age Eskimos of Coronation Gulf in late winter, traveling by sledge in a manner to which the local people were accustomed. We wore fur garments similar to their own, and gave the impression of being not foreign, though strangers. We were able to converse from the first day; for Eskimo is one language from Greenland to Bering Sea across the northern frontier of the New World.

In culture the Gulf Eskimos went back not thousands but tens of thousands of years; for they were just emerging from the age of wood and horn into the earliest period of stone. They knew that certain berries and roots could be eaten, although they did not consider them as real food, but only as a substitute for food in an emergency. Their proper diet was wholly animal tissues. Through two-thirds of the year it was chiefly seal, with an occasional polar bear. During the summer they lived mainly on caribou, with some fish. There was no clothing except from the skins of animals. The tents were of skin and so were the boats. There were kayaks, the small boats used for hunting; there were none of the large skin boats in which other groups of Eskimos travel. The only domestic beast was the dog, and he was mainly a hunting animal. There was usually not more than one dog for each hunter; so that, although the dogs were hitched to sledges in traveling, there were so few of them in comparison with the people that essentially the Eskimos themselves were the draft animals.

The Coronation Eskimos knew of the Bear Lake forest but did not like it as a country to live in and made journeys to it only to secure timber for sledges, tent poles, and for a few other uses. They considered the treeless prairie north of the forest the best possible land in summer, and they considered the ice of the gulf and strait a proper and desirable home in winter. They were satisfied, then, with both their country and their climate, believing that any change would be for the worse.

These Stone Age people considered not only that the one proper food is meat but also that the most delicious things in the world are the preferred parts of animals. They had the highest average of good health which I have ever found in any community of like size; most of the deaths among them came from accident or old age. They had a religion by which they believed themselves able to control their environment; but it was a religion neither of hope nor of fear. There was no permanent future life; there was nothing resembling heaven or hell. The spirits were powerful but they were not in themselves good or evil, though they might do the good or evil bidding of men or women who controlled them—this Stone Age attitude toward spirits was something like the modern attitude toward explosives or steam power: things neutral in themselves but capable of being used for good or ill. They had as much desire to live as any of us but less fear of dying than most of us have.

Of the seven hundred or so Stone Age people about two hundred had been in contact with whaling ships for a few days each of two years, 1906–7 and 1907–8. Our visit to them was in 1910. There were a dozen or less who had seen David Hanbury when he passed along the southern edge of their district in 1902. Another dozen had seen for an hour or two at close range some Slavey Indians a few years before our visit, and of course they had seen groups of them frequently at a distance. But at least four hundred had never heard the noise which gunpowder makes when it explodes or seen the lighting of a match. They had seen pieces of cloth and believed them to be skins of animals. They had received many guns by tribe-to-tribe trade, but had secured them only when the neighbor groups had run out of ammunition. They hammered and cut up the guns to make things which they wanted, such as knives, spear points, and especially needles.

When we first lived with these people they envied us greatly just one thing we had with us, our sewing needles. Among themselves the most valuable single possession was a dog. I purchased a dog for a large knife, worth about three dollars at American wholesale prices. Later that day the man returned with the knife and with a second dog—if I would take the knife back he would give me two dogs for one needle. They explained that, although they had seen the Eskimo woman member of our party sewing before we made the first trade of the knife for the dog, they had not then realized that she possessed two needles. Now they understood that she had not only two but several, and she had told them that, with my consent, she was willing to give up one.

We inquired and found that by local standards a No. 1 size sewing needle was worth much more than any knife and was well worth, in the common estimation, two good dogs. So we made the trade.

The point of the trading story is that these Stone Age Eskimos were as yet not discontented with their copper knives, although they had been familiar for decades with the better iron knives which they themselves had made through Stone Age technic from rifle barrels and other pieces of iron.

But they were far from content with their copper needles, for the shafts were necessarily stout in comparison with the size of the eye, which made it difficult to sew a waterproof seam.

Waterproof sewing is apparently one of the early discoveries of man. There may not be any people on earth to-day except the Eskimos who still remember how to make, and do make, a really waterproof seam. For most or all other sewers rub grease into a seam to waterproof it, or use some trick of that sort; but the women of the Stone Age Eskimos considered it an insult if they saw anybody rubbing grease on the seam of a water boot which they had made. However, in spite of their skill, waterproof sewing was difficult with the use of a copper needle; but it was easy with one of our steel needles.

Perhaps we have gone too far already before saying that we have no thought of deriving the health, happiness, and other details of the good life of the Copper Eskimos from their backward state—from their being still thousands of years behind us in technological development. We are merely trying to sketch briefly, and without any necessary causal relation, how these people lived who were to all appearances so much happier than any other people whom I have ever known.

We were the first of European civilization to live with these Eskimos, and we saw during the first year the gradual, and later rapid, increase of discontent—which was a decrease of happiness. Discontent grew not always along lines that might have been expected. For instance, you would think that our matches would have been coveted, but this was not the case. Their method of lighting fires by knocking together two pieces of iron pyrite had advantages which to their minds (and even to mine later on) compensated for the disadvantages. Certainly a match is handier for a cigarette; also for lighting a fire in good weather our matches were better. The advantage of the pyrite we discovered when we had to kindle a fire in a gale or in a rainstorm. It came to be our practice when we traveled with the Stone Age people to light fires with matches in good weather and to borrow their technic when the weather was bad. Then another advantage of pyrite was of course that two pieces of it, each the size of a lemon, would last you for years, if not for a lifetime. Nor did you have to worry about keeping these lumps of rock dry.

The Stone Age people had been discontented with their needles before we came. The first discontent after that was connected with the insect pests. They had never conceived of a mosquito net that would protect your face during the day and that might be used to cover your bed at night. At first they considered our face nets and bed nets frivolous. But after a few weeks of association they began to say what a fine thing it would be if a white trader should come in with enough mosquito nets so that everybody could buy one.

There were also the black flies. Eskimo garments are loose, somewhat as if the coat were a Russian blouse and the trousers in the style of our pajamas. Besides, in the heat of the summer, with temperatures sometimes running above 90° in the shade, they practically had to have rents and holes in their skin clothing. Through these holes, up their sleeves and down their necks would crawl the black flies as if they were fleas, stinging so that the hurt was greater than the itch. Against these pests we wore knitted cotton shirts and drawers, with long arms and long legs, the elasticity making them tight and flyproof round the wrist and ankle. A longing for this kind of underwear to use in summer was perhaps the basis of the second of the new discontents.

There grew slowly through the first summer an appreciation that a cloth tent was better than one of skins—lighter, less bulky, and less difficult to preserve from decay. It was not until perhaps the second or third year that there was any real discontent with the bow and arrow for caribou hunting and a desire for rifles. The appreciation of the value of fish nets, as compared with spears and hooks, developed somewhat more rapidly than the longing for guns. During the first few years of Copper Eskimo association with Europeans there was no discontent on the score of diet. The local conception was, as said, that meat is real food and that things like cereals and vegetables are makeshifts.

II

The picture of Stone Age life which we have begun to sketch might not seem attractive to the reader even if we could spread it over a large canvas with the details completely presented. We endeavor to bring out our meaning in part by making a contrast between the Copper Eskimos of 1910 and those of 1939.

Perhaps the only thing with which the Coronation people are still content is their climate. You cannot describe to them the weather of Hawaii or California in such terms as to get a more favorable reply than that no doubt Europeans like that sort of thing but they themselves would never like it. They still prefer boiled meat to any imported food; but they now feel ashamed if they do not have, especially for visitors, a few of the costly imports to offer, among them tea, coffee, sugar, salt, bread, and syrup. They are as discontented now with the sewing machines which they own as they formerly were with the copper needles. They are less content with the best rifles they can get than they were with their bows and arrows. They still enjoy their own songs most, but they feel a social need of phonographs, and there is a developing need for the radio. They know that their skin clothes are best for the climate, but fashion has laid such hold upon them that they must have clothes of silk and other materials.

In 1910 they believed in keeping up with the Joneses. In this they used to be approximately successful; for under their communistic anarchy everyone shared the best of the foods and the best of all materials. There was scarcely any difference between garments except that one woman could make a more attractive dress than another out of a given material, or a man correspondingly could make a slightly superior bow or spear. To-day keeping up with the Joneses wears a different aspect. Formerly in that contest they had no problems which we classify as economic; now they compete, or want to compete, in things which are beyond their economic reach, some of them known through hearsay but not obtainable in their country.

The breakdown in native economy, and thereby in self-respect, is more easily described, at least so far as my own experience goes, from the Mackenzie River district, several hundred miles to the west of the Copper Eskimos.

Mackenzie habits of life began to change with the entrance of the New England whaling fleet in 1889. I arrived there in 1906. Between that year and 1918 I saw much change; the rest to date is known to me from dependable reports.

Comparing the reports of Sir John Franklin with what I saw a hundred years later, I would conclude that two thousand delta people had decreased in a century to less than two hundred. The chief cause was measles, one epidemic of which, in the memory of those still living, had killed something like two out of three within a few weeks. Tuberculosis had been rare or absent; now it was prevalent. Digestive troubles had been few, but now they were common. Tooth decay had been unknown, but now their teeth were as bad as ours. There is no reasonable doubt that in 1820 the Mackenzie people, then in the Stone Age, were on the average as healthy as my Copper Eskimos were in 1910; but when I reached the Mackenzie district in 1906 the average Mackenzie health was probably not better than that of our worst slum districts.

The Mackenzie people, however, were not living under a slum level of poverty in 1906. They still had their economic independence and the respect which goes with it. How this later broke down can be shown by the story of Ovayuak, who still held to the old ways of life and who was still a heathen.

Steamers come down the Mackenzie River in midsummer, usually arriving at Macpherson during early July. The first steamer brought the Bishop. It was known among the converts in the Mackenzie district that the Bishop wanted to see them on his annual pastoral visits. The people liked the Bishop, they wanted to purchase goods that had been brought by the steamer, and they enjoyed the outing of the two-hundred-mile trip south to the Hudson's Bay post. So they streamed to Macpherson in late June.

But, said Ovayuak, the Bishop's visit came in a fishing season. Not being a convert, he stayed behind and fished all summer with his family and a few who still took their lead from him. Most of the others went to meet the Bishop and the traders. By the time the religious ceremonies, the feasting, and the trading were completed and the return journey made to the coast, the fishing was nearly over.

But that was only part of the difficulty. The trader had said to the Eskimo husbands that they ought to dress their wives in the best possible garments. When the reply was that the Eskimos had nothing with which to pay, the trader said that he knew them well, that they were reliable, that he would be glad to trust them, and that they could take as much cloth as they wanted, paying him next year.

However, when the cloth had been sold the trader would give these men a talking to of another sort. He would remind them that now they were in honor bound to pay for the goods a year later. They must not, therefore, spend all their time down on the coast fishing and gorging themselves; they would now have to go up into the forest or to certain promontories on the coast so as to catch the mink of the woodland or the white foxes that frequent the shore floe. These would now have to be their chief concern; for they were pledged to see that the dealer should not suffer through having trusted them.

Accordingly, said Ovayuak, when the people returned from their summer visit to Macpherson they would explain to him that they had made promises not to stay very long at the fishing but to go to the promontories or the forest in time to be ready for the trapping season. And, said Ovayuak, naturally he could not argue against this; for, like them, he believed that a promise ought to be kept. So most of the families would scatter for the trapping districts, leaving him and his few adherents still at the fishing.

Ovayuak told me this just after the New Year. He forecast that when the mid-winter days began to lengthen, visitors would begin to arrive. The trappers would now be running short of food and they would say to one another, "Let us go to Ovayuak; he has plenty of fish."

Sure enough, they began to gather. At first we took them into our house, where twenty-three of us had been living in one room; but that accommodation could not be stretched for more than ten extras. So the others had to pitch tents or to build snowhouses in the neighborhood of our cabin. The stores of fish that seemed inexhaustible began to melt rapidly. There was not merely a steady increase of people; they all had their dog teams to feed, also.

Everybody went out fishing every day, we locals and the visitors, but we caught perhaps only one-tenth as much as was being consumed. This went on till the fish store was nearly gone. Thereupon everybody who had a sledge loaded it heavy with the last of the fish and then we scattered in all directions, to hunting and fishing districts. We went in small detachments, for it is a principle of the hunting life that you must not travel in large groups.

The system which I watched breaking down under the combined influence of Christianity and the fur trade was on its economic side communism. Natural resources and raw materials were owned in common, but made articles were privately owned. The blubber of a seal that was needed for light and heat, or lean and fat that were needed for meals, belonged no more to the man who secured them than to anyone else. A pair of boots belonged to the woman who made them until she presented or sold them to somebody else. A meal that had been cooked was in a sense private property, but it was open to everyone under the laws of hospitality—it was very bad form to start a meal in any village without at the least sending a youngster outdoors to shout at the top of his voice that the family were about to dine or breakfast. If the houses were scattered and the people indoors, then messengers, usually children, would be sent to every household. People would come and join the family at their meal, either because they wanted the food or else for sociability. If the house was too small to accommodate everybody, then portions of cooked food were sent out to the other houses.

It is a usual belief with us that this type of communism leads to shiftlessness. But that was certainly not the case in any Eskimo community known to me so long as they still followed the native economy.

Among the Eskimos of northern Canada there was no law except public opinion. Although no one had authority, each person had influence according to the respect won from a community which had intimate knowledge of everybody. Nobody was supposed to work if he was sick; and still the permanently handicapped were expected to work, each according to his ability. Among the Copper Eskimos, for instance, I saw a man of about forty who had been blind since childhood. He was one of the most cheerful and constant workers, but naturally could do only a few special things.

It has been a part of European ethics that a debt of honor should be paid before other debts. Thus a debt which could not be collected through legal machinery was a heavier obligation than one which had behind it the penalties of the state. With the Stone Age Eskimos every debt was a debt of honor; for there were no police, judges, prisons, or punishment.

The same force that compelled the Eskimo to pay his debts compelled him to do his share of the work according to his recognized abilities. I never knew even one who didn't try his best, although there were of course the same differences of energy and aptitude which we find among ourselves. If there had been a shirker he would have received the same food; but even in a circle of punctilious courtesy he would have felt that he was not being fed gladly. It is nearly impossible, when you know how primitive society works under communistic anarchy, to conceive of anyone with that combination of indolence and strength of character which would make it possible for a healthy man to remain long a burden on the community.

In the few cases where strength of character is enough for running against public opinion the issue is seldom or never on any such low plane as that of indolence. I have known one situation where a man was condemned to death. For there was no punishment among the Stone Age Eskimos except the disapproval of the community or death—nothing in between.

III

We may now summarize those things in the Stone Age life which we judge make for happiness more than do the corresponding elements of our own civilization:

The successful man stood above his fellows in nothing but their good opinion. Rank was determined by the things you secured and turned over to the common use. Your importance in the community depended on your judgment, your ability, and your character, but notably upon your unselfishness and kindness. Those who were useful to the community, who fitted well into the community pattern, were leaders. It was these men who were so often wrongly identified by the careless early civilized traveler and the usual trader as chiefs. They were not chiefs, for they had no authority; they had nothing but influence. People followed their advice because they believed it to be sound. They traveled with them because they liked to travel with them.

There was of course the negative side. If you were selfish you were disliked. If you tried to keep more than your share you became unpopular. If you were persistently selfish, acquisitive, and careless of the general good you gradually became too unpopular. Realizing this, very likely you would try moving to another community and starting life there over again. If you persisted in your ways and stayed where you were there would come a period of unanimous disapproval. You might survive for a year or even a few years as an unwanted hanger-on; but the patience of the community might at any time find its limit, and there would be one more execution of a troublemaker.

Because few understand the workings of a communistic anarchy it is necessary to insist that most of the supposed difficulties which fill our theoretical discussions of communism and of anarchy do not arise in practice.

Under the communism we are describing you don't have to accumulate food, apart from the community's store; for you are welcome to all you reasonably need of the best there is. You do not have to buy clothes; for they will be made for you either by some woman member of your family or by some woman friend who will feel about your wearing a coat of hers just the way any number of our women feel when they see their men friends wearing a garment they have knit or a tie they have sent as a Christmas gift. You do not have to accumulate wealth against your old age; for the community will support you as gladly when you are too old to work as it would if you had never been able to work at all—say because you had been blind from infancy.

One common arrangement of ours, however, is useful under communism, though not quite as necessary there as under rugged individualism. It is a good thing to have a family, for your children and grandchildren will look after you even more thoughtfully than mere friends.

The nearest thing to an investment among the Stone Age Eskimos, the one means of providing against old age, is children. For that reason a widow without a child would have to be loved for herself alone. A widow with one child would be a desirable match. To marry a widow with three or four children was, among the Stone Age people of Coronation Gulf, the New York equivalent to marrying the widow of a millionaire.

On the basis of my years with the Stone Age Eskimos I feel that the chief factor in their happiness was that they were living according to the Golden Rule.

It is easier to feel that you can understand than to prove that you do understand why it is man gets more happiness out of living unselfishly under a system which rewards unselfishness than from living selfishly where selfishness is rewarded. Man is more fundamentally a co-operative animal than a competitive animal. His survival as a species has been perhaps through mutual aid rather than through rugged individualism. And somehow it has been ground into us by the forces of evolution to be "instinctively" happiest over those things which in the long run yield the greatest good to the greatest number.

My hope for the good life of the future, as I have seen it mirrored from the past by the Stone Age of northern America, does not rest wholly on a belief in cycles of history. It rests in part on the thought that a few more decades or centuries of preaching the Golden Rule may result in its becoming fashionable, even for the civilized, to live by the Golden Rule. Perhaps we could live as happily in a metropolis as in a fishing village if only we could substitute the ideals of co-operation for those of competition. For it does not seem to be inherent in "progress" that it shall be an enemy to the good life.

---

5   The Scientific Aspect of the Pacification of Papua

SIR HUBERT MURRAY

New Guinea, the world's second largest island, was one of the last large areas of self-sufficient tribal peoples to be brought under state control in this century. In 1900 probably a million tribal people, speaking some 700 languages, were totally self-sufficient in New Guinea. Sir Hubert Murray was the principle architect of an official policy of "peaceful pacification" during the 33 years of his administration of Papua New Guinea from 1907 to 1940. He advocated the gradual penetration of tribal areas by armed patrols and the introduction of government-backed law and order. After administrative control was established, taxation, backed by the threat of jail, was to prod the natives out of their basically Neolithic economy into a plantation labor, market-oriented economy. This selection, origi-

Reprinted with permission from *Report of the Twenty-first Meeting of the Australian & New Zealand Association for the Advancement of Science* 21 (1933): 1–11. Copyright © 1933 Australian & New Zealand Association for the Advancement of Science Incorporated.

nally presented as the presidential address to the annual meeting of the Australian and New Zealand Association for the Advancement of Science in Sydney in 1932, describes in detail how native resistance to government intrusion was overcome. It is obvious that this "pacification" process, the first step in economic development, was a matter of military conquest. Murray, then Lieutenant Governor of Papua, was remarkable for the great humanitarian restraint with which he carried out this conquest, but he apparently never doubted the basic necessity for it. In contrast the respected New Guinea explorer A. F. R. Wollaston (see part IX) in 1920 questioned the justice of the entire New Guinea pacification program. The ethical justification for Murray's policy is further discussed in this volume by Williams (see part IV).

SCIENCE AND HUMANITARIANISM

In the government of primitive races Science, as is so often the case, has marched hand in hand with humanitarianism; and it is recognised nowadays that the old methods of slaughter and slavery were not only inhuman but also unscientific. . . .

PRINCIPLES OF PACIFICATION

A scientific method of pacification postulates firstly some knowledge of the people whom you propose to pacify, and secondly some idea of what you are going to do with them when they are pacified. Native races are no longer deliberately exterminated, and the possible methods of dealing with them have been classified as subjugation, assimilation, and association. Subjugation may be said to be a thing of the past, and assimilation is perhaps the method of the future. Assimilation, in so far as it neglects the obvious facts of race, can perhaps never be realised, but, in so far as it insists upon the common humanity of both black and white, and the comparative unimportance of the points of divergence, it may contain the secret of the ultimate adjustment of racial differences. . . .

. . . In these days of the "dual mandate" and the "sacred trust" the duty of governments towards subject races has become a commonplace of administration; and we may perhaps flatter our national pride by the reflection that this duty has been discharged in the British colonies at least as faithfully as anywhere else. The method adopted in those colonies has been that of association and collaboration, and we have followed the same policy in Papua. We are not trying to make the brown man white; we are trying to make him a better brown man than he was before.

ESTABLISHMENT OF ORDER

But, whatever method you are going to adopt, whether it be assimilation or association or anything else, your first duty is the establishment of order; for this is the foundation upon which all administration must rest. And here, perhaps more than anywhere else, the importance of the scientific method appears. What I have elsewhere called the "swift injustice" of the punitive expedition may conceivably, under some circumstances, be capable of excuse, but it has always seemed to me to be the last word in unscientific bungling. The punitive expedition ignores the individual and makes war upon the tribe, some member of which is suspected of having committed an offence, and returns, perhaps, flushed with victory, "after killing the offender's uncle, ravishing his second cousin, and stealing his grandmother's pig." We consider this method unscientific for two reasons. The first reason is that it is an abandonment of our principle of individual responsibility, and an adoption of the savage's crude idea of tribal vengeance, which we consider to be a lapse into barbarism and a sin against civilisation. And the second reason is that the punitive expedition is inconsistent with the peaceful association which is the end that we have in view. . . .

PROBLEM IN PAPUA

Order must be maintained at all hazards but it must not be order of the kind that once "reigned in Warsaw", and it must be established with the maximum of despatch and with the minimum of friction; and here again the scientific method guides us on the quickest and easiest way. In a country of great chiefs and settled forms of government you would, I presume, go to work by subduing or making friends with the most powerful rulers, in order, with their assistance, to extend your influence over the rest; such at least is the method which has been commonly adopted by European powers in the past. It is in fact a practical application of the maxim *divide et impera*. But you cannot do this in a country like Papua, where there are few chiefs with any power to speak of, and where there was no settled native government. Indeed I have found it very difficult to discover a close parallel to our task in Papua. The work done on the mainland of Africa, and in Madagascar, with which the names of Lord Lugard, Marshal Galliéni, Marshal Lyautey, and others of various nationalities will always be remembered, was on so much larger a scale that it really affords no guidance. We had in Papua no enemy like Rabah Zobeir, or Samory, no kingdoms like Kano and Sokoto, no marauding Arabs to fight, no slave trade to suppress. The labour of these great Africans was on a heroic scale compared with ours, and yet it may be that our task was, in some ways, the more exacting. The occupation of Kano and Sokoto brought about the pacification of the whole of Northern Nigeria, but in Papua every district was a separate problem; there was no centre of government which we could occupy, no ruling chieftain with whom we could treat. The whole territory must be occupied step by step.

ESTABLISHMENT OF POLICE FORCE

There was little organised resistance in Papua, but, unfortunately, a population of the Stone Age, head-hunters for a great part and cannibals, can not be induced by fair words alone to adopt a more peaceful life. We had before us only small scattered bands of savages, armed with sticks and stones; and sticks and stones, however cleverly fashioned and skillfully handled, can never be a match for modern fire-arms. But the difficulty and the pity of it was that the Papuans could not, until too late, be brought to realise the impossible odds against which they were contending. Probably the natives of each district imagined that the particular detachment of police with which they had to deal was all that we had at our command, so that, when once these were disposed of, there would be an end of the Government altogether. A native could have no idea of the power that lay behind the small body of men whom he saw before him, and he could, unfortunately, only learn by experience. And it was doubtless the best and the bravest of the Papuans who fell in the hopelessly unequal contest.

Force being, unfortunately, necessary in order to maintain even the slightest semblance of order, an instrument had to be provided for its display, and also, if occasion demanded, for its use. So the Papuan Armed Constabulary was established, a body which consisted originally of a dozen Solomon Islanders, recruited in Fiji, and two Fijian Non-commissioned officers. At present the force is entirely Papuan. Sir William MacGregor, our first Lieutenant-Governor, speaks of the Armed Constabulary as one of the institutions of which he was particularly proud; and his pride has been fully justified.

CHARACTER OF THE ARMED CONSTABULARY

In training a body of men like the Armed Constabulary the most important thing is to inculcate such ideas as loyalty to the Government, pride in their uniform, and, eventually, a tradition of service; and I think I may say that we have succeeded in doing this. A Constable will stand up against any odds, for the police tradition does not allow him to run away; and he will go to certain death rather than disgrace his uniform. For instance, I remember the case of a Constable who was under orders to report at a Government station on a certain day, and who could just arrive in time if he could get round a point where the sea was breaking heavily. It was a rough night, and he was warned that no one but a very strong swimmer could get past the point. He was a bush native and could not swim at all; but he wore the police uniform and must obey orders. So he braved the passage, and was drowned.

Then a short time ago a party of three, a police cook, an interpreter, and a Constable, was sent from a police camp in the mountains to a village to collect food. On their way they saw signs of the preparation of an ambush to cut them off on their return, and the cook offered the eminently reasonable suggestion that they should go back to the camp and report. But the Constable would have none of it—his orders were to go to the village, and he would go, ambush or no ambush. So they went on, and when they came back the ambush was ready and the Constable was killed. They all put up a plucky fight, and the cook and the interpreter got away.

Our police have developed a strict sense of duty, but they are also very human. They will weep bitterly out of sympathy with a prisoner whom they have arrested, though, for all their tears, they would not dream of letting him go. And a few months ago a traveller in the almost unknown country at the back of the Albert Mountains might have come upon a police camp where all hands were engaged in nursing a baby and attending to a wounded man. The wounded man was one of a party who had attacked the camp, and the baby had been found in the bush, deserted by his father and mother and crying his heart out. Both the man and the baby were carefully tended for many days, and were then restored to their friends.

Some years ago four policemen were murdered on the South Coast, and the murderers fled inland, across the sago swamps, hotly pursued by the rest of the detachment, who passed through the swamps by the light of firesticks, giving the fugitives no rest, and capturing those who fell by the way. Women and children joined in the flight, and so hot was the pursuit that many babies were thrown away by their mothers—but only to be picked up and nursed by the police; and when I came to the station shortly afterwards, I found it like a baby farm, full of small children, who were being fed by policemen on condensed milk, administered through quills. The mothers came back at last, collected their offspring, and departed in peace.

They are a strange mixture these Papuan police, and they are regarded with mixed feelings by their countrymen. When in deadly peril natives have been known to call instinctively upon the Sergeant of the detachment for protection, though the Sergeant was far away; just as in the old days they used, in their last extremity, to call upon their father and their mother. But, on the other hand, I have known prisoners to burst into tears and to beg for death when I have told them that they must not attack a police patrol. "Let us be hanged," they sobbed, "let us be hanged. What is life to us if we can not throw spears at the police?"

Stories like this could be multiplied indefinitely, but they are of no particular interest to one who is not himself a policeman; what really is interesting, I think, is that we have succeeded in creating a sentiment of loyalty and esprit de corps in such apparently unpromising material as these head-hunters and cannibals of the Stone Age. And I feel at liberty to call especial attention to this, since it is mainly the work, not of myself, but of the Magistrates and Patrol Officers, who, from the nature of their service, have been in closer personal touch with the police.

POLICY OF THE "OIL STAIN"

Marshal Galliéni in Tonkin and Madagascar adopted a policy which he called "the policy of the oil stain"—la tache d'huile. Under this system the French influence percolated from certain fixed centres throughout the surrounding country; and, if one may compare very small things with great, I may say that a similar policy has been followed in Papua. Isolated posts have been established throughout the Territory, and from these posts patrols have been made into the neighbouring districts. Each post has become a centre of ever widening influence, and it has been our practice to link them up by a series of patrols, each patrol following a different route so as to cover as much of the Territory as possible. The patrol has generally been a small one, consisting of from six to ten police and one white officer. There is a risk in sending a single officer, and, if the numbers of our Service had permitted, we should always have sent two; but, as a matter of deliberate policy, I think that a small patrol is preferable to a large one. A large patrol has the advantage that it overawes opposition, and is less likely to invite attack; but it has the disadvantage that it requires a big transport, which is always a difficulty in Papua, and that the carriers are likely to get out-of-hand and to cause trouble with the local natives. Unfortunately we must rely upon human transport, for animal transport is out of the question in the mountains of Papua.

The system of isolated posts, too, with which these patrols are connected, is not without its dangers, for there is always a risk that a post may be attacked and overwhelmed before assistance can arrive; and this actually happened at the Tamata Station, near the Mambare River. The Government Officer at Tamata was killed, and the station was occupied by natives of the surrounding district; and it was not without difficulty that the station was recaptured and order restored. But this was long ago, in 1897, and nothing of the kind has happened since.

DANGER OF PATROLLING

The immediate object of these patrols is to examine the country, and to impress upon the natives the ubiquity of the Government. The patrols may meet with little difficulty so long as their object is merely exploration and general investigation; but even when everything seems peaceful one must be on the look out for a possible attack. For there is always a party of die-hard conservatives in a native community, and these will be suspicious of the strangers and hostile to them; and, if they succeed in bringing round the rest of the village to their view, things may go hard with the patrol. On the other hand the younger men are often urged by curiosity and love of novelty to accept the visitors as friends; and my experience is that a good deal depends upon the attitude of the women, especially the older women.

It may make a great difference if you are the first to visit the village; for, if others have been before you, you cannot tell what they may have done, and what wrongs, real or imaginary, the natives may have to avenge. A good instance of this is supplied by an incident in the very successful expedition which Mr. Humphries, one of our Magistrates, made from Nepa, a station of ours on the Lakekamu Goldfield, across the main range, to the North-east Coast on the other side of the island. The mountainous nature of the country drove him north into what is now the Mandated Territory of New Guinea, which was then under military occupation, among tribes who had never been visited before. With these he had no difficulty at all; his troubles began when he reached tribes who had been visited. These were uniformly hostile, and readers of Mr. Humphries's very interesting book, "Patrolling in Papua", will remember how he was saved from a dangerous position by the sudden appearance of a *deus ex machina* in the shape of a strange native, conspicuous among the armed and hostile throng by his peaceful garb of singlet and knickerbockers. This apparition addressed Mr. Humphries in English; he knew the Papuan Government well, and was kind enough to express approval of it. It was, he said, a good Government. The apparition's name was Auda, and he belonged to a coastal tribe; he was, at the moment, staying as a guest with a local chief called Kewawi. Peace was soon made through the good offices of Auda, and Kewawi and his people gave the party every assistance. Mr. Humphries asked why everyone had been so hostile at first, and Kewawi, rather dramatically, produced a handful of cartridge clips and shells. "That is the reason", he said. The district had been visited before.

ABRUPT CHANGE TO BE AVOIDED

Abrupt changes in native life should, if possible, be avoided; but the establishment of order, which is the very basis of administration, involves, in Papua, a very abrupt change indeed, if not a complete revolution. Here we seem to have a dilemma from the horns of which we can hardly escape; for how are these two opposing principles to be reconciled?

The problem may be solved readily enough if the natives have Courts of Justice of their own, however primitive, and an administration, however unsatisfactory; for in that case all that need be done is to strengthen the Courts and to stiffen the existing administration. This is the policy known as "Indirect Rule," which has, I believe, been traced back to the days of Alexander the Great, though it is generally applauded as a recent discovery of British Administration in Africa.

But this solution was not open to us in Papua, for there were no native Courts, and, unless very exceptionally, nothing like a native administration; so that we have had to establish Courts and an administration of our own. This is Direct Rule of the most barefaced kind, and we have been duly taken to task for it by zealots of the Indirect method, who are sometimes inclined, as Sir Hugh Clifford says, to exalt their favourite policy into a fetish. We agree that Indirect Rule is useful as a general policy, but, like Mr. Victor Murray in the "School in the Bush" (p. 273) we have thought that it should not be hardened into a formula. In short we think that Indirect Rule was made for Man, and not Man for Indirect Rule; and we refuse to apply it where it is not applicable. It is interesting to note that Madame van Maanen Helmer commits herself to the statement that all territories under C. Mandate are administered by Direct Rule.

PRESERVATION OF NATIVE CUSTOM

However in so far as Indirect Rule implies a regard for native custom we may claim that we have been faithful to this method in Papua, and indeed one of the stock charges against us is that we have gone too far in this direction, but, as another charge is that we have not gone far enough, we may perhaps congratulate ourselves that we have hit the happy mean. Still, great as has been our respect for these customs, we have thought that it should be tempered with common sense. It is no part of our duty to keep what Mr. Julian Huxley has called "a human Zoo", or to maintain practices which would hamper us in the discharge of the "sacred trust"; and, in particular, we feel that no administration could tolerate the welter of blood-shed which once prevailed throughout Papua, and indeed still continues outside the limits of Government influence. Readers of Mr. Riley's description of the return of the raiders, or of Dr. Wirz's account of his visit to the head-hunters of Dutch New Guinea, will understand, perhaps, the fascination exercised upon these Stone Age savages by the prospect of blazing villages, bleeding trunks, and blood boltered heads; but again the Science of Administration bids us beware. We must remember that it is our conception of law and order that is to prevail, and not that of the native. Head-hunting and other atrocities may interest us in a hundred different ways—as part of a fertility cult, as a means of placating the spirits of the dead, or of winning the favour of the tribal gods, or in any other way that the imagination may suggest—but we must resist the temptation to trifle with our duty. We may sympathise as much as we please with the head-hunter and the cannibal, we may formulate any theories we like about the magic properties of human flesh and the true significance of a severed head; but head-hunting and cannibalism must cease, and must cease at once. And no admiration for the picturesque or the bizarre, no interest in curious customs of infanticide, no sympathy with the gay abandon of the raiding party, can excuse a neglect of the essential duty of establishing and maintaining order.

HOSTILE COLLISION WITH NATIVES

And this means a violent collision with the native population, for it is when the police start to make arrests that the spears and arrows begin to fly in earnest. And naturally so. Public law and order is a conception which is new to the Papuan. He has little idea of individual responsibility, and an attempt to arrest a man who has committed an offense is easily misconceived as an attack upon the village. The attack must be repelled, and so all spring to arms, and grasp spear and club, and begin the hopeless fight of the Stone Age against the Twentieth Century.

And then there are two courses open to the police. They can either blow their opponents to pieces with rifle fire, burn their village, lay waste their country, and cow the survivors into subjection; or, in the alternative, they can concentrate their efforts upon the arrest of the individuals who are believed to be guilty, and seek to bring them to trial with as little disturbance as possible.

The former, that is the violent method, is certainly the easier and the less dangerous, and it brings kudos to the Officer concerned, who will be praised as a "stout fellow", and held up to admiration as one who "will stand no nonsense"; but we have regarded it as unscientific, inasmuch as experience shows that it retards the policy of association which we have in view. So we have preferred the slower, less showy, much more dangerous, but more scientific alternative.

Contact with a strange tribe is a good test of character. Forcible subjugation is, as a rule, easy enough; but there are not many problems more difficult than the conciliation of members of a strange community with whom you have no common language. These people are probably in an agony of apprehension as to what is going to happen to them, and distracted with doubt whether they should choose peace or war. To calm their fears requires courage, for the first sign of timidity will invite attack; it requires almost infinite patience; and it requires constant care and watchfulness. For, if the natives are going to attack, you must know their intention in time; otherwise your small force may be caught divided and overwhelmed in detail. That cautious and experienced leader, Sir William MacGregor, was nearly caught in this way at the village of Kairu, in the Purari Delta, and it is a danger which confronts everyone who is dealing with new tribes. And a very insidious danger it is, for it may not arise until your police are off their guard, and, with the insatiable curiosity of the Papuan, have begun to wander about the strange village, poking their noses into every nook and corner in their search for something new.

It is not always easy to tell when natives are going to be actively hostile. The disappearance of women and children is not a certain sign of danger; nor, if they remain, is their presence a sure token of peace. Women may assist an attack by bringing up fresh spears and arrows; they have occasionally remained to cheer their husbands on to victory; or they may be kept on hand in order that their attractions may throw the visitors off their guard. On the other hand their disappearance may be nothing more than a very reasonable precaution. The Officer in charge of the party must weigh all these considerations and must come to the best conclusion he can. It is not safe to rely upon the experience of the police; they are probably "spoiling for a fight", and may see hostility where there is really none.

In practice the natives always have the first shot, for a Government party does not open fire until it is attacked, and not always even then. It is difficult to stop a fight when it has once begun, although, until then, even if spears are poised and bows are bent, there is still a chance of preserving the peace and of making friends. But it is a chance that a timid man would not care to take. Mr. Karius took such a chance in his celebrated expedition across New Guinea, and took it successfully. But Mr. Karius is not a timid man.

LANGUAGE DIFFICULTY

One of our greatest difficulties comes from the diversity of language. Papua is a regular tower of Babel, and ranks with the Sudan and one or two districts in America as one of the stock instances of linguistic multiplicity (Kroeber, p. 98). Generally you can find interpreters, but sometimes you can not, and, in that case, anything like intelligent intercourse becomes practically impossible. Dr. Wirz, in his fascinating book, "Daemonen und Wilde in Neu Guinea," says that bird-hunters and police in Dutch New Guinea have elaborated a system of signs by means of which they can converse freely with natives whose language they do not understand; but we have not reached this stage. The difficulty has been surmounted in some cases by the enlistment of police from the more remote of the outside districts. These men serve for twelve months, and only in the Division in which they are recruited. They are rarely of much use as police, but they are valuable as interpreters, and as messengers of peace when they return to their villages. It is largely through the influence of time-expired police that our penetration has been as peaceful as it has been.

RETURNED PRISONER AS AN AMBASSADOR OF PEACE

Another very valuable ambassador is a returned prisoner. For instance, a murder is committed far away in the interior, and the police, after a pursuit of perhaps months, have at last arrested the guilty persons. The prisoners are marched off, and their friends can have but a very hazy idea of the fate which awaits them; they think perhaps that they are taken away to be fattened up and killed and eaten, and probably the prisoners themselves think the same. So when, instead of being eaten, they are sent back to their village after a short term of imprisonment, they are likely to give the Government a good character, and their fellow villagers will be more amenable to our influence. The reports of the patrols who return the prisoners to their homes are often very interesting. They describe how all the villagers are on the watch as the patrol comes in sight, and how they dance with joy as they see the prisoners returning, and they tell of the delight of the mother when her son is given back to her, apparently from the grave, of the children when they see their father again, and of the wife when her husband is restored to her. It is "roses, roses all the way", the patrol is welcomed with transports of enthusiasm, all that the village has is at their disposal, and the popularity of the Government is at its height. The critic may say that we are too lenient;

but native offences do not often call for heavy punishment, and the rarity of second convictions supports our practice.

CONCLUSION

Such are the methods by which we are pacifying the Territory of Papua. I trust that I have succeeded in establishing my claim that these methods are scientific, but what I fear I have not been able to convey to you is the intense interest of the work. Years ago, when I was younger, and my "foot was swift and steady", I was able to take an active part in it myself, and the memory of those days still remains with me, and has enabled me to appreciate all that is being done by the younger men. The fascination of the work is, I think, largely due to the fact that our resources in Papua are so limited. To use a military expression, we are all in the firing line; we have no reserves either of men or money, and if anyone failed in his duty the consequences would be serious. Fortunately our men do not fail. They get little reward for what they do, and little credit, outside the Territory; but, as the Founder of all science, "the Master of those who know", would say, "they do a man's work manfully."

---

6   The Indian Protection Service: 50 Years of Work for the Indigenous Peoples

DARCY RIBEIRO

In 1900 the Amazon region of South America was still controlled by large numbers of fully independent tribal peoples, as New Guinea was. For Brazil alone Darcy Ribeiro estimated that 105 tribes were still enjoying a completely independent existence in 1900, and another 57 groups were only just beginning to lose their autonomy. ("Culturas e Línguas Indígenas do Brasil," *Educação e Ciências Sociais* 2, no. 6 (1957): 5–102). Only a third of the total known tribes in Brazil at that time had surrendered their autonomy. As in New Guinea, official

Reprinted from Darcy Ribeiro, "The Social Integration of Indigenous Populations in Brazil," *International Labour Review* 85 (1962): 325–46, 459–77. Copyright © 1962 International Labour Organization. Reproduced in abridged form by permission of the author and the publisher.

policy called for the conquest of tribal territory to be conducted as humanely as possible. In the following selection Ribeiro shows that "pacification" was the first step in opening the resources of tribal territory to exploitation by the national society. It was hoped that stopping Indian resistance would ultimately save lives. The personnel of the Indian Protectorate Service (IPS) carried out their directive of "die if need be, never kill" with great courage and noble intentions; however, in the end the Indians who surrendered lost the bulk of their resources along with their independence. By the mid-1960s the original ideals of the IPS were no longer being followed, and the agency was engaging in direct genocidal attacks to remove Indians. In 1967 the IPS was replaced by the National Indian Foundation (FUNAI), and more humane pacification procedures were again adopted.

Darcy Ribeiro (b. 1922) is an internationally respected Brazilian anthropologist and academician. He conducted ethnographic fieldwork in Brazil from 1947 to 1957 and was a founder and first rector of the University of Brasilia in 1962. Ribeiro served as Minister of Education and Culture in 1963 but went into exile after the Goulart presidency ended in 1964. Ribeiro signed the Declaration of Barbados in 1971, proclaiming his support for Indian self-determination. He is currently Vice Governor of the State of Rio de Janeiro. He deals with the issue of Indian policy more fully in his book *Os Índios e a Civilização*, which is published in Portuguese, Spanish, Italian, French, and German.

In any critical review of the 50 years' work done by the Indian Protection Service since its foundation in 1910,[1] regard must be had to the two kinds of problems that have faced the Service:

(1) the problems of Brazil's expanding society, for which "pockets" of hostile Indians were the last obstacle to complete occupation of the national territory; and

(2) the problems of the indigenous population caught up by this expansion, struggling for survival and seeking adjustment to the new conditions of life which are being forced upon it.

"DIE IF NEED BE, NEVER KILL"

As for the first group of problems, there is no doubt that the Indian Protection Service (I.P.S.) has entirely reached its objectives without betraying the slogan of its founder, General Rondon: "die if need be, never kill." Thanks to its efforts, huge regions of this country, including some which now play a leading part in national farm, ranch and mining output, were peacefully occupied by the Brazilian community; and the people who had lived in those regions were settled in special "Indian Areas" on small sections of their former tribal land.[2]

In order to pacify these groups the Indian Protection Service has had to face trials of every sort. First of all, the size of the tribal territory; then—and perhaps most important of all—the difficulty of facing warlike Indians with the weapons of persuasion (the Kayapós, for instance, in order to protect themselves against attack, had armed themselves with 44-calibre rifles won from their enemies by every kind of sacrifice); thirdly, the hostility of the neighbouring civilised population, hot with resentment and hatred, unable to grasp why the Government should take pains to defend people whom they considered incapable of adjustment and meriting nothing but extermination; lastly, the greed of local magnates who coveted the Indians' land.

Pacification is, in essence, deliberate intervention in an open conflict between Indians and civilised groups, each moved by unbridled mutual hatred and suspicion. The Indian conceives the settlers as ferocious enemies who must be resisted or escaped: and he identifies the servants of the I.P.S. with these enemies, these invaders of his land, moving onward through the forests, scaring the game with powerful noisy weapons, attacking the Indian villages and slaughtering whatever inhabitants they come across.

The first task of a pacification team, therefore, is to convince the Indians that it is made up of people very different from all the white men they have met before. This is an extremely difficult task because the action must start with a daring advance into the Indians' territory, for two reasons—so that the team may make its impact far ahead of the foremost pioneer outposts, thus avoiding outside interference; and as a deliberate provocation, to attract the Indians' attention and hence their hostility.

When Rondon went into the interior at the head of the Mato Grosso-Amazon Strategic Communications and Telegraph Commission, he developed the pacification techniques which were later to guide the Indian Protection Service in similar enterprises. These consist, first of all, in recruiting a team among the local population, explaining to them what they will have to do, warning them of the care they must take if the Indians react violently against the penetration of their land, and convincing them of the justice and efficiency of persuasive methods. The leadership of these pacification teams is allotted to men having experience of work in the bush and of dealings with Indians. Whenever possible, the teams include partly integrated Indians belonging to the same language groups as the neighbouring population, to serve as guides and interpreters.

When the team has been formed, it moves to a carefully chosen point within the tribal territory, near means of communication (rivers or roads) that are definitely open, so as to ensure a retreat if necessary and a constant supply of food and gifts. The point chosen should be readily accessible to the Indians so that, once they have discovered it, they will tend to return, and contacts in sufficiently safe conditions will be possible.

Once the provisional shelter for the "attraction post" has been built, the team makes a wide clearing and constructs in the middle an "armoured" house (zinc plating is best) surrounded by a barbed-wire fence, to protect the personnel against the inevitable attacks and volleys of arrows. At the same time, maize, manioc, potatoes, peanuts and other crops are planted to serve not only for the subsistence of the team but also—and indeed, chiefly—as an attraction for the Indians. In the case of a very "tough" group, the field should be placed at a good distance from the post itself, so that individuals can help themselves without feeling watched. During the work of setting up the post the use of firearms should be avoided, even for hunting, so as not to scare the Indians or arouse their hostility.

Immediately after the establishment of the post, the team leader or assistants whom he fully trusts (accompanied by interpreters) "beat" the neighbouring bush, identify the tracks and water holes most used by the Indians, put up little shelters near by, and leave behind them knives, axes, scythes, shears, choppers, daggers, glasswork and other gifts. Wherever possible, the Indians' own deserted huts or hunting shelters are used for this purpose.

Once they have discovered the post, the Indians watch the team constantly, while remaining invisible, and will often attack a careless individual who strays from the group. Luiz Bueno Horta Barbosa, who directed the pacification of the Kaingángs in São Paulo, made the following comment on the state of mind of a pacification team in the long months preceding contact:

> No one could ever imagine how much moral strength a man must display to keep down the terrific nervous irritation which is caused by the sense of constant encirclement, the sense of being watched and studied in his smallest actions by an unknown number of people whom he cannot see, whom he does not want to scare or annoy but rather to please and attract, while all they seek is the best moment to attack and kill him.[3]

The next stage—that of initial contact—is one of open hostility on the part of the Indians, who make every effort to expel the invaders in a series of attacks. These early incidents are of capital importance, for they give the newcomers an opportunity of proving their friendly disposition and firm intention not to make war. It is essential at this stage to couple a serene and peaceful air with a certain firmness, to demonstrate that the team has arms, knows how to use them, is well defended, and only abstains from attacking the Indians because it does not wish to hurt them. The team acts accordingly—firing into the air when the attacking Indians come too close to the house and threaten to break in, avoiding hurried retreats, leaving in the gift shelters game killed with gunshot to show its skill with firearms.

After the first fruitless attempts to dislodge the intruders, the Indians generally move their villages further back, so as to provide greater safety for the women and children. Groups of well-armed warriors then proceed to harass the pacification team with periodic attacks, usually at first light, each following several days of vigilance.

It is against this background that the equipment of the fortified building has to be completed, the clearing planted and supply arrangements made—all of which amply shows how much personal courage, equanimity and persuasive spirit are required to "attract" a hostile indigenous group.

Only after months of effort will the Indians be convinced by events—

contradicting all their previous experience—that *these* whites are different from the others, for though armed and in a strong defensive posture they never take hostile action, not even to repel an attack. Only then do the boldest individuals begin to slip into the clearing, helping themselves to the maize and the manioc made ready for them. Next, cautiously, they come closer still. Instead of destroying the gift shelters and accepting the contents under the guise of capture, they begin to leave objects of their own in exchange for what they take. Members of the team will also then grow bolder, letting themselves be seen when they know that Indians are near, and calling on them—through the interpreters—to fraternise.

It is customary to call this period *namóro*—the "flirting" stage; the Indians have begun to accept gifts as such, and even to ask for more, leaving in the shelters wooden models of knives, shears or other objects to indicate what they want. Any abuse of confidence at this time is extremely dangerous, because most of the Indians are still terrified of all white people, whom they have learned to regard as bloodthirsty and treacherous. A misunderstood movement may cause them to renew their attacks, cancel out the progress already made or even require the whole undertaking to be dropped.

The "flirting" stage leads on to fraternisation, which may develop rapidly into a sound relationship, after the team's first visit to the Indians' village, or collapse if their fear of the white man is revived by an untoward event.

This gradual approach to hostile tribes which the I.P.S. has adopted no doubt involves risks for the staff; but the method's efficiency has been proved each time it was used with the proper amount of care. Perhaps the best evidence is the impression left on several tribes that it was in fact they who were softening up the white men.

Indeed, after the pacification of some of the most warlike groups it was found that they had made quite moving efforts in that very direction. The Kaingángs of Sao Paulo, the Xokléngs of Santa Catarina, the Parintintíns and other groups, when fraternising with the I.P.S. attraction teams, were convinced that they—the Indians—had done the pacifying. For the first time they had had an opportunity of acting by the rules of their own etiquette without suffering injury. Several of the pacification reports prove, in fact, that these tribes were either peacefully settled or at least wished to establish relations with the whites: They merely did not know how to approach them, for previous attempts in this direction had been met with bullets.

Actually, it is practically impossible for a tribal group to bring off any kind of successful approach to the whites. Their standard of relationships with strangers, their etiquette for the treatment of potential enemies, apt though they may be for the handling of groups with the same cultural traditions, fail with white people. One only has to recall the warlike gestures that serve as greetings in some tribes to appreciate the impossibility of a friendly contact.[4]

Even the dreaded Kayapó hordes, which decimated such neighbouring tribes as the Kuruayas, Tapirapes and Jurunas and kept the farming settlements of the Xingu and Araguaia rivers in constant alarm from the early days of the century, made several attempts at establishing friendly relations with the civilised population, sending them prisoners of war as peace envoys and subsequently coming forward peacefully of their own will. Nimuendajú refers to some of these attempts, all frustrated by the settlers' bitter hatred for the Kayapós whom they considered "wild beasts", "instinctively perverse" and "only fit for reduction by bullets".[5]

The Kaingángs of São Paulo told those who pacified them of their bids to "soften" groups of railway workers on the Brazilian north-western railway as these advanced across the tribal territory. In one such case a Kaingáng chief walked unarmed towards a group of workers, carrying a child in his arms as a pledge of his peaceful intentions. He was greeted with a volley, despite every gesture towards the child and to his own unarmed condition; the volley was repeated and, as he withdrew, a bullet laid the child dead.

This event shortly preceded the arrival of a pacification team and the establishment of peace; it did not prevent these very Indians from approaching the team in the same manner. In this case, however, they had good reason to believe that they had softened the hearts of the intruders, for it was a group of Indians, entering the camp of their own will, which made the first friendly contact.

This brief review of Brazilian relations with the Indians shows that the I.P.S. has been worthy of Rondon's slogan: "die if need be, never kill." All the tribes encountered by the moving frontier of Brazilian society were brought into peaceful co-existence without the killing of a single Indian by bullets, although more than a dozen I.P.S. workers fell pierced by arrows as they went about their work of pacification.

As each team completed its tour of duty, another relieved it to carry the job further. These facts bear witness to the moral potential of the Brazilian people even more than to the qualities of the I.P.S. itself. Courage, perseverance and readiness for sacrifice were the essential qualities needed, and the Service found them in abundance whenever it required them.

But what was to be done with the Indians thus pacified? How should they be led down the paths of civilisation, and how should the physical vigour and love of life which tribal liberty had brought them, despite all the backwardness of traditional methods of subsistence, be preserved? How could they be introduced to the new life they would have to live? Teach them to farm, when many already had bigger and better fields than those of the post? Teach them to dress, when there was no certainty that they could be provided with clothes, once they had learned to use them?

In truth, "pacification" is adjusted more to the need for expansion of Brazil's organised society than to the specific needs of the Indians. It is by "assistance" that these latter needs are met: and in the work of assistance and protection the I.P.S. has frequently failed. Called in to save the tribes from destruction which would have been inevitable, had they been left to their own devices in ecological competition with infinitely larger and culturally more advanced populations, the Service has not been able to prevent the Indians, once disarmed, from descending to conditions of utter destitution and losing their happiness with their independence.

Pacification brought about at the cost of many lives, of heroic effort to bring peace to further tribal groups, has been a source of frustration to its very authors: they have seen victory perverted into the defeat of their ideals, for the Indians have not even been assured possession of the land and peaceful co-existence has brought them hunger, disease and disappointment.

NOTES

1. For an excellent historical study on the Service, see David Stauffer, "Origem e Fundação do Serviço de Proteção aos Indios, 1889–1910", in *Revista de Historia* (São Paulo), No. 37, 1959, pp. 73–95; No. 42, 1960, pp. 435–453; No. 43, 1960, pp. 165–183; and No. 44, 1960, pp. 427–450.

2. The lands of the famous Kaingángs of western São Paulo, pacified in 1912 by Manoel Rabelo and Luiz Bueno Horta Barbosa, are now occupied by some of the biggest coffee estates in Brazil. Those of the Xokléngs of Santa Catarina, pacified by Eduárdo de Lima e Silva Hoerhann, have become a prosperous region, the richest in the state. The Botocudos (Krenak, Pojitxá and others), pacified in 1911 by Antonio Martins Estigarriba, lived in the Doce River Valley (Minas Gerais and Espiritu Santo) on territory covered today by innumerable estates and townships. The pacification of the Umotinas on the Sepotuba and Paraguay rivers, achieved by Helmano Dos Santos Mascarenhas and Severiano Godofredo D'Albuquerque in 1918, opened up the greatest ipecac forests of Brazil. The Parintintíns kept the wide savanna of the Madeira River and its tributaries closed until they were pacified by Curt Nimuendajú in 1922. The Urubus-Kaapors had almost all the Gurupí valley from Pará to Maranbão in a state of war until 1928, when they were pacified by Benedito Jesus de Araújo after 18 years of I.P.S. effort. The pacification of the Xavantes (Akwes) of the Rio das Mortes—completed by Francisco Meireles in 1946—cost the lives of a whole mission under Genesio Pimentel Barbosa, but it opened up the natural pastures of the island of Bananal and the Rio das Mortes. The war raids of the Kayapó-Kubén-Kran-Kégn, of the middle Xingu Valley, ranged from the Tapajos to the Araguaia until they were pacified by Cícero Cavalcanti at the end of 1952. The Kayapó-Xikris, whose attacks carried to the Araguaia farmlands, to the farthest nut groves and savannas of the Itacaiuna River, to Marabá and against the Asurinís, were pacified by Miguel Araújo and Leonardo Vilas Boas in 1953. Another band of Kayapó, Txukahamãi or Mentuktíre—on the left bank of the Xingu River at the level of von Martius falls—used to attack the rubber planters of the Xingu River and the Juruna Indians until pacified in the same year by the brothers Claudio and Orlando Vilas Boas. The Parakanã, Asuriní and other Tupí groups on the left bank of the Tocantins, which had kept the Tocantins railway line in a state of constant interruption, came into peaceful contact with I.P.S. teams led by Telesforo Martins Fontes. Today efforts are continuing to strengthen peaceful relations with, among others, the Gaviões on the right bank of the Tocantins in Pará state; the Pagaa-novas and further Guaporé groups (reduced in size nowadays); and the Uaimiris of the Jauaperi Valley (Amazonas state).

3. Report of São Paulo Inspectorate to Director of I.P.S., 1912 (manuscript in I.P.S. archives). See also L. B. Horta Barbosa: A *Pacificação dos Caingangs Paulistas. Habitos, Costumes e Instituçoes desses Indios* (Rio de Janeiro, 1913). Reports on pacification of other tribes by the I.P.S. may be found in Curt Nimuendajú: "Os Parintintín do Rio Madeira," reprinted from the *Journal de la Société des américanistes de Paris* (Paris), N.S., Vol. XVI, 1924, pp. 201–278;

Joaquim Gondim: A *Pacificação dos Parintintíns—Koró de Juirapa*, Rondon Commission Publication No. 87 (1925); and Lincoln de Souza: Os *Xavantes e a Civilização. Ensaio histórico* (Rio de Janeiro, 1953).

4. Among the Umotina, for instance, on the upper Sepotuba River, etiquette prescribed the following initial approach to any group of strangers—whether a village of the same tribe or a frontier township: to simulate an attack as realistically as possible, going so far as to draw bows and half-release arrows—which were only withheld at the last moment. Evidently no group which does not share the same etiquette could take such an apparent attack for a friendly greeting, the first step towards establishment of peaceful relations.

5. See "Os Górotire: Relatório apresentado ao Serviço de Proteção aos Indios, em 18 de Abril de 1940", in *Revista do Museu Paulista* (São Paulo), Vol. VI, 1952, pp. 427–463.

III

The Shock Phase:
Assessing Initial Impact

The most critical period in the development process begins as soon as routine contact is established between previously autonomous, relatively isolated tribals and representatives of the national society. During this "shock phase" the potential for rapid cultural collapse and even physical extinction of the tribal population is very high. This first phase of development means the surrender of political autonomy and for many groups the loss of territory as well. An "uncontrolled frontier" is often involved, where unregulated traders and settlers may instigate quite brutal exploitation, but the impact may be just as severe when a regular military force or a peaceful civilian authority intervenes. The usual impact of this phase may include increased mortality, subsistence disruption, kin group dispersion, a breakdown of the social support system, the emergence of new religious movements, and in some cases armed tribal resistance.

It is important to recognize that we are really referring here to the trauma and immediate aftermath of armed invasion and conquest by an alien power, even though in the popular mind the negative aspects may be masked by euphemisms about frontiers and development progress. The war of conquest between tribes and states has been underway for some 6000 years, and it still continues in a few remote corners of the globe where the whole process described here is still actively underway.

Tribes held up reasonably well until industrialization tipped the balance in favor of states. As recently as 1800, less than 200 years ago, tribes still controlled roughly half of the globe and perhaps 20 percent of the world's population. However, they have lost ground rapidly since then. Perhaps 50 million tribal peoples died as industrial states expanded between 1800 and

1950. This is a staggering figure, representing perhaps two-thirds of the total tribal population at its peak during the prestate Neolithic; it averages out to more than a quarter million people killed every year for 150 years. Economic development of tribal areas by the industrial state has thus clearly involved genocide on a grand scale. However, the reality of this genocide has been somewhat obscured by the paradoxical fact that in the end, after the state consolidated its control over conquered tribal territories, the surviving tribal population often actually increased. Today's estimated 200 million tribals, or ethnically distinct "near tribals," is a population perhaps two and a half times the tribal population during the Neolithic. However, many surviving "tribals" may have maintained their ethnic identity but no longer display all the characteristics of the tribal cultural type discussed in part I. "Ethnocide" has also, without a doubt, been a significant long-range outcome of development, but it is a more gradual, less dramatic process extending into the second "integration" phase of development.

The following selections document the official discovery of the devastation that the expanding colonial frontiers were causing in tribal areas; they also illustrate the later attempts of anthropologists to understand and moderate the process. The House of Commons Select Committee Report is the first global impact assessment of the shock phase. Originally issued early in the nineteenth century, it is still a definitive overview of the problem. Writing nearly a hundred years later, Mills and Rivers present detailed case studies of the consequences of development intervention in tribal areas from the perspective of British colonial functionalist anthropology.

7 Official Report of the Select Committee on Aborigines

HOUSE OF COMMONS
SELECT COMMITTEE

By the 1830s it had become apparent that the expanding British colonial empire was destroying tribal peoples throughout the world. Not only was this morally unacceptable, it also meant the loss of valuable sources of labor and often led to costly military intervention. In response to the crisis the House of Commons established a 15-member select committee to investigate the problem and issue recommendations. The committee spent some ten months interviewing expert witnesses from all corners of the empire in order to establish precisely what was happening. The official report, issued in 1836–37, was a truly impressive document. It contained more than 1000 oversize pages and some eight pounds of testimony detailing the outrages being committed worldwide against tribal peoples. A very obvious pattern emerged: unregulated frontier expansion was creating a "calamity" for native people. The committee's findings were remarkably thorough and insightful, and they continue to be verified by the experience of tribal peoples throughout the world up to the present time. The World Bank review of the same problem, issued in 1982, provides an amazing modern parallel (see Goodland selection in part IX). The World Bank study was conducted for precisely the same reasons, reviewed the same evidence, and reached the same conclusions. Unfortunately, but not surprisingly given their biases, both agencies recommended hopelessly inadequate "safeguards" that they felt would humanely protect tribal cultures in the face of large-scale economic development.

The Select Committee "appointed to consider what Measures ought to be adopted with regard to the Native Inhabitants of Countries where British Settlements are made, and to the neighbouring Tribes, in order to secure to them the due observance of Justice and the protection of their Rights; to promote the spread of Civilization among them, and to lead them to the peaceful and voluntary reception of the Christian Religion;" and to whom the Report of the Committee of 1836 was referred; and who were empowered to report their Observations thereupon, together with the Minutes of Evidence taken before them, to The House; Have examined the Matters to them referred, and have agreed to the following Report:

The situation of Great Britain brings her beyond any other power into

Reprinted from *Report of the Select Committee on Aborigines (British Settlements)*. House of Commons, Imperial Blue Book, nr VII, 425 (1837), pp. 3–6, 74–76.

communication with the uncivilized nations of the earth. We are in contact with them in so many parts of the globe, that it has become of deep importance to ascertain the results of our relations with them, and to fix the rules of our conduct towards them. We are apt to class them under the sweeping term of savages, and perhaps, in so doing, to consider ourselves exempted from the obligations due to them as our fellow men. This assumption does not, however, it is obvious, alter our responsibility; and the question appears momentous, when we consider that the policy of Great Britain in this particular, as it has already affected the interests, and, we fear we may add, sacrificed the lives, of many thousands, may yet, in all probability, influence the character and the destiny of millions of the human race.

The extent of the question will be best comprehended by taking a survey of the globe, and by observing over how much of its surface an intercourse with Britain may become the greatest blessing, or the heaviest scourge. It will scarcely be denied in word, that, as an enlightened and Christian people, we are at least bound to do to the inhabitants of other lands, whether enlightened or not, as we should in similar circumstances desire to be done by; but, beyond the obligations of common honesty, we are bound by two considerations with regard to the uncivilized: first, that of the ability which we possess to confer upon them the most important benefits; and, secondly, that of their inability to resist any encroachments, however unjust, however mischievous, which we may be disposed to make. The disparity of the parties, the strength of the one, and the incapacity of the other, to enforce the observance of their rights, constitutes a new and irresistible appeal to our compassionate protection.

The duty of introducing into our relations with uncivilized nations the righteous and the profitable laws of justice is incontrovertible, and it has been repeatedly acknowledged in the abstract, but has, we fear, been rarely brought into practice; for, as a nation, we have not hesitated to invade many of the rights which they hold most dear.

Thus, while Acts of Parliament have laid down the general principles of equity, other and conflicting Acts have been framed, disposing of lands without any reference to the possessors and actual occupants, and without making any reserve of the proceeds of the property of the natives for their benefit. . . .

. . . the Address of the House of Commons to the King, passed unanimously July 1834, states, "That His Majesty's faithful Commons in Parliament assembled, are deeply impressed with the duty of acting upon the principles of justice and humanity in the intercourse and relations of this country with the native inhabitants of its colonial settlements, of affording them protection in the enjoyment of their civil rights, and of imparting to them that degree of civilization, and that religion, with which Providence has blessed this nation, and humbly prays that His Majesty will take such measures, and give such directions to the governors and officers of His Majesty's colonies, settlements and plantations, as shall secure to the natives the due observance of justice and the protection of their rights, promote the spread of civilization amongst them, and lead them to the peaceful and voluntary reception of the Christian religion."

This Address, as the Chancellor of the Exchequer observed, so far from being the expression of any new principle, only embodies and recognizes principles on which the British Government has for a considerable time been disposed to act.

In furtherance of these views, your Committee was appointed to examine into the actual state of our relations with uncivilized nations; and it is from the evidence brought before this Committee during the last two Sessions, that we are enabled to compare our actions with our avowed principles, and to show what has been, and what will assuredly continue to be, unless strongly checked, the course of our conduct towards these defenceless people.

It is not too much to say, that the intercourse of Europeans in general, without any exception in favour of the subjects of Great Britain, has been, unless when attended by missionary exertions, a source of many calamities to uncivilized nations.

Too often, their territory has been usurped; their property seized; their numbers diminished; their character debased; the spread of civilization impeded. European vices and diseases have been introduced amongst them, and they have been familiarized with the use of our most potent instruments for the subtle or the violent destruction of human life, viz. brandy and gunpowder.

It will be only too easy to make out the proof of all these assertions, which may be established solely by the evidence above referred to. It will be easy also to show that the result to ourselves has been as contrary to our interest as to our duty; that our system has not only incurred a vast load of crime, but a vast expenditure of money and amount of loss.

On the other hand, we trust it will not be difficult to show by inference, and even to prove, by the results of some few experiments of an opposite course of conduct, that, setting aside all considerations of duty, a line of policy, more friendly and just towards the natives, would materially contribute to promote the civil and commercial interests of Great Britain.

It is difficult to form an estimate of the population of the less civilized nations, liable to be influenced for good or for evil, by contact and intercourse with the more civilized nations of the earth. It would appear that the barbarous regions likely to be more immediately affected by the policy of Great Britain, are the south and the west of Africa, Australia, the islands in the Pacific Ocean, a very extensive district of South America at the back of our Essequibo settlement, between the rivers Orinoco and Amazon, with the immense tract which constitutes the most northerly part of the American continent, and stretches from the Pacific to the Atlantic Ocean.

These are countries in which we have either planted colonies, or which we frequent for the purposes of traffic, and it is our business to inquire on what principles we have conducted our intercourse.

It might be presumed that the native inhabitants of any land have an incontrovertible right to their own soil: a plain and sacred right, however, which seems not to have been understood. Europeans have entered their borders uninvited, and, when there, have not only acted as if they were undoubted lords of the soil, but have punished the natives as aggressors if they have evinced a disposition to live in their own country.

"If they have been found upon their own property, they have been treated as thieves and robbers. They are driven back into the interior as if they were dogs or kangaroos."

From very large tracts we have, it appears, succeeded in eradicating them; and though from some parts their ejection has not been so apparently violent as from others, it has been equally complete, through our taking possession of their hunting-grounds, whereby we have despoiled them of the means of existence. . . .

CONCLUSION

Your Committee cannot recapitulate the evils which have been the result of the intercourse between civilized and barbarous nations more truly, than in the summary contained in the interrogation and responses of the secretaries of the three Missionary societies most conversant with the subject, and to which we have already referred.

> To Mr. *Coates.*] Is it your opinion that Europeans coming into contact with native inhabitants of our settlements tends (with the exception of cases in which missions are established) to deteriorate the morals of the natives; to introduce European vices; to spread among them new and dangerous diseases; to accustom them to the use of ardent spirits; to the use of European arms and instruments of destruction; to the seduction of native females; to the decrease of the native population; and to prevent the spread of civilization, education, commerce and Christianity: and that the effect of European intercourse has been, upon the whole, a calamity on the heathen and savage nations. In the first place, is it your opinion that European contact with native inhabitants, always excepting the cases in which missions have been established, tends to deteriorate the morals of the natives?—Yes.
>
> To Mr. *Beecham.*] Do you concur in that opinion?—Yes.
> To Mr. *Ellis.*] Do you concur in that opinion?—Certainly.
> Does it tend to introduce European vices?—Mr. *Coates.*] Yes.— Mr. *Beecham.*] Yes.—Mr. *Ellis.*] Yes.
> Does it tend to spread among them new and dangerous diseases?—Mr. *Coates.*] Yes.—Mr. *Beecham.*] Yes.—Mr. *Ellis.*] Yes.
> Does it tend to accustom them to the use of ardent spirits?—Mr. *Coates.*] Yes.—Mr. *Beecham.*] Yes.—Mr. *Ellis.*] Yes.
> And to the use of European arms and instruments of destruction?—Mr. *Coates.*] Yes; but might I add a word which would go rather to express a doubt whether the ultimate result of that be injuri-

ous to the savage nations? but that it has the tendency suggested in the question, I have no doubt.—Mr. *Beecham.*] Yes.—Mr. *Ellis.*] Yes.

To the seduction of native females?—Mr. *Coates.*] Yes.—Mr. *Beecham.*] Yes.—Mr. *Ellis.*] Yes.

To the decrease of population?—Mr. *Coates.*] Yes.—Mr. *Beecham.*] Yes.—Mr. *Ellis.*] Yes.

Does it tend to impede that civilization which, if Europeans properly conducted themselves, might be introduced?—Mr. *Coates.*] Certainly.—Mr. *Beecham.*] Yes.—Mr. *Ellis.*] I have no doubt that it does.

The same as to education?—Mr. *Coates.*] Certainly.—Mr. *Beecham.*] Yes.—Mr. *Ellis.*] Certainly.

The same as to commerce?—Mr. *Coates.*] Certainly.—Mr. *Beecham.*] Yes.—Mr. *Ellis.*] Yes.

It is your opinion that it tends to prevent the spread of the Christian Gospel?—Mr. *Coates.*] Most assuredly.—Mr. *Beecham.*] Yes.—Mr. *Ellis.*] Yes.

Is it generally your opinion that the effect of European intercourse, saving where missions have been established, has been, upon the whole, hitherto a calamity upon the native and savage nations whom we have visited?—Mr. *Coates.*] That I have no doubt about.—Mr. *Beecham.*] Yes generally.—Mr. *Ellis.*] Generally, I should think it has.

As far as you know, in instances of contention between Europeans and natives, has it generally happened that the Europeans were in fault?—Mr. *Coates.*] Universally, so far as I have information upon the subject.—Mr. *Beecham.*] Yes.—Mr. *Ellis.*] I have not met with an instance in which, when investigated, it has not been found that the aggression was upon the part of the Europeans.

These allegations have, we conceive, been clearly proved in the evidence of which we have given an abstract; and we have also seen the effects of conciliatory conduct, and of Christian instruction. One of the two systems we must have to preserve our own security, and the peace of our colonial borders; either an overwhelming military force with all its attendant expenses, or a line of temperate conduct and of justice towards our neighbours.

"The main point which I would have in view," said a witness before your Committee, "would be trade, commerce, peace and civilization. The other alternative is extermination; for you can stop nowhere; you must go on; you may have a short respite when you have driven panic into the people, but you must come back to the same thing until you have shot the last man." From all the bulky evidence before us, we can come to no other conclusion; and considering the power, and the mighty resources of the British nation, we must believe that the choice rests with ourselves.

Great Britain has, in former times, countenanced evils of great magnitude,—slavery and the slave-trade; but for these she has made some atonement; for the latter, by abandoning the traffic; for the former, by the sacrifice of 20 millions of money. But for these offences there was this apology; they were evils of an ancient date, a kind of prescription might be pleaded for them, and great interests were entwined with them.

An evil remains very similar in character, and not altogether unfit to be compared with them in the amount of misery it produces. The oppression of the natives of barbarous countries is a practice which pleads no claim to indulgence; it is an evil of comparatively recent origin, imperceptible and unallowed in its growth; it never has had even the colour of sanction from the legislature of this country; no vested rights are associated with it, and we have not the poor excuse that it contributes to any interest of the state. On the contrary, in point of economy, of security, of commerce, of reputation, it is a short-sighted and disastrous policy. As far as it has prevailed, it has been a burthen on the empire. It has thrown impediments in the way of successful colonization; it has engendered wars, in which great expenses were necessarily incurred, and no reputation could be won; and it has banished from our confines, or exterminated, the natives, who might have been profitable workmen, good customers, and good neighbours. These unhappy results have not flowed from any determination on the part of the government of this country to deal hardly with those who are in a less advanced state of society; but they seem to have arisen from ignorance, from the difficulty which distance interposes in checking the cupidity and punishing the crimes of that adventurous class of Europeans who lead the way in penetrating the territory of uncivilized man, and from the system of dealing with the rights of the natives. Many reasons unite for apprehending that the evils which we have described will increase if the duty of coming to a solemn determination as to the policy we shall adopt towards ruder nations be now neglected; the chief of these reasons is, the national necessity of finding some outlet for the superabundant population of Great Britain and Ireland. It is to be feared that, in the pursuit of this benevolent and laudable object, the rights of those who have not the means of advocating their interests or exciting sympathy for their sufferings, may be disregarded.

This, then, appears to be the moment for the nation to declare, that with all its desire to give encouragement to emigration, and to find a soil to which our surplus population may retreat, it will tolerate no scheme which implies violence or fraud in taking possession of such a territory; that it will no longer subject itself to the guilt of conniving at oppression, and that it will take upon itself the task of defending those who are too weak and too ignorant to defend themselves.

Your Committee have hitherto relied chiefly on arguments, showing that no national interest, even in its narrowest sense, is subserved by encroachments on the territory or disregard of the rights of the aboriginal inhabitants of barbarous countries; but they feel it their duty to add, that there is a class of motives of a higher order which conduce to the same conclusion.

The British empire has been signally blessed by Providence, and her eminence, her strength, her wealth, her prosperity, her intellectual, her moral and her religious advantages, are so many reasons for peculiar obedience to the laws of Him who guides the destinies of nations. These were given for some higher purpose than commercial prosperity and military renown. "It is not to be doubted that this country has been invested with wealth and power, with arts and knowledge, with the sway of distant lands, and the mastery of the restless waters, for some great and important purpose in the government of the world. Can we suppose otherwise than that it is our office to carry civilization and humanity, peace and good government, and, above all, the knowledge of the true God, to the uttermost ends of the earth?" He who has made Great Britain what she is, will inquire at our hands how we have employed the influence He has lent to us in our dealings with the untutored and defenceless savage; whether it has been engaged in seizing their lands, warring upon their people, and transplanting unknown disease, and deeper degradation, through the remote regions of the earth; or whether we have, as far as we have been able, informed their ignorance, and invited and afforded them the opportunity of becoming partakers of that civilization, that innocent commerce, that knowledge and that faith with which it has pleased a gracious Providence to bless our own country.

---

8   The Effect on the Naga Tribes of Assam of Their Contact with Western Civilization

J. P. MILLS

In the 1930s the Naga hill tribes of northeast India were virtually a textbook example of a controlled experiment in the impact of government control on independent tribal peoples. At that time the vast forested uplands in what was then the British Indian province of Assam and adjacent portions of Burma were controlled by hundreds of thousands of tribespeople who either had never been effectively conquered by any state or had only recently accepted partial control. During the early period of British rule in India there was little interest in developing

Reprinted with permission from *Proceedings of the Fifth Pacific Science Congress* 4 (1933): 2871–82. Copyright © 1933 Pacific Science Association.

the hill territories, and eventually a formal decision was made to avoid unnecessary conflict by stabilizing the frontier. In 1873 the British administration established an "inner line" in Assam beyond which no government control would be extended and outsiders were prohibited. There were also zones of full and partial government control. In many respects this was an ideal response to the problems identified by the select committee of 1836–37. Here was a carefully regulated development program designed to minimize the damage to tribal people. In spite of all the good intentions, however, serious problems were still occurring in the zones under government influence. According to Mills, the "pax Britannica" ended intertribal fighting but actually increased tribal mortality in quite unexpected ways. Nevertheless, despite the adverse impacts, the culture still flourished in the uncontrolled and partially controlled areas. The later struggle of the Naga to retain their autonomy after India gained her independence from Britain is described in part VII by Ovesen.

J. P. Mills (1890–1960) was educated at Oxford. He served as an administrator in Assam and other tribal areas of India from 1916 to 1947 and published several ethnographic accounts of the Naga. From 1948 to 1955 he was a Reader in the University of London School of Oriental and African Studies.

The Naga tribes inhabit the northern half of the great mass of hills lying along the south-east border of Assam and dividing that province from Burma. My reasons for selecting this area for special consideration are two. Firstly, I have served in it in daily and intimate contact with Nagas for the greater part of the last fourteen years. Secondly, we have here materials for comparison which can exist in few other places in the world. At one extreme there are Nagas dressed as Europeans, speaking excellent English and working as medical assistants, skilled clerks, and so on, and at the other there are tribesmen still taking heads as of old, and entirely unaffected by any Western influence. This is due to political reasons. The administrative district of the Naga Hills consists of a long strip of hill country running parallel with the plains. It was taken over in order to protect the plains from raids, and had reached almost its present extent by 1890. The two hundred thousand Nagas who inhabit it are fully administered. Head-hunting is prohibited and a network of bridle paths covers the country. Beyond the administered district, to the south-east, is another zone. Here the tribes are independent, but are expected to obey orders to a certain extent. They still occasionally make war on each other, but the tendency is for them to bring more and more of their quarrels for arbitration. Beyond them is a third zone in which no control whatever is exerted. Beyond that again lies Burma's area of control.

I have been fortunate enough to visit a large number of independent Naga villages, in some of which a white face has never been seen before or since, and I am constantly receiving individuals from across the frontier and settling their disputes for them. In considering, therefore, the changes wrought by civilization we are not hampered, as is so often the case elsewhere, by having to compare the conditions of to-day with an almost mythical past. Instead we have the unaltered Naga always at hand for reference.

Though the tribes are many, and their divergencies of custom great, the race has a real homogeneity, and I think it is possible to give a picture of a typical untouched village and the life lived in it. This will serve as a standard when the time comes to discuss the changes being wrought in areas where external influences are strong.

Life in the independent area is lived thus. The Naga social unit is not the tribe, but the village. Confederacies of villages may be formed, but they are usually ephemeral. To kill a man or woman of another village is no great crime, even if the villages are bound with definite ties of friendship. If there are no such ties it is a meritorious act. On the other hand, to take the life of a fellow-villager (and so weaken the village) is the greatest crime a Naga can commit—a crime for which the only punishment is death or exile. Each village is inhabited by two or more clans, usually occupying each its own area. Between these, bitter feuds are frequent. These feuds go on from generation to generation, and are never settled, there being no external authority which can make a decision and enforce it. The clans intermarry freely, however, and the feuds usually remain below the surface. Each clan has in its area of the village one or more bachelors' halls where the unmarried men sleep and men of all ages congregate and gossip. They are regarded as the nurseries of warriors. Few tribes have real chiefs. Sometimes wealth and strength of character will give a man pre-eminence. More usually the older men guide the destinies of the village in informal council. War is normal; peace is abnormal. Sentries guard the village continually and scouts reconnoitre the ground before parties go down to the fields to work in the morning. From time to time raiding parties go out and try to obtain heads from villages with which they are not at peace. By his prowess in war is a man judged, and no girl looks kindly on a suitor who has not taken part in a successful raid. Agriculture is the sole means of livelihood and all wealth is in grain and cattle. Money is unknown. Weapons are made only in a few villages and are obtained by barter. Every girl marries as a matter of course. Prostitution is unknown; there is no need to seek this means of livelihood, and no girl could pursue it with her relations living all round her. There is no destitution; orphans and aged people are looked after by their clans. Nor is there any pointless accumulation of wealth; grain and cattle are valued not to be hoarded, but to be distributed in ceremonial feasts which entitle the giver to wear certain coveted ornaments. Crime is punished by a fine in goods. As the clan of a criminal are responsible for his fines they exercise a beneficial control over him. An incorrigible rogue, for whom his clan will pay no more, is liable to be put to death. On the whole the life of a Naga is incomparably better than that of a Western city dweller.

The annexation and pacification of what is now the Naga Hills district has brought inevitable changes, and Western civilization has had its effect on Nagas coming in contact with it. The term "Western civilization" is used in this paper in the widest possible sense. By it is meant not only the direct influence of European officials and American missionaries, but the influence of all whom administration has brought in its train—foreign shopkeepers in the bazaar, Gurka sepoys of the garrison, Indian clerks in the offices, and all the strangers who have been brought or attracted to the area for various reasons. Entrance to the hills is not unrestricted and every foreigner has to obtain a pass. Even so there is a considerable foreign population, though it is strictly concentrated in certain areas. There has always been contact of a kind with foreigners. The hills run for many miles along the edge of plains inhabited by Indians, and Nagas from the outer ranges have frequented the bazaars in the plains from time immemorial. But administration of the hills brought about a change, the significance of which it is essential to realize. Before his hills were taken over, contact was at the option of the Naga; now, in certain areas, he cannot avoid contact with the foreigner. In the old days the Naga could go down to the bazaars when he wished, but the foreigner could not visit the Naga at will; his head would have been forfeited had he tried. Now the Naga living near a centre of administration brushes shoulders with foreigners every day, and even those living in the more remote parts of the administered area are visited from time to time by touring officials. (Tours by casual foreigners are strictly prohibited.)

Some changes can be definitely assigned to particular agencies or combinations of such agencies. These agencies are: officials engaged in administration, the battalion of Assam Rifles stationed in the district, foreign traders, missionaries of the American Baptist Mission, and servants, retired sepoys and other foreigners living in the district. These influences emanate from two centres only—Kohima, which is the headquarters of the district, and Mokokchung, which is the headquarters of the subdivision of that name. There was a tendency in the past to allow Gurkhas to settle promiscuously, and they have left their mark. This has now been stopped and, except near the two centres, a stay-at-home Naga does not on the average see a foreign face more than once in two years.

Other changes are more subtle, and it is difficult to assign them to any particular agency. The most interesting and important of these is the increased use of coin. Villages still exist where coin is unknown, but they are remote, and are probably getting rarer every year. Coin must have long been known to villages near the plains, but the opening up of the district has immeasurably increased its circulation. Wages, payments for work done on roads, *etc.*, trade, and a thousand causes bring coin into the district. Increased circulation of coin has led to a serious fall in the birth rate of one tribe and may cause its extinction. This admittedly startling statement illustrates how utterly unforeseen are the effects of civilization on primitive peoples.

The tribe in question is the Lhota Nagas. It is the only tribe in the area that shows definite signs of dying out. The possible causes of this have occupied my thoughts for a very long time. Naturally I sought some characteristic or custom which the Lhotas alone have, and which has not obtained from a sufficiently remote past to have exterminated the tribe before it ever came in contact with Western civilization. I found it in their present-day marriage customs. Nearly all tribes marry when both sexes are fully mature. A few, such as the Naked Rengmas, marry when neither partner has reached maturity. Among the Lhotas alone is there a very strong tendency for mature men to marry immature girls. My own observations convince me that many of these marriages with very young girls are sterile. Even when children are born they are often sickly, and easily fall victims to the malaria which is so prevalent in the Lhota country. Were this custom of marrying young girls an old one, the tribe would have died out long ago if it was going to do so (a point often forgotten by those who recklessly condemn "evil" customs among savages). It is not an old one. On this old men are quite definite. They say that it has developed comparatively recently and that formerly girls did not marry till they were mature.

The reason for the change is that marriage prices (*i.e.*, payments made by the bridegroom to the parents of the bride) used to be made in cattle and rice, and are now made in coin. It is far easier to make a prompt lump payment in cash than in rice which may take several seasons to grow or cattle which it may take some years to breed. (Among the Thado Kukis, where adult marriage is the invariable rule, payments are still made in cattle, and it is quite common for a man to pay the final instalments of his own grandmother's marriage price.) Nor does a man really welcome a large sudden payment of rice and cattle. His storage room for rice is limited and it will not keep good for long; if he receives all the cattle due at once they may all perish together in one of the frequent epidemics of cattle disease. He greatly prefers instalments, which also give him a pleasing hold over the bridegroom. With cash it is far otherwise. The girl's father welcomes prompt payment in a convenient, easily stored, and imperishable medium of exchange. The sooner his daughter is married off, the less chance there is of the death of such a valuable asset. The bridegroom, on the other hand, ready and able to pay at once, is eager to secure possession of the girl of his choice. Thus has grown up a tendency for girls to be married off earlier and earlier, with disastrous effects on the strength of the tribe. Steps have recently been taken to check the tendency.

The growing use of money has had other effects more easy to foresee. There has been a great increase in indebtedness, especially among the Angamis in and round Kohima. Men who have made money have set up as money-lenders and offer loans at exorbitant interest to ever-ready borrowers. Land is, if possible, taken as security and there is a tendency for it to pass into fewer hands. In the old days loans were invariably in rice, as they still are in most parts of the district. These could, of course, only be repaid by growing rice, and debtors were rarely pressed and were never driven off the land. Loans of money have to be repaid in money, and a class of landless men, perpetually trying to earn money, is coming into existence. In this respect too, old customs are changing for the worse. In the untouched Naga village a landless man can always be adopted by a wealthy villager. He works on his land and is bound by certain ties, and in the event of the failure of other heirs, he inherits as a son. In any case he is treated as such, and is fed, looked after and protected in return for his services. There is no such thing as an "unemployment problem." Lastly, coin enables the possessor thereof to gratify his taste for novelties, and the more the taste is gratified, the more it grows. The result is that foreign-owned shops at Kohima and Mokok-chung do a roaring trade in foreign clothes and other rubbish.

The presence of a body of officials and of a battalion of Assam Rifles has inevitably caused a small town to grow up at Kohima. From certain points of view it might be regarded as a cesspool, and though its influence lessens as the distance from Kohima increases, it has caused and still causes most undesirable changes. With so many men there is naturally a demand for women. Any Naga girl who lives reasonably near can run away from home if she quarrels with her parents, and can always find some old hag who will take her in and teach her how easily she can make money by prostitution. Such girls rarely return home. There are, too, a number of women who form semi-permanent alliances with members of the large staff of inter-preters and other government servants who leave their wives in their villages while working at headquarters. Men and boys drift in, too, to pick up odd jobs. The life is regarded as an easy one. There is no daily going down to the fields to work. The women, instead of carrying countless heavy loads of water from springs below the village, can draw it from taps. Food and tawdry finery can be bought. All that is wanted is money, and that they see that the men provide. The result is a considerable number of Nagas of many tribes living without village discipline, and without religion—for Naga animism presupposes a village community to practise it as a whole. Worse still, a younger generation of men and women of every sort of mixture of blood is growing up entirely without tribal or village ties. It is difficult to see any future for them but that of bazaar wasters, who will beget children like themselves. It is the old problem of the detribalized native.

Shops are unknown to the untouched Naga. Now, besides being places where money can be pleasantly wasted, they have brought a considerable number of hillmen to a limited, but definite, extent, under the influence of world markets. In this year of trade depression I have sat in villages which outwardly looked entirely primitive and listened to grumbles at the present shortage of money. Nagas bring in a considerable quantity of cotton and a fair quantity of lac for trade. When prices rise they behave as if the boom would go on for ever, and when prices fall they are hard hit.

The battalion of Assam Rifles which is permanently stationed in the district is composed of Gurkhas, Thado Kukis from west of the district, and Assamese of the Mech and similar castes. Nagas do not take kindly to discipline and are rarely recruited. There is nothing about this body of troops that the Naga can imitate, and the social changes wrought by them are slight, apart from the increase in prostitution inevitably resulting from their presence. They are, however, the instrument of the greatest deliberate change brought about by government, namely the suppression of war and head-hunting. While readily conceding that this is inevitable in a directly administered district its effects have not been altogether good. On the one hand there has been a definite loss of alertness and vigour, and on the other there has been little or no saving of life. The Naga raider depends on surprise, and an attack on a forewarned enemy is very rare. Where all are at war all are wary, and the number of lives lost is very small indeed. Visits to other villages are infrequent and every village remains almost permanently segregated. This undoubtedly lessens the loss of life from epidemics.

All is otherwise under the *Pax Britannica*. People wander freely at will, and disease spreads. On the day I am writing these lines I have heard of a party of Semas who visited Kohima last month. All went down with influenza when they got back to their village, and four are dead. The visit has had the effect of what Nagas would regard as a serious raid. Not only has administration unknowingly facilitated the spread of infection, but foreigners have brought with them diseases hitherto rare or unknown. Kohima town is full of venereal disease, and men visiting women here spread it in distant villages. Tuberculosis is also increasing. Fortunately cholera is very rare. For this we have to thank the perfect natural drainage of the hills and the scrupulous care the Naga takes to prevent pollution of his water supply.

Against this is to be set the skilled medical treatment now provided free at dispensaries scattered over the district, and the precautionary measures, such as vaccination, that are systematically taken. As a result the Nagas are more than holding their own and in the census of this year the figures for the Lhota tribe alone give cause for anxiety.

Concomitant with the pacification of the hills has been the opening up of roads. There is a motor and cart road from the plains through to Manipur State, and a net-work of bridle-paths over the district. A wise prohibition has made these bridle-paths altogether a blessing; the impossibility of applying it to the motor road has made it almost a curse. The prohibition is that forbidding tourists, traders, and other non-official foreigners to use the bridle-paths. The result is that foreign vices, foreign habits, and foreign trash have not been spread over the district, and except to officials and a few missionaries, the interior of the hills remains a *terra incognita*. But the roads are freely used by Nagas, and they and the peace we enforce have brought about an interesting expansion of real Naga trade. The Naga is a great man for barbaric finery, and the full dress of some of the tribes must be as striking as is to be found anywhere. The makers of ornaments are specialists, and it is rarely that the Naga brave can buy all he wants in his own village. Some villages are famous for their makers of ornamented spear-shafts, others for cane helmets, others for baldricks, others for gauntlets, others for human hair tails, and so on. Roads always passable without fear of ambushes, and bridges across swollen torrents, have enormously helped the interchange of local manufacturers and so have stimulated their production. In a village where in the old days perhaps half a dozen men owned baldricks or other finery which had come by slow barter from village to village, every man who can afford them can now possess what he likes. There are certainly far more true Naga ornaments of the old traditional patterns worn now than there ever were in the day of independence and constant war.

The influence of the motor road is far otherwise. It is the through road to Manipur State and is used by foreigners of many races. All along it one sees foreign clothes and corrugated iron roofs. Not only does it, too, spread venereal disease through prostitution, but malaria-carrying mosquitoes are undoubtedly brought up in the lorries and have caused the disease to be firmly established in Kohima and elsewhere.

I have touched on clothes, and these are usually the first and greatest outward sign of the contact of primitive peoples with civilization. Let it be said at the outset that the percentage of Nagas that wear foreign dress is still very small indeed. The vast majority still retain their scanty, but becoming, national costume. But there is no doubt that the Naga with a smattering of education yearns to put on foreign clothes. A pair of shorts is regarded almost as an M.A. gown and a complete suit as a doctor's robes. On the other hand, the very best of the educated men, of which there are only too few, have minds above mimicry and wear their national dress with proper pride. Both government and the Mission have in the past been guilty of encouraging, or at least condoning, the tendency to scorn and discard the old dress. Except for a few departments government has now changed its ways. For instance the interpreters, who are unquestionably the *corps d'élite* of the hills, all wear Naga dress. No one would be accepted who did not. The views of the Mission are changing too. "Clothes, and yet more clothes" was their slogan of old. Even now there are members who do not readily abandon it, and I shrewdly suspect that the home-supporters of the Mission on whom it depends for funds, insist, in their abysmal ignorance of local conditions, on evidence of "civilizing influence" in the form of photographs portraying converts garbed in chemises, shirts, trousers, and so forth. There is no uniform policy, but the wiser members now see the folly of the old method and are trying to control the taste of their converts and especially of their schoolboys. I say "boys" advisedly, for foreign clothes, in the form of "shirt-waists", are almost universally worn by girls and women under strong Mission influence. One still hears the old talk about "decency", and no missionary is as yet sufficiently advanced to admit that what is wrong for women is wrong for men.

The strongest opponents out here to the welcome change of heart on the part of some members of the Mission are the pastors trained under the old system. Boys under their influence will still say that they wear shorts "because they are Christians". My conclusion is that things have gone too far. We rightly put the brake on, but the influences on the other side are the strong ones of desire to imitate a culture considered superior, and of cease-less propaganda by ignorant pastors working far from the control of the enlightened missionaries. Foreign clothes are spreading and will spread slowly. It remains to be seen if the new Nagas who have absorbed education without losing their national pride will in time leaven the lump and cause a reaction.

This brings us to education, which has brought in its train changes which have rarely been for the better. I can sum up the situation by saying that I now receive petitions for government posts from Nagas of villages with ample land awaiting cultivation who solemnly describe themselves as unemployed. Education, whether given by government or the Mission, has been far too literary, and too entirely divorced from the natural environment of the Naga. It has been regarded merely as the means of obtaining what a Naga aptly describes as "a sitting and eating job". Any suggestion to a youth from a high school that his education ought to make him more fitted for his ordinary village life is received with surprised disdain. There are, of course, far too few posts to go round, and a class of discontented youth is growing up, unable to find work he considers suitable to a man of his attainments and unable to fit happily into village life. A few indulge in trade, but they are no match for the foreigner with generations of experience behind him, and usually bring disaster on themselves and any friends foolish enough to entrust money to them. The position is fraught with danger, and the only hope is that more and more Nagas will take advantage of the useful primary education taught in village schools and that fewer of a calibre that can never profit by it will risk their money in investment in a worthless higher education that brings no return.

Probably our courts of law directly affect more individual Nagas than any other institution for which we are responsible. In an untouched Naga village disputes drag on interminably. Often they are never settled. Sometimes the older men of the village voice the feeling of the community and decide that one party must pay compensation of, say, a cow to the other. Even then the matter is not ended, and months, or even years, may elapse before the animal is handed over. This is bad enough. But when the parties happen to belong to different villages settlement is almost impossible, for even if the elders of the two villages meet each body will back its own side. Courts, therefore, which can come to a quick decision and enforce it constitute a blessing of which the Naga has not been slow to take advantage. Tribal custom rather than the law of British India is administered. There are no legal fees and litigation costs nothing. Cases brought for the sheer love of it sometimes recoil upon the bringers' heads, and frivolous litigation is thus checked to a certain extent. This would no longer be possible were the written codes of the plains to be brought into full force and lawyers allowed to appear to argue the minute points of law and carry every decision to a higher court on appeal, as is the usual practice in India. May this change be long in coming.

While the feeling of security in his rights that our courts give the Naga is a change all to the good, there is another side to the picture. Nagas are inclined to rush to court with every quarrel instead of first laying their case before the village elders. This tends to undermine the authority of the elders. Were this to be allowed they would very soon cease to be useful, and with no effective traditional authority permanently operating in each village, administration would become well-nigh impossible and officials would be overwhelmed with a mass of detail. Care is therefore taken by magistrates to see that disputes which ought first to be heard in the village are thrashed out there before being admitted in court. This is easy enough with such tribes as the Semas and Konyaks, who have chiefs, or the Aos, who have elaborately organized indigenous village councils, with real authority. With others, such as the large and powerful Angami tribe, it is more difficult. Among them every man is inclined to be a law unto himself. Even so they have means of making the general feeling of the village felt, and cases are sent back to them till some sort of decision has been arrived at. But in spite of these checks a great change has been wrought, and one which is bound to become greater year by year, be its effects good or bad. The Naga no longer feels that his fellow-villagers can pass final judgment on his actions.

Lastly, I come to the highly controversial subject of the effects brought about by the religious teaching of the American Baptist Missionary Society, the only mission working amongst Nagas. Their secular educational work has already been touched upon.

One important change they have brought to which the nature of their message is entirely irrelevant. It would have come about had they taught Voodooism or any other religion instead of Christianity. Till they came, such a thing as conversion was meaningless to a Naga. They first led the Nagas to see that a man can change his religion. More than that, the change was proclaimed to be for his advantage. Salvation from otherwise inevitable hell-fire was one of the benefits offered. To this the Nagas themselves in many places soon added good crops, freedom from disease, and other advantages in this world. At first the tendency was for the message of the Mission to be accepted or rejected as a whole. Now, and only very recently, hearers of the message are becoming critical and selective. Having definitely and finally reached the stage of believing that a man can change his religion and may gain benefits by so doing, the Naga now is beginning to wonder if the whole message of the missionaries is the only alternative, or whether other even more beneficial religions cannot be devised containing only parts of that message or even composed of elements wholly alien to it. In other words, there are distinct signs that we are at the beginning of an era of what are vulgarly called "fancy religions", with their inevitable consequences of sectarian strife and wasted effort.

I have before me a report of a sect founded by a Sokte Kuki just over the border in Burma. God, dressed in European clothes, appeared to him in a dream and gave him the rules for a church he has founded. It is a caricature of Christianity. Again, there is a little girl in the Naga Hills who has begun to receive visits from "Jihovu" in dreams. He is also dressed in European clothes. There are no Christians in her village and her hallucinations arise from rumours she has heard of Baptist teaching. The "Commands of Ji-hovu" that she issues have already led to a certain amount of trouble and she will have to be kept under proper control. Again, a man recently arose among the Kabui Nagas inhabiting part of the hill country of Manipur State who claimed kingship over the Kabui, Zemi, and Lyengmai tribes. He introduced a very debased Hinduism in imitation of what he had seen while on visits to the plains. His promises of invulnerability and bumper crops gave him great influence. He is now awaiting execution for human sacrifice.

Most of the changes brought about by the Mission, however, are the direct consequences of the nature of the religion they teach. Western Protestantism comes into direct contact with Oriental Animism. The most far-reaching effect of this contact is the disintegration of the body politic of the village, the Naga social unit. To the Naga the village comes first, and the individual second; the man is definitely subordinate to the society in which he lives. This is incompatible with the Christian emphasis on the supreme importance of the development of the individual character and the salvation of the individual soul. Naga converts do undoubtedly become less amenable to village discipline and more ready to assert themselves as individuals. Cases of unnecessary breaking of taboos, merely to show independence, have been far too frequent; instances occur of Christians refusing ordinary village duties, such as service on the council of elders; little acts of social kindness are omitted, such as the old custom in Ao villages of maintaining a constant supply of dry torches for strangers travelling at night; I have more than once noticed, where Christians have split off from the main village and founded a little community of their own, that they even build their houses farther apart than is the custom of their Animist brethren. This growing individualism, unless checked by the still existent racial instincts, will be disastrous to the Nagas. As closely knit social units they might withstand the impact of civilization. As undisciplined individuals they cannot do so.

Another problem brought about by the Mission is that riddle of the Western world, the surplus woman. She does not exist among the unconverted Nagas. Some tribes are polygamous and some monogamous. Polygamous tribes easily absorb all women and among monogamous tribes divorce is so frequent and easy that though a number of women are always without husbands they are only temporarily so. And, quite apart from marriage, considerable pre-nuptial license in all tribes makes sexual repression a thing unknown. Christianity, on the other hand, has always sternly suppressed polygamy and among Christian Nagas there is a considerable number of definitely surplus women. The Naga does not take kindly to prolonged virginity and it is pathetic to see young women with blotchy faces waiting in vain for husbands long after the ordinary age of marriage. A few find jobs at the mission stations, but most of them can only expend their surplus energy in prolonged singing of hymns. No solution for the problem has been found, or even sought.

So far I have dealt with what might be called the unconscious changes brought about by the Mission. Now I come to those deliberately imposed on their converts. All have far-reaching effects in different ways and it is impossible to assign to them an order of importance. I will take first the abolition among converts of the ceremonial feasts commonly spoken of as "Feasts of Merit". Though the details vary from tribe to tribe, the custom of holding these feasts is universally observed throughout the Naga country. Each tribe has its own series, definitely laid down by tradition. The first feast a man gives will probably consist of the killing of a pig. Thence they increase in importance and expense till, at the final feast, domestic *mithan* (*bos frontalis*) are killed. It is the ambition of every man to proceed as far as he can in the series, and most well-to-do men complete it. Not only is merit increasingly acquired as the giver rises from stage to stage, but certain feasts confer on him the right to wear certain body-cloths and ornaments, and to build a house of a particular shape. Finally he is allowed to set up one or more monoliths, or, in some tribes, carved posts. He thereby gains social eminence in this life and is assured of immortality in the songs of his clan. Not only do these feasts provide the chief breaks in a village life which is otherwise liable to be very monotonous, they involve also frequent distributions of wealth in which the very poorest in the village may share. They are, too, now that head-hunting has been abolished in administered territory, the chief interest in life left for a Naga. To complete them is the ambition of every man. A Christian who is forbidden to give them has no means of distributing his wealth and of earning the right to wear gorgeous clothes of the old tribal patterns. Instead he has to hoard his rice and money and wear dull clothes.

Though probably no actual prohibition has ever been issued by the Mission, their converts have been brought to feel that the wearing of ornaments is wrong. The women are as they are all the world over, and often insist on wearing their beads, Mission or no Mission. But the men, quite apart from the clothes they can only earn by giving "Feasts of Merit", usually will not wear even the ornaments that anyone is allowed to buy. I remember a Christian told me that he was severely reprimanded by the assembled elders because he attended a large church meeting complete with ivory armlets, cowrie apron, and scarlet-shafted spear. This change wrought by the Mission has definitely added to the drabness of life and tends to kill the Naga's very real artistic taste.

Another prohibition is that on the use of bachelors' halls. These are the supreme architectural effort of the race. They are often huge buildings, with the posts boldly carved in high relief with tigers, elephants, and other animals. The Christians build nothing half as fine, and there is no place for carving in their tin-roofed chapels. It is noticeable that the more important the part played by bachelors' halls in tribal life, the better is the discipline of the tribe. At one end there are the well-disciplined Konyaks and Aos with their huge buildings, and at the other the utterly undisciplined Angamis who merely use private houses for the purpose. In the bachelors' halls the boys maintain a system very like that of "fagging" at an English public school. It is most valuable and salutary, and a boy learns to do what he is told and do it quickly. The Mission provides dormitories for boys in the villages, but there is no tradition of discipline behind them.

Another prohibition which adds to the dullness of village life is that on singing (except hymns) and dancing. Neither the songs nor the dances are in any way indecent, and they seem to have been prohibited because they are old and have always been indulged in at heathen festivals. The loss of the genealogies and traditions embedded in the old songs is itself a serious one.

Lastly, there is a prohibition which seems a small one but which will prove important in time. I refer to that on oaths. The majority of Naga disputes are settled by oath. In some tribes the matter is left to the arbitration of the deities, which is signified in various ways. In others, one side offers to swear on so many lives to the truth of a claim, and on the oath being sworn the other side admits it. Cases brought to court are settled by oath every day, and if this custom be abolished it is difficult to see how any decision can possibly be arrived at in many of them. In some there is absolutely no evidence either way, and in others, such as traditional ownership of land, no living man has personal knowledge of past transactions, and the matter can only be settled by one side swearing to the truth of what has been handed down to them.

Reading this paper through, I wonder if it does not give a distorted view. The subject before me has inevitably led to an emphasis on what is changing rather than on what is unchanged. It must be realized that the areas in which change is apparent are limited and few. There are whole tribes never effectively reached by the Mission, which contain not one single convert. It is easy to travel for days, or weeks, even in the administered district without seeing a shred of European clothing or any outward sign of Western civilization except the bridle-paths and the absence of war. The vast majority of Nagas live as they have always lived, save that they are at peace. They wear the clothes they always wore, they give their "Feasts of Merit", their villages are still hilltop strongholds, the old taboos are observed and are respected by officials, the old festivals come round with the seasons and the old songs are sung. There are villages where men still go mother-naked, and others where the girls wear nothing till the time for marriage approaches; no one comes to make them ashamed. There can be few places in the world under direct Western rule where primitive life is so vigorous and healthy. To this the credit is largely due to the deliberate administrative policy of the last 20 years. It would have been easy to have encouraged indiscriminate change and to have spread a thin veneer of civilization over this intelligent and fascinating race. But fortunately wisdom prevailed. It has always been recognized that Nagas cannot be preserved as anthropological specimens. Change is inevitable. But all the officials who have loved the Nagas—and that means every official who has been in charge of them—have striven their utmost to make change as slow as possible. All the time the national pride of the Nagas has been stimulated by the affection they know they win, and by constant sympathetic inquiries into their customs and ceremonies, resulting in a valuable series of monographs generously financed by the government of Assam. Our hope has been that the Naga, imbued with healthy self-esteem, will never blindly imitate the new fashions he sees, or greedily snatch at every bauble the West offers him, but with wise discrimination will choose the thing that is good.

REFERENCES

Butler, Major J. Sketch of Assam, London, 1847.

Butler, Major J. Travels and adventures in the Province of Assam, London, 1855.

Peal, S. E. The Nagas and neighbouring tribes, J. Roy. Anthrop. Inst., vol. 3, pp. 476–81, 1874.

Butler, Captain J. Rough notes on the Angami Nagas, J. Asiatic Soc. Bengal, pt. 1, 1875.

Woodthorpe, Lt. Col. R. G. Notes on the wild tribes inhabiting the so-called Naga on our N.E. frontier of India, J. Roy. Anthrop. Inst., vol. 11, nos. 1, 2, and 3, 1881 and 1882.

Peal, S. E. Fading histories, J. Asiatic Soc. Bengal, pt. 1, 1894.

Hodson, T. C. The Naga tribes of Manipur, London, 1911.

Hutton, J. H. The Angami Nagas, London, 1921.

Hutton, J. H. The Sema Nagas, London, 1921.

Mills, J. P. The Lhota Nagas, London, 1922.

Smith, Wm. C. Missionary activities and the acculturation of backward peoples, J. Appl. Sociology, vol. 7, no. 4, Los Angeles, U.S.A., 1923.

Smith, Wm. C. The Ao Naga Tribe of Assam, London, 1925.

Tanquist, Rev. J. E. Missionary attitude toward the welfare of primitive peoples, Baptist Missionary Review, vol. 31, no. 4, 1925.

Mills, J. P. The Ao Nagas, London, 1926.

9 The Psychological Factor in the Depopulation of Melanesia

W. H. R. RIVERS

By the early 1920s the destructive frontier processes docu-mented by the select committee of 1836–37 were dramatically reducing the native population of Melanesia. In the Solomons local populations that had numbered 500 people before 1900 were reduced to less than 100. Where there were 46 villages, there were now only 3. Some areas were totally depopulated. This was occurring throughout the Melanesian region to such a degree that authorities were becoming alarmed over the threat to the future labor force.

In this selection W. H. R. Rivers refutes charges that such depopulation was caused by problems in tribal cultures themselves and instead shows how colonial intervention increased mortality and decreased fertility. He assumes that under traditional conditions a relative demographic balance existed. According to Rivers, labor recruiting along with a variety of changes in traditional housing, clothing, politics, and domestic life, introduced by well-meaning government administrators and missionaries, caused enormous disruptions. People were losing interest in life. Rivers is apparently not opposed to intervention as such; he merely thinks that introduced changes should be minimally disturbing. For example, in his policy recommendations not included in this selection, Rivers suggests that pig heads might be substituted in rituals requiring human heads and that canoe races might replace the excitement and competition of warfare. Administrators were quick to appreciate the possibilities of these insights, and in 1926 the functionalist anthropol-ogist Radcliffe-Brown was brought to the University of Sydney to begin a five-year program of training administrators for service in New Guinea and the Pacific. In 1927 the Rockefeller Foundation and the Australian National Research Council established a special Anthropological Research Fund to sponsor more fieldwork. Williams (see part IV) represents the policy approaches that logically followed.

Rivers (1864–1922) held a medical degree and lectured in experimental psychol-ogy at Cambridge. He was a member of the Torres Strait ethnological expedition of 1898, and he conducted ethnographic fieldwork among the Todas of India in 1902 and in Melanesia in 1908 and 1914. He was president of the Royal Anthropological Institute at the time of his death in 1922.

The papers by members of the Melanesian Mission and other workers in Melanesia published in this book show conclusively that this great archipelago is undergoing a process of depopulation. In some

Reprinted from W. H. R. Rivers, *Essays on the Depopulation of Melanesia* (Cambridge: Cam-bridge University Press, 1922) by permission of the publisher. Copyright © 1922 Cambridge University Press.

parts the decline is taking place so rapidly that at no distant date the islands will wholly lose their native inhabitants unless something is done to stay its progress. . . .

Various causes have been given to account for the dying out of the people, different factors having been stressed by different authors. I propose to attempt a more complete survey of the causes which lead to decrease of population.

Before beginning this survey it will be well to deal briefly with a supposed fact which has frequently been brought forward as a means of accounting for the decrease of the population of Melanesia. It has been supposed that the Melanesians were already a dying people before the European invasion, and that their decline was due to faults inherent in their own culture. In the first place there is no evidence of any value that the people were decreasing in number before the advent of Europeans.

It may be true that here and there the people already showed signs of diminution on the arrival of the missionaries.[1] It must be remembered, however, that the people had already been subject for many years to certain European influences, such as that of the sandal-wood hunters, which were far from being of a harmless kind.

When apologists for the effects of their own civilisation give reasons for the supposed original decadence, these often bear their own refutation on the face. Thus, one writer blames the heathen custom of polygamy, but in the same paragraph states that the practice is confined to the few.

Another cause which has been put forward is the special kind of consanguineous union known as the cross-cousin marriage.

This marriage is orthodox in several parts of Melanesia and is especially frequent and important in Fiji. This subject was fully investigated by the Commission which more than twenty years ago inquired into the decrease of the native population of Fiji. In their *Report* (1896), which forms a storehouse of most valuable facts concerning the topics of this book, it is shown conclusively that this factor had not contributed towards Fijian decadence, but rather that these consanguineous marriages were more fruitful than marriage between wholly unrelated persons.

I shall deal presently with native customs in relation to our subject and hope to show that it is rather the indiscriminate and undiscriminating interference with them which stands forth prominently among the causes of decay.

I can now consider the conditions to which real efficacy in the process of destruction can be assigned. In studying this subject the first point to bear in mind is the double character of the factors upon which fluctuation of population depends, a double character which holds good of Melanesia as of more civilised parts of the world. Diminution of population may be due to increase of the death-rate or to decrease of the birth-rate, or to both combined. I can bring forward evidence to show that both factors have been active in Melanesia. I will begin with the conditions which have affected the death-rate.

In a subject in which we can find little on which to pride ourselves, it is satisfactory to be able to exclude one cause of depopulation which has contributed in no small measure to the disappearance of native races in other parts of the world. There has been no deliberate attempt to exterminate the people such as has disgraced the history of our relations with regions more suited to European habitation than the sweltering and unhealthy islands of Melanesia. The injurious influences due to European rulers and settlers have been unwitting. Owing to the need for the labour of those accustomed to the tropics, it has always been in the interests of the settlers that the native population shall be alive and healthy. In so far as native decay is due to European influence we have to lay the blame on ignorance and lack of foresight, not on any deliberate wish to destroy.

In considering the death of a people as of an individual, it is natural to think first of disease. Disease is the name we give to a group of processes by which the size of a population is adjusted so as to enable it best to utilise the available means of subsistence. Before the arrival of Europeans, Melanesia had its own diseases, by means of which Nature helped to keep the population within bounds. Everything goes to show that the population of Melanesia was well within the limits which the country was capable of supporting, but it is not so certain that it was far within this capacity in relation to the very simple means the people possessed for exploiting its resources. So far as we can tell, there had been set up a state of equilibrium between the size of the population and the available resources of the country. Recent knowledge goes to show that the diseases due to infective parasites tend to set up a state of tolerance and habituation which renders a people less prone to succumb to their ravages, and there is no reason to suppose that Melanesia was any exception in this respect. Thus the people are largely habituated to the malaria which certainly existed among them before the coming of European influence.

Into this community thus adapted to the infective agents of their own country, the invaders brought a number of new diseases: measles, dysentery, probably tubercle and influenza, and last but unfortunately far from least potent, venereal disease. These maladies had effects far more severe than those they bring upon ourselves, partly because they found a virgin soil, partly because the native therapeutic ideas were not adapted to the new diseases, so that remedies were often used which actually increased their harmfulness. Many of these introduced diseases are still drawing a large toll on the numbers and energies of the people, the two which seem to be exerting the most steady influence, so far as my observations show, being dysentery and tubercle.

A second group of introduced causes of destruction is composed of what may be called the social poisons, such as alcohol and opium. Though it is possible that the people use tobacco somewhat to excess, the only poison which needs to be considered in Melanesia is alcohol. In certain parts of Melanesia there is no question that it has exerted in the past and is still exerting a most deleterious influence, but it is satisfactory to be able to say that its noxious influence has been reduced to negligible importance in those parts of the archipelago wholly subject to British rule, where it is penal to sell or give alcohol to a native. Alcohol is still, however, potent as a cause of disease and death in the New Hebrides. In those islands there are regulations against the sale of alcohol to natives, but under the present Condominium Government they are not obeyed.

A third direct cause of increase of death-rate is the introduction of fire-arms, by means of which the comparatively harmless warfare of the natives is given a far more deadly turn. This cause is still active to some extent in the New Hebrides owing to breaking of the regulations of the Condominium Government, but fire-arms have never had great importance as an instrument of destruction in Melanesia.

I come to a more serious cause when I consider European influence upon native customs. I begin with one which excites perennial interest whenever native welfare is discussed. Before the advent of Europeans the people of some islands went wholly nude or wore only garments, if they can be so called, which fulfilled neither of the two chief purposes for which the clothing of civilised people is designed. In other parts the native clothing consisted of petticoats, loin-cloths, or other simple garments thoroughly adapted to the necessities of the climate. One of the first results of European influence was the adoption of the clothing of the visitors, and clothes were adopted in such a manner as to accentuate the evils which they necessarily brought with them. The Melanesian is not uncleanly. He bathes frequently, and where he preserves his native mode of clothing, his ablutions are amply sufficient for cleanliness. When he wears European garments, he fails to adopt measures, such as the frequent change of clothing, which then become necessary. He continues to bathe in his clothes, and instead of changing his garments frequently, wears them continuously till they are ragged, and even when new clothing is obtained, it is put over the old.

It is a great mistake, often made, to blame the missionaries for this use of foreign clothing. It is true that its use was directly encouraged by the early missionaries, but this encouragement was unnecessary. To the native, trousers and coats are the distinctive mark of the white man, and nothing short of prohibition could have prevented their use. Where we can now see the missionaries to have been at fault is that they did not recognise the evil of the innovation and set themselves steadily to minimise it. They should have insisted upon attention to the elementary principles of the hygiene which the use of clothes involves.

At the present time the influence of missionaries is steadily directed to this end. Having been privileged to live among missionaries of different schools of thought in Melanesia, I can testify that no subject is more frequently discussed and more thoroughly and anxiously considered than how to lessen the use and injurious influence of European clothing.

Another modification of native custom, which is less widely recognised, but in my experience quite as much in need of consideration at the present time, is housing. The native Melanesian house is usually rain-proof and of good proportions, while owing to its mode of construction it is well ventilated and thoroughly adapted to the climate. Instead of being content with houses of similar construction or with houses of the kind used by Europeans living in other tropical countries, settlers have built houses with thick walls and very imperfect means of ventilation. These have in some cases been copied by the natives, or even built by the missionaries for the use of their followers. Such buildings might have been specially devised for the propagation of tubercle, and if they are allowed to be built will certainly increase the already far too heavy ravages of this disease.

The modifications of housing and clothing which I have just considered touch especially the material side of life. I have now to consider a number of modifications and interferences with native custom which I believe to have been quite as important, if not more important, in the production of native decadence. When Melanesia became subject to Europeans, magistrates and missionaries were sent to rule and direct the lives of the people. They found in existence a number of institutions and customs which were, or seemed to them to be, contrary to the principles of morality. Such customs were usually forbidden without any inquiry into their real nature, without knowledge of the part they took in native life, and without any attempt to discriminate between their good and bad elements. Thus, in the Solomon Islands the rulers stopped the special kind of warfare known as head-hunting, without at all appreciating the vast place it took in the religious and ceremonial lives of the people, without realising the gap it would leave in their daily interests, a blank far more extensive than that due to the mere cessation of a mode of warfare. Again, in Fiji, the custom according to which the men of the community slept apart from the women in a special house, a widespread custom in Melanesia, seemed to the missionaries contrary to the ideals of the Christian family, and the custom was stopped or discouraged without it being realised that the segregation of the sexes formed an effectual check on too free intercourse between them.

In the New Hebrides again, the missionaries put an end to, or where they did not destroy, treated with a barely veiled contempt, a highly complicated organisation arising out of beliefs connected with the cult of dead ancestors. In some cases it was apparent enough that the institution with all its elaborate ceremonial was heathen and prejudiced church attendance, while elsewhere stress was laid on occasional revels and dances which gave opportunity for licence. It was not recognised that in forbidding or discouraging without inquiry, they were destroying institutions which had the most far-reaching ramifications through the social and economical life of the people.

If these and similar institutions had been studied before they were destroyed or discouraged, it would have been found possible to discriminate between those features which were noxious and needed repression or amendment, and those which were beneficial to the welfare of the community. Even when their destruction was deemed necessary, something could have been done to replace the social sanctions of which the people were thus deprived. The point I wish to emphasise is that through this unintelligent and undiscriminating action towards native institutions, the people were deprived of nearly all that gave interest to their lives. I have now to suggest that this loss of interest forms one of the reasons, if indeed it be not the most potent of all the reasons, to which the native decadence is due.

It may at first sight seem far-fetched to suppose that such a factor as loss of interest in life could ever produce the dying out of a people, but my own observations have led me to the conclusion that its influence is so great that it can hardly be overrated. I venture therefore to consider it at some length.

When you inquire of those who have lived long in Melanesia concerning the illness and mortality of the natives, you are struck by the frequency of reference to the ease with which the native dies. Over and over again one is told of a native who seemed hale and well until, after a day or two of some apparently trivial illness, he gives up the ghost without any of the signs which among ourselves usually give ample warning of the impending fate. A native who is ill loses heart at once. He has no desire to live, and perhaps announces that he is going to die when the onlooker can see no ground for his belief.

The matter becomes more easy to understand if we consider the ease with which the people are killed by magic or as the result of the infraction of a taboo. The evidence is overwhelming that such people as the Melanesians will sicken and die in a few hours or days as the result of the belief that an enemy has chosen them as the victim of his spells, or that they have, wittingly or unwittingly, offended against some religious taboo. If people who are interested in life and do not wish to die can be killed in a few days or even hours by a mere belief, how much more easy it is to understand that a people who have lost all interest in life should become the prey of any morbid agency acting through the body as well as through the mind. It is this evidence of the enormous influence of the mind upon the body among the Melanesians and other lowly peoples that first led me to attach so much importance to loss of interest as the primary cause of their dying out. Once this belief has been formulated, there is seen to be much definite evidence in Melanesia to support it.

Certain islands and districts of Melanesia show a degree of vitality in striking contrast with the rest. These exceptional cases fall into two classes: one includes those islands or parts of islands where the people have so far been fierce and strong enough to withstand European influence. There are still certain parts in Melanesia which as yet the footprint of the white man has not reached, and others where, after successful encounters with punitive expeditions, the people still believe themselves to be a match for the invader. Here the old zest and interest in life persist and the people are still vigorous and abundant.

The other group of peoples who show signs of vitality are those who have adopted Christianity, not merely because it is the religion of the powerful white man, but with a whole-hearted enthusiasm which has given them a renewed interest in life. Here the numbers are increasing after an initial drop. Christianity and the occupations connected with it have given the people a new interest to replace that of their indigenous culture, and with this interest has come the desire to live.

The special point I wish to make in my contribution to this book is that interest in life is the primary factor in the welfare of a people. The new diseases and poisons, the innovations in clothing, housing and feeding, are only the immediate causes of mortality. It is the loss of interest in life underlying these more obvious causes which gives them their potency for evil and allows them to work such ravages upon life and health.

I can pass to the second of the two groups of influences by which a people decline in number, having so far dealt only with those which increase the death-rate. I have now to consider those which produce decline by diminishing the birth-rate and will begin by stating briefly the evidence that this factor has played and is playing a part in the dying out of the Melanesians. This evidence has been gained by a mode of inquiry adopted originally for purely scientific purposes. When in Torres Straits with Dr. Haddon twenty-four years ago, I discovered that the people preserved in their memories with great fidelity a full and accurate record of their descent and relationships (Rivers 1910). It was possible to collect pedigrees so ample in all collateral lines that they could serve as a source of statistical inquiry into such features as the average size of a family, infant mortality, and other subjects which furnish the basis for conclusions concerning fluctuations of population. I have found this interest in genealogy wherever I have worked, and the collection of pedigrees has always formed the basis of my ethnographic inquiries. In Melanesia this instrument shows conclusively that the fall in numbers is due quite as much to decrease of the birth-rate as to increase of the death-rate. . . .

The two islands which show this striking fall in birth-rate are of especial interest in that in them, and especially in Eddystone, the chief factors to which the dying out of peoples is usually ascribed are absent. In Eddystone, about which a residence of several months enables me to speak with confidence, there is no record of any very severe epidemics. Tubercle and dysentery, the two most deadly diseases in Melanesia, do not appear to be, or to have been, especially active; and though both the chief forms of venereal disease exist in the island, they do not seem to have done any great amount of mischief. The island has never had a white missionary; the people still wear their native dress and live in houses of native build. Alcohol is little known and other poisons not at all, while any effect of fire-arms on mortality is negligible. Few of the people have left the island as labour or for any other reason. All the factors to which other writers in this book ascribe the decrease of the population of Melanesia are practically absent, and yet we have a striking diminution of population, due in the main to decrease of the birth-rate.

If now we pass from material to mental factors, the decrease in the birth-rate becomes easier to understand. No one could be long in Eddystone without recognising how great is the people's lack of interest in life and to what an extent the zest has gone out of their lives. This lack of interest is largely due to the abolition of head-hunting by the British Government. This practice formed the centre of a social and religious institution which took an all-pervading part in the lives of the people. The heads sought in the head-hunting expeditions were needed in order to propitiate the ancestral ghosts on such occasions as building a new house for a chief or making a new canoe, while they were also offered in sacrifice at the funeral of a chief. Moreover, head-hunting was not only necessary for the due performance of the religious rites of the people, but it stood in the closest relation to pursuits of an economic kind. The actual head-hunting expedition only lasted a few weeks, and the actual fighting often only a few hours, but this was only the culminating point of a process lasting over years. It was the rule that new canoes should be made for an expedition to obtain heads, and the manufacture of these meant work of an interesting kind lasting certainly for many months, probably for years. The process of canoe-building was accompanied throughout by rites and feasts which not only excited the liveliest interest but also acted as stimuli to various activities of horticulture and pig-breeding. As the date fixed for the expedition approached other rites and feasts were held, and these were still more frequent and on a larger scale after the return of a successful expedition. In stopping the practice of head-hunting the rulers from an alien culture were abolishing an institution which had its roots in the religion of the people and spread its branches throughout nearly every aspect of their culture, and by this action they deprived the people of the greater part of their interest in life, while at the same time they undermined the religion of the people without any attempt to put another in its place.

I need only consider here very briefly the agencies to which this fall in birth-rate is due. It is well known that certain forms of venereal disease will produce sterility, and it is noteworthy that the dying out of the people of Vulua is ascribed by their neighbours to the ravages of this disease brought by returning labourers from Queensland. There is little doubt, however, that if we take Melanesia as a whole, causes of this kind are trivial or of slight importance as compared with voluntary restriction. Throughout Melanesia the people are acquainted with various means of producing abortion and also practise measures which they believe to prevent conception, and processes of this kind almost certainly form the main agencies in lowering the birth-rate. We have here only another effect of the loss of interest in life which I have held to be so potent in enhancing mortality. The people say themselves: "Why should we bring children into the world only to work for the white man?" Measures which, before the coming of the European, were used chiefly to prevent illegitimacy have become the instrument of racial suicide.

It is satisfactory that before I leave this subject I am able to point to a brighter side. I have already said that in certain parts of Melanesia the downward movement has been arrested and that the people now show signs of growth. I mentioned also that this was occurring especially in islands where the people have really taken to their hearts the lessons of their Christian teachers.

The teachings of the missionaries concerning the evils of racial suicide may possibly have contributed in some degree to this recovery, though I doubt whether in general they have been aware of the part which voluntary restriction has taken. I believe that their influence has lain much more in the fact that the religion they have taught has given the people a renewed interest in life which has again made it worth while to bring children into the world.

Until now I have said nothing of a cause of depopulation which has been especially active in Melanesia. The causes I have so far considered have been treated under two headings, according as they have enhanced the death-rate or lowered the birth-rate. The labour-traffic which I have now to consider is more complex and involves both of these factors.

In dealing with this cause of depopulation it is well that it is possible to begin by distinguishing between the traffic as it was and as it is. It would be difficult to exaggerate the evil influence of the process by which the natives of Melanesia were taken to Australia and elsewhere to labour for the white man. It forms one of the blackest of civilisation's crimes. Not least among its evils was the manner of its ending, when large numbers of people who had learnt by many years' experience to adapt themselves to civilised ways were, in the process of so-called repatriation, thrust back into savagery without help of any kind. The misery thus caused and the resulting disaffection not only underlie most of the open troubles in the recent history of Melanesia, but by the production of a state of helplessness and hopelessness have contributed as much as any other factors to the decline of the population.

I must not, however, dwell on the crimes and mistakes of the past. Our object in this book is to call attention to existing evils in the hope that they may be remedied before it is too late. At the present time Melanesians are only recruited as labourers to work within the confines of Melanesia, and both the recruitment and the conditions of labour are subject to Government control. Its grosser evils have been removed, at any rate in those parts of Melanesia which are wholly governed by Great Britain, though it would appear that there are still very grave defects in those parts of Melanesia under the control of the Condominium Government. But however closely and wisely the traffic is controlled, the removal from their own homes of the younger men, and still more of the younger women, of a declining population is not a factor which can tend to arrest the decline or convert it into a movement in the opposite direction. Even in its improved form, and limited to Melanesia though it be, the labour traffic continues to act as a cause of depopulation. It acts directly by taking men and women away from their homes when they should be marrying and producing children, while other evils are that, as at present conducted, the traffic tends to spread disease and to undermine an influence which I believe to be at the present time the most potent for good in Melanesia, the work of the missionaries. Moreover, the use of natives as labourers on plantations fails to give that interest in life which, as I have tried to show, forms the most essential factor in maintaining the health of a people.

NOTE

1. In some cases this decrease in early times is almost certain. Thus, there is little doubt that the northern end of Ysabel in the Solomons was decimated by the activity of the head-hunters of Ruviana and Eddystone, but this decrease was purely local and had no appreciable influence on the general population of Melanesia.

IV

Intervention Philosophy

If independent tribals are doing a reasonable job of taking care of themselves, as suggested in part I, and if the first phase of development requires outside intervention and causes enormous problems for tribals, as suggested in parts II and III, then some special justification must be found for intervening at all in tribal cultures. The issue is not whether change should occur, because everyone agrees that change is a normal, ongoing cultural process, but rather whether uninvited outsiders ought to take the lead in guiding tribal cultures in specific directions.

Interestingly enough, the basic belief underlying intervention in tribal societies, whether by missionaries or by government representatives, has remained the same for over a hundred years. It is assumed that in the long run, development intervention will benefit tribal peoples. Clearly, not everyone agrees that independent tribal cultures are doing a good job of providing for basic human needs. The more extreme ethnocentric position, represented in the following selections by Merivale and Raglan, argues that it is the duty of the "advanced" society to elevate the "backward" one. Put more delicately by Williams and Richardson, the position claims that since all cultures are changeable and imperfect, when outsiders recognize that individuals are being hurt by an imperfect culture, it is their responsibility to intervene. Furthermore, well-intended outsiders must intervene, because others who are not so well intended have already caused trouble or soon will. Such justifications may be perfectly valid in many cases, but they may not pay sufficient attention to other, equally serious issues, such as the long-range cost of development intervention, the wishes of the people themselves, and the possibility of "protective nonintervention."

Merivale, writing in the mid–nineteenth century, assumed without question that the superiority of the colonizing power both justified and compelled intervention. In the first selection in this part he attempts to rank culture traits to help administrators decide which changes to insist upon, and in this regard his discussion is surprisingly in line with the modern literature of culture change. He makes a convincing case for the seeming inevitability of the relentless advance of the frontier into tribal areas. In the next selection Williams presents a very thoughtful discussion of the intervention issue. He takes an open-minded view of the value of tribal culture, and he accepts the necessity of imposed change only when it will clearly enhance individual welfare. He argues that tribals have a right to maintain their cultures and develop autonomously but that outsiders should provide education to guide their development.

Raglan is much less tolerant of tribal culture and has little difficulty justifying rapid and overwhelming development. He even concludes that the existence of "barbaric" tribals anywhere merely retards progress for the whole world. This is an extreme view but not without its modern supporters. Richardson neatly exposes the hypocrisy of much of the criticism of missionary intervention. His is a compelling argument along the lines taken earlier by Merivale and Williams. Richardson argues that enormous and devastating changes have already taken place in tribal cultures because of outside intrusion. Furthermore, tribal cultures were probably never perfectly humane. According to Richardson, the presence of missionaries, who are responsible and devote many years to studying language and culture and to providing humanitarian assistance to particular tribes, is more justified than is that of their frequent anthropologist critics who visit a tribe and move on.

Hippler's views fit in comfortably with those of Merivale and Raglan. Among contemporary anthropologists his position is extreme, but it no doubt finds wide popular sympathy. His position is simply that tribal cultures stunt individual potential and modern civilization fosters it. There is therefore no justification for attempting to shelter tribal cultures in any way. Weiss challenges the assumptions of the development interventionists and persuasively argues that tribal peoples ought to be allowed to decide their own futures.

10 Policy of Colonial Governments Towards Native Tribes, as Regards Their Protection and Their Civilization

HERMAN MERIVALE

After the report of the select committee of 1836–37 was issued, many colonial authorities rejected the possibility of maintaining intact native communities, but they of course felt that outright extermination was unjust and inhumane. Herman Merivale (1806–1874) was an influential professor of political economy at Oxford (1837–42) when he delivered the series of lectures on colonialism from which this selection is drawn. In 1848 he became the permanent Undersecretary for Colonies, and in 1859, permanent Undersecretary for India. Merivale became an outspoken proponent of rapid "amalgamation," or integration, of natives. Any attempts to protect traditional communities, by such means as reservations, for example, would only prolong the agony, he believed. He could think of no real justification for denying the land and resources to colonists who were eager to develop it. His directness on this point is remarkable. He is the ultimate political "realist" who sees development as the prime objective and considers tribal peoples obsolete. In this view there is no possibility of gradually "improving" the culture from within because tribals are basically "feeble survivors of an obsolete world." European culture is unquestionably superior, and it is the humanitarian duty of Europeans to save these individuals.

Surprisingly, Merivale points out that if Europeans really wanted to treat tribals as equals, which for him they are not, they would prevent settlers from invading tribal territories. That would clearly be unthinkable. Merivale even argues that the 1840 treaty of Waitangi with the Maori was a mistake because it appeared to grant an aboriginal title to the entire northern island of New Zealand. This mistakenly left open the possibility of a viable Maori existence. Twentieth-century exponents of Merivale's point of view include Raglan and Hippler, who are also represented in this part.

I shall not detain you over the wretched details of the ferocity and treachery which have marked the conduct of civilized men, too often of civilized governments, in their relations with savages, either in past times, or during the present age, rich almost beyond precedent in such

Reprinted from Herman Merivale, *Lectures on Colonization & Colonies* (London: Green, Longman & Roberts, 1861), 487–90, 492, 494–503, 507–12, 522–23.

enormities. They have been of late the subject of much attention, and of much indignant commentary. You may study them in the accounts of travellers and missionaries, in the reports of our own legislature, in the language of philanthropic orators and writers. . . . To dwell on all this would be a painful, and I am sure an unnecessary, task. The general features of the subject are by this time sufficiently known, and perhaps regarded with sufficient abhorrence: it remains for us now to act; and with a view to that purpose, it is perhaps desirable that we should cease to dwell so exclusively on the dark side of the picture, as many have hitherto done; still more, that we should not rest contented with vague and general desires of good, or imagine that the evil influences at work are to be counteracted by great undirected efforts—by proclaiming principles—by organizing societies—by pouring forth the lavish contributions of national generosity, without examining for ourselves the channels into which they are to flow. All this is little better than mere idle philanthropy; or, it should rather be said, than the mere fulfilment of certain ceremonies, by which the mind relieves itself of the sense of a debt. But the subject is one of which the consideration peculiarly requires practical and dispassionate views; while to act upon those views requires, in addition, patience under discouragement, contentment with small successes and imperfect agents, faith in sound principles, zeal without blindness, and firmness without obstinacy.

And, in truth, there is something extremely painful in the reflection with which we are driven to conclude all our speculations on this subject— namely, that the evils with which we have to contend are such as no system, however wise and humane, can correct. Our errors are not of conception so much as of execution. Nothing is easier than to frame excellent theories, which, if they could be carried out, would go far towards removing the stigma under which we lie, and redressing the miseries which we have occasioned. But we cannot control the mischief which is going on at a far more rapid rate of progress than we dare expect for the results of our most practicable schemes of improvement. Of what use are laws and regulations, however Christian and reasonable the spirit in which they are framed, when the trader, the backwoodsman, the pirate, the bushranger, have been beforehand with our legislators, poisoning the savage with spirits, inoculating him with loathsome diseases, brutalizing his mind, and exciting his passions for the sake of gain? Desolation goes before us, and civilization lags slowly and lamely behind. We hand over to the care of the missionary and the magistrate, not the savage with his natural tendencies and capacities, and his ancestral habits, but a degraded, craving, timid, and artful creature, familiarized with the powers and the vices of the whites, rendered abject or sullen by ill-treatment, and with all his remaining faculties engrossed by the increasing difficulty of obtaining subsistence in his contracted hunting grounds. What success could the ablest and most zealous philanthropist promise himself out of such materials? And what must be *our* expectations, who have mainly to rely on agents necessarily removed from close control and responsibility, and often very imperfectly qualified for the work we have to undertake? All the anticipations of success which a reasonable man can frame to himself from schemes of reform and amelioration must necessarily be subject to one reservation—namely, if they be not thwarted by the perverse wickedness of those outcasts of society whom the first waves of our colonization are sure to bring along with them. If their violence and avarice cannot be restrained by the arm of power—and it must be confessed that there appears scarcely any feasible mode of accomplishing this—it is impossible but that our progress in the occupation of barbarous countries must be attended with the infliction of infinite suffering. Nor is this state of things peculiar to our own times, though increased demoralization, as well as increased energy and activity in colonizing, may, of late, have rendered it more conspicuous than heretofore. The history of the European settlements in America, Africa, and Australia, presents everywhere the same general features—a wide and sweeping destruction of native races by the uncontrolled violence of individuals, if not of colonial authorities, followed by tardy attempts on the part of governments to repair the acknowledged crime. . . .

In preliminary dealings with savages, whose independence is recognized, common justice and Christian humanity will readily point out the leading rules to be observed; the rest is far more matter of tact, prudence, and firmness in each separate emergency, than for previous deliberation. On this part of the subject therefore I will not touch, but take it up at what may be termed an advanced stage. When the colony is founded, and already extending itself over a considerable tract of territory, the period has arrived at which a more systematic course of proceeding becomes absolutely necessary.

The duties of the colonial government towards the natives comprised within the limits of the colony, then seem to arrange themselves under two heads—protection and civilization.

It is of course true, and must be stated in the outset, that any rules which can be laid down must vary in their application according to the different character, degree of civilization, and numerical force of the tribes with whom we have to deal in the wide circuit of our colonial enterprise. . . .

For the protection of aborigines the first step necessary is, the appointment in every new colony of a department of the civil service for that especial purpose, with one or more officers exclusively devoted to it. . . . A single individual, thoroughly qualified for the task, can accomplish more good among savages in a given time than the best code of regulations which ever was put upon paper.

The obvious duties of these officers, in the protection of the natives, are the detection and prosecution of offences against them: the regulation of contracts between them and the whites, particularly that of master and servant, which requires careful supervision: and here it may be observed that some have proposed fixed laws on the subject, as, for example, that no such contract should in any case exceed half a year; all which appears much better left to the discretion of the protector, if he can be relied upon for the proper execution of his office. He should also, it has been proposed, be the ex officio defender of the natives, or appoint defenders for them, in all cases where complaints are preferred against them by whites. It has been suggested, in addition, that he should have the right of controlling the summary power which travellers, and others who employ natives for temporary purposes, seem often apt to assume, of inflicting corrections upon them.

And here the important question opens itself: how far, and in what mode, are natives, resident or found within the limits of an English colony, to be brought within the pale of English law? That all crimes committed against them should be tried by its provisions, and that all the protection which it extends to the life and property of Englishmen should be also extended to theirs, is admitted on all hands, shamefully as the principle has been neglected in former times by colonial governments. But are the savages themselves to be considered amenable to British criminal justice, conducted according to forms of British law, for acts committed by them against the colonists? "Whenever it may be necessary to bring any native to justice," says Lord Glenelg, in a dispatch to Sir J. Stirling, "every form should be observed which would be considered necessary in the case of a white person." It is easy to understand the benevolent feeling which suggested this direction: namely, that such forms should be interposed as a shield between the savage and the summary justice which an injured colonist would be likely to exercise towards him. But how far is the principle to be carried? Are "ignorant savages to be made amenable to a code of which they are absolutely ignorant; and the whole spirit and principles of which are foreign to their mode of thought and action?" Are they to be punished, in short, with all the forms of justice, for actions to which they cannot themselves by possibility attach the notion of crime? Whatever temporary expediency may suggest, the moral feeling on which all criminal codes must rest for sanction cannot but receive some shock by the straining of their enactments to comprehend persons as incapable of incurring voluntary guilt against them as the lunatic or idiot, who are in all societies exempted from their infliction.

So long as the natives remain in their uninstructed state, the first purpose for which they are to be brought within the pale of criminal justice is that of deterring them from attacks on the persons and property of colonists. Until this is done, other considerations are premature. And perhaps this result would be better attained by placing them, in the first instance, under a species of martial or summary law, to be administered by the chief police functionaries; with opportunity for defence, or for application in mitigation of punishment, in serious cases, by the protector and his agents. Such a scheme, besides avoiding the extreme inconvenience and striking absurdity of formal process in such affairs, would have the additional advantage of removing the white settlers themselves from any share in judicial proceedings against the natives, with whom they have already too many causes of collision; which with a jury system is inevitable. And it would have this further advantage,—that it would leave an opportunity for the admission of the native to full civil rights at a future period, when converted and instructed, and able to satisfy some sufficient test of his fitness for full participation in the rights and duties of civil society. Of the nature of the punishments to be inflicted, the colonial government must probably judge. It has been recommended that in no case should death or corporal punishment be inflicted on a native; but merely confinement in prisons and penitentiaries. I doubt the practicability of this humane suggestion. Although, in most of the regions in which we are brought into contact with savage races, it does appear that the settlers are very rarely exposed to acts of violence from the savages, unless they have themselves given the first provocation, yet it must be remembered that all savages are habitually pilferers; that the difficulty of securing movable property and stock against their depredations is one of the greatest with which colonists in exposed situations have to contend; and that a mode of punishment so expensive and inconvenient may not always be found adequate for the exigencies of the moment. But with respect to death, one thing appears plain; that if it must be inflicted at all, it should be confined, as far as possible, to cases in which it may follow immediately upon the act as a consequence; as when the murderer is taken in the manner—that it may strike terror as a retribution, not appear as an act of deliberate justice; a view of capital punishment which no uncivilized mind can possibly entertain.

But a more important question remains:—how far ought the natives to be brought at once within the jurisdiction of English criminal law, in respect of their conduct towards one another?

Upon this subject I shall take the liberty of transcribing the words of an observer, who has studied with no common diligence and success the characteristics of the natives of the regions visited by him. What he says is intended to have application to the case of the Australian aborigines, but it will be seen at once that it bears equally on other instances.

He observes, that the principle which has hitherto regulated us in our dealings with native races has generally been the following:—that, although the natives should, as far as the persons and property of Europeans were concerned, be made amenable to British laws, yet, so long as they only exercised their own customs among themselves, and not too immediately in the presence of Europeans, they should be allowed to do so with impunity.

"This principle," he goes on to say,

> originated in philanthropic notions, in total ignorance of the peculiar traditional laws of this people. . . . They are as apt and intelligent as any other race of men I am acquainted with: they are subject to like affections, passions, and appetites as other men; yet in many points of character they are apparently totally dissimilar to them; and, from the peculiar code of laws of this people, it would appear not only impos-

sible that any nation subject to them could ever emerge from the savage state, but that even no race, however highly endowed, however civilized, could remain long in a state of civilization, if submitted to the operation of such barbarous customs."

This is very nearly equally true of the New Zealanders, and, to a great extent, of the American Indians.

The plea generally set up in defence of this principle is, that the natives of this country are a conquered people, and that it is an act of generosity to allow them the full power of exercising their own laws upon themselves. But this plea would appear to be inadmissible: for, in the first place, savage and traditional customs should not be confounded with a regular code of laws; and, secondly, when Great Britain ensures to a conquered country the privilege of preserving its own laws, all persons residing in this territory become amenable to those laws, and proper persons are selected by the government to watch over their due and equitable administration. Nothing of this kind either exists, or can exist, with regard to the customs of the natives. Between these two cases, then, no analogy is apparent.

I would submit, therefore, that it is necessary, from the moment the aborigines of this country are declared British subjects, that they should, as far as possible, be taught that the British laws are to supersede their own; so that any native who is suffering under their own customs may have the power of an appeal to the laws of Great Britain; or, to put this in its true light, that all authorised persons should, in all instances, be required to protect a native from the violence of his fellows, even though they be in the execution of their own laws.

So long as this is not the case, the older natives have at their disposal the means of effectually preventing the civilization of any individual of their own tribe; and those amongst them who may be inclined to adapt themselves to the habits and mode of life of Europeans will be deterred from so doing by their fear of the consequences that the displeasure of others may draw down upon them.

So much importance am I disposed to attach to this point, that I do not hesitate to assert my full conviction, that whilst those tribes that are in communication with Europeans are allowed to execute their barbarous laws and customs upon one another, so long will they remain hopelessly immured in their present state: and however unjust such a proceeding might at first sight appear, I believe that the course pointed out by true humanity would be to make them, from the commencement, amenable to the British laws, both as regards themselves and Europeans: for I hold it to involve a contradiction, to suppose that individuals subject to savage and barbarous laws can rise to a state of civilization, which their laws have a manifest tendency to destroy and overturn.

This is a passage which opens a wide field for speculation to the inquirer. The reasons which Captain Grey gives for at once suppressing by law injurious customs, instead of waiting for the operation of conversion, or of

European example, undoubtedly appear very strong. But it may be easy to apply a rule to so ignorant and defenceless a race as the aborigines of Australia, which would be very partially practicable in the case of more numerous and powerful communities. If however his principle be correct, it will scarcely suffice to extend it to such customs as Lord John Russell designates as "violations of the eternal and universal laws of morality," such as cannibalism, human sacrifice, and infanticide. It will be necessary to apply it also, with discretion, to customs less horrible, yet, from the greater frequency of their operation, perhaps still more injurious and incompatible with civilization: such as the violent abuse of the authority of husbands over wives, and barbarous ill-usage of the weaker sex in general; and some of the features of slavery among the New Zealanders, if not the practice itself. It will be necessary, in short, that the colonial authorities should act upon the assumption that they have the right, in virtue of the relative position of civilized and Christian men to savages, to enforce abstinence from immoral and degrading practices, to compel outward conformity to the law of what we regard as better instructed reason. . . . We have been so far taught by the experience of our predecessors, and, I may add, sentiments of humanity and justice have so far gained ground among us, that in recent settlements reserves of land have been invariably made *at once*, and appropriated to the natives. But it is plain that the evil day is only postponed by such measures as these, unless they are combined with a fore-seeing and far-reaching policy hitherto altogether unknown. For whether or not the natives, residing on these reserves, attain in their insulated condition to a certain degree of civilization, the same result will inevitably follow. After a time, the colonists will cast an eye of cupidity on the native lands; they will complain, and with perfect truth, of the economical disadvantages which attend the interposition of large uncultivated or half cultivated tracts between populous districts; of their own sufferings by the proximity of the natives; of the political mischiefs produced by these little inert republics, stagnant in the very centre of a rapidly-moving society. And government will find itself, as it always has been, unable to resist these importunities, and cajoled by the thousand plausibilities advanced in favour of removing these unfortunates a farther stage into the wilderness; it will comply with the exigencies of the times, and the natives will be transported to some other region, to be followed there again with sure and rapid steps by the encroaching mass of European population.

Removal is therefore, inevitably, only a temporary remedy for permanent evils, and must be continually repeated; but, besides this, nothing is more destructive of those first elements of civilization, which may have been implanted at the expense of time and toil. The proofs of this truth are almost too obvious to need any statement. In the first place, the loss of capital and of comfort entailed on the removed is very great. Next, a tribe, become agricultural, is thus placed in a country far more abounding in game than its former seats, and exposed to the strongest temptation to relapse into the hunting condition. Again, the price of those articles which have become necessary or convenient to them, especially those which are useful in their acquired habits of industry, is higher the farther they are removed from the civilized frontier; so that here, again, a temptation is held out to be content with inferior substitutes, and to unlearn one by one the habits and the arts which they had acquired. It is precisely as if a savage had been nurtured in European habits and costume until his own were forgotten, and then turned naked into the wilderness, and told to thrive as he did before. And, as the last and greatest of all these causes of degeneracy, we must not fail to estimate the insecurity, the despair of permanence, the conviction of approaching annihilation, which are inevitably engendered in their minds, and drive back into sullen apathy spirits in which the Promethean spark of enterprise had been for a moment elicited.

One only way suggests itself by which this fatal consummation can be avoided; and, in order to consider it, we must look steadfastly at the broad outlines of the question, What is the ultimate destiny of the races whose interests we are now discovering?

There are only three alternatives which imagination itself can suggest:

The extermination of native races.

Their civilization, complete or partial, by retaining them as insulated bodies of men, carefully removed, during the civilizing process, from the injury of European contact.

Their amalgamation with the colonists.

Those who hold the opinion that the first is inevitable, are happily relieved from the trouble of all these considerations. Their only object must be to insure that the inevitable end be not precipitated by cruelty or injustice.

The second alternative I cannot but believe to be impossible. Reason seems to demonstrate this, and experience abundantly confirms her conclusions. If it be possible to civilize the savage at all, in a state of insulation from Europeans, except his own instructors (which, after the ill success of the Spanish and Portuguese experiments, may be regarded as very doubtful), it must, at all events, be a slow, uncertain process, liable to be interrupted at any moment, and only to be carried on under the defence of laws hedging them in from all foreign intercourse with a strictness impracticable in the present state of the world. The savage thus educated may be morally a more innocent creature, but, intellectually, he must be feeble and dependent, and quite unable to resist extrinsic influence, when brought to bear upon him. And (which is of still greater consequence, and is the peculiar cause that renders such projects certain of failure) long before the seeds of civilization have made any effectual shoot, the little nursery is surrounded by the advance of the European population; the demand for the land of the natives becomes urgent and irresistible, and pupils and instructors are driven out into the wilderness to commence their work again.

There remains only the third alternative, that of amalgamation; and this I am most anxious to impress upon your minds, because I firmly believe it to be the very keystone, the leading principle, of all sound theory on the subject—that native races must in every instance either perish, or be amalgamated with the general population of their country.

By amalgamation, I mean the union of natives with settlers in the same community, as master and servant, as fellow-labourers, as fellow-citizens, and, if possible, as connected by intermarriage. And I mean by it, not that eventual and distant process to which some appear to look, by which a native community, when educated and civilized, is to be, at some future period, admitted *en masse* to the full rights of citizenship; but I mean an immediate and an individual process—immediate, if not in act, at least in contemplation. To answer the view which I am anxious to lay before you, each native must be regarded as potentially a citizen, to become such in all respects as soon as possible. To this end, every step in his instruction and management must conduce. It must be the object in framing every law, in making every provision for his support. Nay, the first steps of the actual operation should rather be accelerated than retarded. I mean that, although prudence must be the guide in all cases, it must be a fixed principle, that less evil is likely to be done by over haste than by over delay.

These views must undoubtedly appear somewhat wild and chimerical. Be it so. I will endeavour presently to develope them a little more fully: at present I am chiefly anxious to point out to you, that, however improbable the success of any particular project of amalgamation may seem, amalgamation, by some means or other, is the only possible Euthanasia of savage communities. And one negative lesson even the most cautious may draw from this plain truth, namely, that all endeavours to civilize the savage, in which this end is not kept in view, are useless, or worse than useless, and must end in disappointment, as they ever hitherto have ended. And we have this advantage at least, that we are on untrodden ground. The experiment of amalgamation, or even of taking means tending to this as their ultimate result, cannot be said to have been hitherto tried in earnest by any government. . . .

And, lastly, there should be no hesitation in acting on the broad principle that the natives must, for their own protection, be placed in a situation of acknowledged inferiority, and consequently of tutelage. This is the old Spanish system of which much has been already said in the course of these lectures, and the only one which has success to appeal to in its favour. It has been in later years too much the fashion to rely on phrases; to imagine that by proclaiming that all fellow-subjects of whatever race are equal in the eye of the law, we really make them so. There cannot be a greater error, nor one more calculated to inflict evil on those classes whom it is intended to benefit. The Caffre or the Maori may be rendered equal in legal rights with the settler, but he is not really equal in the power of enjoying or enforcing those rights, nor can he become so until civilization has rendered him equal in knowledge and in mental power. But a state of fictitious equality is far worse for him than one of acknowledged inferiority, with its correlative protection. If we intend to deal with the aborigines of countries of which we have taken possession as equals, then we must exclude settlers from contact with them. We must adopt what in these lectures has been called the policy of insulation—that of the United States—and leave them, in their allotted reserves, subject to their own laws and usages, so far as our established morality may allow of these prevailing. There we may entrust them to the good offices of the missionary, and the "protector," so far as these can reach. But, if we adopt the opposite policy, that of "amalgamation," then we shall assuredly find that they can only meet with the whites in the same field of hopeful industry on the footing of inferiors, and that, if such subordinate position is not recognized by law, and compensated by legal protection, it will be enforced, at a heavy disadvantage to them, by the prevailing sentiment of the conquering race.

11 Creed of a Government Anthropologist

F. E. WILLIAMS

Anthropologists who accepted the basic premises of functionalism, such as Rivers (see part III), stressed the equilibrium and integration of culture and advised only cautious intervention in tribal cultures. If functionalist anthropology were taken too literally, there would be no justification for intervention in traditional cultures at all. Francis Edgar Williams (1893–1943) was an Oxford-trained Rhodes scholar who had served as a government anthropologist for 17 years in Papua New Guinea when he wrote the paper reproduced here. He was trained in functionalist theory but considered himself only a "limited functionalist." He stressed that cultures were only partly integrated, that they contained "confusion," and that they really only approximated a system, one that sometimes worked badly. The role of the government was to foster the welfare of individuals. If a given tribal culture appeared not to be promoting individual welfare properly, the government was duty bound to intervene. The government anthropologist was therefore a reformer.

This emphasis on individualism is a common and very important justification for intervention; it allows policy makers to sidestep the more basic issue of the right of communities and societies to control their own destinies. Although Williams does endorse the right of native communities to decide things for themselves, he appears to believe that the rights of individuals still take precedence over the interests of the tribal society. Williams also maintains that people need to be educated before they can make decisions about their future and that it is simply not possible for natives to "go their own way." Williams clearly had the welfare of the tribal people in mind, and he had considerable respect for traditional culture, but he was not prepared to question the basic justice of colonial intervention. Part of his ambivalence may derive from the fact that his salary as a government anthropologist came directly from taxes levied on natives. Such taxes were designed to promote economic development by forcing natives into dependence on the market economy.

ANTHROPOLOGY AND TRUSTEESHIP

I shall now attempt to discuss—though still, I fear, in abstract terms—how anthropology may be applied in a somewhat more positive manner. We may presumably dispense with the idea of culture as something to be preserved for its own sake. I have sought to show that it is at best only partially organized; and if this be granted it would seem to follow that it is in some degree inefficient. And we may go further. It is also laden with unhappiness no less than with happiness. For if man is born to sorrow it is largely sorrow of his own making, and he is far from being solely responsible as an individual. Many at least of his sorrows are prepared for him by the culture into which he is born: he is condemned thereby to some suffering, and the luckiest of the lucky will not escape entirely. And I should go further still. Culture is plainly a thing which has nowhere reached its potential limits of development. Some, notably those which we study as anthropologists, are more backward, more restricted, than others. It is notorious that within our own society there are individuals who do not get their fair chance; but, more than this, there are whole societies which have not had their chance. As I see it, then, the best of cultures is not devoid of muddlement; it carries the seeds of unhappiness; and it is only the embryo of what it might be.

Now according to the modern notion of trusteeship it is the duty of the administrator, as it has long been the self-appointed duty of the missionary, to try to improve things. In view of the extreme difficulty and danger of deciding for other people what is good for them, it is a duty which we trust they will always face with proper humility; but it is one which they are not likely to shirk. It becomes necessary for anthropologists, therefore, to recognize this obligation on the part of others even if they decline to participate in it themselves. As for a government anthropologist, he might even be expected as part of his duty to participate. At any rate I think he would make himself more useful if, besides observing and recording things merely as they are, he could also, in his other character, consider them with respect to their value. He might even feel called upon to set things right himself, though I feel sure he would approach that task with all the reluctance of Hamlet. But fortunately for everyone, perhaps, the actual responsibility is not his. His advice may be taken or left.

Assuming, however, the practical necessity for judgments of value, I should begin by declaring an article of faith, viz. that in the application of anthropology, as in any other phase of social work, the primary, indefeasible values are those of the individual human personality. To the administrator, trustee for their welfare, the human animals under his care, both European and native, represent the end; their various cultures are merely means, good, bad, or indifferent, for the satisfaction of their needs and the expression of their potentialities.

This, which seems to me a fundamental postulate, provides him with his charter. For cultures, obviously imperfect and changeable things, are no more than the best means evolved hitherto by the societies to which they belong: and there can be no denying that they stand in need of tidying-up, purging, reconciling, blending, and developing. To this task, tremendous both in difficulty and responsibility, the administrator and the missionary are already actually addressing themselves. The extent to which their interference is justifiable is certainly debatable, and to that point I shall return.

But it falls in with the view I am trying to expound that they have some right at least, indeed that some interference amounts to a necessity. And, whether this be so or not, the policy of interference has come without doubt to stay, so that the anthropologist, even if he disapproves, might bow gracefully to the inevitable and do his best service by criticism, constructive as well as destructive, of its methods.

I have elsewhere stated[1] what seem to me the three general tasks of native education in the broadest sense of that word—which might indeed be taken to embrace all the essentials of a native policy. They are the tasks of Maintenance, Expurgation, and Expansion—not perfectly suitable words, but the best I could think of. I shall go over these briefly and in the reverse order.

First, then, regarding Expansion, by which I mean the enrichment of a culture both by development and by the introduction of new factors. There are, of course, arguments against the introduction of new things—so-called gifts of Western civilization—or at least cautions to be observed. For they may do more harm than good. But I am bound to think that it is the duty of the educator, and through him of the administrator, to give the native a chance of fuller development than has hitherto been possible for him. To take literacy for a concrete example, I cannot think the arguments against it, though they may dictate caution, can absolve us from the responsibility of giving it ultimately to the native as his right. And there are many possible advances in the spheres of economics, politics, art, and religion towards which we might assist him. I would dare say of morality also, except for its suggestion of the pot and the kettle and the fear that anthropologists might think I was thrusting this unfamiliar burden on them. Ideally speaking, however, it is the anthropologist, provided he will deign to think sometimes in terms of value, who is best qualified both to criticize and to suggest the ways and means of adding to an existent primitive culture; for not only should he be the best judge of what is suitable and assimilable, but he should be best aware of the shortcomings of the culture as it stands.

Now for the more ticklish and contentious subject of Expurgation. Allow me first to point out that the theory of culture as a semi-integrated, imperfect whole will allow for the process of expurgation (as well as expansion) in a way that seems hardly possible if we postulate a full, or even a very high, degree of integration. Experience surely shows that cultures possess a good deal of plasticity; that they possess the power to change, to slough or forget old things on the one hand, and to absorb or find room for new things on the other. It is only necessary to give due heed to the warnings which the functionalists have uttered regarding the danger of disruption, the upsetting of balance, and so on, without going so far as to admit such perfection of balance or integration as would seem to make any interference a disaster. For culture as I now see it is the kind of watch that does not necessarily stop for the removal of a reasonably small wheel, but may on the contrary go all the better.

It is true that some things are so deeply embedded and possess so many ramifications that they may justly be called 'indispensable' or 'vital'. And here, unless adequate substitutes can be provided, our interference is likely to bring about serious dislocation—a prospect which should certainly give us pause. But I cannot concede the functionalist plea that everything is vital. There are many things for which no such claim can be made and which would probably be better away. When we seek to eliminate them we may perhaps trust to the adaptive or recuperative powers of the culture to enable it to heal over the breach and survive, when it will be all the better for the change.

While I believe it justifiable to eliminate some things from the primitive cultures that lie, so to speak, at our mercy, I should not dream of suggesting that we should do so merely because they 'outraged civilised notions of propriety'. That common argument is itself an outrage on propriety. But there may be good reasons of other kinds. Our much wider experience and scientific knowledge may enable us to see defects which remain hidden from the native himself. It may be something that hinders the satisfactory living-together of black man and white man which we have to aim at and which certainly requires some adjustment on both sides—for it must be remembered that the white man also has his rights in applied anthropology. But what concerns us more obviously are the defects within the bounds of the primitive culture itself. A time-honoured but mistaken method of agriculture or stock-raising, for example, may be eating into a community's resources; an equally time-honoured method of sanitation may be a danger to its health. Such things are fit subjects for expurgation.

In these cases, however, it is the whole community that suffers through its own age-long mistake embodied in its culture; and I want to draw your attention to a sort of defect that may not be quite so obvious. I have declared my own belief in the primary rights of the human personality, and I think accordingly that wherever we detect the existence of abuse, injustice, exploitation, repression, pain, and suffering—in short, the victimization of the individual by the society—then once more we are called upon to interfere. I should say from my own observations that sorcery (to use a somewhat threadbare subject for illustration) despite its functional connections is responsible for much more harm than good. It is the prime source of suspicion, fear, dissension, and strife—things which seem the very negation of satisfactory living-together and which undoubtedly entail unhappiness. I think we are called upon to remove this form of victimization by the best means in our power.

Similarly with head-hunting, by way of a more extreme and equally hackneyed example. A good defence on functional lines can be made out for this also; no one will deny that it may play a highly important part in a general way of living on the Middle Fly. But, to adopt the individual's rights as a criterion, what of those unfortunates who play the less desirable part of the two roles necessary to a head-hunting scene? Can any more drastic infringement of a man's rights be conceived than to fall on him in his sleep and cut off his head?

Whether, then, in the interests of the whole community or of certain individuals within it, I am bound to think that some interference may be justified. And if it is I should regard it as good service on the part of anthropologists in general, and even as the duty of government anthropologists, to lend their aid. For once again they are in a very favourable position to detect abuses. While it is happily beyond their scope to perform cultural excisions or amputations, they should not hesitate to recommend them where they think fit; for they, in theory at least, are the best qualified not only to diagnose the complaint but to judge whether the general constitution of the patient will stand an operation.

Thirdly, we come to the task of Maintenance. In this anthropologists have always willingly lent their assistance, and the primitive peoples of the world, if they realized it, might perhaps be grateful to those field-workers who must so insufferably have bored them. In fact I repeat that this providing of argument for maintaining existent cultures has been the greatest contribution hitherto made by applied anthropology. And incidentally I think it the best general result of a training in our science that it should broaden the student's mind, teaching him liberality and tolerance, so that he realizes there are other ways than our own, possibly as good and possibly better.

The anthropologist's tendency to cherish the old cultures is so common and so strong that one suspects, as I have mentioned already, a sentimental bias in their favour—for anthropologists are seldom so cold-hearted as they would like to be. I do not imagine that I am wholly free from this bias myself. But there are some very good reasons for maintenance other than sentimental ones.

In the first place there is the general argument of the functionalists that culture represents a working whole in which interference may bring about stoppage or dislocation. One may appreciate the value of this argument without following it to a logical extreme.

The second reason lies in the intrinsic merits of backward cultures as we find them. Those researchers who have cut themselves off from their own world for long periods and immersed themselves in the strangely different world of the so-called primitives always, I believe, find much therein that is truly admirable. They admire it more than do outsiders for the simple reason that they know it better; and they are not necessarily cranks for doing so. Further than this, the sharp comparison which all are able to make between Western civilization and primitive culture is not in the eyes of anthropologists, who see both sides, so unquestionably favourable to the former. In short, primitive cultures may seem worthy of preservation, as far as may be, for their own sakes.

CULTURAL SELF-DETERMINATION

But there is still another reason for preserving them—or, to put it more cautiously, for letting them be—and this brings me to my final point, in which perhaps we step right out of the accepted sphere of anthropology as a science.

We may in wisdom or in arrogance believe that the native and his culture stand in need of reform. But let us never forget that he is himself and his culture is his own. The very fact that we may feel bound to provide scope for a fuller development of the native's personality should imply, one presumes, a genuine respect for that personality. And this means first and foremost a recognition of his right to freedom. By this, of course, I mean nothing so crudely obvious as the denial of slavery. I mean the right to live as he himself thinks good; and this implies also the right of a primitive society as such to enjoy its own culture.

I can conjure up only two justifications for repressive or destructive interference. One is that the culture itself contains abuses which stifle or frustrate the human personality. The other is that in its wider relations it may infringe the rights of others, whether native or European, with whose interests it must be reconciled. Granted, however, that liberty of individual or group must stop short of making itself a nuisance to others, it remains a principle which we choose to regard as sacred. If this is really so, then the native's liberty is no less sacred than our own. He also should have that right, which we prize so highly, of self-determination.

It is mainly on these ethical grounds that I would protest against any definite policy of moulding the native after our own pattern. This policy is sometimes justified on the assumption that we are all moving in the direction of a single united world civilization, to which is added the further tacit assumption that our civilization will provide its model. Even if this be the case I cannot see how it is compatible with the principle of freedom to set about deliberately working for conformity—though to be sure, if the native chooses in the long run to copy our model, then we shall all no doubt be satisfied. There may, however, be quite a different and perhaps more satisfactory future in store for us, viz. one of unity in diversity; and if the vast native populations of the world choose to remain something very different from us it is doubtful whether we should question their right—as it is wholly doubtful whether we should question their taste.

Nevertheless there is a widespread campaign, explicit or inexplicit, direct or indirect, to do away with the native's old way of life and substitute our own. Needless to say it may be motivated by good intentions, even by altruism. But it often appears that the native may have but little say in his own future; for though coercion may be absent, he is nevertheless carried helplessly along with the tide of propaganda and suggestion. In so far as the choice lies between the two extremes of remaining as he is or becoming Europeanized I think that, under certain conditions at present in existence, he is bound to veer strongly towards the latter because the two alternatives are not placed before him fairly.

Let us for a moment try the boots on our own feet and see how we should like to wear them. It is a fact unquestioned that we are deeply and strongly attached to the institutions of our own culture, e.g., private ownership, democracy, and individual liberty. Each one of these institutions or ideals is now subject to attack by rival systems to whose propagandists we should be unjust if we denied their true missionary zeal. Thus we find Fascist on one side and Communist on the other both pouring scorn on the outworn system of democracy.

It is happily unnecessary to declare one's personal opinions upon any of these rival systems, though it seems obvious that our present civilization is so far from being a satisfactorily working whole as to demand some fundamental readjustments. Whatever these may be, however, it is certain that we shall fight hard against any interference with the system we are used to.

I ask you now to imagine hypothetically a band of missionaries, whether Fascist or Communist, in our midst. They are armed with overpowering influence and prestige; and they have sole control of the weapons of education and propaganda. Picture our initial resentment and indignation, but recognize that these in due course would die down; that certain of our cherished ideals would disappear; and that our children would eventually embrace the new order with open arms, convinced that it was their free choice to do so. This hypothetical parallel may throw some light on the justice of similar methods in so far as they involve the displacement of primitive cultures.

The Devil may quote Scripture to his purpose, and I give you another parallel. I recently listened to a sermon on the following text: 'Be watchful, and strengthen the things which remain, that are ready to die'. It was taken from St. John's inspired admonition to the church in Sardis, and the preacher succeeded in giving this somewhat obscure utterance a plausible interpretation. The Church, which had forgotten the essentials of the Christian faith, was to hold fast, pending its rejuvenation, to the superficialities, the mere rites, material emblems, and so forth, which had their value and which were themselves threatened with extinction. An inattentive anthropologist might well reflect that this advice was applicable in a wider sphere. Nearly 2,000 years have passed since the shrewd apostle wrote those words; and by now, in some widely represented opinions, the essentials of Christian faith have themselves become superficialities, trimmings on the face of civilization—something which it might, if it wished, cast off. Indeed revolution in one country and another is at this moment engaged in casting it off.

Once again it is happily unnecessary to declare one's own opinion as to whether a changing civilization could fittingly dispense with the Christian faith; though I would go so far as to assume that that faith has no divine protection to ensure its continuance. That, or its decay and extinction, must depend solely on the present and future generations of humanity; and one may prophesy a long struggle between those who are for it and those who, with perhaps equal sincerity, are against it.

Its vast importance, historically and now, both in our civilization and those of other so-called Christian nations, goes without saying. Nor need I draw attention to the place it holds in the people's affections and all their conservative sentiments. Its maintenance or otherwise is therefore a burning question of applied anthropology—though somewhat bigger than we are accustomed to tackle—and a functionalist from Mars could hardly do other than echo the apostle's words, 'Strengthen the things which remain'. Whatever their religion or lack of it, that is a policy which most anthropologists, if they could transfer their spirit of championship from primitive cultures to advanced civilization, might feel bound to endorse.

But let us imagine once again a situation in which the enemies of Christianity were politically dominant and in absolute control of education and propaganda. They would possibly succeed in blotting Christian belief out of the people's mind; and strange to say the generation which saw it disappear would believe that they had freely willed its disappearance.

Now this would be cultural displacement; it would at least create a serious void; it would be the end of a great human achievement for which no one, whatever his beliefs, would deny admiration; and—which is my point—it would be a denial of self-determination. The ordinary citizen, so strong a champion of his own institutions, might therefore, if he could change places in imagination, question the methods which are sometimes brought to bear against the weaker, more defenceless, cultures of the backward peoples.

All our positive efforts for the welfare of native peoples, therefore, have to reckon with this right to personal freedom and self-determination. I do not think it is a solid wall against which they must all dash themselves to pieces. I believe on the other hand that our scientific knowledge and our wider experience of social rights and obligations should qualify us to help, advise, and perhaps to guide; though the very experience which gives us such an advantage should have taught us how hard it is to know what is good for ourselves, and how more than hard to know what is good for others.

Freedom, the right to think for ourselves and to do what seems good to us, we regard as the highest prize of our civilization. But the possession of it, as we know too well, is insecure: it depends on two complementary factors. On one hand, as we are told, the price of freedom is eternal vigilance; and no one deserves to keep it who has not the courage to fight for it. On the other hand, it can only live by tolerance; and this, in the present connection, is plainly the aspect which we have to consider. The limits which we impose on native liberties are not to be dictated by our own arbitrary sense of propriety, but by consideration for the rights, in fact the liberties, of others, whether individuals or societies. While, then, we undertake the high-sounding obligations of trusteeship, we should impose those limits with a hand as light as it is firm, recognizing that the native's way of living is his own, that he is much devoted to it, and that, if it does nobody any harm, he has a right to it.

If, as I suggested earlier, the native chooses in the long run to conform to our pattern, we should of course be prepared to abide by his choice. It seems wholly probable that he will conform to greater or less extent; and while it would be unfair to lead him deliberately away from a path that might suit him better, I think we should not deny him the opportunity of conforming. Our course then—and it seems to me the most vital part of a native policy—is to educate him. And by education I mean far more than is meant by the word in popular currency; in fact the sort of liberal education which relates itself both to the new things of Western civilization and to the existent things of his native condition. It would well become the anthropologist to co-operate with the educator in formulating the ideal methods which would make, not for any specific type of our own choosing, but rather for straight and independent thinking, critical appreciation, and, in the spheres of action and conduct, vigour, efficiency, and consideration for others. However distant and idealistic these may sound, it is only as the native advances along the path towards them that he will become fit, or indeed able, to choose his future for himself.

Should anyone ask, 'What are you aiming at? What are you trying to make of the native?' I think the only proper way to answer this at first staggering question is to side-step it. Our purpose need be no more than to give him, by education and by respect for his rights, a chance to make something of himself. Provided he plays the game by respecting others' rights, then he can make of himself just what he pleases.

It may seem as if what was said in the earlier parts of this address has been unsaid in the last. But I do not think this is the case. I was at pains to show that things may be far from right in any primitive culture. It needs no pains to show that they are far from right in the world at large. Administrators engage in a bigger field of operations than, as a rule, do anthropologists; they have a wider variety of factors to consider than may occur to us; they recognize that the native problem is only part of a larger one; and they are pledged to the everlasting, if not hopeless, task of reconciling rights. While, then, we might be only too glad to let the native go his own way, it is not wholly possible. His way of life must somehow enter into relation with the affairs of the world. It is to be hoped that we may leave him his fair share of freedom; but to leave him entirely to himself would be to funk the issue and neglect our duty.

NOTE

1. Williams, F. E.: *The Blending of Cultures*, Govt. Printer, Port Moresby, 1935.

12   The Future
of the Savage Races

LORD FITZROY R. S. RAGLAN

Lord Fitzroy Richard Somerset Raglan (1885–1964) was an old-fashioned ethnological scholar. He was a Sandhurst-trained, professional military man who joined the Grenadier Guards. He became interested in ethnology while on military service in the Sudan and Palestine; he became a fellow of the Royal Anthropological Institute in 1921 and was president from 1955 to 1957. His main interest was in the origin of religion, and he remained an uncompromising and outspoken diffusionist even though this ran counter to the prevailing functionalism of the time. His view on tribal policy must have found broad popular support, but it did not represent mainline British functionalist anthropology. It is remarkable for its bluntness: "savagery and superstition" are a plague that anthropologists must help eradicate to make the world safe for progress and civilization. Raglan had no patience with cautious reform policies and emphatically rejected any possibility of nonintervention. His confidence in the superiority of Western civilization would have been quite familiar to Merivale more than a hundred years earlier, but it was not shared by the more sensitive Williams.

This selection was published as a letter in the British anthropology journal *Man* in 1940. It does not appear to have been directed at any specific person or issue, but just two years earlier Donald Thomson had argued in a paper presented to the Royal Anthropological Institute in London that the Aborigines of Arnhem Land in northern Australia should remain free to enjoy their independent tribal existence. It is likely that Raglan heard Thomson's paper, and this letter may be an indirect response to it.

Sir,

It has often been urged against anthropologists that they wish to keep certain parts of the world—those inhabited by interestingly peculiar savages—as 'anthropological museums.' Whether or not this is true, it seems to me that anthropologists have given insufficient thought to the future of savages in general.

We all of us wish to see the world a better place, a place where wiser people than ourselves will lead happier and fuller lives, and it is surely desirable that anthropologists should make their contribution, theoretical as well as practical, towards this end.

Reprinted with permission from *Man* 40 (1940): 62. Copyright © 1940 Royal Anthropological Institute of Great Britain and Ireland.

What exactly makes for wisdom and happiness may be disputed, but there can at any rate be no doubt that one of the chief causes of folly and unhappiness is that complex of beliefs and practices which we describe as 'magic.' That nobody is wiser or happier as the result of belief in demons, witchcraft, and the evil eye, or the practice of human sacrifice, torture, and mutilation, will hardly be disputed, yet anthropologists often plead for the preservation of cultures of which these are prominent features. The British government has abolished human sacrifice throughout its dominions, and no scientist has pleaded for its retention, yet, although more sensational, it is no more irrational and inhuman than many other features of every savage culture.

Progress can be achieved in two ways only, that is to say, by improving the best and by eliminating the worst, and by the worst we can only mean that which is the least humane, rational, and scientific.

It may be urged that savages have now so little influence on human affairs in general that their survival in a state of savagery can have no effect on the general progress of the race. This seems extremely doubtful. The ease with which men relapse into savagery and superstition is only too obvious, and the continued existence of reservoirs of undiluted savagery and superstition must make such relapses easier. Plague spots will remain from which the rest of the world, if it should ever get a clean bill of health, will inevitably be reinfected.

The worst evils of the day arise from the survival of savage beliefs, and of the habits of mind with which such beliefs are associated. We can never be really civilized until we are all civilized.

Our proper course, then, in dealing with the savage races of our empire, is to try to civilize them as rapidly as possible. By this I do not mean that they should be deprived of their ancestral lands or exploited in any way, but that we should bring to them our justice, our education, and our science. Few will deny that these are better than anything which savages have got, but many claim that, though good for Europeans, they are bad for Asiatics or Africans. That certain features of our civilization are bad for Asiatics and Africans cannot be disputed, but these are also bad for Europeans; it is surely impossible to maintain positively, as many do by implication, that up-to-date medicine, surgery, sanitation, and scientific agriculture are bad for anyone.

Some maintain that good as these things are, they are good for savages only if the savages develop them for themselves. We must then conclude that our own educational and health services are bad for us, because they have in almost every case had to be forced on local authorities by the central government. It is possible, though highly improbable, that in a hundred years' time the Solomon Islanders will discover the method of making chloroform; must we therefore deprive them of it now?

To attempt to lay down any general scheme of advancement would be absurd, since conditions differ so enormously, but it is greatly to be desired that anthropologists should array themselves on the side of progress, and not allow their science to be linked, in the minds either of European administrators or educated non-Europeans, with a policy of deliberately keeping savages savage.

Raglan

---

13   Do Missionaries Destroy Cultures?

DON RICHARDSON

As a missionary for the Regions Beyond Missionary Union (RBMU) Don Richardson in 1962 entered the territory of the still-independent Sawi people in the Asmat lowlands of what was then Netherlands New Guinea. His objective was to convert them to Christianity and to "preadapt" them for civilization by convincing them to end intertribal conflict and cannibalism. The story of his successful effort is told in a film and in his widely read popular book *Peace Child*, published in 13 languages and as a Reader's Digest condensation. The present selection was written in response to a journalist's accusations (*Washington Post*, August 3, 1976) that Protestant missionaries in West Irian were insensitively destroying native culture. It is a very persuasive defense of missionary work. In Richardson's view intervention by missionaries in even the most isolated tribal cultures is justified because such "directed change" will soften the inevitable transition to civilization and will help ensure physical survival. Indeed, missionary work has often reduced the destruction and exploitation that have accompanied the development of tribal areas. Missionary-trained tribal individuals have also sometimes become prominent spokespeople for the human rights of tribal communities. However, there may well be other routes to tribal self-defense than change "directed" by Christian missionaries. Richardson's approach is certainly humanitarian, but it does not question the basic assumptions that external development of tribal areas is inevitable and that development must be directed by outsiders.

There are reasons why the missionaries had to go into isolated areas like Irian Jaya as soon as they could. History has taught them

Reprinted by permission of Don Richardson, author of *Peace Child*, *Lords of the Earth*, and other books.

that even the most isolated minority cultures must eventually be over-whelmed by the commercial and political expansion of majority peoples. Naive academics in ivy-covered towers may protest that the world's remaining primitive cultures should be left undisturbed, but farmers, lumbermen, land speculators, miners, hunters, military leaders, road builders, art collectors, tourists, and drug peddlers aren't listening.

They are going in anyway. Often to destroy. Cheat. Exploit. Victimize. Corrupt. Taking, and giving little other than diseases for which primitives have no immunity or medicine.

This is why, since the turn of the century, more than ninety tribes have become extinct in Brazil alone. Many other Latin American, African, and Asian countries show a similar high extinction rate for their primitive minorities. A grim toll of five or six tribes per year is probably a conservative worldwide estimate.

We missionaries don't want the same fate to befall these magnificent tribes in Irian Jaya. We risk our lives to get to them first because we believe we are more sympathetic agents of change than profit-hungry commercialists. Like our predecessor John Sargent, who in 1796 launched a program which saved the Mohican tribe from extinction, and like our colleagues in Brazil who just one generation ago saved the Wai Wai from a similar fate, we believe we know how to precondition tribes in Irian Jaya for survival in the modern world. The question, "Should anyone go in?" is obsolete because obviously someone *will*.

It has been replaced by a more practical question: "Will the most sympathetic persons get there first?" To make the shock of coming out of the stone age as easy as possible. To see that tribals gain new ideals to replace those they must lose in order to survive. To teach them the national language so they can defend themselves in disputes with "civilizados." And yet produce literature in their own language so it will not be forgotten. To teach them the value of money, so that unscrupulous traders cannot easily cheat them. And better yet, set some of them up in business so that commerce in their areas will not fall entirely into the hands of outsiders. To care for them when epidemics sweep through or when earthquakes strike. And better yet, train some of them as nurses and doctors to carry on when we are gone. We go as ombudsmen who help clashing cultures understand each other.

We missionaries are advocates not only of spiritual truth, but also of physical survival. And we have enjoyed astonishing success in Irian Jaya and elsewhere. Among the Ekari, Damal, Dani, Ndugwa, and other tribes, more than 100,000 stone agers welcomed our gospel as the fulfillment of something their respective cultures had anticipated for hundreds of years. The Ekari called it *aji*. To the Damal, it was *hai*. To the Dani, *nabelankabelan*—an immortal message which one day would restrain tribal war and ease human suffering.

The result: cultural fulfillment of the deepest possible kind. And it opened the door to faith in Jesus Christ for tens of thousands.

Along with our successes, there have been setbacks. Nearly two years ago one of our colleagues from a European mission, Gerrit Kuijt, left some coastal helpers in charge of a new outpost while he returned to Holland. In his absence, a few of the coastals began to molest the surrounding tribespeople for private reasons. Thirteen coastals were killed in retaliation.

Sympathize. Sometimes it is not easy to find responsible helpers willing to venture with us into these wild areas. At times you have to trust someone; you have no choice.

Earlier, in 1968, two of our buddies, Phil Masters and Stan Dale, died together while probing a new area of the Yali tribe. But then Kusaho, a Yali elder, rebuked the young men who killed them, saying: "Neither of these men ever harmed any of us, nor did they even resist while you killed them. Surely they came in peace and you have made a terrible mistake. If ever any more of this kind of men come into our valley, we must welcome them."

And so a door of acceptance opened through the wounds of our friends. It was a costly victory. Stan's and Phil's widows were each left with five small children to raise alone. Yet neither widow blamed anyone for the death of her husband, and one of them still serves with us in Irian Jaya today.

Ours is a great work, and a very difficult one. It is not subsidized by any government, and can succeed only as it has sympathetic support from churches, private individuals, and the public in general. That is where correspondent McDonald could have helped. Instead . . .

McDonald now transferred to a Mission Aviation Fellowship helicopter loaded with sweet potatoes contributed by Christians from the Dani tribe and rice from Indonesian government stores. Pilot Jeff Heritage thought McDonald seemed surprisingly uninterested in the many tribal hamlets stranded like islands in the midst of uncrossable landslides, their inhabitants on the edge of starvation. After only a few hours in the interior, he returned to the coast and wrote his report.

Wielding the cliche "fundamentalist" with obvious intent to stigmatize and nettle us, McDonald launched a scathing yet baseless attack which appeared as a major article in the *Washington Post* and was relayed by wire service to hundreds of newspapers around the world. Citing the loss of Gerrit Kuijt's thirteen helpers and the murder of Phil and Stan eight years ago, he made the absurd accusation that we are "provoking hostile and occasionally murderous reactions from primitive tribesmen." He continues: "The missionaries are also coming under attack by anthropologists and other observers for attempting the almost total destruction of cultures. . . ."

Who are the anthropologists and other observers? Within our ranks we have a number of men who hold degrees in anthropology, and they have not warned us of any such attack by members of their discipline. We have cooperated with a number of anthropologists in Irian Jaya over the past twenty years, and have had good mutual understanding with them.

Perhaps McDonald is referring to the three remaining members of a

German scientific team he met on one of his helicopter stops in the interior. Some of them, reportedly, have been critical toward us, not on the basis of wide knowledge of our work, but because of anti-missionary sentiments they brought with them to Irian Jaya.

Their problem is that they hold to an old school of anthropology, still current in some areas, which favors isolating primitive tribes from all change in zoo-like reserves. A new school, now rising in America, has at last recognized the futility of this approach, and advocates instead that primitive tribes be exposed to survival-related "directed change," in order that they may learn to cope with encroachment, now seen as inevitable.

Directed change is exactly what evangelical missionary John Sargent practiced back in 1796 and what we are practicing in 1976. In fact, missionaries are virtually the only persons who do. Anthropologists don't remain with tribesmen long enough. And humanists aren't sufficiently motivated. But if, indeed, we are under attack, a careful reporter should have asked us for our defense, if any. McDonald did not do this, though he had opportunity. What evidence does he present for his charge that we are "attempting the almost total destruction of local cultures" in Irian Jaya? He writes: "The first action of a missionary . . . in Valley X recently was to hand out shirts to the tribesmen."

The tribesmen concerned had just lost most of their homes in the earthquake. Indonesian officials had provided shirts to help them stay warm at night in their crude temporary shelters at mile-high elevations. No one wanted a rash of pneumonia cases complicating the relief operation. Johnny Benzel, the missionary, cooperated with the government directive by handing out the shirts.

Nowhere have we ever provided Indonesian or Western-style clothing until demand for it arose among the tribal people themselves. This usually took from seven to fifteen years. Tribal church elders preached in the open or under grass-roofed shelters, wearing their penis gourds, and no one thought anything of it. Even today the vast majority of men still wear gourds and women wear grass skirts.

It is the Indonesian government, not missionaries, which tries to shame tribals into exchanging gourds and grass skirts for shorts and dresses under *Operation Koteka*. But they do it for understandable reasons. They want the tribesmen to become part of Indonesian society as soon as possible, find employment, etc.

At Nalca, McDonald snapped a photo of a native with a ball-point pen stuck through the pierced septum of his nose. This photo appeared in some newspapers with the ludicrous caption: "Ball-point pen replaces nosebone; fundamentalist preachers destroy culture." A native forages a used ball-point pen out of Johnny Benzel's wastepaper basket, sticks it through his nose, and presto! Johnny is accused of destroying culture. Very tricky, McDonald.

McDonald slams Johnny again: "At Nalca mission, women have been persuaded to lengthen their grass skirts to knee-length. . . ." What actually happens is that families of the Dani tribe follow missionaries to places like Nalca, and over a period of years the Nalca women begin to imitate the style of their Dani counterparts, which happens to be longer.

Do we, then, approve of everything in the local cultures? No, we do not, just as no one in our own Western culture automatically approves of everything in it.

We are out to destroy cannibalism, but so also is the Indonesian government. The difference is, we use moral persuasion, and if we fail, the government will eventually use physical force. Our task is to give the tribals a rational basis for giving it up voluntarily before the guns of the police decide the issue with traumatic effect.

We also want to stop the intertribal warfare that has gone on for centuries. In view of all they have to go through in the next fifty years, it is imperative that the tribes stop killing and wounding each other *now*. Often we are able to stop the fighting by emphasizing little-used peace-making mechanisms within the cultures themselves. Or we simply provide the third-person presence which enables antagonists to see their problems in a new light.

We are against witchcraft, suspicion of which is a major cause of war. Killing by witchcraft is contrary, not only to Christian concepts of goodness, but also to the humanist's, isn't it?

We are against sexual promiscuity, and not for religious reasons only. In 1903, Chinese traders seeking bird-of-paradise plumes landed on the south coast of Irian Jaya. They introduced a venereal disease called lymphogranuloma venereum among the 100,000-member Merind tribes. Since group sex was widely accepted, the disease spread like wildfire. It wiped out 90,000 lives in ten years.

McDonald attempts to antagonize us still further by comparing our methods unfavorably with "the more adaptive policies of Roman Catholic and mainstream Protestant groups."

Only one "mainstream" Protestant mission works in interior Irian Jaya, and they have experienced the same problems McDonald uses as grounds to incriminate us. For example, that mission's director was seriously wounded with three arrows eight years ago, and eight of his carriers were killed, while trekking through a wild area. Such incidents are merely an occupational hazard, and should not be used to levy blame.

As far as I know, Roman Catholic missionaries have not been wounded or slain by tribals in Irian Jaya. This is due, not to "more adaptive policies," but to the fact that they limit their work mainly to areas already well-controlled by the government. But they have counted their martyrs across the border in Papua New Guinea, and this is no shame to them.

If McDonald had taken time to visit Roman Catholic and evangelical Protestant areas of operation and compare them, he would have found the degree of culture change at least as great if not greater in the Roman Catholic areas. For example, in all Roman Catholic areas primitives are expected to give up their tribal names and take Latin names like Pius or Constantius, whereas in evangelical Protestant areas they still use their Irianese name, like Isai or Yana. But here again, if it is survival-related directed change, it cannot be faulted on anthropological grounds.

McDonald continues, "Nearly all Roman Catholic missionaries in Irian Jaya are required to hold degrees in anthropology." Actually, the percentage of Roman Catholic and evangelical Protestant missionaries holding degrees in anthropology is approximately equal, and when it comes to prowess in learning tribal dialects, the evangelicals excel by far. The majority of Roman Catholic priests teach in Indonesian even where it is not understood.

McDonald describes the lime-scattering dedication of a new Catholic church at Jaosakor. Surely if this is the limit of their cultural penetration, our Catholic friends must be far from satisfied. Cultural penetration, to be effective, must go far deeper than mere externals like scattering lime. Not until you come to grips with internal concepts in the category of the Ekari tribe's *aji* or the Dani tribe's *nabelankabelan*, are you getting close to the heart of a people. And in matters of this category, we evangelicals have been spot on. As one of our members said to McDonald, "What we are looking for is the cultural key. . . ." McDonald quoted his words, yet failed totally to appreciate them.

Another point of McDonald's article calls for refutation: Gerrit Kuijt raised funds for a helicopter for general service to all tribal peoples in Irian Jaya, not for "aerial evangelism." In fact, it was this helicopter which was on hand just in time to help in the earthquake relief operation and which bore McDonald on his reporting mission. Thank you, Gerrit, for your foresight. The rest of us are not unappreciative like McDonald.

McDonald, your article was erroneous, inept, and irresponsible. You have made a perfect nuisance of yourself. You and the *Washington Post* owe us a printed apology.

Do missionaries destroy cultures? We may destroy certain things "in" cultures, just as doctors sometimes must destroy certain things "in" a human body, if a patient is to live. But surely as we grow in experience and God-given wisdom, we must not and will not destroy cultures themselves.

14 Comment on "Development in the Non-Western World"

ARTHUR E. HIPPLER

In many respects the argument presented by Arthur Hippler is a sophisticated modern version of Merivale's and Raglan's views. Hippler is a psychological anthropologist with a Ph.D. from Berkeley. Since approximately 1968 he has conducted research among native groups in Alaska; he is an associate professor at the Institute of Social and Economic Research at the University of Alaska in Anchorage. He feels that it would be both morally wrong and impossible to stop the advance of civilization into tribal areas. In the first place he argues that "culture" is an abstraction and not an entity to be protected. Furthermore, he considers tribal cultures to be backward, oppressive ways of life that limit human potential. These views may seem blunt and even inappropriate for a contemporary cultural anthropologist, but they represent honest opinions that still prevail in many development circles. Recently Hippler has been very outspoken on native issues as a conservative newspaper columnist in Alaska. He has argued against granting natives special rights to fish and game resources on the basis of the assertion that there is "nothing vaguely resembling" a "traditional" native culture in Alaska. Such views have been so unpopular with both natives and anthropologists that in 1981 22 anthropologists working in Alaska took the remarkable step of running a notice in the Anchorage Daily News to disavow publicly Hippler's views. Following the selection by Hippler in this volume is a detailed critique of his views by anthropologist Gerald Weiss.

In a thought-provoking review of a number of works on development in the non-Western world, Gerald Weiss (*American Anthropologist* 79:887–893, 1977) has, besides raising important issues, articulated a position (essentially a plea) that we as anthropologists must undertake "a determined effort" to "save" tribal cultures from extinction. In context, it seems reasonably clear that Weiss is not arguing that people be saved from personal death but that "tribal cultures" somehow be preserved.

Weiss's overall scholarly intent in the rest of the article is clear. He takes an even-handed view, presenting the arguments favoring and opposing development as far as they relate to "third world" areas, which he usefully defines as statal societies already emerged from tribal organization.

Also emerging reasonably from this analysis is his recommendation for pressure to implement the Declaration of Barbados, which favors cultural autonomy. That concern is extended in his apparent agreement with Bodley that statal governments must *choose* to ensure the continued existence of tribal peoples.

It is in his plea for protection of such societies that I have some difficulties understanding his meaning.

Anthropologists make their livings and have substantial intellectual interest in cultures, yet cultures are abstractions. I need hardly remind anyone of the historical difficulties that have attended attempts to define this elusive yet intuitively useful concept. Culture is what people do.

If people seem to find (and many seem to) rifles more efficient than spears, religion more benign than the terrors of shamanism, or a broadened knowledge of all mankind more interesting than their traditional intellectual horizons, how can that be reversed? Should it? Who can decide to do that to someone?

Technology is powerful. The underlying intellectual processes that create it are exciting. Once exposed to them, people seem to want to move in the new directions as far as they are capable. We are all aware of the pressures to resist modern thought by elders or those in power in some tribal societies. Objectively, when we see equivalent behavior in advanced societies, we are quick to note the vested self-interest involved and its constriction of human possibilities to other persons, and we rightly condemn it. It seems rather a slippery yardstick.

Why is some tribal elder's decision to maintain his power and perquisites so much more appealing to anthropologists? Indeed, most of the concern I hear voiced about the issue is from Western intellectuals, who, surprisingly enough, seem willing to warrant internal oppression in favor of some concept of cultural autonomy for some societies, yet seem unwilling to do so for others, such as South Africa.

Tribal societies can be kept walled off. We call that sort of thing oppression, or concentration-camp thinking. But why should anyone want to do that, and by what right? What about the individuals in such communities who desire change? Is oppression by members of one's own cultural or racial group morally superior to other forms of oppression?

It is difficult to find nonethnocentric scales by which to measure human cultures. But, if we assume that human beings have vast potential, then cultures that foster a wider variety of human potential should attract many people.

A real objection could be voiced to the way in which third-world governments treat dissenters or smaller cultural groups. It is only recently in human history, and then only in that Euro-American culture in which we live, that large numbers of people have supported kind treatment of "outsiders." And we well know the continuous need to struggle to support such freedoms. Perhaps many third-world cultures have not reached that point. Is that admirable?

If we are concerned about diversity and great variety in the human experiment, I suggest that our own culture has vastly more of that than any tribal society. It does so because of its great ability to create more and more options for people. Trying to preserve people, which would entail some degree of force, merely forces people to stay in conditions that do not support great varieties of human expression.

Instead of assisting people in change, which is inevitable and seemingly provides for human growth as well as pain, Weiss seems to be arguing that we somehow join in an effort to keep them in some backward state. I am aware that many would bristle at the label "backward," but that is not an unrealistic statement.

It is possible that I misread Weiss's concern. He does note approvingly his opposition to the "human zoo" concept. I find it difficult, however, to determine, first, how the content of his general suggestion differs from the human zoo idea, and I would like to know in what way it does. If he means political autonomy, at what levels? And how is it to be enforced? If it is physical protection, that takes armies, often intruding on some other sovereign space. If it is cultural autonomy, it is not only a nebulous concept but, as I suggested above, likely not realistic. What pieces of a culture should be preserved? Which groups in a society should decide?

If this all seems harshly put, it is because I am deeply interested in the issue of freedom and choices. In the spirit of scholarly inquiry, I would like to know what Weiss actually proposes.

---

15   The Tragedy of Ethnocide: A Reply to Hippler

GERALD WEISS

Gerald Weiss is professor of anthropology at Florida Atlantic University. He obtained his Ph.D. from the University of Michigan in 1969, and since 1960 he has conducted extensive fieldwork among the Campa (Ashaninka) Indians of the Peruvian Amazon. Weiss is a cultural anthropologist who has specialized in tribal myth and cosmologies and theories of cultural systems. In this selection, originally written in 1979, he approaches the problem of development policy from an entirely different perspective than does Hippler. Weiss assumes that cultures are physical systems incorporating people and that people can be seriously

Reproduced by permission of the author.

harmed when their cultures are changed against their wills. Weiss is a firm advocate of tribal self-determination. Although not all anthropologists would accept Weiss's theoretical assumptions about culture systems, most would now agree that tribal cultures represent valid ways of life and that forced change is often detrimental.

In his "Comment on 'Development in the Non-Western World,'" Arthur Hippler writes: "In the spirit of scholarly inquiry, I would like to know what Weiss actually proposes" (1979, 349). I wish to respond to Hippler in that same spirit in order to explain the meaning of passages in my review article (1977) that Hippler finds puzzling.

This appears to be one of those situations in which one's theoretical viewpoint makes all the difference in even recognizing that a serious problem exists. Understanding my remarks about the tragedy of ethnocide (the destruction of cultural systems) requires that one read my earlier paper, "A Scientific Concept of Culture" (1973). To be moved by my remarks one might have to accept the argument presented in that paper. Someone operating with a different concept of culture could very well find my remarks on ethnocide largely meaningless, as Hippler appears to.

When I speak of the destruction of a culture, I have in mind much more than what Hippler seems to understand by such an expression. For Hippler, "cultures are abstractions" and "culture is what people do" (1979, 348). He seems to imply that people can doff their old culture and don a new one as if they were changing shirts. For me, the designation of a culture as an abstraction conveys no meaning. A culture either exists or does not exist. I see a culture not as a mental construct of the observer but rather as a reality in the observable world. What I choose to call a culture, or a cultural system, is what some others call a "sociocultural" system. For me, a cultural system has an objective reality—which many have had difficulty perceiving, to be sure—but a reality best comprehended in terms of level theory (see Weiss 1975), as a material system composed of human and nonhuman material components, modified neurally and physically and organized socially and technically. *That* is the reality with which we are faced and to which I believe the term *culture* in its traditional anthropological sense properly applies.

A shirt, then, is an item of culture, and it *can* be doffed and replaced by another, or by another type of garment altogether. But a culture also includes the most deep-seated understandings and feelings of its human components, internalized by them as part of the enculturation process existing in every culture. Those understandings and feelings come to the individual from the common fund of understandings and feelings already existing in the culture, so that in this sense as in every other the individual must properly be viewed, not as an independent entity capable of doffing and donning cultures at will, but as a part, a piece, or a fragment of the cultural system itself, which created and shaped him. It has long been recognized (and here I quote a medieval author) that "custom [i.e., habit] is a second nature" (Graystanes 1929, 93). And excising that second nature, once it is ingrained, is exactly like excising one's primary nature—a wrenching experience with devastating psychological effects.

There are occasions when individuals voluntarily migrate from one cultural system to another, yet even for them the culture shock can be considerable, with full assimilation into the new culture occurring only in a later generation. And for these voluntary migrants there is always the possibility of returning to the embrace of the culture they left. It is something else when human beings, as parts of a larger cultural system, survive the destruction of that cultural system, still imbued with the understandings and feelings proper to that lost system and with no real place for themselves in the cultural system that destroyed theirs. The incomprehension, the demoralization, the despondency, the hopelessness—this condition might even be judged worse than death. It is the condition we observe in cases in which tribal people have survived the destruction of their tribal cultures (see, for example, Rivers 1922, for a report on the Melanesians and more recent reports for Amazonia, including Hanbury-Tenison 1971; Amazind 1974; Indígena, Inc., and American Friends of Brazil 1974; Cultural Survival, Inc., 1979; and continuing coverage in *Survival International Review*).

But, it might be countered, at least the people survive. Yes, *some may*, but at what cost? And if one is indifferent to ethnocide conceived in such terms, one could entertain a similar indifference about genocide—after all, what are a few human beings more or less? The loss of one's cultural system is the most devastating event short of death that a human being can experience, and to be forced to relinquish the entire set of understandings and feelings within oneself derived from that lost culture is to lose an intrinsic part of oneself—the cultural part. It is a partial death, perhaps the most meaningful part of complete death.

Having taken Hippler to task for his inability to comprehend what ethnocide signifies in human terms, I would now like to remonstrate with him for his ethnocentrism. Hippler argues that statal cultures—*our* kind of culture—are superior to tribal cultures. I see in his remarks a clear cultural bias. Let us consider the points he makes one by one.

Hippler states: "People seem to find . . . rifles more efficient than spears." Someone from an extremely militaristic culture such as our own might well consider this a telling argument, but another view might be that the less efficient the instruments of war, the better. If it is hunting that is under consideration, firearms are not always as efficient as other weapons (hence the Plains Indians continued to hunt bison with bow and arrow rather than firearms after these were introduced), or they are too efficient, endangering the game supply (see, for example, Lizot 1976, 13–14).

Hippler states: "People seem to find . . . religion more benign than the terrors of shamanism." What are these terrors? And what is religion if it does not include shamanism? Hippler apparently has a very limited conception of what properly can be called religion. We are reminded of the utter ethno-centrism of a fictional character in one of Fielding's novels in this regard: "When I mention religion I mean the Christian religion; and not only the Christian religion, but the Protestant religion; and not only the Protestant religion, but the Church of England" (1943, 84). It has been a long time since Boas wrote, "Our knowledge of . . . tribes the world over justifies the statement that there is no people that lacks definite religious ideas and traditions" (1940b, 627). Has this understanding been lost in anthropology?

Hippler states: "People seem to find . . . a broadened knowledge of all mankind more interesting than their traditional intellectual horizons." But it may be questioned whether and to what extent the horizons of people by and large in our own culture have been so broadened. Hippler, for example, may well have something yet to learn about spears and shamanism and all that may be found in tribal cultures alien to what *we* are familiar with and respect. I am not sure exactly what Hippler is referring to, but I see nothing that would preclude people in tribal cultures from taking on "a broadened knowledge of all mankind"—comprehended, of course, within each of those cultures in a distinctive way, just as each Western culture compre-hends that "broadened knowledge" in its own distinctive way. The tribal cultures need not be destroyed for that to occur.

Hippler states: "Technology is powerful. The underlying intellectual processes that create it are exciting. Once exposed to them, people seem to want to move in the new directions as far as they are capable." But there is a technology in every culture. *Our* technology is indeed impressive, not be-cause of the underlying intellectual processes (which are no different from those in other cultures) but because of the overt results, and many non-Western peoples, both tribal and statal, have found it attractive. Yet they may be unwilling or reluctant (as is widely reported) to give up the remain-ing part of their traditional cultures—the social relationships, the values, and so on, that mean so much to them—in exchange for complete accep-tance of Western technology. And who can blame them? Nor is the resis-tance to change just from "elders or those in power in some tribal societies." Hippler is operating with a stereotype that bears no relation to tribal reality, certainly as I know it. In my own fieldwork (among the River Campas of eastern Peru), where the culture is in its death throes, I have observed all degrees of acculturation preparatory to actual assimilation, but still there are children who refuse to speak any but their own native language at home, girls who refuse to don alien dress, boys who speak contemptuously (among themselves) of the alien statal culture that has engulfed them and of its representatives. The resistance is from young and old, male and female, layman and shaman.

Hippler states: ". . . cultures that foster a wider variety of human po-tential should attract many people. . . . If we are concerned about diversity and great variety in the human experiment, I suggest that our own culture has vastly more of that than any tribal society." Perhaps Hippler has occupational diversity in mind, because if the Campa case is typical, then temperamental diversity is as great in any tribal culture as in ours, although the permitted range may differ. The assessment of tribal cultures made by an earlier generation of anthropologists is not entirely beside the point: "Their simplicity only seems so to our ignorance. They are in truth enormously complex, and, psychologically speaking, as rich, full, and complete as ours" (Dorsey 1931, 235). Or perhaps Hippler has in mind some concept of freedom of choice—yet he is then being quite unrealistic in not seeing that for many if not most in our own society the options are in fact limited. There are, to be sure, great diversity and heterogeneity in our culture, but no one in the culture can experience all of it, and mobility, despite the popular view, is limited in many ways. Does Hippler have a conception of the narrow range of expression in tribal cultures while being oblivious to the beam in his own cultural eye? We should be reminded of Boas' caution in this regard: "The life of the Eskimo as seen from my point of view as well as my life seen from the Eskimo point of view was not free, for objective observation from the point of view of one culture shows the restraints imposed by life in another type of culture" (1940a, 376).

Moreover, if by "our own culture" Hippler means that of the United States (which is commonly conceived by its citizenry in terms of unlimited opportunities, whatever the reality), it should be pointed out that the tribal peoples about whose fate we are arguing will not be assimilated into *our* culture but into other statal cultures to which Hippler's glowing characterization may not apply, certainly not with the same force. And in those other statal cultures, the survivors of destroyed tribal cultures are hardly being offered all the "good things" of Western culture. Instead, they are being forced to enter the statal culture at the lowest social level, where they can expect a lifetime of poverty, misery, and disrespect—even generations of the same, until the group achieves oblivion in one way or another (absorption or extinction). This is a general statement, to be sure, and would not necessarily apply to the life experiences of a few especially fortunate individuals. In any event, given the real options faced by tribal peoples, it does not make sense to contrast tribal life with idealized American middle-class existence. (If by "our own culture" Hippler means not the United States cultural system but what he elsewhere calls "Euro-American culture," I would say he is confusing culture, or cultural system, with culture area. I shall not attempt to disentangle here what his argument then becomes.)

One thing should be made clear: in arguing against the destruction of tribal cultures I am not arguing against change *within* those cultures. In my earlier paper I distinguished between *entity change* and *compositional change* (1973, 1404). Ethnocide is one case of that type of entity change to which we can give the name of *termination* (or fusion that amounts to termination): the entire culture ceases to exist as a distinct, separate cultural system—indeed, it becomes obliterated. Ethnocide occurs when one cultural system destroys another through either genocide or cultural assimilation. Internal, compositional change can be extensive in a tribal culture; all manner of culture traits can be taken over from the statal cultures with which it is in contact; yet that would not constitute ethnocide, and I for one would find nothing necessarily objectionable in such change. Compositional change through internal innovation or through interaction with other cultures is normal; entity change in the form of termination is disaster.

Hippler misconstrues what I am proposing with respect to the last surviving tribal cultures, perhaps inevitably, since he misunderstands the theoretical framework in terms of which I have urged that we look at the situation. I advocate, not walling off tribal societies, but guaranteeing to them the territory they occupy and allowing them self-determination to choose for themselves the path they take. No force at all is proposed here (as in Hippler's thought that "trying to preserve people . . . would entail some degree of force") except whatever force would be needed to keep *out* the encroachers and poachers, the exploiters and opportunists—the types that in other instances in the past have flooded pacified tribal lands to corrupt and swindle and divest. Whatever kind or degree of "physical protection" may be necessary, I am unmoved by Hippler's argument that such means would "intrud[e] on some other sovereign space." That space, on the periphery of existing tribal lands, would have been usurped by the statal culture in the first place.

I now come to answer the questions scattered through the paragraphs of Hippler's comment. "If people seem to find . . . rifles more efficient than spears, [and so on] . . . how can that be reversed? Should it? Who can decide to do that to someone?" Let me first answer with my own series of questions: How can *what* be reversed? The preferences listed by Hippler? What does it mean to reverse a preference? If the members of a tribal group prefer rifles to spears (*and* can get them), "religion" to shamanism, or "broadened knowledge" to their traditional world view, I would have no objection. Who can decide? Who else but the tribal people themselves, and not under external duress!

"Why is some tribal elder's decision to maintain his power and perquisites so . . . appealing to anthropologists?" I reject this view of the source of resistance to ethnocide within any tribal culture. Can Hippler provide documented cases in which such a scenario is reported? Offhand, I can think of none.

"But why should anyone want to do that ["wall off" tribal societies], and by what right? What about the individuals in such communities who desire change? Is oppression by members of one's own cultural or racial group morally superior to other forms of oppression?" I do not grant that guaranteeing a tribe its territory is walling it off. I am opposed to the "human zoo" concept not because I reject the possibility of keeping statal cultures at a distance from tribal territories (quite the contrary) but because I reject the invidious term *human zoo* as an accurate descriptive term. It is not setting up a human zoo to guarantee one's proprietary right to the place where one lives. When the law protects my home from invasion by my neighbors, it has not made a human zoo of my house. The argument can be extended to a tribe's territory, and that is all that Bodley's concept of "tribal autonomous regions" calls for (1975, 169). Individuals in such autonomous regions who desire change for themselves or for everyone can work for it and would have entire freedom to work for it, under conditions that I believe would prove Hippler's fear of "oppression" by the more traditionally minded to be a chimera. Certainly, if there is a tribal culture somewhere in the world that is oppressive, we would hope that the oppressed in that society would find a solution to their problems through culture change, either internally or even as imposed from without; but this is just to say that we need to look at the conditions of each individual case to decide whether the destruction of that particular culture is merited. And I know of no tribal situation in the present day resembling conditions in South Africa, despite the analogy that Hippler draws.

"Walling off" tribal societies is described by Hippler as "concentration-camp thinking." But let us consider something similar. For all their inadequacies, Indian reservations in this country are *not* concentration camps. They are havens for traditional Indians. They would only have to be larger and better located to permit their occupants to be self-sustaining and to serve as a model for the autonomous regions envisioned by Bodley. No, it is in connection with *forced assimilation* that there arises the danger of "concentration-camp thinking," of suggesting an expeditious means of providing a final solution to the tribal problem. The following proposal was once advanced by one well-meaning believer in forced assimilation regarding the surviving tribal peoples of eastern Peru:

> With individuals so degraded nothing or almost nothing can be done either for religion or for the state. I believe that we could finish in relatively very few years with this blemish of humanity by forming something like concentration camps and gathering them there willy-nilly. As the savages are not many, . . . I estimate that two or three camps of that kind would be more than sufficient to hold them all; and I even believe that a single camp would suffice. In those concentration camps, they would be under the vigilance of missionaries, with the help of the police, subjecting them to discipline and seeing in a gentle but persistent manner that their matrimonial unions are made with civilized people, so that they receive an injection of new and healthy blood, charged with history, tradition and civilization. The regeneration of these poor people, under the conditions indicated, would be easy, gentle, and efficient; and possibly within very few years we will be finished in a dignified and Christian manner with this race of degenerates (Olarte 1942, 21–22; my translation).

This proposal, happily, was not put into effect in Peru, but something closer to the Nazi model has come to exist in Paraguay (see Münzel 1973, 1974; Lewis 1975; Arens 1976, 1978).

"If he [Weiss] means political autonomy, at what levels? And how is it to be enforced?" Clearly, I would claim that political autonomy should be at the level of the cultural system (an arrangement that I do not view as nebulous and that I believe to be possible whatever the difficulties). This would be established by law in the encroaching statal culture and enforced as all laws are supposed to be enforced. Every means should be taken at this time to persuade the statal governments involved to take such a step—through international public opinion, the United Nations, and so on.

"Perhaps many third-world cultures have not reached that point [that is, of tolerance toward tribal groups]. Is that admirable?" Not at all. It is so unadmirable that every effort should be made to impress upon third-world statal governments and people that ethnocidal intolerance is reprehensible and unacceptable to the international community.

"What pieces of a culture should be preserved? Which groups in a society should decide?" What part of a tribal culture's content ought to be preserved from compositional change should be decided through self-determination by the human components of that cultural system, not by external force or cataclysm. Which elements of a tribal society should have or will have most influence in making decisions over time regarding culture change is probably none of our business.

If advocating self-determination for the surviving tribal peoples of the world is "an effort to keep them in some backward state," that may be a commentary on how tribal peoples may view the cultural accomplishments of which we are so proud. Hippler never contemplates the possibility that many tribal peoples would be happy to remain as they are, for they admire their own culture as much as Hippler admires his own. Hippler writes that his use of the label *backward* is "not . . . unrealistic," but I would say that it is false and misleading, and it is in perfect harmony with the pervasive ethnocentrism of Hippler's article. With its very negative connotations this label prejudges all; it conforms to the habits of thought engendered by what I have called simplistic unilinear evolutionism; and it implies that when type A gives rise to type B in a sequence of change, every A that does not become a B is ipso facto "backward" rather than, properly speaking, *primary*.

The views I expressed in the article to which Hippler responded are those that I believe the anthropological community in all good conscience must come to espouse: the custodians of the anthropological tradition in the Western cultures have a moral obligation to act on behalf of the world's tribal cultures and the tribal peoples within them. Bodley argued this eloquently in his own way; I attempted to make the point in terms of my earlier statement about the nature of culture and the reality of the cultural system. If my theoretical approach is not accepted, I would hope that any obdurate rejecter of that approach will be led by some other route to the same conclusion about our responsibility toward tribal cultures. And if I have not been sufficiently persuasive to convince Hippler and other readers, I hope that I have at least made clear how I would defend the position I have taken against the objections that Hippler raises.

REFERENCES

Amazind
1974   *Amazind Bulletin* 2. Geneva: Amazind.

Arens, Richard, ed.
1976   *Genocide in Paraguay*. Philadelphia: Temple University Press.
1978   *The Forest Indians in Stroessner's Paraguay: Survival or extinction?* Survival International Document IV. London: Survival International.

Boas, Franz
1940a   Liberty among primitive people. In *Freedom: Its meaning*, ed. Ruth N. Anshen, 375–80. New York: Harcourt, Brace.
1940b   The aims of ethnology (1889). In *Race, language and culture*, ed. Franz Boas, 626–38. New York: Macmillan.

Bodley, John H.
1975   *Victims of progress*. Palo Alto: Mayfield.

Cultural Survival, Inc.
1979   *Special report—Brazil*. Number 1. Cambridge, Mass.: Cultural Survival.

Dorsey, George A.
1931   *Man's own show: Civilization*. New York: Blue Ribbon Books.

Fielding, Henry
[1749] 1943   *The history of Tom Jones, a foundling*. New York: Modern Library.

Graystanes, Robert de
[14th century] 1929   Chronicle. In *Life in the Middle Ages*. 2d ed., ed. G. G. Coulton, vol. 3, 92–95. Cambridge: Cambridge University Press.

Hanbury-Tenison, Robin
1971   *Report of a visit to the Indians of Brazil on behalf of the Primitive Peoples Fund/Survival International, January–March, 1971*. Survival International Document I. London: Survival International.

Hippler, Arthur E.
1979   Comment on "Development in the non-Western world.", *American Anthropologist* 81:348–49.

Indígena, Inc., and American Friends of Brazil
1974   *Supysáua: A documentary report on the conditions of Indian peoples in Brazil*. Berkeley: Warren's Waller Press.

Lewis, Norman
1975   The horrors of Cecilio Baez. *Tropic* (The *Miami Herald* Sunday Magazine) 9(16): 16–23.

Lizot, Jacques
1976   *The Yanomami in the face of ethnocide*. IWGIA Document No. 22. Copenhagen: International Work Group for Indigenous Affairs.

Münzel, Mark
1973   *The Aché Indians: Genocide in Paraguay*. IWGIA Document No. 11. Copenhagen: International Work Group for Indigenous Affairs.
1974   *The Aché: Genocide continues in Paraguay*. IWGIA Document No. 17. Copenhagen: International Work Group for Indigenous Affairs.

Olarte, Antonio M.
1942 *El Vicariato Apostólico del Ucayali (Perú): Descripción y estado actual* (1942). Lima.

Rivers, W. H. R., ed.
1922 *Essays on the depopulation of Melanesia.* Cambridge: Cambridge University Press.

Weiss, Gerald
1973 A scientific concept of culture. *American Anthropologist* 75:1376–1413.
1975 Culture and the theory of levels. Abstract. In *Abstracts of the 74th Annual Meeting of the American Anthropological Association,* 162. Washington, D.C.: American Anthropological Association.
1977 The problem of development in the non-Western world. *American Anthropologist* 79:887–93.

V

Tribals and Contemporary Development Policy

In many parts of the world today the most intense arenas of conflict between tribals and national governments involve the development of natural resources on tribal lands by outside interests. Tribal populations invariably occupy territories that are but lightly exploited and then only for local, tribal use. National governments, often driven by trade deficits and gigantic foreign debts, are understandably eager to extract as much wealth as possible from their entire national territory. Thus we see highways, mining operations, giant hydro-developments, lumbering, agri-business, and planned colonization projects, all intruding on tribal territories. These developments often cause serious problems and may be strongly opposed by the tribals.

The following case studies discuss the policy issues and impact of specific contemporary development projects on diverse tribal groups. Even though these case studies include examples from Africa, the Philippines, New Guinea, Australia, and North America, there are striking similarities among them. The most obvious parallel is that large-scale projects are invariably introduced into a tribal area in the first place to meet the needs of other segments of the national society. Improving the quality of life of tribals can easily be seen as a rationalization for a project that would have been pursued regardless of its impact on local people. It is apparent that many of these projects were designed with virtually no input from the tribal people to be affected and little consideration of tribal interests. Fortunately, there are exceptions to this generalization, but the exceptions primarily reflect official concern for the potential of tribal people to disrupt or even block a project that has not adequately addressed their legitimate concerns.

135

Thus, as shown in the following selections, in Alaska (Lee), Canada (Lee; De'Ath and Michalenko), and Australia (Lee), where natives were in a position to use the courts to block or delay development programs that they opposed, we see policy adjustments in their favor. In the Philippines (Drucker) and the Sudan (Lako), tribal groups have stalled enormous development projects by armed rebellion. The example from West Papua (Nietschmann) suggests that where tribal legal claims are not recognized and the threat of armed resistance is manageable, official development policy reflects only minimal concern for tribal interests.

16

The Impact of the Jonglei Scheme on the Economy of the Dinka

GEORGE TOMBE LAKO

For millenia the pastures of the Nilotic Dinka/Nuer cattle herders in the Sudan's upper Nile have depended on seasonal flooding of the vast Sudd swamps, which supported a complex and finely tuned human ecosystem described in Evans-Pritchard's classic work, *The Nuer*. Soon after the Anglo-Egyptian Sudan was established in 1898, government planners in Khartoum labeled this seasonal flooding "wasteful" because as much as half of the floodwaters were "lost" to plants and evaporation, when they could be channeled to export crops such as cotton. The fact that this water supported cattle was irrelevant to planners because few of these cows ever entered the marketplace. In 1904 the construction of a lengthy canal to bypass the great bend in the Nile was proposed to reduce the "loss" and promote agricultural development, but such a program was not actually initiated until 1974. The Jonglei canal, as it is called, is to be 360 kilometers long; it will be one of the largest engineering projects in the world. The actual excavation was begun by a French company using a gigantic machine.

George Tombe Lako, who lectures at the University of Juba, describes the Dinka in the early 1980s as still basically self-sufficient farmers and herders. The government hopes that the Jonglei project will increase their involvement with the national economy, and it has attempted to convince the Dinka that the project will be highly beneficial for everyone. As Lako shows, the ultimate impact of these developments on the Dinka will be enormous but difficult to predict precisely. The Dinka themselves are divided: many villagers doubt the governments claims, but the urban elite who stand to make immediate gains are strong supporters. Lako's assumption that the canal will be completed may be premature. In 1984 construction on the canal was halted following attacks on Sudanese army units and construction camps by the Sudanese People's Liberation Army, which is apparently composed largely of disaffected Nilotic people who consider the canal to be an invasion from the Moslem-dominated north.

The Jonglei Scheme is the most ambitious project currently being undertaken in the Sudan. Its social, political and economic impact on the country will obviously be great; but in particular, it will affect the lives of the people living there dramatically.

The main aim of the Jonglei Scheme is to provide additional irrigation

Reprinted from *African Affairs* 84, no. 3 (1985): 15–38. Copyright © 1985 The Royal African Society and Contributors. Reproduced in abridged form by permission.

water to the North and Egypt. But it is hoped by the planners that the scheme will also create social development and increase wealth amongst the societies that live in the canal zone. This paper sets out to examine some of the ways in which the scheme will affect the Dinka transhumant pastoralist way of life. Most of the data was obtained during a field survey of 110 Dinka households carried out between January and June, 1981, in various villages in the canal area, particularly Kongor. In addition, my previous research experience in the area as a member of a government-sponsored research team between November 1975 and July 1977 augmented gaps in my 1981 fieldwork. . . .

THE DINKA

An analysis of the present social and political organization of the Dinka is important for understanding the various ways in which the Jonglei Scheme may affect their lives. Full accounts are available in the works of Lienhardt (the leading authority on the Dinka) and of Deng (himself a Dinka), amongst others.[1] Thus, the following discussion will be brief and selective, but hopefully adequate to enable discussion of the impact of the Jonglei Scheme on the Dinka.

The Dinka are a Nilotic people numbering about two million. Although known to the world as Dinka, they refer to themselves as *Jieng* (singular *Jang*) and they refer to all 'foreigners' or non-Dinkas as *juur* (singular *jur*), a term often used with contempt. In all there are about 25 mutually independent tribal groups forming the *jieng*, but all of them can be regarded as a largely homogeneous ethnic and cultural whole. . . .

An important feature of Dinka country is the seasonality of its climate, being characterised by the succession of dry and wet seasons. The dry season lasts from November to April. During this period there is virtually no rain, and temperatures may rise up to 40°C, especially before the onset of the first rains in late April or early May which gradually intensify to reach their maximum in August and September. However, the onset and the amount that falls vary with the years.

The same general physical and climatic characteristics apply to all Dinka country which, and particularly the Jonglei area, can be divided into three parts. Firstly, there is the narrow strip roughly the area along the Bor-Malakal road which provides the land suitable for human settlements. Most of the lands that remain above the flooded areas are to be found within this narrow strip and are together called the *Highlands*. Secondly, there are the *toiches* (or *Lowlands*) on the western fringes, which extend up to the main channel of the Nile and provide dry-season grazing and water. Thirdly, in between the highlands and the *toiches*, there is a vast stretch of land known as the Intermediate Land. When moving to and from the *toiches*, the Dinka cross the intermediate land and use some of the grass and water that is still there for their animals.

The conditions of land and climate make transhumance inevitable and give rise to the mixed economy of cattle herding, cultivation, fishing and hunting and gathering. The Dinka have developed their own specific political and social system which is suited to transhumant pastoralism.

The social and political system of the Dinka is very much centered around cattle and their use. Feelings of nationhood and togetherness among the Dinka hardly extend beyond the tribal group or descent groups. Conflict and rivalries over grazing land and water for animals are frequent. The *wut* (cattle-camp) is the arena where much of the Dinka political expression takes place. . . .

The political significance of the *wut* emanates from the fact that it provides the pattern through which members of a tribe are segmented into subtribes, sections and descent groups. Important decisions regarding war or peace and reconciliation as well as social matters are determined in the cattle camp.

The resolution of conflict over grazing and other activities in the cattle-camps is the responsibility of the 'leaders of the cattle-camps' and the 'masters of the fishing spear', who have ritual and religious functions as well as playing important political roles. The 'leaders of the cattle-camps' organize seasonal migration to the *toiches*, and generally advise and help in the management of the cattle-camps. In addition, when disputes over grazing arise between cattle-camps, they have to work out a solution. If they fail, and fighting occurs, then they have the difficult task of bringing it to an end through negotiation. Similarly, the 'masters of the fishing spear' plan and organize fishing trips in the *toiches*, as well as being involved in the resolution of conflicts that may arise over fishing areas.

Cattle dominate a Dinka's life since he derives his livelihood from, and identifies with, them socially and politically. Their importance is much more than just as a source of livelihood.

A Dinka is very much tied to cattle in a spiritual and even 'sensual' manner. Herdsmen enjoy spending hours with a favourite animal, usually a bull, singing to it and deriving satisfaction from merely watching it. Sometimes Dinka treat their animals as almost human. An animal is addressed by name before being slaughtered in sacrifice. Cattle are even differentiated in terms of intelligence in that those with short horns are regarded as stupid, and those with long horns as intelligent. When dancing, Dinka curve their arms in a way that imitates the curvature of their favourite ox. The Dinka do not count their herd; nor allow that to be done by anyone else. People rarely give the correct figure of the size of their herd when asked. Cattle, like children, are not to be counted. Any person who attempts to count cattle is considered as bewitching the herd, and often failure in marriage negotiations is attributed to some malicious gossip that has 'numbered' the cattle being bargained for.

The most important role of cattle is their use as bridewealth. Marriage cattle range from as few, by Dinka standards, as 40 head to as many as 200, particularly if the bride is educated, education being regarded as having increased the 'value' of the girl. My fieldwork survey showed that few men marry much before 30 and that the divorce rate (0.3 per cent) is negligible. . . .

AGRICULTURE

The mainly subsistence economy consists of three main components. Cattle rearing is rated the most important, followed by crop production and then fishing, hunting and gathering; but crops provide the bulk of a family subsistence.

The Dinka cultivate a number of crops, namely: dura (sorghum), tobacco, pumpkins, maize, okra, lubia (type of bean), groundnuts and sesame. . . .

Almost all crops are consumed by the household, except some tobacco (25.5 per cent of the crop) and maize (16.0 per cent of the crop, mainly in the case of households with poor tobacco yields). Significantly, although some crops may be lent or given to kinsmen suffering from poor harvests or sold in the market (e.g. tobacco and maize) no barter takes place in crops.

Crop production and yields are affected by a number of factors, of which rainfall is the most important. The sequence and intensity of rains expose crops to floods or droughts, with floods being the more common problem. The clay soils have poor water percolation and, in the absence of run-offs, the problem of water-logging becomes acute and an obstacle to cultivation on a greater scale. In addition a variety of pests and diseases affect crop yields. Those affecting dura include birds, grasshoppers, worms, the stem borer and dura head smut. Tobacco is mostly affected by frog eye and leaf wilt. Maize yields are affected largely by birds as well as floods and drought. The commonest hazard for the groundnut crop is drought. Untimely planting of groundnuts and sesame often results in poor yields. Of course weeds are a common problem for all crops and much time is spent in weeding. There are no problems with labour, all members of a family take part in cultivation.

ANIMAL HUSBANDRY

The seasonal activities of the Dinka are integrated with the climatic changes throughout the year. In general, the wet season is devoted more to cultivation than to cattle care since animals graze around the *luaks* or in cattle-camps nearby. The dry season is almost entirely devoted to cattle care and, to some extent, fishing and hunting. Cattle are driven to and from the lowlands in synchronization with the availability of grass and water along the traditional routes.

The organization of this migratory process is based on the tribal, subtribal, clan and family units. Members of these units graze their animals over well defined areas and follow routes that belong to the tribe at the wider level, and to a clan or family or groups of these more specifically. The role of the 'leaders of the cattle-camps' and 'masters of the fishing spear' is very crucial in this process. . . .

. . . the emphasis of the Dinka is on rearing cattle and less so on sheep and goats which are slaughtered on various sacrificial, social or religious occasions as well as being killed for meat. Cattle are mostly sacrificed at large feasts such as marriages or very serious social occasions like the settlement of tribal disputes over grazing areas.

However, the Dinka do part with their cattle in a way that is contrary to the view that is still currently expressed, despite all that Lienhardt and others have written, that they suffer from a 'cattle complex'. Ring has described how Dinka not only sell cattle in the market for profit, but also how a special group of what he called 'wealth seekers' is emerging.[2] The important point to note here is not how large or small the size of the commercial off-take is, but rather that it is taking place mainly as a result of indigenous or 'internal' forces of change in the traditional economy.

The main reason why a Dinka may sell an animal is to buy food (usually dura, the staple food) with the cash. Other reasons are to buy clothes and veterinary drugs. . . .

The traditional economy is being gradually transformed through the influence of trade in modern sector goods not locally produced, e.g. cooking oil, salt, clothes, household utensils, etc. Furthermore, some Dinka have joined the retail trade, tailoring in the market centres, beer brewing for profit and the sale of tobacco. We mention this aspect of the monetization of the traditional economy because the picture painted above might be mistakenly construed to mean that Dinka society is stagnant and not responsive to change and modernization. Certainly, the use of money is becoming more and more common. However, it is a fact that the basis of Dinka society is still largely traditional animal husbandry and agriculture. Both are conditioned by seasonality and the migratory nature of cattle husbandry.

GOVERNMENT INTENTIONS AND ATTITUDES

The present Jonglei Canal Project is viewed by the Sudan Government as being capable of transforming the traditional subsistence economy. The government hopes that people like the Dinka will become part of the modern economy. Modern irrigation will be introduced, particularly in Phase Two of the project. The people would retain their livestock, but in modern ranches using better animal husbandry techniques. Clearly, government policy towards the people of the canal area entails a radical transformation of the economic and social basis of these societies.

In following such a policy, the government hopes that the response of the people to such a radical change will be positive, because they are also assumed to be dissatisfied with the existing natural hazards.[3] In the event of people rejecting such a radical change in their semi-pastoralist way of life, that would only mean that 'people do not necessarily know what is best for them' to quote the words of an official of the Executive Organ.

The dissatisfaction with and outright dismissal of the subsistence economy is coupled with a determination to impose the canal on the people as the only way that can and will lead to development or modernization. 'If we have to drive our people to paradise with sticks, we will do so for their good and the good of those who will come after us.'[4] The government has little faith in the ability of the subsistence economy to modernise through its own internal dynamism. This is believed to be so because of the 'alleged' inherent weaknesses and impotence of the subsistence economy to extricate itself from the environmental and physical constraints affecting both agriculture and animal husbandry. In addition, the present social and political organizations of the people are considered too 'primitive' or 'rudimentary' to suit the needs of a 'modern' society.[5] For example, people are deemed unwilling to increase the commercial off-take from livestock because of their 'cattle-complex', at a time when they are apparently willing to part with their animals for social, ritual and cultural purposes.

To convince people of the benefits of the canal, a massive 'enlightenment' campaign has been conducted in the villages of the canal zone. These campaigns have been carried out by the 'Basic Units' of the Sudanese Socialist Union (SSU), the country's only political party. The basic 'attractions' being presented to the people are apparently clear solutions to the hardships and deprivations that they normally face. People are told that the canal would put an end to the present shortage of water for themselves and their animals during the dry season. More pastures would be available and so the quality and numbers of the livestock would be improved. Veterinary services would be readily available. Obviously, nothing touches a Dinka's heart more than the cure or prevention of the diseases that beset his animals.

In the sphere of agriculture the government is persuading the people by encouraging them to believe that the canal project would bring them the prosperity of the Gezira Scheme in the North. Their land would become 'a second Gezira' through the introduction of modern irrigation and new commercial crops (e.g. cotton, sugar cane, rice, etc.). It is further argued that, of course, hunger, which is not an uncommon phenomenon at present, would cease to exist. This argument is further instilled in people's minds by statements made by those Dinka who had seen developments in the Gezira.

Further 'attractions' are those regarding health and education, which are included in the development programmes associated with the canal project. The canal project purports to lead to the development of easier and better roads linking the villages. This would be possible, since a major road is being constructed on the eastern side of the canal and all other roads would be linked to it.

The above contentions of the government contrasted sharply with those of the Dinka we talked to in the canal area (especially in Kongor).

DINKA ATTITUDES

It is by no means an easy task to measure people's attitudes, but it is important to try to do so. We held guided interviews and lengthy discussions with fifty Dinka (both sexes) in Kongor and other villages, as well as some of those working in government or the private sector. These talks were mainly about attitudes towards the canal project and how people might respond to the changes that might occur in their way of life.

Over three quarters of the villagers interviewed had first heard of the project from lorry passengers who travel up and down the road between Juba and Khartoum. Some had heard from educated Dinka who made home visits to the villages and others from returning migrants. A few had heard from the radio or read it from newspapers. Later on, various research teams and the SSU 'enlightenment officers' visited the permanent settlements, preaching the merits and benefits of the project to the villagers. Thus, most people are aware of the project and in fact some (who live close to the mouth of the Sobat river) have seen the cut.

Although most people know of the impending reality of the canal, their views and response often differ from those desired by the government. While the government regards the canal as an alternative that would end or reduce drastically the annual dry season migration to the *toiches*, most of the people considered it an addition to the already existing wells and boreholes. Most people think that they would like to continue travelling to the *toich*, since it is there that they can catch fish. Moreover, it is in the cattle-camps in the *toich* that the 'masters of the fishing spear' and the 'leaders of the cattle-camps' have their influence. Since so much of their socio-political organization centres around these figures, it is not surprising that most people interviewed, do not contemplate an end to, or even disruption of, the working of these institutions.

People also do not see that the reorganization of animal husbandry along the lines of modern ranches and irrigated agriculture is not commensurate with their present practice and may, in fact, lead to them having to abandon their traditional system of subsistence as well as their social and political organization. One of their most prominent chiefs in Kongor summed up their feelings as follows:

> We do not know how the government wants us to change our way of looking after cattle and digging the land; and so we shall wait and see. If it turns out to be bad for us, then we shall refuse although I do not know how we can fight the government. You know the government is very powerful. I was told by the people in Bor (meaning the provincial commissioner and his officials) that things will be alright and better for us.

The Dinka also fear the settlement of other tribes who might come to work on the scheme. Most people questioned the need for such settlement and proposed that if this was necessary at all, then these newcomers should settle in the east of the canal line and their number should be kept small, so as not to 'disturb' their way of life. A thirty-five year old man in Panyagoor village told us that: 'if other tribes come and they don't cause troubles, then we can stay with them in peace; but if they don't maintain peace, then we can easily clash.'

One of the often cited aims of the Jonglei Scheme is the improvement of land and river transport in the area. Thirty of the fifty people interviewed expressed indifference towards these proposed improvements. Again the paramount chief of Kongor summed up: 'We do not wish to leave our land and so we do not need roads or steamers. We want schools for our children and more medicines for us and our animals. That dispensary over there has remained as a mere foundation for five years. You see that ruin over there? We used to receive drugs for our cattle from there before the war with the Arabs. Why has it not been rebuilt?'

Most of the interviews and discussions with the Dinka in their villages were generally cordial and frank. This was not the case with the educated Dinka, who form a substantial number of the civil service in the South and work in towns like Juba, Bor and Malakal. Those in top positions of authority in government preferred to recount the familiar 'benefits' of the project as stated by the government. However, most of the Dinka elite expressed private doubts about these 'benefits', but only agreed to air their views if they were assured of anonymity. I can only offer a general outline of their attitudes. They feared the canal could lead to the destruction of their tribal system of social and political organization, at a time when such institutions in other tribes remain undisturbed. They fear that the Dinka would lose their identity, in which they pride themselves so much.

Moreover, in their opinion, the resources earmarked for the construction of the canal could have been used better for the provision of more health and educational facilities, as well as for the improvement of agriculture and livestock production. In this they were close to the position of the elder cited above. In addition, they refer to the likely adverse environmental effects of the project such as the drying up of the lakes and swamps, the reduction in fish supplies and the 'desertification' of the area through the reduction in conventional rainfall caused by the vast swamps.

A third group of Dinka, comprising big and also small businessmen, cattle traders and top civil servants, whose eyes were set on owning large farms in the forthcoming Jonglei Irrigation Scheme, expressed total and unqualified support for the project. Their model of development for the Dinka is the Gezira Scheme just as propagated by the government. A typical expression of this group's position is the following statement by a Dinka merchant, who owns four shops and a fleet of lorries and trucks in Bor and Juba:

> Our people (Dinka) are too lazy and will never develop. The canal will enable us to invest in irrigated agriculture, commerce and agro-industries. We shall make them work and pay them well and so their standard of living will improve. Why worry about adverse environmental, social and political effects when we shall all be richer?

Clearly, then, different groups have different views of the canal depending on their economic and educational positions. However, on balance, the views and attitudes of the Dinka in the villages (who form the majority of Dinka and are most likely to be affected immediately by the canal) do not indicate any great enthusiasm for or anticipation of the completion of the canal. They have not been persuaded of the need for it.

IMPACT OF PHASE ONE AND TWO

It is not possible to predict how all the wide ranging changes planned (particularly in Phase Two) will occur. However, we can identify some of the socio-economic impacts the project is likely to make on the livelihood of the local inhabitants.

Impact on Human Population and Settlements

There is no exact figure of the population living in the Jonglei Canal area. The 1955/56 census estimated this to be 130,620 persons. A more recent figure from the 1973 census puts it at 260,746 persons. Perhaps the distribution of this population is more important to note than its size. Although population and human settlements in the area are scattered, they nevertheless lie along the narrow strip of land we earlier referred to as the highlands where alone such settlement is possible.

Since the canal is still being dug, it is not possible for us to analyse its impact on the human populations and settlements throughout the canal zone. However, the cut has already had a serious impact on the Shilluk, Dinka and Nuer living around the Sobat mouth and southwards to the point reached by the earth-digger.

Some 200 or more households have already been forced to move from their traditional homesteads because the canal has crossed over their land.[6] Although the actual width of the canal is 54.5 metres, an area of about a quarter of a mile on both sides is also being cleared for the construction of cross-drainage works.

The government has formed a Compensation Committee, headed by a Dinka judge, which assesses the economic and social cost of displacement and the subsequent resettlement of the people away from the canal line. At present the compensation is in monetary terms, i.e., between L.S. 50 and L.S. 250 per household.[7] After receiving this money, the displaced persons have to find new sites, well out of the way of the canal line, for cultivation and construction of new homesteads, without government assistance. They have to find new land suitable for cultivation and grazing during the rainy season around the *luaks*. New wells and water points have to be constructed for them by the government.

As the digging progresses, the canal will cross more densely populated areas around Duk Fadiet, Duk Faiwel, Kongor, Maar, Jale, etc. Although the Eastern Alignment was adopted precisely in order to avoid this eventuality, it is nonetheless possible that displacement will occur and the number affected may on aggregate be quite substantial. In this case some social and political unrest may occur, although this has not so far been recorded in the area where the canal has been dug. Given that the attitude of the Dinka towards the canal is at best sceptical if not hostile, people may not be willing participants in any government-sponsored resettlement programme.

Impact on Livestock and Seasonal Migration Routes

The impact of the canal on livestock, particularly their movement in search of water and grazing, will be quite substantial. The displacement of people from their settlements, as is the case now where the canal has been dug, means that new areas for settlement have to be found. An important factor determining where such areas will be situated, is the availability of water and grazing for the animals. Either people and their animals will have to travel back to the canal itself for water or the government will have to provide wells or reservoirs in the new settlements. This latter alternative has been included in the Phase One programmes, but has not so far been implemented, even where some people have been displaced already.

But even if wells or reservoirs are constructed in the new settlement areas, these would be used mainly during the wet season when there is grazing around the homesteads. When the rains stop and the grass dries up, the animals will have to be driven to the *toich* for grazing. Whether this will be possible depends on whether the canal becomes a barrier to the seasonal movement of humans and animals or not.

There are so many seasonal migration routes that no one, including the Dinka themselves, can enumerate them. In general, migration along these routes takes place at the beginning of the dry season with the return at the beginning of the wet season.

The authorities of the Jonglei Project argue that seasonal migration can continue because animals and humans will be able to cross the canal using the crossing points (about 20 along the Eastern Alignment) and the bridges and barges that will be constructed. The determination of the location and number of crossing points was based on the following factors: (a) the number of present migration routes; (b) the size of the human and livestock population that would cross the canal; and (c) the expected future crossing needs.

Regardless of the actual number of crossing points based on these factors it seems that unless we take into consideration the present system of the organization of the seasonal migration to the *toich* and the way in which cattle-camps are set up and managed, a number of problems are likely to arise.

We have seen that the *wut*, (cattle-camps), provides the key to the understanding of the Dinka view of their political and social organization. The danger in considering only the numerical distribution of migration routes and the numbers of people and animals using them, in the determination of crossing points, is that these may actually become areas in which conflicts over grazing and cattle-camp sites develop.

It is not any Dinka with a herd who can use a particular migration route. The individuals who use a particular route are close kinsfolk and old neighbours who know each other and the animals they are droving. Besides, we have mentioned that the total number of routes is large and unknown, so that the planned number of crossing points is unlikely to be sufficient to make crossing orderly and free from disputes.

The establishment of crossing points might also lead to the devastation by overgrazing of the available pastures at the sides of the crossing points, as a result of the congestion of livestock on smaller areas. This possibility has been underestimated by the canal authorities.

There is also the possibility that cattle diseases and human ones (such as bilharzia and malaria) might spread more easily and might be more difficult to control due to the greater concentrations of animals and humans in small areas. The Jonglei canal authorities argue that 'if such adverse conditions occur, their rectification will demand additional planning work from the Executive Organ.'[8] The authorities, therefore, seem to imply that they would rather see the problem arise first, before they consider any remedial or preventative action.

Impact on Fisheries

Although this is not a study of the effects of the Jonglei Project on the environment, climate, and wildlife, nevertheless fisheries have a special importance to the livelihood of the people and so some comment on the possible effect of the canal on fish resources seems in order. The Jonglei Investigation Team (1954) concluded that the Equatorial Nile Project would undoubtedly cause a reduction in fishery resources in the area. The planners of the present canal argue that since the reduction in Sudd waters would be only 25%, the effect on fisheries would be negligible. However, a recent study[9] has demonstrated that a reduction in the swamp level would have adverse effects on fish breeding and growth. The reasons given are that 'there are very little fluctuations in water level in the permanent swamps and also vegetation overgrowth are widely dispersed as substratum for oviposition and as sanctuaries and feeding ground for juvenile fish.'[10]

If fish retire into deeper waters, and since any reduction in these waters, as shown by the Hydro-biological Research Unit of Khartoum University, would have adverse effects on fish supplies, then the local inhabitants are likely to lose an important component of their diet. The planned commercial exploitation of fisheries resources does not necessarily mean that fish would be available to the Dinka households. On the contrary, people would have to obtain for cash (which is in very short supply) what they are at present able to obtain using their own labour and traditional means to the extent that they satisfy their domestic requirements and even sell. Perhaps it would be more appropriate to improve on the present system of fish exploitation, which has developed without any reduction in resources, rather than embark on a new system which may not benefit the households as well as the present practice does.

CONCLUSION

The idea of reclaiming the waters lost annually in the Sudd through evaporation and transpiration was conceived by Egypt, Britain and the Sudan Government for their interests and not those of the people living there. This is true for all the various canal proposals including the present one in its initial stage in 1974. It is only because of Southern Sudanese fears and opposition to the project (as demonstrated by the riots in Juba following the announcement of the present scheme in November, 1974), that concern for local development was included in the project plan and costs.

The Sudan Government regards the Jonglei project as an opportunity for transforming the local subsistence economies and modernizing them. A two-pronged strategy has been adopted under the Phase One and Two programmes. The government has shown a willingness to implement them, particularly the actual excavation of the canal, even without local consent and participation.

In general, the Dinka in villages appear to welcome the canal but for reasons other than those held by the government; principally they hope the canal will become an effective barrier between them and hostile neighbouring tribes. Their apparent receptiveness towards the improvement programmes in Phase One (e.g. new seeds, vaccination and cure of animal diseases, health and education services, etc.) should not be construed to mean that they are aware of the radical nature of the Phase Two changes, or are willing to take part in them.

We have seen that most Dinka in villages are at best sceptical about the canal's projected benefits, if not hostile towards them. This position is shared by students and lower rank civil servants who also worry about likely adverse environmental effects, and the loss of their tribal and cultural identity. The educated elite in top civil service jobs or rich Dinka in towns, on the contrary, give unqualified support to the project. This category of Dinka is not worried about adverse effects on the total ecosystem or the disappearance of the present way of livelihood. As mentioned, their model of development is the Gezira Scheme, and so they await the implementation of Phase Two with enthusiasm.

There are many ways by which the scheme may have an immediate impact on the lives of the Dinka. The canal itself has already caused the displacement of people from their settlements. Although at present the numbers affected are small, these are likely to increase as the digging reaches more heavily populated areas.

The impact of the canal on the movements of livestock in search of grazing is likely to be tremendous. Despite crossing points, barges and bridges, crossing may be physically impossible for livestock given that the canal itself and the ramp road (6 metres high) east of it are sizeable barriers. An additional water channel and irrigation schemes, as planned for in Phase Two, would further exacerbate the difficulties of crossing for livestock. It is also possible that conflicts over the use of land for irrigation or grazing may also arise.

Crossing is not only necessary and important for animals but also for humans. Much of the organization and decision making concerning social and political life takes place in the cattle-camps. To stop seasonal migration completely, might, for example, reduce or eliminate the role of the 'masters of the fishing spear' and 'leaders of the cattle-camps' and thus create a vacuum in social and political organization.

Since the canal is likely to become a reality, it seems proper that we make some proposals that may minimize the many adverse effects on the people. Firstly, there is need for more planning of Phase One projects than the government have undertaken. Such planning should be on the basis of full and open discussion with all the affected peoples as well as Dinka, so that they can bring their knowledge to bear on questions like resettlement, compensation, crossing, etc. Secondly, Phase Two should be regarded as completely open, i.e., only to be decided on after a very extensive study and discussion of the needs of the people and of the best way to bring modernization to them. If these points are not considered, it is almost certain that tribal life may disintegrate with nothing worthwhile arising in its place.

NOTES

1. Lienhardt, G., *Divinity and Experience: The Religion of the Dinka*, Oxford, Clarendon Press, 1961. Lienhardt, G., 'Western Dinka' in Middleton and Tait, eds., *Tribes Without Rulers*, Routledge and Kegan Paul, London, 1967. Deng, F. M., *The Dinka of the Sudan*, Holt, Rinehart and Winston, 1972. Seligman, C. G. and B. Z., *Pagan Tribes of the Nilotic Sudan*, Routledge and Kegan Paul Ltd., London, 1932.

2. Ring, M. N., 'Dinka Cattle Trade: A Study of Socio-Economic Transformations in a Semi-Pastoral Society', unpublished MA Thesis, University of Nairobi, 1980.

3. 'Jonglei Canal—A Development Project in the Sudan', *Executive Organ*, Khartoum, 1982 Edition, pp. 9–12.

4. Alier, A., *Statement to the People's Regional Assembly on the Proposed Jonglei Canal*, El Tamaddon Press, Khartoum (undated), p. 20.

5. People are considered uneducated, unskilled and often clinging to social values that are regarded unsuited for a 'modern' society.

6. The figure of 200 households is an estimate based on interviews and informal discussions we had with some of the tribal leaders and some Jonglei Project officials and workers whom we met on the site in April, 1981.

7. We obtained these estimates from the surveyors working about 20 miles in advance of the earth-digger. Officially, no member of the Executive Organ or the Compensation Committee was willing to disclose the size of these compensations, let alone the criteria they used in deciding how much money a household deserved.

8. Executive Organ, 'Comparative Socio-Economic Benefits of the Eastern Alignment and the Direct Jonglei Canal Line', *Executive Organ*, Khartoum (undated), p. 13.

9. Hydro-biological Research Unit, University of Khartoum, 'Investigations of the General Ecology of the Sudd Area', *Executive Organ*, Report No. 12, Khartoum, February, 1979.

10. *Ibid.*, p. 18.

17 Dam the Chico: Hydropower Development and Tribal Resistance

CHARLES DRUCKER

The Chico Dam development program in the Philippines is an outstanding case because it illustrates utter insensitivity to the interests of tribal peoples by government planners, and it demonstrates that such projects, even the megamillion-dollar ones, do not inevitably go forward. The Chico project threatened the rice terraces of many of the Igorot, or mountain tribes of Luzon. The dams would have destroyed a highly productive tribal engineering system of water and soil management that has been called a "wonder of the world" and that in this specific case supported some 90,000 people. From the moment the project began in 1974, the Igorot protested it. They obtained broad popular support in the Philippines and internationally. They were also supported by the anti-Marcos New People's Army. The successes of this initial tribal resistance movement contributed to further resistance. Tribal groups throughout the mountain provinces of Luzon formed a united organization, the Cordillera People's Alliance (see part IX), which pressed for tribal autonomy from the central government. Ultimately, the Igorot resistance contributed to the fall of Marcos himself and opened the way for genuine tribal autonomy under the terms of the new constitution sponsored by the Aquino government. Following the collapse of the Chico project, the World Bank, which had originally funded it, was forced to reassess its view of tribal peoples and development issues (see Goodland selection, part IX).

Charles Drucker conducted fieldwork in northern Luzon in 1972 and 1973 and obtained his Ph.D. in 1974 from Stanford University. In 1985 he was working with Friends of the Earth in San Francisco, California.

In 1973, the Philippine government announced an ambitious plan to develop the hydropower resources of the mountainous interior of Luzon, the archipelago's principal island. The Chico River Basin Development Project called for the construction of five dams: four large impoundments to generate an aggregate of over 1,000 megawatts, and a smaller diversion dam to irrigate 52,000 hectares of downstream agricultural land.

Twelve years later, the Chico Project is in total disarray. One of the

Reprinted from *The Ecologist* 15, no. 4 (1985): 149–57. Copyright © Ecosystems Ltd. Reproduced in abridged form by permission.

power dams has been cancelled; the other three have been postponed at least until the 1990s; the irrigation dam is under construction, but in a dramatically scaled-down version that will service little more than a third of the land area specified in the original design.

The Philippine Martial-Law government—and President Ferdinand E. Marcos himself—made numerous, heavy-handed attempts to get the dam project under way, over the strenuous objections of the Chico region's indigenous, tribal inhabitants. The dams would inundate ancestral lands and threaten the tribal peoples' traditional way of life. Their opposition has, over the past decade, escalated into an armed, bloody struggle that the government must somehow resolve before the dam projects may proceed.

One of the tribal peoples' principal allies in this confrontation is a nation-wide revolutionary movement, which provides arms and guerrilla training. The Chico Dam issue has become so politicised that many observers see it as "the most important conflict yet between the Marcos administration and the communist insurgents."[1] As we shall see, the project is also one of the Philippines' most blatant manifestations of enforced, misguided development.

THE PRICE OF POWER

The Chico Dam Project was spawned by the widely held belief that national economic growth requires increased consumption of energy, particularly in the form of electricity.[2] Although the Philippines is abundantly endowed with natural resources, inexpensive energy from fossil fuels is not among them. Historically, the country has been dependent upon imported oil for 95 per cent of its energy supply,[3] and three-quarters of its electricity.[4] Even before the OPEC price hike of 1973, the Philippines' oil import bill had risen to a troubling $231 million (US) annually.[5] Although oil then cost only one-tenth what it does today, both the government and the World Bank perceived the development of domestic energy sources as a virtual economic necessity.[6]

The country's most accessible, conventional energy resource is hydropower, with a theoretical potential five times greater than the present electricity demand.[7] From the development planner's perspective, dam projects are doubly attractive because they serve both the energy demands of the Philippines' prominent, extractive industries, and the irrigation needs of its plantation agriculture.

A technical feasibility study, financed by the World Bank, and conducted in 1973 by Lahmeyer International, of West Germany, identified four gorges in the Chico River Valley as candidates for thin-shelled, concrete arch, high dams. The generating capacity of the four dams would be 1,010 megawatts, making the Chico Dams the largest hydroelectric facility in all of Southeast Asia.[8] Even in industrialised nations, where thousand-megawatt nuclear and thermal plants are fairly commonplace, hydropower projects of this magnitude are rare. And although the Philippines had ten hydro-electric plants operating in 1973, the largest of these was only 212 megawatts. The Chico Dam Project, once completed, would triple the country's installed hydroelectric capacity, increase the power available to the Luzon grid by 50 per cent, and, by itself, could run most of the city of Manila, where the majority of Philippine electricity is consumed.[9]

By any reckoning, the Chico Project would be a monumentally ambitious undertaking, with an equally monumental price tag at 1983 prices, it will cost over 1,000 million (US) dollars, the bulk of this in foreign exchange.[10] The Lahmeyer study did not include a detailed, economic cost/benefit evaluation of the Chico Dams, though it recommended that such an assessment be the project's next phase. But the Philippine government, lured by the Chico's vast potential to reduce foreign oil imports, ignored the recommendation. It secured preliminary project funding from the World Bank in 1974, and wasted no time in signing another contract with Lahmeyer International, this time to design the dams.[11]

RISING WATERS

With equal insouciance, the government ignored the protests of the Chico River Valley's indigenous inhabitants, for whom the dams spelled disaster. The Central Cordillera mountains of northern Luzon, which are drained by the Chico, are the ancestral homelands of several strongly traditional, ethnic minority cultures, known collectively as Igorots, or "people of the mountains". Unlike their lowland neighbours, the Igorots of the Chico area remained fiercely independent during the centuries of Spanish colonial rule in the Philippines, and the eight decades of American administration and economic domination that followed. Although the modern market system has, in the last decades, made significant inroads into their nonindustrial economy, the Igorots retain their distinctive language, dress, religious ritual, and village social organisation.[12]

At the heart of the Igorot way of life is a form of subsistence agriculture that revolves around the intensive cultivation of rice in irrigated terraces. Chiselled from the rocky slopes, with retaining walls up to ten metres in height, the rice terraces in some places ascend a thousand metres from the river bed, forming an unbroken stairway to the peaks of the Cordillera. The terraces dominate the mountain landscape, and the lives of the Igorots who occupy it. Bishop Francisco Claver, himself an Igorot, maintains that the culture of his people "is linked inextricably with the land: with their fields, their burial grounds, their sacred groves, hence with the particular piece of land their villages are built on."[13]

Despite centuries of high-intensity food production, the Igorot rice terraces show no signs of exhaustion. For generation after generation of highland farmers, they have produced consistently abundant harvests—without chemical fertilisers, herbicides, insecticides, or elaborate farm machinery.

Impeccable maintenance, and the complex ecology of the pondfield, combine to make the Igorot subsistence system stable, self-perpetuating, inherently conservative, and nearly indestructible. Even high population pressure does not damage the terrace, because rice yields can be increased by more intense cultivation practices.[14]

The only way in which this stable alliance of culture and environment could be disrupted is by the physical destruction of the terraces themselves. This is the threat posed by the Chico Dam Project. It would create four immense reservoirs, inundating the land upon which Igorot life is based. Sixteen Igorot villages would be partially or totally destroyed, and 2,753 hectares of prized rice terraces would disappear beneath the rising waters.[15] All told, as many as 90,000 Igorots, principally from the Bontoc and Kalinga ethno-linguistic groups, would be affected. Many of them would be forceably resettled "in some other environment where they fear their folkways would be irrelevant, their traditions meaningless, and their future that of cultureless refugees."[16]

TRIBAL PROTEST

The plight of the Bontoc and the Kalinga—their lands encroached upon, and their traditional way of life endangered by a national government eager to expropriate and exploit their resources—is the shared condition of many of the world's remaining tribal populations. The Philippine situation is especially critical, because most of that country's remaining natural resources are concentrated on the ancestral lands of the national minorities.[17]

Throughout the country, national minority groups now find themselves pitted against the machinery of the state. What makes the Igorots' story unique is the intensity of their opposition, the nature of the political alliances they have formed, and their dramatic success in postponing the dams' construction.

The National Power Corporation (NPC) of the Philippine government intended construction of Chico II Dam, in Mountain Province, to initiate the project. In February 1974, survey teams arrived in the provincial capital of Bontoc amidst a storm of protest. Clergy, Municipal Councillors, and Provincial Government officials publicly objected to the dam project in letters to the NPC and to President Marcos. The official position, then as now, is that the displacement of tribal peoples for the sake of development is an unfortunate necessity. According to Dr. Placido Mapa, Minister of National Planning and Development (now head of the Philippine National Bank), "there is a greater good to be derived from the setting up of the dam, for the benefit of the society . . . and each group has to be willing to make some sacrifice for the benefit of the entire society."[18]

The Bontoc and Kalinga people, though, were well aware of the government's poor record in assisting those tribal people who had sacrificed for the "greater good." Every instance of dam construction in northern Luzon has involved displacement without adequate compensation or resettlement. The residents of Anabel and Betwagan wrote, in an open letter:

> We have of our own accord quietly gone to check on the government's performance at Pantabangan, Binga and Ambuklao regarding the promises made to the former inhabitants of those places. At Pantabangan, we saw people without a will to live. They are still crying over the loss of their land. At Ambuklao we spoke with householders who up till now, twenty years later, are still waiting for promised compensation for destroyed property. How can we deal with a government that promises everything, but whose word cannot be trusted?[19]

When their peaceful appeals to halt the Chico Dam Project failed, Bontoc villagers began harassing the survey teams by dismantling their campsites and equipment. Finally, NPC crews were attacked by the villagers, whose long tradition as warriors limited their tolerance for insult and abuse. With the banks of the Chico River no longer safe, the survey work had to be completed from the air.

Even though only a few Bontoc villages would lose property to the dams and undergo the trauma of displacement, the entire province mobilised behind the resistance effort. A long history of village intermarriage contributed to their mutual concern, and the Bontoc people also recognised that economic and environmental disruption in one municipality would affect the region as a whole. Political organisation of the opposition effort followed the lines of the traditional "peace pact" system, or *bodong*. This was, historically, a network of non-aggression agreements between individual villages, intended to prevent hostilities and foster trade. In the face of massive, external threat, the *bodong* was transformed into a consortium of mutual defence treaties, designed to create a united opposition front.

With the entire province of Bontoc in an uproar, the National Power Corporation shifted its attention to the Chico IV Dam site, in the province of Kalinga-Apayao. This time, the Philippine Constabulary accompanied the surveyors as they went about their work. Five delegations of Kalinga elders travelled to Manila during 1974, hoping that by direct appeal to President Marcos they could forestall construction, but they were not received. Their peaceful protest frustrated, the Kalinga villagers followed the lead of the Bontocs, and began dismantling the surveyors' camps.

The next year, at a church-sponsored conference in Manila, religious and human rights groups listened to the arguments that the nation's president had refused to hear. These meetings ended with peace pact ceremonies, among both Bontoc and Kalinga villages, which prohibited cooperation with the NPC, and stripped those Igorots who dared to work on the dam project of their customary peace pact protection. This regional peace pact, staged with the assistance of non-Cordilleran groups and institutions, marked the entry of the Chico Dam issue into the national political arena.

The ceremony that sealed the Bontoc-Kalinga pact included a butchering and feast, as is customary when alliances are forged. The liver of the sacrificial pig, scrutinised for omens and portents, proclaimed that "the struggle will be a protracted one, but the people will triumph in the end."[20]

DIVIDE AND CONQUER IN KALINGA

A few months later, the National Power Corporation received instructions from President Marcos to terminate its work in the Chico River Valley. But the battle for the Chico, far from being over, was only entering a new and more dangerous phase. Moving in the wake of the departing NPC, the Presidential Assistant on National Minorities (PANAMIN) came to Kalinga in the Autumn of 1975.

> PANAMIN started out in 1968 as a well-meaning if paternalistic effort to help tribal Filipinos. . . . Today, PANAMIN has become the primary instrument in the Marcos regime's attempt to move tribal Filipinos out of their lands to make way for agribusiness expansion and the government's ambitious hydro-electric projects. It is PANAMIN that is herding tribal Filipinos into Native-American-style reservations.[21]

PANAMIN'S ambitious and self-aggrandising head, Manuel Elizalde, Jr. arrived by helicopter, with a convoy of freight trucks, buses, jeeps, and a PANAMIN entourage of some 60 assorted armed soldiers, doctors, lawyers, film-projectionists, hostesses, and magicians. Elizalde induced villagers far from the Chico IV site to endorse PANAMIN as their representative in future dam negotiations. Other villages followed suit, after receiving bribes or promises that construction would not be resumed.

Their first encounter with PANAMIN divided the Kalinga and shook the inter-regional peace pact against the dam. At a meeting of Chico Valley leaders, just after the PANAMIN intrusion, Bontocs castigated their Kalinga counterparts for having given PANAMIN so much power and authority.[22]

The debate over PANAMIN'S intentions heightened when the agency arranged a meeting between Kalinga representatives and President Marcos. Once in Manila, the delegation was sequestered and not permitted to see Marcos until they had signed blank sheets of paper, even though they had not been empowered by their villages to enter into binding agreements. When they were finally taken to the President, the blank sheets had become statements consenting to the construction of Chico IV Dam.

To add to the confusion in Kalinga, PANAMIN embarked on an intimidation campaign against the most active villages within the anti-dam movement. Their traditional enemies were organised and armed with 40 high-powered rifles, reviving feuds that had simmered since the days of uninhibited inter-village conflict. Numerous people, including several local leaders, were injured and killed in the PANAMIN-initiated conflict. And to further suppress the opponents of the dams, the government moved a battalion of 700 Philippine Constabulary to the site of Chico IV, to back up the 150-man Provincial force. Not since the final days of World War II had the Igorots seen so many soldiers.

By mid-1976, Kalinga had become an armed camp, with dam opponents set against both government forces and PANAMIN'S civilian militia. The next few years saw sporadic violence erupting throughout the Chico River Valley. The Philippine Constabulary, subject to periodic sniper fire, became increasingly repressive, until they began to resemble a foreign occupation force. PANAMIN was out of its depth, and in August of 1978 was removed from Kalinga, leaving the Constabulary in charge of dealing with the local resistance.

According to human rights attorney, William Claver (brother of the Bontoc-born Bishop), "the military abuses which naturally followed so hardened the Bontoc and Kalinga opposition to the Chico Dam Project that we, the indigenous natives of the Cordillera, did finally understand that the government had come here with no other purpose but to make our lives more oppressive."[23]

NEW ALLIANCES

In response to the government's intransigence over the Chico Dams, and the increased militarisation of the Cordillera, the dam opposition movement took on a broader, anti-government perspective. Contacts with outside activist and revolutionary organisations began in 1976, when the first cadres of the New People's Army (NPA) appeared in the Chico River Valley. The NPA was established in 1969 as the armed, guerrilla wing of the Communist Party of the Philippines. The Party, in turn, is integrated into a coalition of anti-government organisations, known as the National Democratic Front, which draws much of its support from peasant groups, labour unions, and elements of the Catholic Church. The NPA offered the Bontoc and Kalinga support in their fight against the dams,

> while at the same time winning them as allies in the broader struggle against the Marcos regime. Long resistant to any ties with outsiders, the Kalingas gradually responded to the NPA appeal, because it seemed to offer them hope in the face of the overwhelming forces arrayed against them.[24]

By the summer of 1978,

> NPA songs could be heard around village campfires and in children's playgroups, while old men chanted verses against the dams and the government.[25]

For the next three years, the Chico Dam Project remained at a virtual standstill, while the opposition movement grew stronger. The majority of the Bontoc and Kalinga villages to be affected by Chico II and Chico III established local militia units, which were armed and trained by the NPA and its affiliate groups.

Together with the NPA, and independently as well, the village militia staged periodic attacks on the Philippine Constabulary and on National Power Corporation crews. The military retaliated by harassing, arresting, and ultimately assassinating, suspected NPA members and supporters.[26]

By 1980, the Chico Valley had become a virtual war zone. The *Asian Wall Street Journal* reported that at least six NPC employees had been killed as of June of that year, along with eight government soldiers in the previous four months.[27] This continued, violent conflict between government troops and NPA-assisted villagers made it unsafe and impractical for the National Power Corporation to proceed with Chico IV or any of the other power dams. When the Philippines Five-Year National Energy Programme was announced in mid-1981, no mention was made of the Chico Dams. Placido Mapa, the Minister of National Planning and Development, commented:

> The controversy related to the Chico River Dam Project prompted the government to revise its plans. Instead of forcefully, and over the objections of the people involved, going ahead with the project in Chico, the government instead has decided to postpone it, although that would have been an ideal project from a technical point of view.[28]

The Philippine government had, however, proceeded with the Chico River Irrigation Project (CRIP) dam, some 40 kilometres downstream from the Chico IV Dam site. Near the junction of the Chico and the Cagayan rivers, this fifth dam of the original Chico Project was designed to contain, and divert into canals, the water that passes through the power turbines of Chico IV. With this large reservoir behind it, CRIP could irrigate some 52,000 hectares of agricultural land in the Cagayan Valley. As a run-of-the-river project, without Chico IV, the area irrigated falls to about 19,000 hectares.

The Philippine National Irrigation Administration uncertain as to when the Chico IV reservoir would be built, scaled CRIP down accordingly. At the same time, though, it drafted plans for a second project stage that assumes the prior existence of Chico IV. The World Bank, which has provided principal funding for CRIP, maintains that the first stage is "economically viable on its own and is not dependent on a storage dam or on a second stage irrigation development." Philippine government officials, however, dispute that claim[28], and National Irrigation Administration employees, interviewed at the CRIP site in June of 1982, expressed the belief that it is "only a matter of time" before the project's second stage begins.[29]

Thus the Chico River power dams have not been cancelled, but only postponed. The power lines and the irrigation canals that would feed off the Chico Dams have already begun to march across the neighbouring lowland provinces, carrying with them the certainty of another bloody confrontation, in the not-too-distant future, between the government and the Chico Valley's indigenous inhabitants.

ENERGY PLANNING AND EFFICIENCY

The Chico Dam Project is, unfortunately, not an isolated event in the history of Philippine energy development. Over the next two decades, forty major dams are planned, almost all on lands now inhabited by cultural minority groups like the Igorots of northern Luzon. The National Power Corporation, charged with the construction and operation of these dams, has broad powers over the watersheds involved. It can restrict or prohibit farming, and it can forcibly displace residents, their ancestral lands claims notwithstanding. By one estimate, the lands and the subsistence routines of one and a half to two million minority Filipinos will be affected.[30]

Philippine planners justify the enormous social cost of hydropower development by claiming that it will "hasten the electrification of the country and reduce reliance of the electricity industry on imported oil."[31] Increasing the supply of electricity is, in fact, one of the government's principal planning goals, and one of its most costly, since it is striving toward an annual growth rate in electricity generation of 9.6 per cent. The consumption of energy in all forms is expected to increase at seven per cent per year. Despite this extremely rapid growth, the Philippines hopes to reduce its dependency on foreign oil from 84 per cent of total energy consumed in 1981 to less than 47 per cent by 1986, thereby trimming the huge 1981 oil import bill of $2.6 thousand million.

Curbing oil imports whilst rapidly increasing the energy supply will require a massive effort to develop the country's infrastructure: a major domestic petroleum exploration and production programme; the purchase of a nuclear plant (costing well over one thousand million dollars); the creation, from virtually nothing, of an entire coal industry; the installation of more geothermal capacity than any country in the world; and, a 240 per cent increase in hydroelectric capacity, all within a period of only six years. The price tag on that programme, at 1981 exchange rates, is about $6 thousand million,[32] or about $120 per capita in a country where the average annual income is little more than twice that amount.

Unquestionably, the Philippines needs to reduce its foreign oil bill, which eats up nearly 40 per cent of the country's export earnings.[33] But it is highly questionable whether massive hydropower development is the most cost-effective and most equitable way to achieve that objective. Only about one-quarter of the Philippines' oil is used for generating electricity; almost one-third of the oil is burned by internal combustion engines, and virtually all the rest is used for industrial process heat. Both of those latter uses have high inherent inefficiencies: engine exhaust pipes carry away two-thirds or more of the energy value of the fuel consumed; and heating equipment, while somewhat more efficient, still wastes more than one-third of the fuel's energy.

Over the last few years, largely in response to high oil prices, a new generation of engines, vehicle designs, and process heating equipment has matured. Petroleum-based fuels are used much more efficiently, and renewable energy sources (for instance, solar energy and biomass fuels) are substituted wherever they are cost-effective. In the industrial economies, broad dissemination of conservation and renewable energy technologies could stabilise, or even reduce, primary energy consumption (notably of fossil fuels), while permitting continued GNP growth.[34] Already, most of the economic growth in the United States is 'fuelled' not by new energy supplies but by energy made available through improvements in efficiency.[35]

The same oil displacement strategy could, and should, be followed in developing countries like the Philippines. They offer, if anything, even more fertile ground for improvements, because the existing equipment is of less efficient design.[36] They also possess a greater renewable energy resource potential, because of the higher biomass productivity of their tropical climates. The Philippine Ministry of Energy has, in fact, supported a number of programmes to investigate and develop conservation projects and renewable energy technologies. However, the World Bank and the other international financial institutions show little interest in providing funds for wide implementation of these promising energy alternatives. Even though the technologies involved are proven, commercially available, and cost-effective, they are also inherently decentralised. Loan programmes for decentralised capital investment are thought difficult or impossible to administer and oversee, so they are rarely applied for, and even less frequently approved.

ELECTRIC POWER AND MULTI-PURPOSE DAMS

Philippine energy planning is similarly shortsighted with respect to electricity. At least three quarters of the country's electricity is consumed in lights and motors (including refrigeration and air-conditioning compressors), for which highly efficient and relatively inexpensive technologies have recently become available. Up to fifty per cent of the power used by conventional lights and motors could be saved by retrofits, with payback times that rarely exceed two years.[37] The aggregate potential for electricity savings in the United States, using these technologies, equals the combined capacity of all the nuclear and coal plants now planned or being built.[38] In the Philippines, the savings potential is about equal to the capacity of all the hydropower dams scheduled to go on-line between 1981 and 1986, and possibly the nuclear power plant as well. The capital cost of these savings would be one-half to one-third that of the projects that would be displaced.[39]

This high-efficiency, resource-conserving scenario, however, is extremely unlikely to be realised in practice. Conservation investments require substantial infusions of capital, albeit in smaller doses than with any of the conventional alternatives. The flow of capital to the Philippines is largely controlled by the World Bank, the Asian Development Bank, and a few other international institutions, none of which is interested in loaning the Philippine government funds for an equipment retrofit programme.

Even if financing these technical alternatives were not a problem, Philippine planners would continue to pursue massive hydropower projects for the sake of their irrigation potential. The Chico Dams, along with the recently completed Magat Dam in Isabella Province, and all the other major hydro-electric facilities planned by the Philippines, are multi-purpose projects. They include diversion structures and irrigation canals as part of the design. The government claims that a principal objective of its irrigation programme is to help small farmers increase the yields of their lands. The National Irrigation Administration, echoing official policy, insists that the Chico River Irrigation Project—which is one of the biggest in the country— "is first and foremost for the benefit of the Kalingas themselves."[40]

In fact, the Chico irrigation dam will not work to the advantage of small farmers, nor was their benefit its original intention. The principal aim of the national irrigation programme is to increase the productivity of corporate plantations, which export the vast majority of what they grow. The Kalinga, like most subsistence farmers in the Philippines, lack the capital for irrigation fees and equipment. Throughout the country, the principal beneficiaries of irrigation projects are "landlords, businessmen, and government officials who already have substantial incomes, and surplus capital to invest."[41] In the case of the Chico irrigation dam, the advantages of irrigation will accrue to the Cagayan Sugar Company, and a few other large landowners.[42] The Kalinga and the other rural poor of the lower Chico area not only cannot afford irrigation, they indirectly stand to lose from the programme. Once irrigation is available, the small farmers' lands become more attractive to large, land-owning interests and, in many other parts of the Philippines, this has led to massive displacement and expropriation.[43]

The final irony to the Chico story is that other resource development projects are subjecting the Chico watershed to such environmental abuse that high dams no longer make engineering or economic sense. Extensive mining and commercial logging operations, now under way or planned for the next decade, will carve roads into the most remote areas, denude whole slopes, and greatly increase runoff and erosion. If the Chico Dams are ever built, the high rate of siltation will dramatically reduce their capacity and lifespan. At least one of the northern Philippines' hydropower installations has already been severely damaged by precisely this kind of land mismanagement. The 75-megawatt Ambuklao Dam, built in Benguet Province in 1952, was supposed to produce electric power for 75 years. However, its watershed is dotted with mines, which log the surrounding slopes for shoring timbers. Dumped mine tailings, together with erosion from logging activities, have choked Ambuklao Dam with silt and it is no longer fully operational.[44]

ELECTRICITY AND EQUITY

The National Energy Programme of the Philippines, like its irrigation programme, is designed to favour the largest consumers, while the basic needs of the country's poor receive short shrift. The programme strongly stresses electrification, and even if the government achieves this goal via efficiency and renewable energy sources (rather than more disruptive, conventional technologies for expanding energy supply) the inherent inequities remain.

Industry is by far the major consumer of electricity in the Philippines. After subtracting transmission losses and the utilities' own uses, industry absorbs about 54 per cent of the national total. Most of the industrial energy use, furthermore, is concentrated in heavy, primary industries, such as mining, refining, and manufacturing, the majority of which are foreign-owned or foreign-controlled. In Mindanao, for example, the largest single user of electricity is the Kawasaki sintering plant.[45]

The Philippine government claims that generating more electricity, through projects like the Chico Dam, would foster rural development; it would allow farmers to irrigate their land with electric pumps, grind their rice and corn in electric mills, and develop cottage industries. These claimed benefits, however, are rationalisations rather than realities. Rural Filipinos, by and large, lack the capital to invest in electric equipment and appliances; the majority cannot even afford basic connection charges and fees.[46]

But from the perspective of foreign-based industrialists, Philippine energy is being sold at bargain rates: less than six cents/kWh in Manila, about four cents in other parts of Luzon, and down to a rock-bottom two cents in Mindanao.[47] Such cheap rates encourage electricity-intensive industries to settle in the Philippines, but this unfortunately does little to promote national development. Few jobs are created for local workers; the manufactured and refined products are, for the most part, exported; and the profits from these industries are either repatriated to the investors' home countries, or else retained by a small group of wealthy Filipino entrepreneurs.

Large hydropower projects like the Chico Dams are not true instruments of national development. They constitute, rather, part of an elite strategy to convert the Philippines' natural and human resources into corporate profits, through the medium of international trade. This accounts, at least in part, for the government's prolonged intransigence on the Chico Dam issue, despite the enormous social costs involved, the fervent opposition of the tribal people, and the international disrepute into which the project eventually sank. Only when the Chico River Valley had become an all-out guerrilla front, making construction work impossible, were the dams postponed.

LESSONS LEARNED AND LOST

There are a number of important lessons to be derived from the history of the Chico Dam, though in most instances the wrong lessons have been learned. The National Power Corporation should have realised that the Bontoc and Kalinga people would never accept the Chico Dams, but instead of abandoning the project, the decision was only to delay it. NPC Chairman, Gabriel Itchon, commented that "the studies are there. As to when the project will be implemented the government has yet to decide."[47] The

NPC mistakenly assumes that a few years of continued military pressure will break the alliance between the New People's Army and the Bontoc and Kalinga, thereby weakening the opposition movement sufficiently to permit the project to proceed.

The National Power Corporation should also have learned from its experience in Chico that any lack of candour in dealing with people who will be displaced by development projects, leads to a violent backlash once the full effects are known. But, instead of becoming more open, the NPC has become more secretive. When work began on the Abulug Dam Project, in another part of the Cordillera, the NPC withheld the information that the dams would inundate the Provincial capital of Kalinga-Apayao, and displace thousands of tribal Filipinos.[48] A public outcry was thus avoided, but another large group of people now feel betrayed by the present government, and their support for the militant opposition is growing.

The World Bank, which played an instrumental role in the Chico Project, also "refused to draw the real lessons from the people's resistance."[49] The Chico conflict led to a World Bank re-assessment of its policy regarding tribal minorities threatened by development programmes. Its conclusion was that the Bank would not prevent development of areas inhabited by tribal people, and, moreover, that it would assist national governments in resettling and acculturating tribal minorities who stood in the path of development.[50]

Perhaps the most important lesson of the Chico conflict, according to Filipino analyst Walden Bello, has been learned by other communities "resisting development from above."[51] The opposition of the Bontoc and Kalinga people showed that it is possible to confront a misguided development policy, regardless of its domestic and international proponents; possible to bring the issue to the attention of the international community; possible to enlist strong supporters in the struggle to retain self-determination; and, ultimately, possible to achieve a significant political voice.

NOTES

1. Sheilah Ocampo, "The battle for Chico River", *Far Eastern Economic Review*, October 20, 1978, 32–34.

2. Philippine Ministry of Energy, *Ten Year Energy Program, 1979–1988*.

3. Philippine National Oil Company, *The 7th Year Towards Energy Self Reliance*, 1982.

4. Philippine Ministry of Energy, *Energy Forum*, Vol. 1, No. 1, July–September, 1981.

5. Ministry of Energy, *The National Energy Programme, 1981–86*, p. 3.

6. The political cost of oil dependence was also becoming excessive. Ninety-five per cent of crude imports come from Middle Eastern countries, whose Islamic leaders were, and still are, gravely concerned about the Philippines' Islamic minority groups. Concentrated on Mindanao and the other southern islands, the Islamic Filipinos claim a long history of land expropriation and oppression by the Christian-dominated national government, and have supported a strong secessionist element since the early part of the century. Inter-ethnic relations had so deteriorated by the early 1970s that pressure from oil suppliers on the Philippine government was mounting to grant some measure of autonomy to Islamic Filipinos.

7. Ministry of Energy, *op cit*, p. 5.

8. Ceres P. Doyo, *Philippine Panorama*, June 29, 1980.

9. Ministry of Energy, *op cit*, pp. 22–25.

10. Sheilah Ocampo, *op cit*, p. 34.

11. Anti-Slavery Society, *The Philippines: Authoritarian Government, Multinationals and Ancestral Lands*, Indigenous Peoples and Development Series, Report No. 1, 1983.

12. Charles Drucker, "To inherit the land: Descent and decision in northern Luzon," *Ethnology*, Vol. 6, No. 1, 1977, pp. 1–20.

13. Bishop Francisco Claver, quoted in *The Southeast Asia Chronicle*, Issue No. 67, October 1979.

14. Charles Drucker, "The price of progress," *Sierra*, Vol. 63, No. 8, October 1978, pp. 22–24.

15. Letter to World Bank President Robert McNamara, signed by 1,795 Kalinga leaders, elders, and village residents.

16. William Henry Scott, "Old folkways, new societies," paper read at the Third Folklore Congress, San Carlos University, Cebu City, Philippines, November 28, 1976.

17. World Bank, *Economic Development and Tribal People*, 1982.

18. Dr. Placido Mapa, film interview, San Francisco, California, 1982.

19. Letter, people of Anabel and Betwagan, Sadanga Municipality, Mountain Province, Philippines.

20. Martha Winnacker, "The battle to stop the Chico Dams," *Southeast Asia Chronicle*, No. 67, October 1979, pp. 22–29.

21. Joel Rocamora, "The political uses of PANAMIN," *Southeast Asia Chronicle*, No. 67, October 1979, pp. 11–21.

22. Winnacker, *op cit*.

23. Attorney William Claver, filmed interview in Tabuk, Province of Kalinga-Apayao, June 1982.

24. Winnacker, *op cit*.

25. *ibid*.

26. Amnesty International, *Report of an Amnesty International Mission to the Republic of the Philippines, 11–28 November, 1981*.

27. Dr. Placido Mapa, film interview, San Francisco, California, 1982.

28. Correspondence between Barbara Bentley (Director, Survival International) and Edward V. K. Jaycox (Director, Country Programmes Department, East Asia and Pacific Regional Office, World Bank), *Survival International Review*, Autumn 1981, pp. 68–70.

29. This belief was founded on the allocation of funds for the construction of canals and culverts that could not be utilised unless CRIPs second stage proceeds.

30. Anti-Slavery Society, *op cit*, p. 92.

31. Ministry of Energy, *The National Energy Programme*, 1981–86, pp. 41.

32. *ibid*, pp. 10–11.

33. *ibid*, p. 3.

34. Solar Energy Research Institute, US Department of Energy, 1981, *Toward a New Prosperity*.

35. Jim Harding, "The Nuclear Blowdown," *Not Man Apart*, May 1983.

36. Ministry of Energy, *op cit*, p. 6.

37. Jim Harding, "New Tools Save $," *Not Man Apart*, August/September 1982, p. 20.

38. *ibid.*

39. *ibid.*

40. *Pangawidan ti Amianan*, Newsletter of the National Irrigation Administration, Sector A, March–April 1982, p. 7.

41. Anti-Slavery Society, *op cit.*

42. Barbara Bentley, *Survival International Review*, Autumn 1981, p. 70.

43. Joel Rocamora, *op cit.*

44. Anti-Slavery Society, *op cit.*

45. Anti-Slavery Society, *op cit*, p. 100.

46. *ibid*, p. 95.

47. Geronimo Z. Velasco (Philippine Minister of Energy), "Rationalising the Power Industry," *Energy Forum*, Vol. 1, No. 2, January–March 1982.

48. *Ibon Facts and Figures*, No. 28, October 15, 1979, p. 2.

49. Walden Bello *et al*, *The Development Debacle: The World Bank in the Philippines*. Institute for Food and Development Policy.

50. The World Bank, *Economic Development and Tribal Peoples*, 1982.

51. Walden Bello *et al*, *op cit.*

18

High Technology and Original Peoples: The Case of Deforestation in Papua New Guinea and Canada

COLIN DE'ATH

GREGORY MICHALENKO

In these two case studies from Papua New Guinea and Canada we see a convergence of interests between governments and multinational corporations to promote profitable development programs that disrupt local subsistence economies while providing little compensation. In both cases development of forest resources has resulted in enormous environmental degradation, which has endangered previously viable local subsistence pursuits. Both governments clearly were in a position to profit from their support of the corporations in opposition to the demands of local people for a more reasonable share of the profits and for protection of their subsistence resources. The authors point out that in cases such as this, government policy must explicitly acknowledge that indigenous communities are engaged in "dual economies." If the government is concerned with citizen welfare, it may be just as necessary for it to support local subsistence economies as to facilitate penetration by the market economy. In Alaska government development planners have indeed calculated the cash-equivalent value of bush products to demonstrate the economic importance of hunting and fishing to native communities.

Professor De'Ath, now at the University of Waterloo, Waterloo, Ontario, Canada, is a native of Turua, New Zealand. He holds degrees from universities in his country and in the United States as well as the Certificate of the Australian School of Pacific Administration, Sydney. Dr. Michalenko, his coauthor, studied biology at the University of Saskatchewan and now teaches environmental studies at the University of Waterloo. He has been involved in studies of pulp mills in both Saskatchewan and Ontario.

TECHNOLOGY, CORPORATIONS AND ORIGINAL PEOPLES

Technologies in industrialized countries can be characterized by the following features. First, they have become highly centralized in terms of bureau-

Reprinted with permission from *Impact of Science on Society* 30, no. 3 (1980). Copyright © 1980 UNESCO.

The portions of this article dealing with Papua New Guinea are based on 'The Throwaway People: Social Impact of the Trans-Gogol Timber Project', a monograph to be published in 1981 by the Institute of Applied Social and Economic Research, Port Moresby.

cratic control; second, they rely generally on a narrow spectrum of energy sources; third, organizations responsible for controlling technologies are large and complex, and relatively inflexible especially in terms of setting new goals; fourth, until quite recently such organizations assumed that resources were infinite and that growth and induced consumption by its clientele were unimpeachable goals.

The spread of western technologies has been facilitated by a number of factors. More and more scientists spend their working lives making more and more sophisticated 'things', especially for the military. Through world-wide communication systems, the knowledge of the potential of new technologies becomes known rapidly by corporations. There is growing congruent thinking between transnational firms and national governments in terms of the supposed utility of various technologies. Emphasis in gauging the relevance of a given technology to a particular situation has usually been on whether there is a technological 'fit', rather than a social or ecological fit. There have not been dramatic advances in the social sciences equivalent to those in other sciences and their related technologies; this has led to centrally inspired technocratic fixes in lieu of sound social planning and follow-through. A fatalistic kind of technological determinism has been adopted, implying that the evolutionary trajectories of certain technologies once set in motion are irreversible—until, of course, there is a catastrophe. And, important for our purposes here, the impact of technologies and their associated political institutions have not been adequately publicized.

In the heartlands of Western-type industrialization (whether in Europe, Japan, North America or the Union of Soviet Socialist Republics), there is some appreciation of what effects complex or 'high' technology has on ecological and social systems. Even there, however, technological change can be gradual enough for its participants not to realize what is happening to them and their natural environment. This anomaly is also attributable in part to a distortion in feedback. Because it is in the interests of governments and corporations to promote consumption, the illusion of improvement, growth and profits, it is very difficult for subject populations caught up in specialization, professionalism, machine-like routines, consumerism and 'commodification' to assess the direction in which change is moving.

The deterministic theories and assumptions of engineers, and physical and natural scientists generally, do not encourage ordinary citizens to participate in decision-making—the belief becomes widespread that the experts 'know' what is right and appropriate in terms of resource exploitation and the efficient use of human beings.

Original peoples, such as those in northern Canada and in Papua and New Guinea, tend, in the face of the solvent power of Western money, science and technology, to be very vulnerable to corporate dynamism. In the following sections the results are examined of the playing out of this dynamism by a Japanese corporation, sanctioned by what was formerly the Australian colonial government in Papua New Guinea, and a British transnational assisted by Canadian governments.

THE TRANS-GOGOL

The Trans-Gogol is a tropical river valley about 60 kilometres from the town of Madang in Madang Province. This province is on the north coast of Papua New Guinea.

Although the authors' first study focused on the Gogol Timber Rights Purchase (TRP) area (52,265 hectares (ha)), the Jant (Japan and New Guinea Timbers) had interests in three other adjacent 'TRPs'.

The vegetation is tropical rain forest and somewhat different from that found in Indonesia and elsewhere in South-East Asia. Compared with our knowledge of temperate forests, not a great deal is known about the ecological system. Foresters themselves, because of the role of natural disasters, cannot even agree on whether the forest has ever reached 'climax status'. Because of this knowledge deficit, and because there has never been massive clear-felling elsewhere in lowland forest areas in Papua New Guinea, it is not known what the impact on this complex life-system will be. Although the Man and the Biosphere Programme research in this area is well-intentioned, it has many gaps, particularly in the area of ethnobiological studies. Too, not enough is known about the role of the forest in stabilizing the valley which regularly floods but also goes through droughts, and its influence on the micro-climate. Another area which is of extreme importance is the effect on regeneration of extensive commercial tree-cutting compared with that of the scattered cuttings of subsistence farmers who have been in the area for an unknown number of generations. Human settlements there may go back 50,000 years, although the current linguistic diversity could indicate that some groups are fairly recent arrivals.

The Company and Its Position

Jant is a subsidiary of Honshu Paper. The latter began negotiations with the Australian Government in the late 1960s. At that time, the Australian Government was a United Nations trustee for the Territory of Papua and New Guinea (TPNG). After complex negotiations resulting in the incorporation of a TPNG/Australian/New Zealand saw log company, cutting operations began in 1973. (The subcontractor had been cutting saw logs for some time before this date.) Several agreements were involved in setting up the operation, namely between the local residents (who owned the land and the trees) and the government (which purchased the rights to cut them) and between the company and the government. The company agreed to pay royalties for cutting and entry rights. These agreements had a number of flaws.

It is doubtful whether the people understood what was about to happen to their land, their life-style, and their incorporation in (and exclusion from) an imposed cash economy. The agreements were vague about costs and benefits except for the initial purchase price for the trees.

The company's commitment to reforestation was not clearly spelled out; neither were rigid obligations to diversify agriculturally or industrially included in the agreements. Strict monitoring of company operations, particularly in the areas of staff localization, were not included in the agreement. Social, technological and ecological impact studies were not a prerequisite to setting up the operation.

Impact of the Operations

In Madang town   In Madang town itself, where a chip mill and the saw log facility are situated, probably only about half of the jobs promised materialized. All but two or three top executive positions are held by Japanese executives who live in comfortable housing areas. Most sub-contracting for goods and services is given to non-Papua New Guinean firms. The town, which is in economic decline, has not been revitalized by the foreign firms' presence. The area around Madang—especially in Binnen harbour where Jant and Wewak Timber are located—is very beautiful and an ecologically sensitive area because of its estuarine and coral ecological systems. There was little consultation on the siting of these facilities, with the result that the town is saddled with an eyesore as well as an effluent-producing facility. Waste products include smoke, ash, sawdust and bark, and chemically polluted excess water.

The quarters for mill workers, not far from the mill and in the low-cost housing areas, leave much to be desired. A third of all workers come from outside of Madang Province. Employee turnover is very high. Employment for local women does not exist. There have been complaints about industrial safety and housing conditions, as well as a number of wild-cat strikes. Jant has not paid any corporate tax since its operations commenced. It builds up considerable debts in Japan, and these must be serviced. It is doubtful whether the expertise exists in Papua New Guinea to monitor Jant's transfer costing and accounting practices and to ascertain whether these are ethical in terms of the welfare of a new nation. Jant suggests that its operations are not as profitable as envisaged, partly because of a depressed global pulp market. Much of its equipment, especially its bulldozers and log-hauling trucks, have become aged and unsafe. Because of overloading, the latter vehicles do much damage to the local road system (which is partially government maintained).

The Japanese, because of high staff turnover and their own ethnocentrism, have great difficulty in getting to know their own people. They are generally preoccupied with technical efficiency at the mill and in maintaining production targets. They consider that the welfare of their company is coterminous with the welfare of their employees and that the profitability of the company is always a prior consideration in dealing with workers about pay and working conditions. The philosophy of co-prosperity made very explicit before the Second World War, is alive and well within the firm, i.e. a profitable company automatically means an increase in the welfare of its employees and those involved in supplying resources to the corporation. When there are problems between the employers and local nationals, there is a strong tendency to leave the government the responsibility for their solutions. This has not been hard to do as there is still a strong paternalistic tradition within government, a heritage from the colonial Australians. Problems such as the size of royalty payments tend to take years to resolve.

Within Madang town, the size of the Office of Forestry's operations has grown considerably. A rough estimate for the Gogol TRP shows that between January 1974 and June 1977 the government received K1,398,968 in revenue and spent K1,962,000 in the operation (in March 1978, K1 = US $1.37). Nearly all of this could be classified as a subsidy for Jant's operations. Within the Office of Forestry however, there is some ambiguity in how the local foresters should function, i.e. whether they should be: (a) revenue producers; (b) local royalty paymasters; (c) protectors of the environment; (d) company policemen; (e) facilitators of company activities (especially in times of crisis); or (f) social planners acting on behalf of TRP residents.

From past operations, it becomes obvious that, despite the existence of an interdepartmental working group, the Office of Forestry does place emphasis on (a), (b) and (e). This is probably due to the training of the foresters and to the inevitably close contact which occurs between Jant and the Office of Forestry. Jant, with its entertainment and political contacts, can be a much more powerful lobby than can disorganized subsistence farmers who know little about the ways of transnational firms. Much infrastructural assistance by the government is given to the company through the provision of roads, electricity, harbour facilities, land and forest surveys, research and planning. Yet the company complains about its assessments for some of these items. (No comprehensive analysis has been done on the value of these services.) Local people receive some spin-off benefits but these, in the past, have tended to have an incidental effect rather than lead to a marked improvement in the standard of living in Madang town, whose population is 19,000.

The rural impact   At the commencement of the project there was much discussion on agricultural development—of the development of a small town and of employment prospects for Trans-Gogol inhabitants—and on both deforestation and reforestation. But little benefit has resulted from these proposals. Reforestation did not commence, and then on a very limited scale, until 1978. Local people quickly became disillusioned with labouring for Jant at K25 per week (less than half the urban wage). Currently only about one-sixth of Jant's labour force is recruited in the timber areas. No comprehensive agricultural development occurred, and the small town of Arar is still only a town planner's sketch.

The people's grievances include the following:

The size of royalty payments (they get less than 50t [half a K] per m³. Dressed timber in Madang town costs them K198 per m³. The export value of 1 m³ of wood chips is K16.7, and Jant and Wewak Timber sell logs to one another for K11 per m³).

Payment for road-building gravel; the people receive nothing for the gravel, but elsewhere companies must pay a royalty of 5t per m³.

Indifference of government, researchers and others to the needs of villagers. Villagers say that visits by government officers may have become perfunctory and some social services are worse than they were previously.

Gardening and game. Cut-over areas, because of bad logging practices, are unsuitable for gardening. Game, despite token reserve areas, has declined considerably. Many species of game used for food no longer exist.

The water-table in many areas along levees and roads has been heightened, leading to the death of vegetation and the existence of ponds where mosquito populations can increase. Malaria, consequently, has increased in the area. Some of the malaria is chloroquin-resistant, and some of the mosquito vectors are now resistant to DDT.

The style of Japanese operations: Japanese supervisors tend to believe they are omniscient and, at the beginning of the project, made many mistakes in siting roads and bridges and in their actual construction. Few had any tropical-forest experience and fewer still knew anything about local societies, tropical ecological systems and reforestation. Their operations during the wet season were wasteful, and their initial use of labour profligate. Local folk complain that the Japanese never listen to them and that there are no real employment prospects. The company has been remiss in setting up meaningful training programmes which could lead to complete localization of their operations. In the five years of the company's operation, villagers have never risen higher than foreman.

The company does not tell them enough about its logging plans. Within the Trans-Gogol, the government embarked on a very expensive survey of clan boundaries primarily so that it could acquire land for reforestation and possibly pay royalties on a more equitable basis. But payments for leasing land that will be used for reforestation will be low, and there is a strong possibility that the landowners will again be disillusioned when they realize what valuation is put on their land and labour inputs.

Some other negative effects   A forest station has been established at Baku in the Trans-Gogol, not primarily to benefit the villagers but rather the company's operations. It is situated adjacent to Jant's base camp. The local police station also is sited there.

Many kilometres of roads have been constructed in the logging areas, but after one wet season many of these are washed out or have slumped. Poorly built logging bridges also collapse or may be washed out. Thus, after the company finishes its logging (except where there is reforestation), the roads rapidly become dysfunctional; and the people are in as bad a shape for marketing their crops as they were before the logging. They do not have the means to maintain roads, and the new provincial government has other priorities.

The company initially estimated that it would take twenty to twenty-five years to log its four TRPs. This has now been reduced to eleven years. The firm is seeking extensive concessions in areas nearer the Ramu River, which will mean very long, expensive hauls as well as expensive road maintenance. This will also increase the possibility of a road being linked to the highland roads where people are short of land. The Trans-Gogol and other Madang people are very apprehensive about the impact of such migrants. They have bad memories of land losses earlier to German and Australian occupants.

In many development scenarios it is assumed that technology and built features such as roads will lead to the well-being of all concerned. In the Trans-Gogol it is doubtful whether village people will benefit from Japanese controlled high technology. It is also doubtful whether the town of Madang and its regional hinterland has benefited. The entire nation probably also has been a loser, even if only traditional economic criteria are used. Certainly the ecological system will never recover its integrity. In this instance roads and high technology have led to a net outflow of resources. Because of the myths associated with business and government operations, and because of a colonial past in which these kinds of extractive operations were the norm, it is doubtful whether a great deal has been learned about how to manage—let alone enhance—the functioning of interdependent technological, social and ecological subsystems. The integrity of each of these subsystems, particularly the indigenous social subsystem which has taken thousands of years to refine to a point where it is self-sufficient in terms of food and material culture, has been breached.

The people in the Trans-Gogol, once their forest disappears and their land becomes unsuitable for food staples and game, will be forced into a dependency relationship with the larger system. Even prior to the coming of the foreign timbering firm, the local people did not have great admiration for the exploitative behaviour of outsiders. They managed, at least during the period 1871–1973, despite insistent demands for cash-crop surpluses and their labour, to keep their most valued resources (land and forest) intact. Now, however, the future is problematical.

THE OJIBWAY OF NORTHERN ONTARIO

The Ojibway live in the forested land lying between the Great Lakes and Hudson's Bay. Traditionally they have hunted moose, beaver, hare and fish, and lived in small local groups. Because of periodic or seasonal fluctuations in the resource base, there was always some movement of these small groups. 'Bush' resources were distributed on the basis of reciprocity or mutual sharing within the local group; this had the added effect of extending sharing to other groups of Ojibway in the area.

Contact with fur traders of European origin led to a profound shift to a dual economy—whereby a substantial supply of resources for direct consumption still came from the land, while furs (easily obtained through technological refinements of traditional trapping skills and existing ecological knowledge) were bartered and later sold for trade goods. Traditional seasonal movements of people were modified in accordance with this new dependence on trade goods.

Canadian colonial policy for indigenous peoples followed the pattern in the United States of extinguishing native rights to huge expanses of territory in return for tiny reservations. The Ojibway were one of the last peoples to sign away their land rights. Treaty No. 9 in 1906 ceded their land to the federal state in return for small reserves, guarantees of the viability of and access to game stocks on the alienated territory, and tiny annual monetary grants. The Ojibway never had a concept of legal land entitlement, but rather one of land use. Thus surviving witnesses of the treaty-signing maintain that they thought the treaty was merely a declaration of friendship, not a land transaction.

The dual economy functioned so long as fur prices remained high, but the prolonged depression in prices after the Second World War had drastic effects on original peoples across the country. Federal Government policy encouraged removal towards centralized settlements; pressed for compulsory schooling, even during the crucial seasons when endogenous education in subsistence pursuits such as trapping and hunting was most important; introduced complicated ad hoc systems of subsidiary payments like family allowances, old-age pensions and welfare; and favoured integration into the wage-labour market economy. Thus, by the 1960s, the nuclear family in relatively permanent settlements became the primary economic unit—and one increasingly dependent on the outside state. The contemporary native economy has not solved the problem of dependency on externally controlled agencies: direct government payments have had to replace productive labour as the main resource for obtaining trade goods, and self-destructive coping mechanisms (such as alcohol) have often marked the pace of cultural decline.

Our discussion ignores higher order political and economic shortcomings of the industrialized state—or even Western capitalism as a whole: foreign economic control by huge corporations, regional disparity, exploitation of the hinterland by the metropole, racism, the absence of long-range planning, and the growing severity of inflation linked with chronic unemployment.

The Boreal Forest

The boreal forest of the Ojibway lands is a mosaic of stands of poor species diversity growing in cycles largely initiated by fire. The most common species is the black spruce (*Picea marjana*) which has long fine fibres that are ideal for paper, can grow in both swampy land and on well-drained soils, but may attain a diameter of only 10 cm after 100 years because of the short growing season. Forest exploitation is controlled by the provincial government, which grants large timber licences to individual companies. Theoretically the nationally important pulp and paper industry has not reached maximal capacity, since the mean annual cut of combined operations does not reach the level of 'sustained yield'. This would be the level of cutting that could (ideally) be maintained in perpetuity, because the calculated increment of growth in all areas, no matter how distant from mills or difficult of access, is still greater than the amount taken in intensive operations in preferred, accessible stands.

Thus, official Ontario economic policy for the north is to stimulate quantitative additions to existing resource-extraction industries like forestry or mining, while ignoring apprehensions of foresters, sylviculturists and conservationists that the supply of wood—or at least the wood that can be cut at reasonable cost—will run out by about 2020. What is so quietly ignored is that the Ontario pulp and paper industry cannot compete with the American in wages, productivity per worker, rate of re-growth, and woodcutting and hauling costs. This means that the effective circles of operation lie close to most mills, even if they are within large licensed tracts; necessary artificial regeneration and husbandry are neglected; and up to a third or more of cut-over land becomes unproductive in terms of preferred species.

Two situations result. In the first, old pulp factories are badly in need of major capital investment; they operate inefficiently, are the single greatest source of water pollution in the nation, and must utilize increasingly distant stretches of virgin forest lying beyond the belt of sylvicultural islands that have resulted from past activities closer at hand. Some mills have closed, effectively killing the one-company towns that depend on them. Others have attempted to pass additional cutting costs to the worker, and one company faced a bitter strike with the deployment of imported 'scab' workers, elaborate security, and the ready co-operation of the police. In the other situation, new plants and new cutting operations are designed for maximal technocratic efficiency. Huge machines that cut, strip, prune and stack tree trunks are used over extensive clear-cut tracts. Capital costs are higher, labour is reduced, and the large denuded areas are much more difficult to regenerate than expensive strip cuts which leave intervening patches of seed stock. These practices are often likened to 'mining' the forests.

A Paper Company in North-western Ontario

In 1961, the Reed Paper Company, a subsidiary of the British multinational, Reed International, bought a pulp mill that had been built in Dryden, Ontario, in 1911. In 1970 it was discovered that the English-Wabigoon River system, downstream from the Dryden plant, was seriously polluted by mercury originating from a chlor-alkali unit installed in 1962 to produce bleach. Some 9,000 kg were released into the river, while another 13,600 kg remain unaccounted for. Commercial fishing, especially important to the economy of the two downstream Indian reserves, Grassy Narrows and Whitedog, was closed; sports fishing was allowed to continue, although the number of tourists going on fishing trips declined and some local guides lost their jobs. Fish meat, now often containing thirty times the World Health Organization's limits for mercury, continued to be a major part of the reserve's diet. Government attempts to deal with the situation have been half-hearted, pointless and fumbling. For example, a freezer was given to one reserve to store uncontaminated fish flown in at some expense from distant lakes. One day the freezer was found warm and the fish spoiled. A ranking provincial cabinet minister accused the natives of politically motivated sabotage. It was soon discovered that a child at play had pulled out the electrical plug.

The two Ojibway communities face social destruction in the form of welfare dependency, unemployment, social apathy, and high rates of homicide, suicide, accidental death, crime, alcoholism, and gasoline-sniffing among the young. There have not been any striking cases of mercury poisoning as were seen in Minamata, Japan, but visiting Japanese specialists were able to diagnose a number of cases with definite early symptoms, such as narrowed visual field and muscular incoordination.

In 1974, the paper company announced plans for a new mill using the last unlicensed stands of commercial timber in a 50,000 km^2 block north of the town of Red Lake. Attempts by the newly formed indigenous 'umbrella' organization for northern Ontario, Grand Council Treaty Number 9, to obtain information about the scheme were fruitless, although the provincial government assured the original people that they would be consulted and their interests respected. Secret government documents that were leaked to the press later showed that this was a sham. Treaty 9 was forced to prepare its own information base for land use, treaty history, forest management, timber inventory, and the expected effects of large development projects. By 1976 the issue had become a public scandal, and a growing anti-paper company coalition of leftists, conservationists, organizations supporting native rights, church groups, labour, and independent research groups became increasingly effective.

A memorandum of understanding was signed by the provincial government and the Reed firm in October 1976 for the construction of a 1,000 tonne/day mill that would use wood from the new forest tract. The tract includes several reserves and independent settlements, and also is hunted or trapped by other Indian communities to the north and east. Most of these communities can only be reached by hydroplane or canoe, although one,

Onsaburgh House, is accessible by the only road into the district. Interestingly enough, the residents of Osnaburgh had been deported from their old scattered lakeside houses when a hydroelectric dam was built; the new centralized settlement on the road is suffering rapid social disintegration with chronic alcoholism as the main symptom. Yet even in Osnaburgh, 41 per cent of the Indians' livelihood is still derived from traditional bush pursuits.

Capricious Economic and Social Planning

Ontario government principles for land-use planning stress that 'public participation is an essential part of the planning process', 'fairness is required when dealing with the people concerned', 'plans should be made for the long term and should provide for future options', and 'the public good must take precedence over the private good'. These have proved to be hollow sentiments as far as Ontario Indians are concerned. The natives of the communities affected by the paper firm's mercury pollution continue to be ignored at the best of times and are the subject of arbitrary decision at others.

Although commercial fishing is banned in contaminated waters, sport angling under the slogan 'fishing for fun' (i.e. angling is allowed, but eating the poisonous catch is discouraged), is still promoted. Indian spokesmen stressed that this made it difficult to dissuade their people, many of whom eat fish daily, from eating the deceptively healthy looking fish. There is general agreement that the English-Wabigoon waters will remain badly polluted for many years. In true bread-line style, healthy fish are provided by the government for immediate consumption yet no systematic programmes have been proposed to replace the economic losses suffered by native commercial fishermen.

The indigenous people were eventually forced to resort to legal manoeuvres against Reed; these lawsuits seem destined to drag on until they falter in the complexities of trying to prove a direct link between metallic mercury discharges and social disintegration—suicide, gasoline-sniffing, anomie—against the skills of sophisticated and well-paid company lawyers. What is most sadly lacking in the government is the simple, honest will to admit that a tragedy has occurred and that redress is a moral necessity. The only recognition that either the government or industry has given to the situation is a curious attentiveness to the possibility of legal liability when negotiating the sale of the Dryden mill to another company in 1979.

An investigation of the possibility of Minamata disease occurring in Grassy Narrows and Whitedog was delegated by the government to a specialist, who eventually prepared an inconclusive preliminary report that skirted the main questions. Yet it earned the specialist a prestigious position in occupational health at the University of Toronto and a position on a provincial government board with important powers to review environmental problems. And, in a most macabre misunderstanding of the point of the whole matter, the government licensed fish that were too poisonous for

Canadian consumption to be exported to countries that had no mercury-contamination standards for foodstuffs.

Some third-order consequences   Planning for the new mill is completely contradictory. A new plant was advocated for somewhere in the area, even though it is admitted that too much reliance is put on extractive primary industry, especially forestry with its spectacularly erratic production cycles. It is still not publicly known whether the eventual guidelines for regional development advocating a mill were developed to fit a purely political decision by powerful elected allies of the paper firm or whether Reed's decision was a genuine response to an objective development decision. Negotiations were secret; leaked government memoranda showed that natives were being misled to believe that there would be consultation before any decisions were made.

The government and company both operated from deficient information bases. A 1967 timber inventory that showed a shortage of wood in the proposed area lay hidden until an independent researcher discovered it in 1979. Neither Reed nor the government undertook forest inventories before the agreement was signed in 1976 and Reed's subsequent, much publicized, environmental assessment (1976) was only a site-selection study that ignored the forest the mill would depend on. The government's reaction to information leaks from its disgruntled civil service was to launch an internal witchhunt, take peevish punitive actions against at least one sincere civil servant, and subject Treaty 9 workers and independent researchers to police interrogation.

Alleged police surveillance of outspoken Indian political leaders across Canada became a major topic of conversation among those involved in fighting for native issues. Even the company's timber inventory, conducted as a condition of the agreement, may not be accurate. One of us spent an evening in an isolated northern pub in August 1977 with exhausted members of the survey crew who complained that the exigencies of time, weather, biting flies, and protracted isolation forced them to make quick, subjective guesses of parameters that required objective measurement.

The marginality of native concerns   Although several thousand Ojibway live in or near the new lease, they were intentionally not consulted. When the natives, through Treaty 9, insisted on making themselves an issue, the company offered not to cut in small 130-km^2 blocks around the three reserves in the lease area. Reed was not aware that not all natives live on reserves and a slim volume available on native people, in its environmental assessment, merely displayed maps of official reservations. A query to Treaty 9 would have established that one important, independent community also existed in the lease.

The final lease boundaries also excluded a small strip in the north and a block on the east that were included in an earlier map. These changes conveniently removed a number of reservations from being within the *geographical* boundaries of the lease, while ignoring the existence of the use areas of these same communities within the lease.

In addition, no studies were made of possible direct effects of cutting operations on wild-rice (*Zizania aquatica*) harvesting, fishing, trapping or hunting. Logging roads would also open lakes to outside anglers and forests to big-game hunters, yet the effects of such competition on the traditional economy were not considered.

The Bogy Man of Wage Labour and Development

The government's northern economic policies are based on a 1977 document, 'Design for Development: Initiatives and Achievements'. Key programmes so far have been communications (roads, airstrips, electrification), administration, law enforcement (courts, gaols, police), and schools. All these provide the infrastructure for the development of the national market economy and European culture as well as the infiltration of state control 'from the south'. There has been no job programme to suit endogenous talents, skills or needs.

The place of natives in provincial forestry policy was first admitted in 1972: 'Many kinds of forestry work are well suited to the employment of relatively unskilled labour of the type found in rural areas and amongst the native population—a labour force that is otherwise wasted.' A study by Reed echoes this view and discusses the residents of Osnaburgh not as a community but rather as data of available man-hours of unemployed, able-bodied males between 15 and 64 years of age.

Thus, in the north, natives remain hewers of wood and crushers of rock. At Osnaburgh, they worked as flagmen, blasters, or operators of jackhammers in road construction, or held hot, dusty jobs as rock sorters in the mill at the nearby Union Minière copper mine.

Racism is also important. Natives are disliked by many employers who claim that they are unreliable, leave without notice, have poor stamina, or just cannot manage in 'white' occupations. It may be true that the impoverished diet of some acculturated natives affects their health. But there is evidence that the indigenous can adapt to a variety of jobs, will take to work unrelated to traditional pursuits (and not just 'analogous' activities such as tour guides and fire wardens), and do not show a high turnover rate. Natives have shown that they prefer jobs that are outside, keep them near their families, and are reasonably steady. Thus they are actually a highly selective labour force with an unorthodox emphasis on nonmaterial employment values.

Statistics show that natives usually are given jobs that last only a few months, that are distant from home and friends where they must live in bunkhouse-style social isolation, or are dirty and noisy. Credentialism—preemployment prejudice based on inflated or artificial educational requirements or restricted professional licenses—also bars natives from jobs. It has been found that, for natives, there is no correlation between job quality and years of schooling, but only between having a high-school diploma (secondary-school certificate) or not having one. The most important positive variables in one study of native employment are the work supervisor and identification with the goals of plans and jobs. This suggests that community control of, or involvement in, job-generating activities is essential, and that natives have not yet been acculturated to the condition of classically alienated labour found in industrial societies.

SOME CONCLUSIONS

Wage labour in the market economy poses a subtly invidious threat to the traditional economy and the social structures around it. It could undermine the traditional value of economic equality and create classes of rich and poor, because it is most often young unmarried men who get jobs. This would concentrate wealth in the hands of those with fewest economic responsibilities who may be least willing or able to use it in socially useful ways. Wage labour also helps to undermine the value of, or esteem for, traditional labour that does not produce disposable income. Thus, industry presentations to administrative tribunals considering major projects in the north (such as oil pipelines) give wild meat a low monetary rating.

If valuation were done properly in comparing the two sides of the dual economy, then it would have to be based on use value—or at least on replacement costs of purchased non-indigenous goods or services. If such comparisons were made, it would be realized that natives in viable traditional communities are not impoverished or unemployed because, having some bush income, they do not need as much employment. Their low labour-participation rates, employment levels, and per capita earned incomes cannot thus be fairly used as additional arguments by the corporations for establishing major projects without first examining the prevailing economic characteristics of the communities.

Where the bush economy is stable and significant, wage labour itself may then become the problem, rather than unemployment. In the long run, it is also possible that economic flexibility will be lost if the dual economy is superseded by the narrowed skills of, and dependence on, jobs. In an area solely dependent on an industry with as wildly fluctuating fortunes as forestry, long-run economic survival may actually depend on the ability to switch back to an earlier vocational skill.

REFERENCES

AUSTRALIAN UNESCO COMMITTEE FOR MAN AND THE BIOSPHERE. *Ecological Effects of Increasing Human Activities on Tropical and Sub-tropical Forest Ecosystems.* Canberra, Government of Australia, 1976.

BERNARD, H. (ed.). *Technology and Social Change.* New York, Macmillan, 1972.

BISHOP, C. *The Northern Ojibway and the Fur Trade: An Historical and Ecological Study.* Toronto, Holt, Reinhart & Winston, 1974.

CANADIAN ASSOCIATION IN SUPPORT OF NATIVE PEOPLES. For Generations Yet Unborn: Ontario Resources North of 50. *Bulletin,* Vol. 18, No. 2, entire issue, 1977.

DE'ATH, C. *The Throwaway People: Social Impact of the Gogol Timber Project, Madang Province.* Monograph 13. Boroko, Papua New Guinea, Institute of Applied Social and Economic Research, 1980.

HARTT, E. *Interim Report and Recommendations.* Toronto, Royal Commission on the Northern Environment, Government of Ontario, 1978.

HUTCHINSON, G.; WALLACE, D. *Grassy Narrows.* Scarborough, Ont., Van Nostrand, Reinhold, 1977.

JALEE, P. *The Pillage of the Third World.* New York, Modern Reader Paperbacks, 1968.

MICHALENKO, G., AND R. SUFFLING. Social Impact Assessment in Northern Ontario: The Reed Paper Controversy. In *India SIA: The Social Impact Assessment of Rapid Resource Development on Native Peoples,* ed. G.C. Geisler, D. Usner, R. Green, and P. West, Monograph 3, 274–89. Ann Arbor, University of Michigan Natural Resources Sociology Research Lab, 1982.

ONTARIO PUBLIC INTEREST RESEARCH GROUP. *Quick Silver and Slow Death: A Study of Mercury Pollution in Northwestern Ontario.* Waterloo, Ont., University of Waterloo, 1976.

ONTARIO PUBLIC INTEREST RESEARCH GROUP. *Reed International: Profile of a Transnational Corporation.* Waterloo, Ont., University of Waterloo, 1977.

PAIJMANS, K. (ed.). *New Guinea Vegetation.* Canberra. Commonwealth Scientific and Industrial Research Organization, Australian National University, 1976.

PAPUA NEW GUINEA OFFICE OF ENVIRONMENT AND CONSERVATION. *Ecological Considerations and Safeguards in the Modern Use of Tropical Pulpwood: Example, The Madang Area, PNG.* Port Moresby, Department of Natural Resources, Government of Papua New Guinea, 1976.

SHKILNYK, A. M. *A Poison Stronger Than Love: The Destruction of an Ojibwa Community.* New Haven, Yale University Press, 1985.

SUFFLING, R.; MICHALENKO, G. The Reed Affair: A Canadian Pulp and Paper Controversy. *J. Biol. Conservation,* Vol. 17, No. 5, 1980.

TROYER, W. *No Safe Place.* Toronto, Clarke, Irwin, 1977.

VAYDA, A. *Peoples and Cultures of the Pacific.* New York, Natural History Press, 1968.

WINSLOW, J. (ed.). *The Melanesian Environment.* Canberra, Australian National University, 1977.

19 The Impact of Development on Foraging Peoples: A World Survey

RICHARD B. LEE

Richard B. Lee (b.1935) received his Ph.D. in anthropology from the University of California at Berkeley and taught at Harvard and Rutgers before moving to the University of Toronto in 1972. He is well known for his ethnographic accounts of the San (Bushmen) of the Kalahari. This selection is a comparative examination of the official development policies of contemporary Alaska, Canada, Australia, Botswana, and South Africa toward traditionally oriented hunting and gathering peoples living within their boundaries. Lee uses a series of case studies to explore the political and economic factors that have shaped the outcome of confrontations between development interests, such as multinational corporations, and native peoples. Clearly, these issues can only be understood within national and international contexts. A traditional ethnographic case study of "culture change" or "acculturation" at the band or village level will not adequately deal with the variables that must be considered. Lee also shows how anthropologists have sometimes played an active role in facilitating the political response of the natives, and he cautions that it may be impossible for fieldworkers to remain politically unaligned.

Lee's paper was written in 1981 and presented at the Annual Meeting of the American Association for the Advancement of Science held in Washington, D.C., in January 1982. It is an overview of conditions at that time; it is important to remember that specific situations are changing constantly. For example, natives in Alaska are now seeking major changes in the conditions of their land settlement because of serious problems that have emerged. (Thomas R. Berger describes this situation in detail in his 1985 book, *Village Journal*.)

This is a survey of land rights and political struggles among former hunting and gathering peoples of the world. A good deal of my data and information comes from two world conferences on hunting and gathering peoples, one in Paris in June 1978 and the other in Quebec City in September 1980. We brought together a lot of information from anthropologists working in different parts of the world, and out of this came an informal network of sources.

I'll start out by asking a question. What do the hunting and gathering peoples in widely separated parts of the world have in common? Two things,

Paper presented at the Annual Meeting of the American Association for the Advancement of Science, Washington, D.C., January 1982. Reproduced by permission of the author.

I would argue, one quite obvious and the other not so obvious. The obvious point is that hunting and gathering peoples are band societies, à la Julian Steward, with similar organization, similar kinds of group structure, similar modes of conflict resolution and sharing patterns; and these similarities cannot be due to common historical origins, because we're talking about people as widely separated as the Inuit and !Kung; and they cannot be due to similar habitat or adaptation to similar environment, because one lives in the Arctic and the other in the subtropical desert. So we are left with the conclusion that these similarities are due to the common possession of a way of life, the hunting and gathering way of life.

The second and less obvious thing that hunter-gatherers have in common is multinational corporations. The hunting-gathering peoples of the world occupy the last great resource frontiers of the world. Minerals, oil, gas, and so on, have already been found in all the easily accessible places, and now the inaccessible places are the locales of the last great scramble on the planet. What the !Kung and the Inuit, for example, have in common is that there is major mineral prospecting going on today in both the Arctic and the Kalahari Desert.

This situation is, for better or for worse, going to continue in the future. It is incontestably true that the future of the hunting-gathering peoples is more closely bound up with the behaviour of the multinationals than it is with the behaviour of the seal or the antelope population, or with the availability of mongongo nuts or witchetty grubs.

So the question I want to address is, How do hunting and gathering peoples in very widely separated parts of the world adapt? Do they give way? Do they resist? How does the challenge of having to negotiate with the multinationals or with governments that have the multinationals' interests at heart affect their organization?

I see a wide range of responses. Some hunting and gathering societies have developed strong political organization and have fought for and won massive cash settlements in exchange for their mineral rights; the Alaska and James Bay settlements are examples. At the other pole are people for whom political mobilization has not yet taken place and who have actually lost their land base. Some of the Ge-speaking peoples in the interior of Brazil fall into this category.

The factors at work in determining the outcome of specific struggles are complex. To start out, there are three parties to any agreement. First of all, there is the incoming party, usually a large mineral prospecting company, such as Dome Petroleum in the Beaufort Sea, Falconbridge Nickel in Namibia, or the big uranium explorers in Arnhemland, Australia. The second actor is the government that mediates between the claims of the business interests and the claims of the native people. The position of this government can range from no sympathy whatsoever for native rights to what may be, for various complex political reasons, actually quite a principled stand in favor of native rights. Third is the native peoples themselves and their organizations. You would think that this is the area we know most about; I think it's the area we know least about. I'm intrigued by the concatenation of factors responsible for the fact that some native groups crystallize strong political organization and others never mobilize. Successful groups look to two kinds of human resources. First, they draw on their own cultural, political, and organizational resources, reaching into their roots to see what sources of cohesion they can find. Second, they rely on outside help from two groups: the members of their own community who have gone off and gotten a higher education and sympathetic outsiders—anthropologists, lawyers, and others—who are willing to take up their cause.

Of these three actors, the most consistent and predictable is the first one, the multinationals. They seem to have a rather uniform modus operandi, their goals are clear, their methods are pretty clear, and they don't stray from their goals. Much more variation seems to appear in the responses of the national governments and the native peoples.

Let us look now at the case studies.

ALASKA

Let us look first at the situation in Alaska. In 1971 the native Inuit people of the North Slope were able to get a $962 million, 40-million-acre settlement from the government of the United States over the 40-year lifetime of the agreement. This massive cash settlement was in some way a victory, but it was by no means an unalloyed victory. There is more than one way to destroy a hunting and gathering society, and killing them with kindness, it turns out, is one quite good strategy. The native people got their billion, and the oil companies, for their part, will probably get $15 billion or so by the time the field is played out. So even though the price tag to settle the native land claims looked rather large in the early 1970s, I think most insiders realized that the native people didn't get that great a deal, and in fact the oil companies did quite nicely for themselves.

There has been less follow-up on what happens to native organizations that become million-dollar corporations, which is what the 224 native communities have become. We know that there is a big demand for Inuit business school graduates on the North Slope; we also know that many of the corporations are struggling financially and organizationally. I get the sense that the Alaskan native revenues are underwriting a lot of development projects in Alaska, not necessarily for the benefit of the natives themselves.

Despite the problems, this has not been an overall disaster for native people, because out of even a small proportion of the revenues, they have financed a good deal of infrastructural development in schools, sewage systems, housing, roads—and this is where some of the money has been put to use. The Alaska settlement therefore can be seen as one prototype of the kind of settlements that can be made.

When we move on to Canada, we find a different range of possibilities. I want to look very briefly at James Bay, the Dene in the Northwest Territories, and the Yukon.

JAMES BAY

In James Bay the 1976 settlement between the government of Quebec on the one hand and the Cree and the Inuit on the other, is a sort of mini–North Slope type of settlement. The price tag was nowhere near a billion, but it was in the range of $150 million, again over the lifetime of the agreement. One of the interesting innovations in the James Bay settlement was that a good deal of work was done by anthropologists, and continues to be done in ecological anthropology, concerning the level of wild resource harvesting that the natives had a right to maintain. Here the native people did not sell their hunting and fishing rights or their way of life. They are entitled to harvest resources at a certain level annually, with different species specified in the agreement; if they are unable to harvest at that level, then they receive compensation. Furthermore, only when the natives have taken up to their level are the sport hunters and fishermen allowed in.

This kind of agreement obviously sets up pretty complex problems for regulatory agencies, and, as is the case in the North Slope, a tremendous bureaucratization of native organizations ensues. In James Bay the band councils are pretty much full-time bureaucrats monitoring the different sections of the agreement, on water levels, game levels, geese levels, ptarmigan levels, and so on. So what you see in the James Bay is a massive cash settlement, funding development projects, with the additional factor of some built-in mechanism that enables the traditional economy to continue to play a role in the future life of the people.

DENE

The Dene of the Northwest Territories are interesting because they have not yet struck a deal: they are still in the process of negotiation, and they have basically taken the position that their way of life is not for sale. This sort of strategy has the government and the multinationals flummoxed. They ask, "What's the price tag? Surely there's a price tag here—is it $150 million, $200 million? Name your figure." And the Dene respond, "We don't have a price tag—you can't put a price tag on a way of life." The Dene are trying, so far successfully, to block development until their land claims are settled. If the land claims are settled in their favour, the multinationals face the possibility that they may never get the pipeline. The Dene could say, "Thank you, we now have the land, and we decided we don't want the pipeline."

There's an interesting dynamic in the James Bay and Dene cases between the roles of a negotiating government on one side, the sophisticated native leaders on the other side, and anthropologists and other advisers in the middle. The input of anthropologists, such as the McGill University people in the case of the Cree and Michael Asch and others from the University of Alberta in the case of the Dene, has been very useful to the native cause. It is one of the things I can be most proud of as a Canadian anthropologist. Canadian anthropologists have pioneered some of these new relationships with the native people. But there are dangers. One of the dangers in James Bay is that the whole process will become so sophisticated that when you put a dollar value on the ptarmigan, on the geese, on the ducks, and so on, the end result will be a group of bureaucrats negotiating, not to *sell out* a way of life, but to rationalize it and make it cost efficient beyond recognition. How this process will end up, I'm not sure, but it deserves more careful study than it has received.

So far the Dene have taken another strategy: they are not buying the price tag argument and they are sticking with the land claims case. Now let's look at the Yukon, since there is an important connection between the two areas.

The Yukon Indians were caught in a squeeze between the Canadian government and the oil companies, and the consequence of this squeeze is the Alaska Highway pipeline. After the report of Justice Thomas Berger came down recommending a ten-year moratorium on the Mackenzie Valley pipeline, the Dene got a reprieve, but the government of Canada rushed through the equivalent inquiry in the Yukon with lightning speed. The Lissik Commission did its work in the Yukon in about 90 days, and the result was a glowing recommendation to build the Alaska pipeline. Under this kind of timetable the Yukon Indians didn't have a chance, so the Canadian government evidently learned a valuable lesson from the Mackenzie experience, namely, don't let the natives get organized. If you give the native people access to the media and time to mobilize support in their own communities and in the south, you're going to have a very tough fight on your hands. The Lissik Commission took those lessons in hand in the Yukon and rushed through the report and the recommendation. One of the main anthropologists attached to the Lissik Commission resigned in disgust when he saw what was happening. In November 1981 the Yukon Indians went to Washington and testified before a congressional committee, urging the rejection of the Yukon pipeline route on the grounds that their land claims weren't settled. The congressional committee responded to this deputation by passing the pipeline proposal by a vote of 14–1.

There is a valuable lesson to be learned from the Dene case. The Dene represent, to my mind, the most successful example of native mobilization not only of their own people but of public opinion. Scholars and scientists who want to support native claims should study the Dene case with care. For example, there was a catalyst in the form of idealistic students in a government-sponsored program called the Company of Young Canadians who went up north around 1969 to 1971. They went into native communities and talked to the generation of young native men and women who are now the leaders of the Dene. It's almost a textbook case that native groups elsewhere in the world can use as a model in how effectively to challenge steamroller operations on the part of governments and corporations.

AUSTRALIA

Australia has many similarities to Canada. In the early 1970s a Labour party government was elected that was very sympathetic to native land claims. During the rather short tenure of the Gough-Whitlam government, the aboriginal people of Australia made real advances in the recognition of their claims and in the willingness of the government to build aboriginal rights into the law. Then, with the falling from power of the Whitlam government in 1975, the old Liberal-Country party coalition came back in. But when they tried to turn the clock back, they found that various forces in southern Australia had been mobilized to such an extent that they couldn't go back to square one. In fact well over a half of the Whitlam era gains are still on the books in Australia today, and there's been a very big, exciting movement on land claims, which has had a considerable degree of success.

An interesting aspect of the Australian situation is the outstation movement. Starting in the 1950s and early 1960s the government tried to move the Australian aborigines into large, agglomerated settlements where government services could reach them. By 1966 there were few Australian aboriginal groups living independently, and almost all of them were agglomerated into settlements of from 300 to 1000 people. These rural slums were a stressful environment for nomadic people who are used to moving frequently and to resolving conflicts by fission. In the early 1970s some aborigines began to move back to the bush, in some cases occupying abandoned cattle stations. The first response of the government was quite unsympathetic: steps were taken to get them back. But in the Whitlam era the policy changed. The administrators reasoned, "They're out there, this is where they want to be, and they're actually getting 50 percent of their grub from the land. They're not on welfare, they don't cost us as much."

A certain logic was recognized to this movement, and then, happily, the outstation movement became part of government policy. The government actually went out and provisioned the camps, delivered the mail, and provided services, such as a circuit public health nurse who would come every month to the camps. There was even an attempt to get tutors or teachers out to the camps. Family allowance and old-age pension cheques were delivered for certain categories of people. The experiment was successful and it continues to the present day.

I should add that very similar patterns are found in several parts of Canada, where, for example, Cree families get flown out to their trap lines and are serviced by ski-plane throughout the winter. It's more than worth the price of the aviation fuel to service them on the trap line, compared with the cost of having the same group of 15 living on welfare in the Mistassini all winter. So this has been a very interesting and successful experiment both in Australia *and* in Canada.

Where things have not been so successful is in the areas in Australia where real economic interests, mainly mining, have existed. In the Alligator River region of the Northern Territory, four huge open-pit uranium mines are in production or are coming on stream before 1985, with devastating ecological and cultural effects. The four mines are Nabarlek, Ranger, Koongarra, and Jabiluka. The native people mobilized widespread support in their tribal councils, the Australian labour movement, the media, the universities, and the Institute of Aboriginal Studies. They got everybody mobilized and put up a terrific campaign, and they didn't win a thing. Every time they've gone to court on the uranium claims, they've been met with a stone wall. The lesson to be learned here is, if a mining interest group is powerful enough, there isn't a great deal that native people can do to stop them.

And, if we look more closely at the outstation movement and the land claims that have been settled, we find a rather interesting negative correlation: the outstation movement has thrived in direct proportion to the degree that the cattle and sheep industries have gone downhill. From 1900 to 1950 there was a boom in central and northern Australia, with white ranchers in the interior opening up cattle and sheep stations and hiring aboriginal labour for the stations. Then such factors as structural changes in the world livestock economy, the replacement of wool by artificial fibres, the rising cost of beef production, the introduction of feedlots, and other changes in the industries made these remote stations no longer viable. When they were abandoned some of the aborigines moved into them and occupied them as outstations. So in fact the outstation movement comes at a time when capital is itself withdrawing from the interior of Australia. This conjunction highlights the importance of looking at the outcome of the struggle as a combination of factors, both native and outside.

AFRICA—BOTSWANA

Let's go on now to look at two African examples. Here we shift our ground quite drastically, moving away from the familiar situation found in Canada, Australia, and the United States: advanced capitalist societies with very high levels of accumulation of wealth, very large tax bases, a tradition of large-scale government intervention in people's lives, and highly mobilized press and electronic media. When these variables are in place it is often expedient for governments and multinational corporations to arrive at settlements with native peoples rather than to have them camped on Capitol Hill, dynamiting pipelines, and so on.

But what happens when the country is poor and the media are limited? Botswana is an independent African country, a member of the United Nations, and a front-line supporter of South African liberation movements against the apartheid regime of that country. Economically, Botswana is also heavily dependent on South Africa. In Botswana there is a *Bantu-speaking* majority constituting about 95 percent of the population and a minority of Khoisan speakers of !Kung and /Gwi and other small groups of San or Bushman people.

Here there are interesting contradictions. On the one hand, Botswana would like to be a liberal democracy, with native policies, native reserves, land claims, and so on. On the other hand, they are a front-line state fighting one of the world's most powerful and racist regimes. This puts them in a dilemma, because the San citizens of Botswana objectively hold the same position in Botswana society that native people hold in North American society, namely, second-class citizens, economically and educationally disadvantaged. However, it is difficult for the Botswana state to acknowledge this because they rightfully say that *they* are indigenous people themselves, not settlers. And so here is the dilemma. Botswana has adopted a policy, one might say, of "benign neglect." Botswana does not ignore the claims of San people, but neither does it give them the kind of protection under law that the native people of Canada or Australia are getting.

In 1975, at the urging of anthropologists, such as members of the Kalahari People's Fund, the government of Botswana actually put into their budget a development fund for Basarwa development, Basarwa being the term by which San are known in Botswana. This little fund totals about $250,000 a year, for a clinic here, a school there, and some scholarships elsewhere. The Basarwa Development Fund has done a modest job of at least keeping the people of Botswana aware that they have disadvantaged citizens. The Botswana government has gotten around the racial aspect of this policy by calling their office of development the "Remote Area Dwellers' Office." Technically, anybody who is a cattleless person living in a remote area is entitled to this support. There is some dispute about whether 95 or 99 percent of the people in the remote area category are Basarwa, but it is a large percentage. This seems to be a good system.

Now, as long as the San are in remote areas, far from water supplies, far from the roads, they're fairly safe. But a very rapid development of capitalist ranching by wealthy and influential Batswana is occurring now in Botswana. It isn't multinationals that are threatening in this case but cabinet ministers, wealthy Batswana, chiefs, chiefs' relatives, and other successful members of the budding bourgeoisie. Where do they look for the 20,000-acre tracts of such land? They look not to the heavily overgrazed areas under tribal land tenure but rather to the interior of Botswana, the central Kalahari game reserve, the Dobe area, and other areas in western Botswana, places largely occupied by these remote area dwellers. These areas are completely uneconomical if traditional techniques of getting water are employed, but very economical if modern boreholes are used to reach deep water. Currently, entrepreneurs are moving drilling rigs hundreds of miles into the Kalahari desert, drilling for water and finding it. If they strike water, under Botswana law they may then apply for a 99-year lease to the area. And a 99-year lease that can be sold effectively amounts to freehold tenure.

In this rapidly evolving situation the anthropologists are once again playing an unusual role at the centre of things. A special committee has been formed from a number of ministries to oversee the welfare of the remote area dwellers, and this special committee has done a lot of very good research on San social organization and land tenure. It has also attempted to be an advocate within the government for the land rights of these people. But the committee's main opponent, the main group that is interested in getting that land for ranching, is composed of the very cabinet ministers who are the superiors of these middle-level civil servants. At the moment it's a standoff. The land rights of the remote area dwellers are still being upheld because the land can be gazetted, that is, set aside for the use of the remote area dwellers until the latter are themselves able to apply for a lease to dig a borehole.

On balance and in spite of the conflicts I would say that, given its limited resources, the Republic of Botswana deserves praise for their humane policy vis-à-vis the hunting and gathering people under their rule.

NAMIBIA

The situation in Namibia is entirely different. Namibia is a South African colony, totally dominated by South Africa. Even though the fate of Namibia is being discussed at this very moment in the United Nations and in capitals of Africa and the world, the situation inside Namibia is very grim. In Bushmanland it's particularly grim.

It is not a question of the San being killed by the South African army, but what's happening there almost amounts to the same thing. The South African army has recruited hundreds of !Kung men into the defense forces, forming two battalions, one based in Caprivi, the other at Chum!kwe. In addition the South African Defense Force has turned the tiny Bushman reserve into a little kingdom of its own, and the lives of the !Kung there, about 4000 of them, are almost totally controlled by the military. According to recent observers the social situation in Bushmanland is deteriorating rapidly, with anomie and constant internal bickering and drunkenness. Since the military took over, the homicide rate has tripled as !Kung men armed with new weapons and a new macho image kill and wound each other in Saturday night brawls. There is a split in the administration between the civilians who want to turn Bushmanland into a game park, and the military, who want to turn it into a development area with the people becoming ranchers under military tutelage.

In the fate of the !Kung San under military rule we see some of the worst aspects of the experience of the Montagnards in Vietnam in the period

1960–75. The Montagnards, you will recall, were the tribal people in the highlands of Laos and Vietnam who were recruited by the CIA and the Green Berets in the late 1950s and early 1960s to fight against the ethnically distinct lowland Vietnamese. This is exactly what the South African army is trying to do in Namibia.

Despite the grimness of the situation there does seem to be some cause for optimism. The best hope for the Namibian San is probably a victory by the South West African People's Organization (SWAPO). In my opinion SWAPO has earned the right to rule in Namibia; they are staunchly nonracial and nonethnic, and they have Namibian nationalism as the cornerstone of their policy rather than the sectarian interest of one ethnic group or another. The key difference between the situation in Namibia and that in such countries as Uganda or Chad or Zaire is that in Namibia the SWAPO militants undergo a very rigorous training in Marxism-Leninism. They are systematically trained to see the struggle in class terms rather than in ethnic or racial terms. SWAPO emphasizes that what has to be destroyed is a system, not an individual or a person. For these reasons I think that for the !Kung a SWAPO government could be the best possible outcome. Some people have asked me, "Don't you think that since the !Kung supported the South Africans, they would be victimized by SWAPO once SWAPO came to power?" I reply that this is exactly the argument the South Africans have used to convince the !Kung to stay with them. The South African military commander has been quoted as saying, "If we go, the Bushmen go with us." But the argument is fallacious. I've talked in great detail to SWAPO leaders, and I am convinced that there is no basis for this fear. As they point out, the Bushmen are not the only people who are fighting on the South African side; every major ethnic group has a regiment that is part of the South African army. This is a class issue, not an ethnic one, and I am confident that when SWAPO comes to power, the San will be very reasonably treated by them. It's only through victory by SWAPO that they will be able to have their own cultural survival ensured.

As a contrast, let us look at the fate of the Indo-Chinese Montagnards. Right now there are about 60,000 Mnong Montagnards living in the states of Washington, Montana, and Minnesota and in parts of Canada. The CIA said, "If we go, the Montagnards go with us," and in fact when they went, about 60,000 Mnong came with them to the United States. Would you call that a happy ending to a story of a former tribal people?

A very similar situation, incidentally, is now unfolding in the Philippines, where, according to recent reports by anthropologists, Agta hunter-gatherers are being actively recruited by the New People's Army *and* by Marcos' security forces.

In closing I would like to point out that one of the themes that comes through this case material again and again is that anthropologists and other social scientists have a role to play. There was some talk ten years ago to the effect that societies were changing so rapidly and traditional cultures were disappearing so quickly that the job of the anthropologist was likely to become an antiquarian one. Anthropologists would peruse old field notes and documents and describe what was, but they would not have a role for the future. Happily, we've seen that this is not the case and that some of the most interesting work that anthropologists are doing is aiding native peoples in their struggle toward self-determination. I think that this has given our old discipline a new lease on life. But in order to pursue this work, we have to be very clear about our goals, and we have to be perhaps more politically aware and politically sophisticated than we've been in the past.

20   Third World Colonial Expansion: Indonesia, Disguised Invasion of Indigenous Nations

BERNARD NIETSCHMANN

Bernard Nietschmann is a professor of geography at the University of California at Berkeley. For his doctoral work at the University of Wisconsin he conducted an extensive field study of the subsistence ecology of the Miskito Indians of Nicaragua in 1968–69 and 1971. He continued his contacts with the Miskito after the Sandinista victory, becoming an outspoken advocate of Miskito autonomy and a critic of both Sandinista and United States policy. In this selection he applies his very unconventional approach to an analysis of Indonesian development policy in West Papua, which Indonesia claims as Irian Jaya. In Nietschmann's terminology the Fourth World is composed of individual indigenous "nations," or tribal peoples, sharing a common culture and territory. The Third World consists of so-called developing nation-states that are actually artificial composite states seeking development by invading the territories of Fourth World indigenous nations. Here again we see that tribal development and change are really political issues. Under Dutch rule the tribal nations of West Papua largely retained their independence.

Reprinted from Bernard Nietschmann, "Indonesia, Bangladesh: Disguised Invasion of Indigenous Nations," *Fourth World Journal* 1, no. 2 (1985): 89–126. Copyright © 1985 Center for World Indigenous Studies, P.O. Box 911, Snoqualmie, Washington. Reproduced in abridged form by permission of the author and publisher.

Now their territory is being invaded by the armed forces of a foreign political power, and rapid "development" is taking place. Nietschmann's original article included a parallel discussion of the invasion of the Chittagong Hill tribal areas by Bangladesh. This type of analysis could be applied equally well to many other tribal "development" situations throughout the world, and it often reflects quite accurately the perceptions of the native political organizations that are confronting the invading states.

Third World colonialism has replaced European colonialism as the principal global force that tries to subjugate indigenous peoples and their ancient nations. European colonial empires became powerful through the forced incorporation of distant peoples and territories. Wars of independence and national liberation and post–World War II decolonization created today's Third World countries largely on the artificial outlines of the vanquished colonial empires.

Invasion and occupation of indigenous nations once done by foreign white expansionist powers are now done by foreign brown expansionist powers. The majority of these artificial Third World states can only be maintained by the invasion and physical incorporation of lands and resources of hundreds of indigenous nations. What is called "economic development" is the annexation at gun point of other peoples' economies. What is called "nation-building" is actually state expansion by *nation-destroying*. Territorial consolidation, national integration, the imperatives of population growth, and economic are phrases used by Third World states to cover up the killing of indigenous nations and peoples.

The capture and control of geography, not the extension of politics or economic philosophy is the objective of the Third World invasions. Most Fourth World indigenous nations have maintained the quality of lands, waters and resources while Third World states have not. Systems that do work are being destroyed to prolong systems that don't work. Over one-half of the world's conflicts are being fought over Fourth World geography, not East-West politics, or North-South economics.

DEVELOPMENT BY INVASION

The development and modernization of Third World states is heavily dependent upon the invasion and annexation of Fourth World nations. Duplicating the experience of First and Second world states, exported European socialism and capitalism have both failed to sustainably develop the internal resources within Third World territories. Unable to limit fast-growing populations, unwilling to reform elite-dominated land ownership, and incapable of dramatically increasing food production with more *"green revolutions,"* many Third World governments promote development by invasion. "New" lands and resources are freshly invaded lands and appropriated resources.

The ex-colonial Third World is doing to the indigenous Fourth World what First and Second world states did to it.

Most of the world's largest countries are expansionist and use "nationalized" populations—backed by an army and programs of forced allegiance—to occupy and annex indigenous territory and to claim Fourth World resources. All of the 10 most populous countries are waging expansionist cold and hot wars against indigenous nations. Much of this violence against indigenous nations is hidden by common agreement among states to alter the terminology of conflict: Aggressive conflict between states is called war; a nation's defense against aggression by a state is called *terrorism*; and the aggressive invasion and occupation of a nation by a state is called *development*.

Development by invasion is done by all of the most populous states that together lay claim to 63 percent of the world's peoples and 43 percent of the land area. However, in many of these states, sovereignty and allegiance are only obtained by the use of state army and security forces against nations of peoples (ironically called citizens by the states) who seek to maintain their own distinct and sovereign identities, governments and territories.

An Indonesian Fatherland

Indonesia is a post-World War II state imposed over the artificial outlines of the Dutch East Indies colonial empire (see figures 1 and 2). Spread across a 3000-mile arc of 13,700 islands and at least 300 distinct nations and peoples, the government and army are controlled by Javanese, a people from but one island and one nation. Java has almost 100 million people, some 80 percent of whom live in rural areas where one-third of the land is controlled by only one percent of the land owners. These conditions place further pressure on the agriculture-based peasantry whose population density reaches 5000 people for each square mile in some areas. With Java's population growing at the rate of two million per year and with similar growth rates on the adjacent island-nations of Bali and Madura, the Jakarta-based Javanese government has instituted a state policy of expansion to redirect the backup of the ruling population and to consolidate Javanese control beyond the island of Java.

Aided by the slogan "Unity Through Diversity," Java has moved to expand its domination over unconsenting nations by military invasion and occupation, deployment of Javanese settlers, and compulsory "Javanization" programs to change religion, nationality, language, and allegiance. This has and is being done, for example, in the South Moluccas (invaded in 1950), West Papua (invaded 1962), and East Timor (invaded 1975). Another aspect of Javanese territorial consolidation of huge portions of insular Southeast Asia and Melanesia, is the declaration of an Indonesian *land-and-water fatherland* (*tanah air*) united by the state doctrine of *wawasan nusantara*, Java's concept of an "archipelagic state." This means that Java-controlled Indonesia asserts authority over a vast expanse of ocean waters by claiming 200-mile exclusive zones around each of the more than

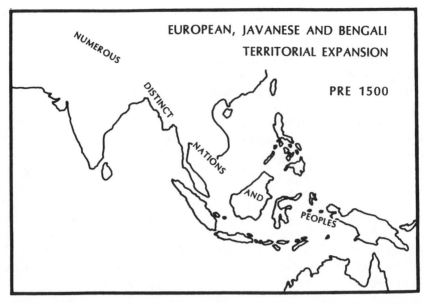

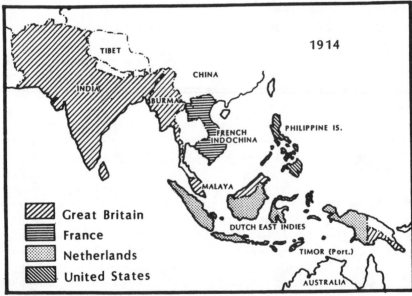

FIGURE 1

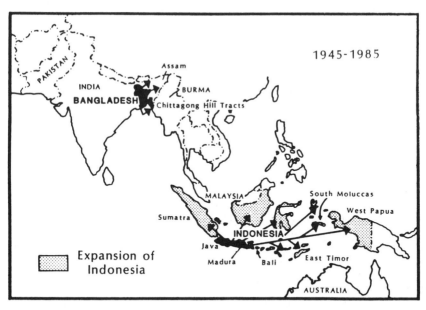

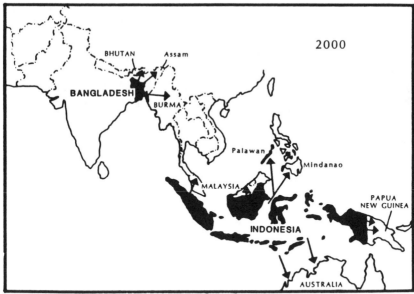

FIGURE 2

13,000 islands within Indonesia's colonial boundaries. These extensions of Jakarta's territorial land and water claims mean that Indonesia has become the world's seventh-largest state in area, potentially sealing off international access to island straits and sea lanes. These commercially and strategically important sea lanes connect the Pacific and Indian oceans and the Asian mainland and Australia. Furthermore, Java's archipelagic "fatherland" is a military-backed geopolitical net that has been cast over hundreds of distinct nations and peoples. Jakarta effectively strips these nations of their own self-determination, land and sea territories and resources, and freedom. The backup and overflow of Java is resulting in the destruction of multitudes of nations, peoples and environments.

Java's population problems and geopolitical aspirations have resulted in a campaign of military-assisted movements of millions of people, island-hopping, and island takeovers, and environmental damage on a geographical scale verging on the 1941–1945 War of the Pacific.

One Country, One People: New Guinea

Comprised of many nations of Papuan peoples, New Guinea, the world's second largest island, has more internal commonality and political consensus than any part of it has with any past or present colonial powers that have asserted control over this natural geopolitical country: Britain, the Netherlands, Germany, Australia, Japan, and Indonesia. One half of the island achieved independence from its colonizer, Australia, in 1975, and became Papua New Guinea, an emerging important power in the Pacific and in Melanesia. Instead of self-determination and independence, the western half of the island was invaded and annexed by expansionist Java as Indonesia's easternmost province.

Papuan people are Melanesian, not Indonesian. Melanesian is a term of identity of free choice; Indonesian is a word that delimits an area and peoples held together by force. The people of West Papua are different in all respects from their rulers from Java: Language, religions, identity, histories, systems of land ownership and resource use, cultures and allegiance. For more than 23 years, the Javanese have tried to take West Papua by force and to incorporate it and its peoples into Indonesia. And the Papuan peoples have continued to resist the takeover and instead wish either to be free to create their own autonomous state or to merge with Papua New Guinea.

The Javanese occupation of West Papua has no legitimacy. Java and West Papua are separated by 2300 miles of ocean waters and numerous island nations. The Dutch ruled the two colonies with separate administrations, similar to the former British colonies of Jamaica and Trinidad, each of which became an independent state in 1962. To acquire West Papua, the Javanese promoted a sham, claiming that half of New Guinea was a "natural" geographic part of "greater Indonesia," and they launched political and military campaigns to secure their bogus claim.

After the Dutch military forces were driven from Java in December,

1949, the Javanese set their sights on claiming all island nations of what once had been the Dutch East Indies. For 12 years the taking of West Papua was a matter of "national pride" for the Javanese. They promised to liberate the Papuans by invading and driving out the Dutch. In 1962 they attacked with a paratroop force at Aru Bay. The Dutch took the problem to the United Nations.

A special UN commission headed by Elsworth Bunker, a ranking member of the Kennedy Administration in the United States, considered the Netherland's complaints and then urged the turnover of West Papua to Indonesia. It was obvious at the time that the decision to turn a blind eye to Indonesia's blatant disregard for the UN Charter was a choice made to enhance U.S. foreign policy interests. Indonesia was a U.S. ally and an important part of Washington's plan for the containment of communism in Southeast Asia. (Elsworth Bunker's UN sanctioned plan to force West Papua into the arms of Indonesia was confirmed in The New York Plan of 1962. It was an agreement similar to Sir Cyril Radcliff's 1947 Radcliff Award which gave the Chittagong Hill Tracts to Pakistan.) Indonesia was to govern West Papua as a trust territory until an election could be held to determine the political future of the Papuan peoples. From 1962 to 1969, Papuan resistance to the Indonesian occupation was widespread.

By 1969, Indonesia felt that it had enough military control over West Papua to hold a phony "Act of Free Choice" (*Pe Pe Ra*, Determination of the People's Opinion). Widely referred to as the Act of No Choice by the West Papuans, only 1,025 (of 800,000 total population) people were allowed to vote on the destiny of their country: Independence or union with Indonesia. Indonesian military units and generals determined the outcome of the vote. Indonesian army Major Soewondo threatened those who were to vote by telling them:

> I am drawing the line frankly and clearly. I say I will protect and guarantee the safety of everyone who is for Indonesia. I will shoot dead anyone who is against us—and all his followers. (TAPOL, 1984:31)

And Brigadier-General Ali Murtopo warned Papuan representatives that Indonesia,

> as the strongest military power in Southeast Asia, is able to strike fear into any country. If we want to be independent, he said, . . . we had better ask God if He could find us an island in the Pacific where we could emigrate. . . .

> . . . General Murtopo impressed upon us that 115 million Indonesians had fought for West Irian for years. They had made many sacrifices in this struggle, and they would not therefore allow their national aspirations to be crossed by a handful of Papuans. Short shrift would be made of those who voted against Indonesia. Their accursed tongues would be torn out, their full mouths would be

wrenched open. Upon them would fall the vengeance of the Indonesian people, among them General Murtopo who would himself shoot the people on the spot. (*TAPOL*, 1984:31–32)

With a gun to her head, West Papua was annexed to Indonesia. In 1969, Indonesian President Suharto declared that West Papua was a province of Indonesia to be called West Irian. In 1973 the province was renamed Irian Jaya and the Papuans were renamed Irianese. A new mythical people—the Irianese—were to be created instantly with this declaration from Jakarta, a people whose identity, allegiance, land and resources were to be given to Java and to Java's self-inflated image of empire and destiny. Use of the word Papuan was forbidden and punishable by imprisonment; use of the geographical name West Papua was also forbidden and censored from radio and all publications. To make Papuans and West Papua Indonesian, the Jakarta central government began programs to obliterate the people and to annihilate their place.

With an area of 160,032 square miles, West Papua has a size larger than Japan or Poland and almost as large as Iraq or Sweden. Its Papuan population of 1,000,000 is larger than one fourth of the states recognized by the United Nations including Gambia, Fiji, Guyana and Cyprus. If West Papua were to join the 3.5 million people of Papuan New Guinea—a goal of many among the West Papuan resistance forces, "One Country, One People"— then the indigenous peoples of New Guinea would have a population larger than almost half of the established states. And, a combined Papuan territory would have an area larger than any Central American or European country.

TRANSMIGRATION: ANNEXATION BY OCCUPATION

An area coveted by expansionist desires and even placed on a *thirty pieces of silver platter* by opportunistic Western countries wishing to establish good relations with new Third World powers, must nevertheless be occupied and subjugated. The strategy used by most Third World states relies on the mass transfer of a civilian population loyal or at least dependent upon the central government, backed by a large and ruthless military force, with almost all expenses lobbied for by transnationals and provided by international development agencies.

Indonesia's Disguised Invasion of West Papua

When Java replaced the Netherlands as the colonial power that claimed sovereignty over 300 Fourth World Nations on 13,700 islands over a 3,000-mile-extent, the expansion of political, military, and economic control was made the top priority. In 1950, President Sukarno said that *migration* to the outer islands was "a matter of life and death for the Indonesian nation." Java's expansionist designs were to extend by moving Javanese settlers and military units, island to island, and to disguise these invasions as the *redis-*

tribution of overpopulation within the confines of a mythical Indonesian state. The invasions are financed by international aid, amounting to some $600,000,000 provided by the World Bank, World Food Program, European Economic Community, Asian Development Bank, Islamic Development Bank, Federal Republic of Germany, France, Netherlands, the United States, and the United Nations Development Program. (Survival International, Bulletin: March 2, 1985)

Transmigration—the resettlement of people loyal to a central government—is the main tactic for "smokeless wars" of invasion and occupation by Third World states against Fourth World Nations and peoples. Java's war on the peoples it claims as Indonesian civilians is called *transmigrasi* (Transmigration). It represents the world's largest invasion force. The 1984–1989 Five Year Plan called for the movement of 5,000,000 people from Java, Madura and Bali specifically to those areas that resist Java's imposed sovereignty: Sumatra, Kalimantan, Sulawesi, South Moluccas, East Timor, and West Papua. Over the next 20 years, some 65,000,000 more people will be moved to Javanize Fourth World territories claimed by Indonesia.

Java no longer gives overpopulation as the principal reason behind transmigration. Centralized political and economic goals—not humanitar-

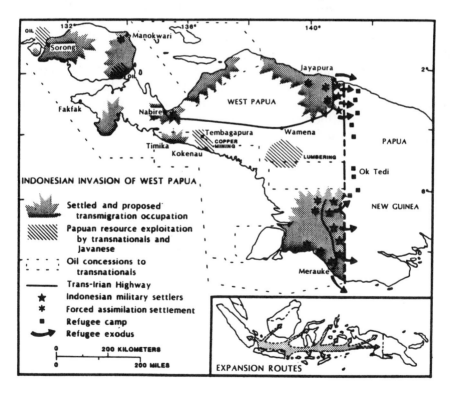

FIGURE 3

ian ones—are the justifications. The Jakarta government lists seven goals for its transmigration program: To promote national unity, national security, an equal distribution of the population, national development, the preservation of nature, help to the farming classes, and *improvement of the condition of local peoples*. (Survival International, Bulletin: March 2, 1985)

What transmigration has actually accomplished is very different: The spread of poverty, forced displacement of indigenous peoples from their homes, communities and lands; deforestation and soil damage at the rate of some 200,000 hectares per year (to total 3,600,000 deforested hectares by 1989); destruction of local governments, economies, means of sustainable resource use; forced assimilation programs; widespread use of military force to "pacify" areas and to break local resistance by bombing and massacres of civilians.

It costs about $9000.00 to move a family from Java and to establish it on 2.5 to 5 hectares of expropriated land in a distant island. People who are forcibly displaced to make room for the transmigrants are not paid for their land; Indonesia asserts that transmigration is a national priority and that national needs for land replace any local ownership: "The rights of traditional-law communities may not be allowed to stand in the way of the establishment of Transmigration settlements" (Basic Forestry Act: Clarification Act 2823, 1967, Clause 17).

Indonesia cannot itself afford to move 65 million people at the present-day cost of $9000 per family. Funds for that will be sought from international sources. The purchase of land would drive the amount far beyond the $10 billion that Java needs to extend its control over non-Javanese islands, nations and peoples. Internationally financed invasions disguised as national priorities and domestic resettlement is the way poor Third World states acquire land and resources.

West Papua is one of the main areas targeted for annexation and incorporation by the military-backed transmigration program. West Papua's abundant forest and mineral resources and offshore oil potential makes it even more attractive for development by invasion. To physically secure West Papua and to transfer control of the area from Papuans to Javanese, Jakarta has imposed a seven-part strategy:

1. Territorial Occupation. Displacement of Papuans by Javanese, Maduran and Balinese settlers that will number 1,000,000 by 1989, and up to 10,000,000 by the year 2000.

2. Relocation of Papuans into Assimilation Camps. The Javanese use two primary types of relocation camps to erase Papuan identity (ethnocide): *Translocal* settlements where Papuans are brought to live with Javanese settlers at ratios of 1:3 to 1:5 in order to "civilize" them with Moslem religion, Bahasa Indonesian language, and Javanese culture and community life; and *Centers for Social Development* where Papuans are brought to remove them from supporting the Papuan resistance forces and to indoctrinate them. The

centers are called PPMs and have the same purpose as "strategic hamlets" widely used during the war between Vietnam and the United States, "model villages" used by the Guatemalan government on Mayan Indians and "relocation camps" used by the Nicaraguan government to control Indians from the Miskito, Sumo and Rama nations.

3. Indoctrination. Within the *translocal*, and community development camps, and surviving Papuan villages, Javanese government people carry out a program of *Pascasila Indoctrination*, to replace Papuan and Melanesian identity and nationality with Indonesian. Called *P4 indoctrination*, its goals "to cultivate national pride, self-respect and broaden people's horizons so as to create a consciousness of being [part of] a nation, part of the Indonesian state, and to defend the state. (*TAPOL*, 1984:10)

4. Territorial Management. Throughout Indonesia the Javanese rely on a doctrine of "territorial management" (*Pembinaan territorial wilayah*) for "national defense." It is based on the belief that the Indonesian army will face warfare of "internal" and "external" guerrilla forces, not conventional armies. Therefore, the army must organize all the peoples within the claimed Indonesian state into "total people's defense" (*hankamrata*) by "management" of each society down to the smallest units. "Territorial Management" is a major part of Java's strategy to occupy West Papua and to use the Indonesian army to reduce opposition from "citizens" claimed by Indonesia.

5. Counterinsurgency. The Papuan defense force is called the OPM (*Organisasi Papua Merdeka*) or Free Papua Movement which has been fighting the Indonesian invasion for almost 25 years. The goal of the Pemka and Vitoria branches of the OPM is to resist the Indonesian invasion as long as it is necessary until world opinion or future allies pressure a withdrawal. OPM's views are encapsulated in its slogan, "One people, one soul." Jakarta does not recognize the OPM as a legitimate guerrilla force, instead calling it the GPK (security disruptor gangs), or GPL (wild terrorist gangs). Jakarta uses the weight of its army—the largest in Southeast Asia—to break the OPM resistance by isolating the Papuan people in either PPM or *translocal* camps, by burning down villages, creation of fear by carrying out arbitrary arrests, beatings, torture, and murders. Indonesian army units make frequent sweeps through villages to arrest and burn. (*TAPOL*, 1984:10)

6. Military Settler Units. An important component in Jakarta's strategy to defend the occupied territory against Papuan guerrillas ("Territorial Management"), and to seal off the West Papua-Papua New Guinea border to deny the OPM sanctuary and access to supplies is the use of military settler units (*transmigrasi saptamarga*) numbering some 90,000 in compounds along the Jayapura-Merauke Trans-Irian Highway which is under construction. Made up of former army personnel and their families, these units—unlike regular army—are permanent settlements that will eventually comprise a "Java Curtain" between Papuan peoples.

7. Prohibition of Free Access and total Denial of Violations. To hide the widespread human rights violations, and genocidal assault on Papuan culture and community life, Indonesia has closed off almost all of West Papua to journalists, and human rights organizations. At the same time, the Indonesian government and army deny the existence of the 25-year-old war, the state of siege against the Papuan people, and the killing of up to 200,000 Papuans. Instead, Jakarta says the armed resistance is being done by "terrorists," who are "separatists" and whose aim it is to "disrupt regional stability" and "development process;" and that Papuan rejection of Javanese assimilation is due to their "backwardness," and "simplistic way of thinking."

Java is waging a war against the Papuan people in order to take over Papuan land and resources for the Javanese, all in the name of a mythical Indonesia, whose state motto is "Unity Through Diversity," but should be "Submit to Java."

The most comprehensive statement on Java's plans for West Papua are contained in a document issued in April, 1984 by Brigadier-General Meliala Sembiring, military commander of the occupying Indonesian army in West Papua.

> The basic strategy for restoring security in Irian Jaya [West Papua] is concentrated on separating the people from GPK ["Security Disruptor Gangs"], inculcating a spirit of non-cooperation/resistance among the people towards the GPK, localizing the security-disruptors, striking out at those disruptors who persist, and consolidating and rehabilitating the region.
>
> The smiling policy implemented by the 17th/Cendrawasih Division before the middle of 1982 was the first step in our efforts to detach the people from the influences of the GPK separatist idea, and this policy must be further developed by means of more basic management. Territorial smiling reflects a territorial attitude guided by the eight duties of the Armed Forces. Territorial smiling means acting with human feelings and outlooks, honest openness and friendship from the [army] apparatus towards the people in its area. This can in practice be done by face-to-face encounters, house-visits, especially in the more remote regions, and other such family activities.
>
> The next step which is now needed is to separate the people from the GPK, mentally and physically, by setting up Centers for Social Development [Pusat Pengembangan Masyarakat], or PPMs, that is to say, setting up settlement locations especially in the more remote regions, taking account of local customs, religious beliefs, life-styles, historical background, inter-tribal relations, and the aspirations of the local community. A program to raise living standards and improve social and economic conditions is a powerful magnet to attract the people in the vicinity to settle in the PPM locations so as to detach them from the influences of the GPK separatists. (TAPOL, 1984:10)

With respect to the Papuan refugees who have fled Indonesia's "smiling policy," PPMs, and territorial management, Sembiring says "we shall generously and open-heartedly welcome back the border crossers as Indonesian citizens if they consciously return to the fold of the Motherland." (*TAPOL*, 1984:10)

Approximately 13,000 to 15,000 Papuan refugees have crossed into Papua New Guinea to seek safety from Indonesian violence. The refugees are living in 16 isolated camps, in terrible conditions, with very limited assistance, most coming from the League of Red Cross Societies. Papua New Guinea's fear of Indonesia has prevented it from meeting internationally recognized standards for the treatment and protection of refugees, and that fear has for the time being silenced the PNG government in Port Moresby from internationally condemning what is happening to Papuan peoples on the other side of the invisible barrier.

Indonesia denies that there are refugees, instead referring to them as "illegal border crossers." Indonesian offers for repatriation have been rebuffed by the refugees who fear reprisals if they were to return. Jakarta is pressuring Papua New Guinea's government to force repatriation in order to close the biggest leak in the "Java Curtain."

STATES CLAIM INNOCENCE AND DENY VIOLENT INTENT

It is commonplace that states refute evidence of their invasion and takeover of Fourth World nations by asserting a sovereign right over "domestic territory;" by claiming that their armies are but dealing with "law and order problems," "terrorists," "separatists," "backward tribalism," or "rebels;" or by outright denials of any wrongdoing, territorial or human rights violations. Because most states claim sovereignty over many nations, and small states fear big states, most states look the other way and do not see state armed and settler forces that have invaded and now occupy Fourth World nations and peoples. Equivalent to the Hans Christian Andersen fairy tale, "The Emperor's New Clothes," where the Emperor's claims were empty but nevertheless were imposed, a new fairy tale of emptiness is being told, "The Emperor's New Claims."

Speaking before the UN Working Group on Indigenous Populations in response to a statement given by the OPM West Papuan delegation, Indonesian representative, Mr. Juwana, rejected all accusations:

The accusation that the objective of transmigration is either to overwhelm the unique identity which exists in Irian Jaya or to "smother local resistance" is preposterous. The objective of Indonesia's transmigration programme, which is a national endeavour already in existence for many years, is to expand development efforts and to evenly spread its benefits to the regions outside of the already overpopulated areas in order to achieve nationally balanced economic progress. The purpose is to utilize the surplus agricultural manpower available to develop land resources in the outer islands. It is aimed at improving the standard of living of the community in general, by increasing regional development and by assisting the people on the outer islands that demonstrate a relative lag in development.

The worthy aims of the transmigration policy are recognized, both nationally and internationally. Assistance for this programme is not only received from friendly countries but also from such international institutions as the World Bank, which recently approved a substantial loan. The implementation of the transmigration programme is not yet perfect. There are many problems left to iron out and many unforeseen difficulties to attend to. But these are almost entirely concerning the agricultural aspects of the project and obstacles to cultural understanding have never been the main hurdles to overcome. As in any country we have experienced difficulties in harmoniously fusing peoples with different backgrounds and different languages. . . .

I must add that allegations of more than 200,000 Irianese deaths during military occupation, bombings, indiscriminate shooting, imprisonment torture, etc. are completely absurd and untrue. . . . (Juwana, 1985)

Melanesia and Indonesia

Consider that there are two major forces in collision worldwide: the expansion of states and the defending nations. Indonesia and Melanesia—two large geographic areas of islands—represent these counterposed forces of political incorporation by invasion, and political liberation by self-determination. Indonesia is a new colonial state built on Javanese expansion by armies and settlers against the peoples of Sumatra, Kalimantan, South Moluccas, East Timor, and West Papua. Melanesia is an equally large area that has an emerging geopolitical identity based on independence from colonial occupation. Indonesia is an archipelago of different nations united by force; Melanesia is an archipelago of similar peoples united by choice.

Independence from colonial rule is spreading throughout Melanesia: Fiji (1970), Papua New Guinea (1975), Solomon Islands (1978), Vanuatu (1980), and Kanaki (New Caledonia claimed by France) will achieve independence in the near future. That leaves the Torres Strait Islands (claimed by Australia), and West Papua, South Molucca and East Timor (claimed by Indonesia).

Melanesia has a very strong internal affinity based on identity and a growing consensus against non-Melanesian control by occupation. Vanuatu is in the forefront of the pan-Melanesian movement. In an address to the United Nations General Assembly (October 11, 1984), Vanuatu Foreign Minister Sela Molisa stated:

We regret that there is some justification to the Israeli and South African complaint that the international community is very selective in its denunciations. It pains us deeply that there is indeed a grain of truth to this argument. How else can we explain the condemnations

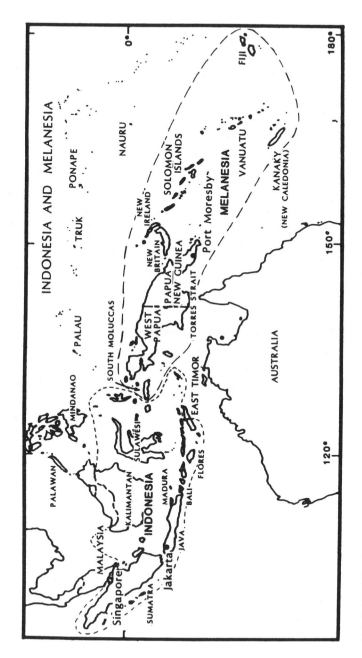

FIGURE 4

of the annexation of Jerusalem and the Golan Heights, but silence on the annexation of East Timor? How else can we explain the condemnations of *apartheid* but the silence on the plight of the Melanesian people of West Papua?

How else can we explain the appeals to sever economic ties with South Africa while a South African company participates in the exploitation of West Papua's oil resources? How else can we explain the concern over Israeli and South African military expansionism, and the indifference to the military expansionism in our region which has already seen West Papua and East Timor swallowed, if not digested, and which now provokes, and threatens the sovereignty and territorial integrity of our good neighbor, Papua New Guinea?

Our region is known for its calm and serene atmosphere. The countries of the South Pacific are populated by peace loving people of diverse ethnic and cultural backgrounds. However, our similar colonial histories have instilled in us all a strong aversion to external interference and foreign rule. On this we are in total accord.

Unfortunately, the international community has not yet taken note of this. Thus, while our support is given as a matter of principle in the struggle against *apartheid*, little is known of our own struggle against the same practices in our own region. (Molisa, October 11, 1984)

FOUR CHOICES INSTEAD OF THREE

The three worlds of capitalism, communism and poverty are not the only choices for the more than three thousand nations that are confronted by political, military and economic expansion. A fourth choice establishes a geopolitical firebreak between aggressive, expanding states. Enduring nations are anchored in their geography, they do not expand beyond the extent of their people or beyond their need.

REFERENCES

"Banking on Disaster: Indonesia's Transmigration Programme." *The Ecologist* 16, no. 2/3 (1986).

May, R. J., ed. *Between Two Nations: The Indonesia-Papuan New Guinea Border and West Papua Nationalism*. Bathurst, N.S.W., Australia: Robert Brown and Associates, 1986.

Mitton, Robert. *The Lost World of Irian Jaya*. Oxford: Oxford University Press, 1985.

The New York Times, January 16, 1986.

Osborne, Robin. *Indonesia's Secret War: The Guerrilla Struggle in Irian Jaya*. North Sydney, Australia: Allen & Unwin, 1985.

Otten, Mariel. *Transmigrasi: Indonesian Resettlement Policy, 1965–1985*. IWGIA Document 57. Copenhagen: International Work Group for Indigenous Affairs, 1986.

"Planned Relocation of the Papuan Population," *TAPOL Bulletin*, No. 66, November, 1984.

"Statement by the Honorable Sela Molisa, Minister for Foreign Affairs and External Trade of the Republic of Vanuatu." Thirty-Ninth Session of the UN General Assembly, New York, October 11, 1984.

"Statement by Mr. Juwana, Observer of the Republic of Indonesia to the Fourth Session of the Working Group on Indigenous Populations of the Sub-Commission on Prevention of Discrimination and Protection of Minorities," United Nations, Geneva, August 1, 1985.

West Papua: The Obliteration of a People. TAPOL, London (1984).

"West Papua: Transmigration: The Invasion of Tribal Lands." Urgent Action Bulletin, Survival International. London (March 2, 1985).

VI

Development, Tribal Society, and Health

Beyond the major disruption and the shock of the initial contact and loss of independence, the further impact of development on tribal society and health is complex and often occurs gradually. Development does indeed disturb previously effective cultural systems, often in a sudden and traumatic way, and drastic long-range adverse effects are to be expected. The most obvious detrimental impacts are caused by a weakening of the subsistence base due to resource depletion and/or breakdowns in the social organization of subsistence activities. Pressures on natural resources may increase immediately as outsiders begin to compete for them or as tribal peoples themselves begin to harvest for the market. The territorial base may be drastically reduced as official policy restricts tribal access to make tribal resources directly available to outsiders. Natural resources may be further stressed by increases in tribal population following the disruption of prior demographic balances and the introduction of modern medical practices.

Increasing population, rising per capita demand for resources, and decreasing territory can cause rapid resource depletion that accelerates even more rapidly as key resources begin to disappear altogether. As subsistence resources decline, tribal people are less well nourished and become vulnerable to many diseases that may have been absent or insignificant in the past. The health effects of subsistence decline may be accelerated by increasing social inequality both internally and in relation to the national society. Under independent tribal conditions adverse subsistence fortunes were shared equally, but in the modern context a few families or individuals may do well while their fellows suffer. Furthermore, some individuals may have easy access to market goods and medical assistance while others will be unable to generate an adequate cash income.

209

One might fairly ask, Why the emphasis on adverse impacts? What about the positive results of development? Justification for this negative emphasis is twofold. In the first place it is to counter the popular wisdom that development improves people's lives. These case studies demonstrate that this is only partially true; development also does enormous, often unforeseen, damage. Secondly, it reflects a concern for total communities in contrast to the common emphasis of development planners on the benefits that will accrue to individuals. It is true that specific individuals may profit a great deal from development, and they may strongly favor it. However, benefits at the community level are much more difficult to find, or promised benefits are measured by culturally irrelevant standards. In the final analysis few development changes are unalloyed benefits, and benefits should in any event be defined by the communities that experience them.

The following selections present case studies from three parts of the world: arctic Alaska (Reinhard), the upper Amazon region of Ecuador (Kroeger and Barbira-Freedman), and highland New Guinea (Grossman). As medical researchers, Reinhard and Kroeger are primarily concerned with the health aspects of development changes on regional populations. Grossman offers an anthropological view of the social consequences of development on a specific native community.

21 Resource Exploitation and the Health of Western Arctic Man

K.R. REINHARD

Karl R. Reinhard (b.1916) holds a Doctor of Veterinary Medicine degree and a Ph.D. in bacteriology from Cornell University. From 1954 to 1960 he was chief of the Infectious Disease Program of the Arctic Health Research Center of the U.S. Public Health Service. Reinhard carried out laboratory-based field studies of infectious diseases among native peoples in Alaska. In the 1970s he served as a consultant to the Norton Sound Health Corporation in Nome, Alaska. From 1969 to 1979 he worked for the Indian Health Service. Reinhard has published extensively on the ecology and epidemiology of disease among arctic and American Indian populations. This selection concisely documents how successive waves of development frontiers in Alaska beginning before 1800 drastically undermined the traditional resource base of the native peoples, causing socioeconomic deprivation and impoverishment that increased disease and social pathology. The fur trade, the exploitation of marine mammals, the establishment of commercial salmon fisheries, and the gold rush all contributed to a peak of "severe disadvantage" to the native Alaskan support system by 1900. The situation since the oil boom of the 1970s is much more complicated, but native control over the subsistence base remains a critical concern and a factor in the physical health and social well-being of native peoples.

I first ventured into the Arctic about 22 years ago, to study the natural history of infectious diseases. At the outset, I held the common belief that the native people of the Arctic, in their prehistoric state, had no serious health problems and that major disease problems were primarily the result of contamination caused by Euro-American adventurers and immigrants. The target was completely susceptible, and the imported microorganisms were irresistible.

Before long this stereotype faded. We found very little clinical poliomyelitis in the native Alaskan population at a time when it was epidemic among urban non-natives. Serological studies revealed the common pre-existence of naturally acquired immunity in the native people of western central and northern Alaska. Entero-viruses were recovered repeatedly from native populations with no clinical evidence of infection. Acute otitis media could be aborted and recurrent or chronic otitis prevented if prompt medical treat-

Reprinted from *Circumpolar Health: Proceedings of the Third International Symposium, Yellowknife, Northwest Territories*, ed. Roy J. Shephard and S. Itoh, 617–27, by permission of University of Toronto Press. Copyright © 1976 University of Toronto Press.

ment was provided. Measles no longer occurred in total-community epidemic form, but were maintained endemically. The epidemiology of tuberculosis suggested not population hypersusceptibility, but rather inadequate health services with widespread undetected and untreated "open" cases. This was confirmed when a few years of intensive casefinding, hospitalization, and ambulatory chemotherapy and chemoprophylaxis drastically reduced the prevalence of this disease. The spectrum of diseases experienced by arctic populations is generally no different from that of temperate zone populations. Why, then, has so much disease been present for so many years? And how had the great problems been generated? This is not merely a "Host vs Parasite" issue; other environmental factors have been at work.

The aboriginal people of the Arctic were originally highly adapted groups, making the most of an area of relatively low biological productivity. Populations were, of necessity, small and diffuse, limited by the ecology. The large and concentrated populations existing in the Arctic today subsist on the resources of more southerly areas. In the aboriginal state, famine was an ever-present threat, precipitated by unusual weather or changes in animal migration. If resources were overutilized, renewal was slow. As a consequence, a nomadic or semi-nomadic mode of existence was developed.

Early explorers describe nosebleeds, "scrofulous" skin diseases and boils, dysentery, neurological disorders, a high infant mortality, snowblindness and other ophthalmias, pulmonary diseases, lousiness, and injuries among arctic natives. Several accounts describe pulmonary disorders that could have been tuberculosis; for example, Zagoskin mentions "consumption" among Kuskokwim people who had had little contact with the outside world. Most observers agreed that the arctic people were relatively healthy in their aboriginal state, although subject to early senility. The greatest dangers to individual and public welfare were untoward natural events, and if there were great epidemics before the advent of the Euro-American, we have no record of them.

In the past 20 years, ecological and sociological concepts have infiltrated epidemiology, and it has become clear that social and economic deprivation and depressed or poor health are directly related. How do such concepts relate to the health status of native Alaskans? How can social and economic deprivation become established among a hunting and gathering society? The answer is simple: if natural resources are depleted, and are not replaced by adequate alternative resources, then the people are deprived of subsistence just like a person without cash or credit in an industrialized society. When Euro-American commerce and industry extended to Alaska, to appropriate renewable and nonrenewable resources, it entered into direct competition with the native people.

THE FUR TRADE

While native commerce had been based on local exchange, Euro-American activities involved exploitation and removal of resources for the benefit of distant shareholders and consumers. Unregulated exploitation of the Aleutian Islands by Russian adventurers brought not only despoilment of resources, but also the massacre of native people who resisted the adventurers. Under the Russian-American Company, homicidal activities were reduced, but the land from the Yukon to the southeast archipelago was denuded of its rich fur resources. Often, the native people participated, either by impressment or out of desire for trade items.

The US-sanctioned monopoly which succeeded the Russian-American Company appeared no better in its treatment of indigenous people. Skins were bought with script, which could be spent only at the company store, at its prices, and early treatment of the fur seal resources was an ecological disaster. It is a miracle that the fur-seal rookeries were able to become re-established and that the sea otter did not become extinct.

As a result of exploitative commerce, the arctic Americans were deprived of primary sources of the traditional clothing needed for protection against their rigorous environment. The excessive kill also depleted food sources and the native people began to substitute commercial articles such as textiles, guns, steel knives, axes, and metal cookware for home-made clothing, utensils, tools, and weapons. Skills needed to make the traditional items faded and the people became dependent upon commerce for the necessities of life. However, there is no evidence that the depletion of fur resources, per se, caused increased death and disability among the Alaskan population.

WHALE, WALRUS, AND SEAL

The major portion of the aboriginal population lived in the maritime regions. In western and southern Alaska, fish and marine mammals were important to the support of human life. North of Norton Sound, marine mammals were more important than fish, while in the Bering Sea Islands and along the Arctic coast, whales, walruses, and seals provided most of the subsistence. Land mammals were also available, but were utilized much less along the coast than in the interior.

In the first part of the nineteenth century, the whaling industry reached the North Pacific. Whalers derived from the large San Francisco fleet moved into the Bering Sea and Arctic Ocean, taking large harvests until the last two decades. Then, low catches, decreasing demand, and multiple shipwrecks caused a rapid decline of the industry. The last commercial whaling effort in the American Arctic took place about 50 years ago.

Catches in the nineteenth century greatly exceeded the levels of sustained yield. In addition to whales, many thousands of walrus were taken for ivory and oil. Depletion was so drastic that nearly 100 years after the peak activity of the whaling industry, none of the affected animal populations has fully recovered. As with the fur trade, native people were motivated to hunt beyond their subsistence needs, obtaining baleen and ivory to trade against store items that had become part of their life-style. The advent of the repeating rifle and bomb lance further aggravated the wastefulness of hunting. Table 1 indicates the rise and eventual fall of the whale-walrus harvest.

Within a couple of decades of the advent of intense commercial whale and walrus hunting in the Bering Sea, Chukchi Sea, and Arctic Ocean, the maritime native population of those areas declined substantially, stimulating concerned comment from members of Arctic expeditions. A massive famine killed at least half the people of St. Lawrence Island and depopulated three of four communities in 1879–80.

In recent years there has been a resurgence of walrus populations and some recovery of the whale population, but the future size and use of these resources remain to be seen. Meanwhile, welfare programs have helped the people eat, albeit a "flour and sugar" diet of limited nutritive value.

TABLE 1
Whale and Walrus Products, 1874–91

Year	Oil (bbl)*	Bone (lb)	Ivory (lb)**
1874	10,000	86,000	7,000
1875	16,300	157,800	2,540
1876	2,800	8,800	7,000
1877	13,900	139,600	74,000
1878	9,000	73,300	30,000
1879	17,400	127,000	32,900
1880	23,200	339,000	15,300
1881	21,800	354,500	15,400
1882	21,100	316,600	17,800
1883	12,300	160,200	23,100
1884	20,373	295,700	5,421
1885	24,884	451,038	6,564
1886	37,200	304,500	2,850
1887	31,714	564,802	875
1888	15,774	303,587	1,550
1889	12,834	231,981	1,506
1890	14,890	231,232	4,150
1891	12,228	186,250	1,000

Source: From Report of Govt. of Alaska 1892.

  * Petrof estimates that the average yield of oil per whale was 40 bbl.

** Petrof estimates that the average yield of ivory per walrus was 5 lb. He estimated further that 7 out of 10 walruses hunted in the open sea were lost after being shot.

SALMON

The salmon fisheries of northwestern United States and western Canada were sufficient to supply world demand in the mid-1800s. However, when those fisheries were depleted, the industry moved north into Alaska (Table 2). Some rivers were completely depleted of salmon by dams or cross-nets. Fish-traps decimated runs of salmon headed into rivers for spawning. Canneries competed for control of the catch and often bought more than could be canned or salted.

T A B L E 2
Salmon Pack, 1883–1908

Year	Canned (cases)*	Salted (bbl)
1883	36,000	
1884	45,000	
1885	75,000	
1886	120,700	
1887	190,200	
1888	439,273	
1889	703,963	
1890	671,000	6,390
1891	688,332	7,300
1892	789,294	9,000
1893		
1894	646,345	21,000
1895	675,041	32,011
1896	619,379	5,502
1897	949,645	10,000
1898	909,538	17,388
1899	1,000,000	15,000
1900	1,098,000	24,922
1901	1,529,569	30,000
1902	2,690,000	
1903	2,400,000	
1904	1,910,000	
1905	1,131,312	
1906	1,500,000	
1907	2,146,000	
1908	2,000,000	

Source: Excerpted from Reports of the Governor of Alaska.

* A case consisted of 48 one-pound cans.

Until the establishment of salmon canneries, the maritime natives had taken the brunt of resource deprivation, but with the rise of commercial salmon fishing, the river peoples also suffered a severe setback. Their subsistence had never been as secure as that of the coastal people, for they had to depend upon seasonal runs of fish and relatively inefficient (but conservatory) means of catching them. Large land mammals were an unreliable additional resource, since their migration routes shifted from one year to another. Each family had to catch, dry, and cache a number of tons of fish during the runs.

IMMIGRATION

At the end of the nineteenth century, the Gold Rush brought a flood of Europeans, Euro-Americans, and Orientals, seeking a quick fortune in the great river valleys and some coastal areas. Immigration doubled or tripled the population competing for natural resources, and caused severe inflation. The native people had little buying power to compete for commercial items they had come to depend upon; Indian communities which had experienced fishing failures could not afford flour, sugar, blankets, or ammunition at the inflated prices. The traditional resources of the native people remain greatly depleted, with no hope for early renewal, and they have not been made partners in the new economy to the extent that they can be self-supporting; in recent years only welfare programs have enabled most of the rural native people to survive.

CHANGES IN WAYS OF LIVING

While their environment was suffering drastic change caused by exploitation, the way of living was also changed in a more subtle fashion by the pressures of the dominant Euro-American "culture." The drift towards commercial procurement of food, hunting equipment, and household articles was discussed above. Many of the items available from the trading post were labour-saving, but not all were well adapted to arctic life. Foods were high in calories but low in essential proteins, vitamins, and other essential nutrients, and high in price. Repeating arms ammunition increased the monetary cost of food gathering and caused decimation of animal populations. Alcoholic liquors blighted the lives of a substantial portion of the native population, both physically and psychologically.

The establishment of fixed trading posts, church missions, post offices, and schools gradually brought an end to the semi-nomadic life. The copying of housing from the dominant culture slowly terminated the use of housing made from local materials. Poverty then determined that families would live most of the year in crowded, poorly ventilated, one-room cabins or shacks, which were hard to keep in repair. The low-grade, permanent housing was inferior, sanitationally, to that of the semi-nomadic life, for temporary shelters were open to the cleansing effects of the natural elements between times of use. Native Alaskan communities became rural slums, with ill-nourished people living in crowded quarters, without adequate sanitation or protection from accumulating pollution and rigorous elements. Concentration of the population greatly aggravated the problems of hunting and gathering and fostered high rates of communicable diseases such as tuberculosis.

Many people of Euro-American extraction respected and loved the Alaskan native people and worked towards their betterment—admittedly, not always with the right methods, but certainly with the right motivation. But over-all, the intruding society was incredibly arrogant and intolerant of the "ways of the savages." The government took a custodial stand. Euro-American society disparaged the native life-style and held up the "way we do it in the States." Some early military ventures were for tactical reconnoitering—to gauge the potential resistance of the native houses to small arms or cannon fire. Among the missionaries, too many purveyed damnation, Euro-American mores, and a pietistic philosophy rather than the Gospel of Grace. Traders robbed, cheated, and intimidated the natives. Such treatment by a dominant culture inevitably degrades the self-image of an overwhelmed people. Is there any wonder that mental health problems are serious among Alaskan natives, and that the current, tardy release of the native people from intellectual and cultural tyranny brings with it overreaction and militancy?

HEALTH AFTER EURO-AMERICAN CONTACT

Devastating epidemics were introduced by seafarers and immigrants, including outbreaks of smallpox, measles, dysentery, influenza and other respiratory diseases, gonorrhoea, and syphilis. As the population gained experience of these diseases, and vaccination was introduced, mortality decreased. But lethal epidemics contributed strongly to the decline of the native population in the western American Arctic during the nineteenth century. Figure 1 shows the fluctuations caused by these factors and those cited earlier.

By the latter half of the nineteenth century, tuberculosis had become hyperendemic—or perhaps epidemic—among the native population. The disease did not sweep the country dramatically, like smallpox or influenza, nor did it decimate villages in weeks like measles. But by the late 1800s, it existed throughout the territory and took a constant, heavy toll of life. As recently as 1960 one could see many households that comprised re-knitted fragments of families broken up by deaths from tuberculosis. The entrenchment and emergence of tuberculosis as the principal infectious cause of mortality correlates well in time with the increasing disjointment of the native economy and way of life.

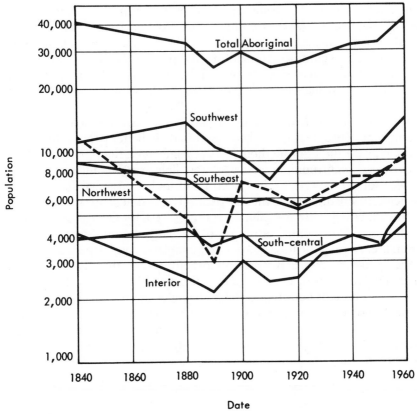

FIGURE 1
Regional growth of aboriginal populations of Alaska, 1840–1960

Source: From *Alaska's Population and Economy*, by George W. Rogers and Richard A. Cooley (University of Alaska, Economic Series, Publication No. 1, Volume 1, 1963).

THE CURRENT SITUATION

The current patho-ecological status of the Alaskan native people is little different from that of disadvantaged people in more southerly climes. Communities have first decreased in number and then grown in size. The initiation of midwifery and immunization programs some 30 years ago greatly reduced foetal wastage and infant and childhood mortality. For many years, the native population has been increasing at a rate about four times the US national average (Figure 2). An aggressive control program has greatly reduced the morbidity and mortality rate from tuberculosis. Current health problems include iron deficiency anaemia, diarrhoeal disease, otitis media, "common colds," enterovirus infections, bronchitis and pneumonia, and, above all, psycho-social problems and accidents. To these we should add an

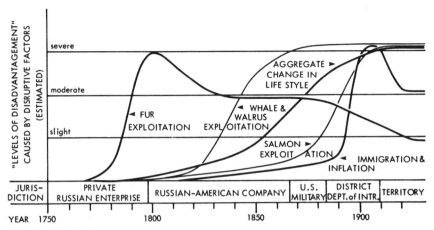

FIGURE 2
Estimate of effects of disruptive ecologic events on the health and security of
Alaskan natives. (The curve for immigration and inflation increases again greatly
in 1940–45 and after 1950.)

indefinable amount of malnutrition. A bourgeoning population is beset with
health issues that cause disability rather than death. The disabling diseases
aggravate social and economic problems, while needs continue to out-dis-
tance efforts to provide services.

THE ROAD TO IMPROVEMENT
Efforts to improve the health of the native people started after the close of
World War II. Medical services were expanded greatly, both for hospitalization and ambulatory care. Recently, regional health corporations have
given the native people themselves a voice in health policy.

Notwithstanding these desirable efforts, it is unlikely that Alaskan native
people will enjoy a health status equivalent to that of the general population
until economic and social disadvantages are corrected.

EPILOGUE
At this period in history, knowing the ecological and sociological aftermath
of unbridled commercial and industrial exploitation, we are not entitled to
point an accusing finger at the exploiters of centuries past who thought they
were dipping into inexhaustible resources. Today a multitude of people
foresee, at least partly, the ecological results of commercial and industrial
exploitation, yet the latter continues with ever greater avariciousness. Even
now a new commercial exploitation of a non-renewable resource is under

way in Alaska, and it is difficult to predict what this will mean eventually to the Arctic environment and the health of its population. The settlement of the Alaskan native claims brings with it more imponderables. Can the new land holdings become bases for the development of local industrial economies capable of ending deprivation among Alaskan native people, or are they merely the beginning of another kind of disadvantaged living "out on the reservation"?

SUMMARY

The high prevalence of disease among residents of the western Arctic, starting in the first half of the nineteenth century and extending through the first half of the twentieth century, appears to have been caused primarily by external, commercial exploitation of the resources necessary for subsistence of the indigenous people. This has been complicated by incomplete industrialization of the native economy, increasing urbanization, great surges of immigration, and economic inflation. The net results have been a defacto pauperization of most of the indigenous population and degradation of their life-style, producing greatly increased morbidity and mortality with social depression. Current health problems among the indigenous racial stocks of Alaska are now similar to those prevalent among the disadvantaged people of more densely populated temperate zones. Increased medical service activity has substantially reduced morbidity and mortality, but health problems remain more severe among Alaskan natives than among the non-native population. Socio-economic disadvantagement seems a prime cause of the continuing problems; therefore, the attainment of good general health depends on the establishment of social parity and a sound economic base of support.

22

Cultural Change and Health: The Case of South American Rainforest Indians

AXEL KROEGER

FRANÇOISE BARBIRA-FREEDMAN

The complex impact of economic development in a tribal territory is well illustrated in this ecological and epidemiological study of the Shuar Indians of eastern Ecuador. The Shuar, popularly known as the Jibaro headhunters, were traditionally manioc-growing, shifting, slash-and-burn cultivators and hunters, living in small, widely dispersed settlements in the rain forest–covered eastern foothills of the Andes. Kroeger and Barbira-Freedman show in concise detail how the recent development of Shuar territory set off a series of cultural and environmental changes that depleted the natural resources, undermined the subsistence base, increased disease, and disrupted the social system. Although these changes were obviously detrimental, the increase in Shuar population density gave them some political power, and they successfully formed a political federation. Ultimately, they were able to retain some of their land, and they turned to cattle raising to help maintain themselves within the cash economy; their long-term prospects, however, are uncertain. Like Reinhard, Kroeger and Barbira-Freedman argue that for tribal peoples public health depends on the maintenance of socioeconomic well-being; it is not merely a medical technology problem. Development disrupts previously established, self-maintaining socioeconomic systems and does not easily replace them.

Recent research conducted among rainforest Indian minorities in Venezuela (25, 29) suggests that in those minorities, the sectors enjoying better health are those in lesser contact with agents of the dominant society. There is however no simple explanatory scheme which can provide local politicians and medical practitioners with an adequate understanding of the problems faced by Indians.

This paper collates some of the main research data on the health implications of acculturation in order to develop an epidemiological model which could aid a better understanding of the problems and point to possible practical solutions, with particular reference to the Upper Amazon. The discussion is based on the case of the Shuar and Achuar (Jívaro) Indians of Ecuador among whom the first author worked as a health officer (1971–74) and did some complementary studies (1975–78). It is illustrated by data from the Peruvian Montaña, where the second author carried out anthropological fieldwork in the southernmost extension of the Jivaroan culture area (Lamista Quechua) 1975–77 and 1980–81. Although we are specially concerned with rainforest Indians, we hope that some points of this paper may also be valid for Amerindian minorities in other areas. . . .

This paper addresses the question of what are the public health consequences of the national integration process and the ensuing "transculturation" of South American rainforest Indian minorities. . . .

CHANGE OF THE DISEASE SPECTRUM IN THE PROCESS OF ETHNIC AND ENVIRONMENTAL TRANSFORMATION

The Destruction of the Ecosystem

During the last few decades, the South American countries which extend into the Amazon basin have rediscovered their vast and so far neglected rainforest regions. Governments have designated them as areas for economic exploitation and they have encouraged people from over-populated agricultural areas to migrate and settle there. Settlement projects in the rainforest are launched as a substitute for land reform in order to solve the problem of population pressure: so far, they have not been very successful and they have given rise to a flood of spontaneous colonists (3, 11, 28). In Ecuador and Peru, settlers are generally poor peasants from Andean areas where a historically fixed system of land tenure kept them below the poverty line. The burning socio-economic conflicts of those areas are transferred into rainforest areas with the migrants. On the eastern slopes of the Andes and along main river valleys, rapid colonization entailed the displacement of the Indian population to further forest areas. The forest cover has been replaced by grass-land for pastures or by cash-crop plantations. Throughout the Upper Amazon region, national and multinational companies exploit timber and search and exploit minerals and petroleum (15, 19, 20).

Displacement of the Indian population   The displacement of the native population from their hunting grounds occurred through unjust transactions and physical force rather than by mutually agreed and respected contracts. The literature on this subject is abundant. . . .

The loss of hunting grounds to the invading colonists—at best the restriction to a fixed piece of land—is one of the major external pressures on the Amazonian Indians' social and economic systems. In Ecuador, the law of colonization of the Amazon region (Ley de la Colonización de la Región Amazónica) and in Peru, the revised Agrarian Reform laws (Ley de Promoción y Desarrollo Agrario, 1980) have accelerated the process of spontaneous colonization by Andean colonists. These pressures result inevitably in a much greater dependence on agriculture, in changes in farming techniques (larger clearings, mono-cultivation) and, at best, in the adoption of stock farming showing an acceptance of the settlers' economic system. These changes have been and are highly disruptive to the Indians' way of life, particularly if it is correct to assume that the more strenuous environmental constraints—as in the case of the rainforest—the more specialized is man's adaptation and hence the more limited the ability to react to new conditions. In a few cases, such as among the Shuar, missions have played a positive role in defending Indian territories threatened by colonists. They have however encouraged other social, economic and cultural changes. The majority of Amazonian Indian minorities have reacted to the invasion of their land by retreating to hinterland areas which are usually of lesser agricultural potential.

Replacement of the forest by grassland or plantations   The erosion of a complex ecosystem results in a simplification of the habitat with a noticeable decrease in the "diversity index" (number of species/number of individuals per species: 20, 31) until the whole system is threatened with extinction (18, 32). At first, while some animal species disappear—particularly the larger game—others thrive (rats, mice, opossum). New species are introduced by man (cattle, pigs, chicken).

Figure 1 summarizes the main consequences of ecological change for the Shuar in particular and Amazonian Indians in frontier areas in general. The consequences are the following:

1. Deep, disruptive changes in the social life and culture of Indian groups, which may remind us of the extent to which a society is conditioned by its subsistence base and the environment is a stabiliser of culture;

2. Increasing nutritional problems caused by a rapid transition from a subsistence economy to a cash one. We must bear in mind that the introduction of livestock does not necessarily entail a better nutrition: Indians breed cattle exclusively for cash and hardly ever drink the milk: the prevalence of lactase deficiency, which might explain a widespread aversion to cow's milk, is unknown among Amazonian Indians. Pigs, and even chickens, are slaughtered at feasts only and to feed a large number of guests. Pigs require a considerable amount of waste food not commonly found in Indian households, or an increase in manioc production. The rearing of poultry on a large scale is successful only in areas where settlement is dispersed: in villages, it is not successful without vaccination, which people often consider a complicated practice. In most cases, Indians do not gain access to stock farming and they are unable to compete with settlers, as shown by FUNAI reports (Brazilian National Foundation, 15);

3. Changes in the potential of disease transmission through an increased density of the host population (animal and human) versus a

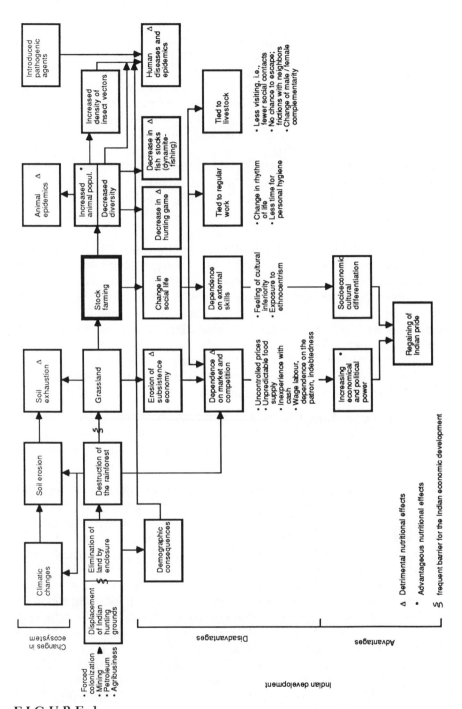

FIGURE 1

Main consequences of ecological change for the Shuar and other Amazonian Indians in frontier areas

limited number of insect vector species: this point is particularly stressed by Dunn (17);

4. Cattle raising entails particular changes which are both negative and positive; they are an increased sedentarization, an exclusively male control on the cattle and on its sale, contrasting with a widespread traditional male-female complementarity in productive activities. On the positive side, cattle raising may be the basis of a new economic stability for Indians; together with intensive farming, it may give rise to a greater political autonomy from outsiders. This is not only true for the Shuar but for many of their Peruvian neighbours, even though herds are very small on average (less than 20 head). . . .

Demographic Implications

As it was mentioned above, physical extinction is one of the main risks of acculturation in an environment such as the rainforest. As an act of despair, some Indian tribes in Brazil are said to have renounced any productive activity in view of a hopeless future (34, 35). Other tribes, after a temporary decrease in population size, have started to grow again (4, 15, 30, 35). Other groups in a more protected environment—the Shuar, for example, supported by their mission initiated self-help organisation "Federación de Centros Shuar" now show a considerable population growth. The Shuar themselves see this growth as a possible factor for increasing their power in the future.

An increased population density, however, presents serious dangers (see Figure 2):

1. Is the agricultural potential sufficient for the land to support a considerable population increase, either through an intensified agriculture or animal husbandry or both?

The ecologically destructive effects of large-scale cattle raising on rainforest soils have been denounced by Goodland (19, 20) among others. Introduced African pastures exhaust the soil after a few years. Rotation is rarely practiced so that the area of fallow land decreases. Shaller (37) reminds us of some African studies which showed that the total weight of game on relatively poor soils is greater than that of livestock on rich soils: "the reason why an acre can support a greater biomass of wildlife than domestic cattle is because natural selection tends to maximize the energy flow in the community. Cattle eat only some grasses; they do not utilize the habitat as fully as the game." Experiments in game farming, successful in South Africa and U.S.A. (41) are still incipient in Amazonia.

2. It can be assumed that the reduction of subsistence agriculture will result in a deteriorated diet. This has been shown elsewhere (5, 13, 16, 21, 27). It is already clear among those Indians who raise cattle, while it seems easier for those who rely on cash crops to preserve their

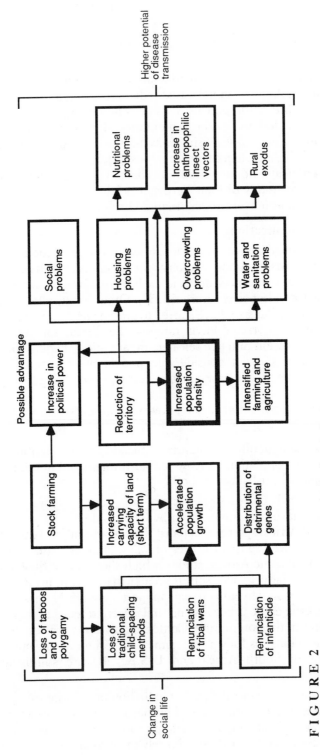

FIGURE 2
Demographic and subsequent consequences of cultural change

traditional diet (2). The cash economy which cattle raising entails does not offset detrimental nutritional effects (Figure 1): the foodstuffs that can be purchased usually consist in industrial foods brought by plane from regional capitals at high prices (canned fish and meat, flour, sugar noodles).

3. An increased population density can both be the consequence of and result in social changes, adaptation to which may be a difficult process. Among the Shuar, such changes are monogamy—associated with a higher fertility rate—reduced households, the construction of smaller houses—often with separate kitchens, and the impossibility of escaping social conflicts through migration because of sedentarization. Among others, Polunin (33) observes the effects of crowding, particularly in the psychosomatic field: "the social process linking high population density to enhanced disease susceptibility is not crowding per se but the disordered relationships that are the inevitable results of such crowding".

"High population density" is of course relative and must be seen from the perspective of the original baseline. For the Shuar, "disordered relationships" mean the loss of their own social order, including for example the acknowledgement of formal authorities for dispute settle-

T A B L E 1

Selected Diseases among Moderately and Highly Acculturated Shuar (Morbidity Survey, 1971)

	"Moderately accult." Zone II (n = 286)		"Highly accult." Zone I (n = 485)		Type of disease	Favoured by
	n	%	n	%		
Bronchitis or pneumonia	40	13.9	95	19.6	droplet infection	Over-crowding
Scabies	4	1.4	7	1.4	contact** infection	
Furuncle	9	3.1	12	2.5	Water-washed disease*	Low water quantity
Conjunctivitis	9	3.1	11	2.3		
Alcoholism (assessment)	(+) +		++***		psycholog-ical	Accul-turative stress

* Classification of water related diseases by Bradley (10). Only the infectious conjunctivitis belongs to this group.

** Scabies is not seen as a water-washed disease; the distribution was markedly clustered in three communities.

*** Alcohol is more easily accessible in Zone I.

  $p < 0.05$ only in the first row

ment (see also 49). For other Indians, the loss of their own social order coincides with the imposition of an alien order by non-Indian political authorities (2) or by missionaries.

4. Will population growth stimulate a phase of innovations (indigenous or borrowed) which may improve long term prospects? Among others, (e.g. 8) Alland and McCay (1) write: "we ourselves are committed to the proposition that increased population is one of the major mechanisms involved in evolutionary change. We see a rather strict correlation between rise of population, stress on the environment and culture change". But these factors work only when there is enough time for gradual evolution and, as MacCormack stresses (26), in the absence of urban capital intrusion in the rural sector. This absence is rare in Amazonia and Indians tend to fall into dependence upon external pressure groups, as both intensive farming skills and extractive activities (logging, mining) come from non-indigenous sources. The consequence is more often disruption than health adaptation. There are only few cases—and never from forest areas—of Indian groups achieving economic preponderance over Mestizo settlers (Otavalo, cf 36; Saraguro, cf 40; Mexican Indians, cf 12): they do so on a specialized economic basis and manage the marketing of their products.

Implications on Disease

Table 1 presents some results of our medical examinations of almost all members of five Shuar communities. It can be seen that the frequency of *water-washed diseases* (10) is almost the same in the communities of Zones I and II—as there is not much difference in the hygienic standards and a similar access to rivers and brooks in the studied communities—but that droplet infections, as examples of diseases linked to over-crowding (smaller houses, closer man-to-man contact) are more frequent in Zone I. Further evidence for the link between crowding and droplet infections is provided by our figures on the prevalence of tuberculosis infection in school children (age group 5–19) in the boarding schools of Cuchanza and Sevilla D.B. (crowded conditions, particularly in the dormitories). We found 43.2% of the 343 pupils to be infected compared with only 20.2% of the 94 pupils (p < 0.01) in the surrounding communities of Kuchankas/Kumanchay and Mutintsa.

The first noticed outbreak of venereal diseases occurred in 1977 (H.P. Franken, personal communication) in a Shuar community in Zone I.

Unfortunately it was not possible to get sufficiently reliable data on diarrheal diseases. According to officials of the Malaria Eradication Programme, malaria has been spreading rapidly since 1976 (personal communication 1978).

So the disease pattern found among the Shuar fits well with the health risks of acculturation as illustrated in Figure 3. These show: an increase in the relative frequency of droplet infections (due to more crowded housing

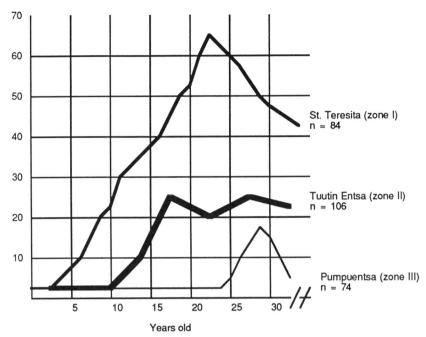

FIGURE 3
Age-specific prevalence rates of tuberculosis infection (PPD-RT23) in three Shuar communities

conditions), an increase of faecal-oral diseases (higher population density leads to water and sanitation problems), an increase in malaria (due to the simplification of habitat and increased density of human and animal hosts) and the spread of TB as an example of a "new" disease.

Nutritional Changes

We have the following evidence of a deterioration of the nutritional status in the process of acculturation among the Shuar:

1. *Observations:* In Zone I, where colonization is now spreading, there is no game left. Very little game is left in Zone II. Domestic animals cannot bridge the protein gap. People have to rely on their traditional crops but gardens are being displaced by pastures. The fact that many girls now attend school increases the work load on adult women, with regards to agricultural tasks and child care.

2. *Survey data* (22, 23): the mean energy intake per person per day measured over two days in two typical Shuar families of Zone I equals only 1,778 Cal, and the protein intake only 12.7 g. These figures may be lower than the average figures for the Shuar as a whole since manioc beer or "chicha", a basic energy source among the Shuar as well as

other Amazonian Indians, was not consumed by the two sample families in Zone I. Settlers condemn this drink as "dirty" and "uncivilized". We found by biochemical examination 50 Cal in 100 g of *chicha*. Berlin and Berlin found 57 Kcal in the manioc beer of the Peruvian Aguaruna Jívaro (6). Under the assumption that *chicha* in the diluted form contains 50% water (i.e. 25 Kcal per 100 ml), an adult would get sufficient energy (i.e. 2,000 Kcal) by drinking 8L per day. This is not an unusual quantity.

The serum Albumin level of a sample of 31 acculturated Shuar was 3.7 g/100 ml. Black et al (8) found a mean of 4.3 g/100 ml among acculturated Cayapa, and Baruzzi et al (4) a mean of 3.3 g/100 ml among Kreen Akorore suffering from destruction of their environment. Using anthropometric measurements in a sample of 126 children (aged 1 to 4 years) we found 0% with 3rd degree malnutrition, 6% with 2nd degree and 30% with 1st degree (weight for age, Gomez classification).

These data from 1971 are of limited value because of the small numbers examined, but they fit well with our observations and with the general opinion of the Shuar themselves. Since 1971, the process of acculturation has advanced at a rapid pace: in 1978, we observed Shuar buying manioc at the market of the urban centre of Sucúa.

Preventive Medicine

The process of acculturation causes some elements of preventive medicine to be lost: on the whole, there is less time for personal hygiene because of the concern with and care of livestock. The animals themselves contribute considerably to environmental pollution. The "avoidance rules" previously observed in the occurrence of some transmissible diseases are forgotten, or they have become impractical. Changes in house-style entail the loss of warming fires at the end of beds, over-crowding and poorer sanitation standards. One of the authors (A.K. 24) has made a comparative study of housing conditions among rainforest and highland Indians in Ecuador as well as of the change of these conditions in time. While populations are undergoing socio-cultural adaptation, there are indications that housing is changing for the worse. . . .

A considerable increase of inter-personal frictions is due to increased promiscuity, to the socialization of children in schools and to the consumption of alcohol. Problems arise particularly when different shamans practice in one village and split the community into factions. Exposure to the ethnocentric, sometimes insulting behaviour of settlers instill feelings of inferiority among Indians (14). Among the Shuar, the extent to which the redistribution of labour between the sexes (men rather than women are now in charge of agriculture in the form of cash-cropping and mainly cattle raising) has created a new social order is not yet clear (39). Traditionally, Shuar women were both physically and ritually responsible for all aspects of fertility and reproduction: the recent changes in the relations of production deprive them of this role. Likewise the substantial alterations in the socialization of Shuar children as a consequence of changes in life style and social relationships have not yet been studied in depth: the possible detrimental impact (psychological and social) of the missions' boarding school system has been assumed by Münzel but without supporting evidence.

DISCUSSION AND CONCLUSIONS

General Considerations

Are the described negative consequences of environmental destruction balanced out by positive effects among South American rainforest Indians in general and the Shuar in particular? In many parts of Amazonia, a negative answer is obvious. This crucial question is, however, difficult to answer because it calls for value judgements where anthropologists, economists and politicians tend to disagree strongly. How can one weigh cultural losses against the gains of "transculturation", i.e. the emergence of a new differentiated culture including new components? Transculturation presupposes an ideal situation where cultural differentiation really occurs: the more common outcome however, is "deculturation", with a dependence upon the external value system.

If increased contact results in the advent of new diseases among Indians, to what extent is this offset by the beneficial effects of vaccines and drugs?

Technological innovation implies a lesser dependence on the ecosystem, but how is this to be balanced against the facts of a new dependence on an external economic system?

Answers to these questions might be helpful to the Indian self-reliance movement. Some of our considerations may help to clarify the issues.

Other questions are more practical: should the future economic basis of rainforest Indian minorities be cattle raising or, in areas of relatively fertile soils, cash crop agriculture? Can an alternative "economic integration" be contemplated, at least for some Indian groups? In the Shuar case, due to massive international aid and to the creation of an Indian self-help organization which has gained considerable political influence over the last few years, the first steps towards an economic balance with—even preponderance over—non-Indian immigrant settlers have been secured. While the short term prospects are encouraging, the long term effects, however, remain unknown. In many parts of Amazonia, particularly on colonization fronts, there have been policies to turn rainforest Indians into cash-croppers and cattle raisers. Due to the pressures exerted by colonists, the survival of many tribal societies depend almost entirely on the goodwill of their respective countries' governments (e.g. case of the Brazilian Xingu Park (15)). The major issues associated with controlled efforts to construct new Indian economies appear to be the following: the attendant risks in destroying the original ecosystem, the definition of bases for a relative political and cultural autonomy of the Indian group, and finally a satisfactory balance with the requirements of the poor immigrants who settle in the area (38). The third issue is the most urgent in those areas of Ecuador and Peru where neither the respective government controls the advance of colonisation nor do missions protect Indian rights and encourage self-help organisations such as the Shuar's. . . . possible governmental measures to improve the Indians' situation and their health status . . . [include] the legalization of the Indians' landholdings, economic aid to start Indian-run farming programmes and education programmes aiming at preparing the population for the imminent changes.

Public Health Considerations

We have seen that the main health risks for contemporary rainforest Indians arise from their social and economic development. Malnutrition and the increase of disease are directly related to the destruction of the environment and the accompanying social changes. It follows then that medicine has a lower priority for Indian well-being than social and economic factors. Nevertheless, medical services, because of direct action on the individual and the community, might be helpful in counter-balancing the worst effects of acculturation—it is a matter of symptoms and causes.

SUMMARY

1. The destruction of the rainforest and its replacement by pastures goes hand in hand with the displacement of the Indian population towards ecologically less attractive areas. Wherever Indians take part in the economic "development" of the region, the disruption of their social life follows, characterized by dependence on the market, on external skills and on cash as well as by an increase in transmissible diseases. The potential advantages of such an economic integration is a new economic independence and an increase in self-reliance.

2. The genetic implications of interethnic miscegenation are still theoretical and not yet supported by evidence.

3. The increase in population density has severe implications for the dynamics of disease transmission as it is accompanied by overcrowding, change in housing patterns, water and sanitation problems, malnutrition.

4. The costs of acculturation include a deterioration in the nutritional status for rainforest Indians in general.

5. The introduction of modern medicine has followed the acculturation process: the use of new drugs has been spread, while sometimes western-trained doctors and local primary health care officers have

attempted to cope with the new situation. Some characteristics of the confrontation between modern and traditional medicine are described, with particular reference to preventive medicine and healing systems.

The paper reaches the following conclusions:

1. The relative advantages of economic development and acculturation for rainforest Indians are questionable. Economic problems, particularly concerning the legalization of land rights have, and rightly so, a higher priority than medicine for the Indian population.

2. Health risks are socio-economically determined to a large extent. A successful medical approach should take into account the specific conditions of the situation we have described. Among the Shuar and other rainforest indigenous populations, there are now some promising health services based on the work of indigenous health workers, but they are small-scale and generally nongovernmental. The training of local health workers able to bridge the cognitive gaps between primary health care and traditional healing systems could limit to some extent the negative consequences of acculturation on health. The existing primary health care programmes, however, still have shortcomings that do not allow the necessary cooperation between formal health services and indigenous communities.

ACKNOWLEDGMENTS

Several parts of this paper have been drawn from the M.Sc. dissertation of the first author. Thanks to all colleagues of the Ross Institute at the London School of Hygiene and Tropical Medicine for their invaluable stimuli, particularly to Prof. David Bradley and to Dr. Carol MacCormak. Mr. David Ashcroft helped in the revision of the first version of the paper. The Federación de Centros Shuar, particularly Marcelino Chumapi, assisted personally; and my co-workers, at different times, have been Dr. Elena Ileckova, Mr. Herbert Heyna, Mrs. Gisela Pawelzig, Mrs. Barbara Blessin and, above all, my wife, Nelly Kroeger. Fieldwork would not have been possible without the consistent help of the Ecuadorian health authorities. Financial support was provided in part by the Deutsche Forschungsgemeinschaft.

REFERENCES

1. Alland, A., McCay, B. (1973): Adaptation in biological and cultural evolution, pp. 143–178 in Honigman, J.J. (ed.): *Handbook of social and cultural anthropology*, McNally College Publ. Comp., Chicago.

2. Barbira-Freedman (Scazzocchio), F. (1979): Ethnicity and boundary maintenance among the forest Quechua of San Martín, Peru. Unpublished Ph.D. thesis, Department of Social Anthropology, Cambridge.

3. Barbira-Freedman (Scazzocchio), F. (ed.) (1980): *Land, people and planning in contemporary Amazonia*, Centre of Latin American Studies, University of Cambridge, England.

4. Baruzzi, R.G., Marcopito, L.F., Serra, M.L., Souza, F.A.A., Stabile, C. (1977): The Kren-Akorore: a recently contacted indigenous tribe, pp. 179–200 in *Health and disease in tribal societies*, Ciba Found. Sympos. 49 (new series), Elsevier Amsterdam-Oxford-New York.

5. Behar, M. (1968): Food and nutrition of the Maya before the conquest and at present time. *Pan. Am. Health Organ. Sci. Publ.*, 165, 114–119.

6. Berlin, B., Berlin, E.A. (1978): Etnobiología, subsistencia y nutrición en una sociedad de la selva tropical: Los Aguaruna (Jíbaro) pp. 13–47 in Chirif, A. (ed.): *Salud y nutrición en sociedades nativas*, Centro de Investigación y Promoción Amazónica, Lima.

7. Black, F.L., Pinheiro, F.P., Hierholzer, W.J., Lee, R.V. (1977): Epidemiology of infectious disease: the example of measles, pp. 115–130 in *Health and disease in tribal societies*, Ciba Found. Sympos. 49 (new series), Elsevier Amsterdam-Oxford-New York.

8. Black, F.L., Hierholzer, W.J., Black, D.P., Lamm, S.H., Lucas, L. (1977): Nutritional status of Brazilian Kayapo Indians. *Hum. Biol.*, 49, 139–153.

9. Boserup, E. (1965): Conditions of agricultural growth, Chicago.

10. Bradley, D.J. (1974): Water supplies: the consequences of change, pp. 81–98 in *Human rights in health*, Ciba Found. Sympos. 23 (new series), Elsevier Amsterdam-Oxford-New York.

11. Bromley, R. (1980): The role of tropical colonization in the twentieth century economic development of Ecuador, pp. 174–184 in Barbira-Scazzocchio (ed.): *Land, people and planning in contemporary Amazonia*, Centre of Latin American Studies, University of Cambridge, England.

12. Cine, H. (1953): *The United States and Mexico*, Harvard University Press, Cambridge, Massachusetts.

13. Collis, W.R.F., Dema, J., Omolu, A. (1962): The ecology of child health and nutrition in Nigerian villages. Part II: dietary and medical surveys. *Trop. Geogr. Med.*, 14, 201–229.

14. Cueva-Jaramillo, J. (1978): Ethnocentrism and cultural conflicts. *Cultures*, UNESCO Press, 3, 19–31.

15. Davis, S.H. (1977): *Victims of the miracle: development and the Indians of Brazil*, Cambridge University Press, Cambridge-London-New York-Melbourne.

16. Dornstreich, M.D. (1977): The ecological description and analysis of tropical subsistence patterns: an example from New Guinea, pp. 245–271 in Bayliss-Smith, Th., Feachem, R. (eds): *Subsistence and survival. Rural ecology in the Pacific*, Academic Press, London, New York, San Francisco.

17. Dunn, F.L. (1968): Epidemiological factors: health and disease in hunter-gatherers. In Lee, R.L., De Vore, I. (eds): *Man the hunter*, Aldine Publishing Co., Chicago.

18. Gomez-Pompa, A., Vasquez-Yanes, C., Guevara, S. (1972): The tropical rainforest: a non-renewable resource. *Science*, 177, 762–765.

19. Goodland, R.J.A., Irwin, H.S. (1975): *Amazon jungle: green hell to red desert?* Amsterdam, Elsevier Scientific Publishing.

20. Goodland, R.J.A. (1980): Environmental ranking of Amazonian development, pp. 1–20 in Barbira-Scazzocchio, F. (ed.): *Land, people and planning in contemporary Amazonia*, Centre of Latin American Studies, University of Cambridge, England.

21. Hernandez, M., Perez, C.H., Ramirez, J.H., Madrigal, H., Chavez, A. (1974): Effect of economic growth on nutrition in a tropical community. *Ecology Food Nutrit.*, 3, 283–291.

22. Kroeger, A., Ileckova, E., Heyna, H., Pawelzig, G. (1976): Epidemiologie der Gesundheitsbedingungen bei den Shuara Indianern von Ecuador. *Th. d. Gegenw.*, 115, 1227–1256.

23. Kroeger, A., Ileckova, E., Heyna, H., Pawelzig, G. (1977): La salud y alimentación entre los indígenas Shuar. *Rev. Ecuat. Hyg. Med. Trop.*, 30, 119–167.

24. Kroeger, A. (1979): Housing and health in the process of cultural adaptation: a case study among Jungle and Highland Natives from Ecuador. *J. Trop. Med. Hyg.* 83:53–69 (1980).

25. Lizot, J. (1977): Population, ressources et guerre chez les Yanomami, critique de l'Antropologie écologique. *"Libre" Paris* 2, 111–145.

26. MacCormack, C.P. (1978): The cultural ecology of production: Sherbro Coast and Hinterland, Sierra Leone. *International Series*, suppl. 47, 197–210.

27. Marealle, A.L.D., Kazungu, M., Kondaki, X.G. (1964): Cross sectional studies on protein calorie malnutrition in Tanganyika. *J. Trop. Med. Hyg.*, 67, 222–229.

28. Martine, G. (1980): Recent colonization experiences in Brazil: Expectations versus reality, pp. 30–94 in Barbira-Scazzocchio, F. (ed.): *Land, people and planning in contemporary Amazonia*, Centre of Latin American Studies, University of Cambridge, England.

29. Montgomery, T.A. (1978): Health care for the underprivileged in the land of affluence: California native Americans. *Pediatrics*, 62, 377–381.

30. Oberem, U. (1980): *Los Quijos*, Colección Pendoneros 10A, Instituto Otavaleño de Antropologia, Otavalo, Ecuador.

31. Odum, E.P. (1959): *Fundamentals of ecology*, 2nd ed., Saunders Co., Philadelphia-London.

32. O'Reilly Sternberg, H. (1968): Man and environmental change in South America, pp. 438–445 in Fittkau, E.J., Illies, J., Klinge, H., Schwabe, G.H., Sioli, H. (eds): *Biogeography and ecology in South America*, Vol. 1, Dr. Junk Publishers, The Hague.

33. Polunin, I. (1977): Some characteristics of tribal people, pp. 5–20 in *Health and disease in tribal societies*, Ciba Found. Sympos. 49 (new series), Elsevier, Amsterdam-Oxford-New York.

34. von Putkamer, W.J. (1975): Brazil's Kreen-Akaróres: requiem for a tribe? *National Geographic Magazine*, 134, 254–268.

35. Ribeiro, D. (1971): *Fronteras indígenas de la civilización*, Siglo veintiuno editores S.A., Mexico.

36. Salomon, F. (1973): Weavers in Otavalo, pp. 463–492 in Gross, D.R. (ed.): *Peoples and cultures of native South America*, The Natural History Press, New York, Garden City.

37. Schaller, G.B. (1969): Man's ecological environment, pp. 116–126 in Sladen, B.K., Bang, F.B. (eds): *Biology of populations*, American Elsevier Publishing Co., New York.

38. Tavener, Ch.J. (1973): The Karajá and the Brazilian frontier, pp. 433–459 in Gross, D.R. (ed.): *Peoples and natures of native South America*, The Natural History Press, New York, Garden City.

39. Taylor, A.Ch. (1981): La riqueza de dios: los Achuar y las misiones, pp. 115–143 in Whitten, N.F. (ed.): *Amazonia, la otra cara del progreso*, Serie Mundo Shuar, Centro de Documentación, Investigación y Publicaciones Shuar, Sucúa, Ecuador.

40. Temme, M. (1972): Wirtschaft ûnd Bevölkerung in Südecuador, Diss., Universität Köln.

41. von Treuenfels, C.A. (1978): Game farming, GEO no.12, Verlag Gruner und Jahr, Hamburg, 34–58.

23

Cattle and Rural Economic Differentiation in the Highlands of Papua New Guinea

LAWRENCE S. GROSSMAN

This case study from Papua New Guinea focuses on the social consequences of a specific development project. Here it is not an invading multinational corporation but individual tribal members themselves who are exploiting communal properties for personal advantage. They do so under a government-sponsored loan program designed to increase cattle production for the market economy. This example highlights one of the principle contrasts between tribal systems and national market economies. Tribal economies assume relative equality. Critical natural resources are communally owned and available to everyone, and differences in wealth tend to be minimized. Economic development promotes participation in a system based on inequality of wealth and unequal access to basic resources. Social inequality in the form of economic differentiation is a frequent consequence of development; it may result in internal conflict and the impoverishment of large segments of the population. Grossman, who received his Ph.D. in geography from the Australian National University in 1979, bases his conclusions on 18 months of research in New Guinea in 1976–77.

Rural economic differentiation is a ubiquitous phenomenon accompanying the incorporation of rural societies of the Third World into the expanding, global capitalist system. In the highlands of Papua New Guinea, a country that is rapidly changing from a classless, subsistence-based economy to a more stratified and monetized society (Howlett 1980), increasing differentiation is well documented (e.g., Finney 1973; Gerritsen 1975; Howlett, Hide, and Young 1976; McKillop 1976a; Connell 1979; Good 1979). In this paper, I examine a major influence on differentiation in the highlands—the introduction of commercial smallholder cattle projects. . . .

THE VILLAGE

The 441 residents of the village of Kapanara live in the Kainantu District of the Eastern Highlands Province, an area of relatively rapid economic

Reproduced in abridged form by permission of the author and the American Anthropological Association from *American Ethnologist* 10, no. 1 (1983): 59–76. Not for further reproduction.

growth. They are speakers of the Tairora language. Within their village territory of 39 km² the population density is 11/km², low for the highlands region, where densities are as high as 300/km². The village is linked by an unpaved road to the nearest town, Kainantu, 26 km to the north.

The economic structure of the village is characteristic of a precapitalist mode of production. The level of development of the productive forces is low, the division of labor is simple, and the household is the basic unit of production. Subsistence, the main form of production, is based on several types of shifting cultivation and pig raising. Villagers maintain control over their major means of production, land, which is rarely sold,[1] can be purchased only by others in the village, and thus is not a fully marketable commodity.

Village social relations of production affected by leader-follower ties have changed significantly in Kapanara since the former Australian colonial administration established control over the region in the late 1940s. In the precontact era, intervillage warfare in the Tairora region was chronic, and leadership was achieved mainly by prowess in warfare (Watson 1967). Leaders, or Big Men, sometimes intimidated and influenced their followers to provide labor or resources for activities or exchanges that enhanced the prestige of the Big Man, and differences in economic position did occur among villagers (Watson 1967). Nevertheless, economic differentiation was not perpetuated from generation to generation for several reasons. Much of the wealth obtained by leaders was given to others to satisfy old obligations or to create new ones. Also, many of a leader's assets were distributed to a wide range of people upon his death, thus preventing differential accumulation of capital within particular families from passing to subsequent generations. In addition, a Big Man's status was achieved and thus not necessarily inherited by one of his sons (cf. Standish 1978); unless an individual displayed the characteristics of a leader, he would not become a Big Man. After the Australians pacified the area in the late 1940s, the traditional basis of leadership was destroyed, and subsequent Big Men have had less control over their followers.

A current Big Man of a clan acquires influence by force of personality, demonstrated competence in certain activities, and generosity. To maintain support from his followers, he must not become "overextractive" (Sahlins 1963); he must not demand too much from his followers and must adequately reciprocate for the help he has received. A current Big Man cannot command or force his followers to help. If overextraction continues to characterize the relationship between leader and follower, the latter can withdraw the support on which the current Big Man depends. A Big Man cannot manipulate and control the labor or resources of others to accumulate substantial wealth for himself. Kapanara Big Men of the three village clans lack the power characteristic of Big Men in many other highland societies (see Standish 1978), perhaps because of the smaller size of the political units here and the absence of large-scale ceremonial exchange systems that are found in most other areas in the highlands. Leaders assert their influence on only a limited number of occasions.

A Big Man does not control the land-use activities of the members of his clan. Rather, he acts as the spokesman and guardian of his clan's territory and performs several generalized functions, such as mediating disputes over land and other property within the clan's area, and he protects the territory against the claims of others. Each clan is associated with a particular tract of land, which is further subdivided into strips associated with a patrilineage or group of patrilineages. These divisions, however, do not imply exclusive control because members of other patrilineages and other clans in Kapanara also have rights in the tracts. The traditional land-tenure system was sufficiently flexible to ensure that all members of the village had favorable access to the productive resources needed to provide for the necessities of life and for full participation in social affairs. With the abundance of land and subsistence-oriented production, differential control of land did not influence the relative economic or political position of individuals. The perceived need to restrict other Kapanarans' access to clan land was minimal; as a result, previously established land rights are now highly intermixed. . . .

Changes associated with the introduction of commercial activities, particularly smallholder cattle projects, have significantly altered the potential for economic differentiation. The Kapanarans have been involved in village-based, cash-earning activities since the mid-1950s. The average amount of wealth in cash and material assets is small, the per capita income in 1977 being less than K80.[2] Much of the money earned is channeled into the traditional system of reciprocal exchange, within which villagers can obtain prestige, thus somewhat limiting the extent of individual variations in capital accumulation. Money is also reinvested in income-producing endeavors, such as raising cattle, transporting passengers, and operating trade stores.

The most important cash-earning activities today are cattle raising and coffee production. Given the abundance of land in the village, everyone has access to productive land for coffee. Both Big Men and entrepreneurs have planted more coffee than others, though these differences are not dramatic. Variations in household coffee production are determined largely by available household labor, the amount of coffee planted, and individual initiative. The use of hired labor in coffee production is minimal. By contrast, access to cattle raising is more restricted.

VILLAGE CATTLE PROJECTS

The previous Australian colonial administration introduced smallholder cattle projects to Papua New Guinea in 1960 to diversify the rural cash economy, improve rural nutrition, limit the amount of beef being imported into the country, and supply beef to expanding urban markets. Since 1959 the number of cattle owned by villagers in Papua New Guinea has risen dramatically, from approximately 300 head to 50,000 head in 1978, though the rate of increase has slowed considerably in the latter half of the 1970s. The growth of the smallholder herd has been greatly facilitated by the Papua New Guinea Development Bank (PNGDB), established in 1967 to provide loans to villagers wishing to start commercial enterprises; a major goal of the bank is to speed the transition to a cash economy (McKillop 1976b:33). The PNGDB has granted loans to approximately 2600 of the 3300 Papua New Guinea smallholder cattle projects functioning in 1978 (Grossman 1980:22). Agricultural extension officers, who are also the bank's field agents, supervise smallholder projects. . . .

Kapanarans established their first cattle project in 1970, two more in 1973, and their last four in 1975. The villagers have enclosed approximately 550 ha—28 percent of the grassland area and 14 percent of the village territory. The patterns followed in the establishment of a project follow certain fairly standardized steps from inception to completion. Once a man of some esteem (a clan Big Man, a successful entrepreneur in cash-earning enterprises, or a more dynamic member of one of the patrilineages) decides to enter the cattle business, he calls together people related to him through various ties of descent, kinship, and friendship, seeks their support to start a cattle project, and suggests that they use a particular parcel of land to which they have a claim. The man who has called the others to the meeting acts as a leader, or "cattle boss," of the project; the others will be his "followers," or "helpers." Three Big Men are cattle bosses. At the same time, the leader usually seeks another person of some repute to join him in the endeavor. This person may be chosen for a variety of reasons, none of which are mutually exclusive. He may have saved money from cash-earning activities, or he may be a close relative. In addition, he or his kinsmen may have a major claim to the land that will be enclosed by the proposed cattle project. This person in turn recruits his own relatives and friends, discusses his intentions, and acts as the leader, or cattle boss, of the second group. Thus, two groups are usually joined together.

The leaders appeal to their followers by proclaiming that the cattle project will enhance the prestige of their group, will earn them a considerable income, and will provide a locally available source of fresh beef. The leaders stress the advantages that will accrue to the group as a whole, though the exact distribution of future rewards is left unstated. The helpers expect to benefit substantially in reciprocation for giving up part of their land and for their contribution of labor and finances to the cattle project. Usually, the bosses and followers reach a consensus to start a project.

Having limited financial resources, cattle bosses and followers must pool money to purchase enough barbed wire to fence the paddock; the average cost of fencing per project was K420. Then they begin the arduous and time-consuming task of building the cattle enclosures. People must fell trees, split fence posts, carry heavy posts from the forest to the grassland, clear a path through the grass for the fence, dig holes and set in the posts, staple and strain barbed wire onto fence posts, and finally construct a stockyard.

The spatial distribution of individual land rights is highly intermixed, and fencing off any large area is bound to impinge on the rights of some people. In a few instances, project leaders defer to certain objections and change the proposed boundaries, whereas in others they ignore them and proceed. Some protesting villagers look on in dismay as their present gardens or past garden sites are enclosed within the boundaries of the cattle project. The fence line, which of necessity is as straight as possible for effective barbed-wire tightening, gives little concession to traditional garden patterns and occasionally bisects producing gardens. Some irate villagers demand compensation for enclosure of their gardens, but this is to no avail. Occasionally, cattle bosses promise to put barbed wire around existing gardens to protect them from the cattle, but they never keep such promises. In extreme cases, violence erupts.

The cattle bosses inform agricultural extension officers stationed in the town of Kainantu of their intentions and of their desire to obtain a loan from the PNGDB to purchase cattle. The loan is needed to finance the enterprise because the villagers do not have enough cash to start an economically viable cattle project. A prerequisite for granting the PNGDB loan is approval of the "Clan Land Usage Agreement." The PNGDB was aware that no single individual within a village community controlled all the land needed to establish commercial ventures such as cattle projects (Gunton 1974:108). Rights in land are vested ultimately in groups, and the land rights of individuals are highly intermixed. Not wishing to lend money for projects on disputed land, the bank introduced the Clan Land Usage Agreement. Two representatives, usually elders of the loan applicants' clan, must indicate on the agreement that the other members of the clan have granted the loan applicants the sole right for life to use the land enclosed by the project boundary fence for cattle raising (Gunton 1974:109). The clan elders give consent to the agreement, even though some disputes concerning use of the land still exist; the clan elders are either closely related to the cattle bosses or believe that the disputed claims should not hinder the project, especially if the complaining party is a member of another clan. The agreement states:

> We, the undersigned, being representatives of the _____ Clan, hereby acknowledge that _____ (Applicant's name) _____ has the right under native law and custom for the whole of his lifetime to use the land known as _____ (or more particularly described in the plan on the reverse hereof) for the purpose of _____ with the right to receive the proceeds of crops, trees and palm grown, livestock grazed and/or business conducted on the said land. We certify that all members of the said clan agree to the truth of this certificate and that we are the persons authorised by the clan to sign it.

To provide a description of the area referred to in the document, agricultural extension officers either make a compass traverse of the boundary or provide a sketch plan. The bank hopes that the agreement will give its borrowers secure tenure to ensure that conflicting claims to land do not hinder repayment of the loan.

The PNGDB approved the loan applications of the cattle bosses of the seven Kapanara projects. . . . The amounts of the loans, which ranged from K1200 to K6010, are typical of PNGDB loans granted to other highland smallholder cattle projects. After loan approval, the agricultural extension officers delivered the cattle to the village.

CATTLE PROJECTS AND LABOR

The nature and scope of the organization of the cattle projects introduce elements without precedent. Given the large scale of the projects compared to traditional economic activities, one man alone in Kapanara cannot start and operate a cattle project, because of limited financial resources, land, and time; he must call upon others for help. The cattle bosses are the project managers. The boss is responsible for making sure that the loan is repaid in part with proceeds from the sale of cattle, and he occasionally seeks the aid of his followers to complete the tasks necessary to maintain the projects, such as clearing regrowth under the fence line. Most people work an average of only one or two hours or less per week on the cattle projects after the arduous task of fence building has been completed.

Labor relationships are influenced in part by the policies of the PNGDB and the agricultural extension officers. On the PNGDB loan application form there is space for up to three loan applicants, though in most cases in Kapanara the two cattle bosses signed as applicants. The names of these two loan applicants are also placed on the Clan Land Usage Agreement, which is read before the villagers. When various forms have to be signed, the agricultural officers contact the cattle bosses. When villagers occasionally sell cattle to the abattoir in Goroka or to the government livestock station in Kainantu, the government sends cash to the cattle boss. . . . Almost all subsequent official contacts from the PNGDB and the agricultural officers to the smallholder projects are made to the loan applicants. . . .

The cattle bosses use their links with the government to their own advantage to mobilize the labor of their followers. If the leaders experience difficulty in obtaining labor, they sometimes inform their helpers that an agricultural officer has told them that they and their followers must all work on a particular task designated by the extension agents, such as fixing the stockyard. At other times, bosses remind their followers that extension officers have told them that if their followers do not help with the cattle project, the followers will lose their membership in the project, forfeit any potential profits to which they would normally be entitled, and have their cattle removed from the project. The followers cannot readily verify the statements made by their project leaders. The cattle bosses' justification of actions and requests by referring to directives from agricultural extension officers is partially effective because it is patterned on the previous form of relationship with the government. Government patrol officers in the past have told villagers what to do for so long that orders from the government have become part of the perceived routine of interaction. Although the cattle bosses do not always obtain compliance from their followers when so justifying their actions, their relationship with the government does give them added leverage in convincing villagers and mobilizing labor. . . .

CATTLE PROJECTS AND SURPLUS

The potential for accumulation and differentiation in the village is heavily influenced by the links with and policies of government agencies—specifically, the PNGDB and the agricultural extension service. The bank prefers to lend money to projects having the capacity to hold 10 to 15 breeders, though smaller projects in Papua New Guinea also received funding. A variety of factors influenced the bank to emphasize relatively large projects.[3] The International Development Agency, an affiliate of the World Bank, provided much of the credit to the PNGDB to finance smallholder cattle projects; it originally stressed the importance of lending money to projects with a 15-breeder capacity to ensure that they would be large enough to be commercially viable. Because extension agents have to complete a complex of forms for each loan application, they encourage larger projects.

> More importantly, the complexity of the credit package oriented extension agents toward large projects which would provide a better return for the effort involved. Unofficially, Development Bank administrators concede that loan applications for less than $500 are too costly to administer . . . (McKillop 1976a:11–12).

Because of the relatively large size of the enterprises, the potential annual revenues of a project far exceed the average household income. In a large project, for example, five to eight progeny can be produced each year, some of which could be sold eventually for K300 per head. . . .

Most of the income from the projects was sent to the PNGDB to repay the loans and was not divided among the cattle project leaders and their followers. Nevertheless, the initial distribution of benefits accruing to the enterprises is revealing. . . .

. . . Aggregated data from the first three projects, which have existed the longest, are instructive: the bosses have contributed 58 percent of the money to start the projects and repay the loans, whereas they have kept 93 percent of the revenues retained in the village for themselves.

The loan repayment process itself enables cattle bosses to accumulate financial wealth. According to disgruntled followers, cattle bosses claim that they could not distribute much revenue from the projects because of the need to repay the loans. However, because of the exclusive nature of contact between cattle bosses and the outside world, the followers are not sure whether cattle bosses actually make loan repayments or keep the money for themselves. Indeed, complaints that cattle bosses have dishonestly kept project revenues intended for loan repayments are common throughout the highlands.

Although it is possible that the followers in each project may eventually receive more money than they have invested, they will never, as a group, receive as much as their two bosses will. Within each project the combined net income of the cattle bosses will always be greater than the combined net income of all the followers. Clearly, the cattle project leaders are and will continue to be the chief beneficiaries of the K500 to K2000 that each project has the potential of generating annually from the sale of its herd, a rather large amount in a village in which the per capita income in 1977 was less than K80. . . .

The cattle bosses are clearly the major beneficiaries of the projects, receiving a disproportionate share of the cash proceeds relative to the inputs made. Many followers feel deceived, cheated, and bitter, a pattern not unique to Kapanara. Fleckenstein (1975:123), for example, notes that in a project near Goroka, a similar imbalance in the distribution of benefits occurred, though the number of people receiving significant returns was greater than in Kapanara. Complaints from followers about the failure of project leaders to adequately share the revenues of their cattle project are widespread throughout Papua New Guinea.

CATTLE PROJECTS AND PROPERTY RELATIONS

In addition to obtaining a disproportionate amount of income from the cattle projects, the bosses have also enhanced their position in relation to land. They now assert more control over land within the fenced paddocks than Big Men do with their clan territory. Changes in control of the means of production are partly related to the villagers' interpretation and manipulation of the meaning of the Clan Land Usage Agreement.

The agreement notes that the cattle bosses have been granted the exclusive right to use the specified area for a cattle project. Many villagers consent to the Clan Land Usage Agreement simply to satisfy a bureaucratic requirement, believing initially that the cattle bosses' rights would not be as encompassing as the agreement suggests. . . . When denying others access to land in the paddocks or refusing to pay compensation for enclosing gardens, cattle bosses refer to both the approval of the agreement and to supportive directives from extension agents. . . .

A villager who previously had a proprietary right or a right of encumbrance in land that has been enclosed by a cattle fence loses all such rights if he is not a member of the project.[4] Given the previous pattern of intermixed proprietary rights, many people have lost rights in land enclosed in projects. The only people who may be able to prepare gardens within the enclosed area are the members, though sometimes bosses either restrict the number of times a garden plot can be replanted or prohibit cultivation altogether. Followers also lose their proprietary rights in land in their own projects; they cannot plant trees of economic importance or transfer rights to land within the projects to others as they could outside the projects. They can only temporarily use the land. However, such rights are often not exercised; under moderate to high stocking rates, most people are hesitant to plant gardens within the fenced areas because of the likelihood of damage by cattle. Several cattle bosses also restrict nonmembers' access to such naturally occurring resources in the enclosures as *Imperata* grass, used for roofing, and the *munah* beetle grub, a relished item in the diet; traditionally, all Kapanarans could gather such resources anywhere in the village territory.

Two trends can be discerned: first, the bosses are restricting the access of nonmembers; second, they are controlling their followers' use of these resources. Their position as leader of a cattle project gives them more influence in determining patterns of resource use and allocation than Big Men exercise in relation to clan land. Because the cattle projects enclose 28 percent of the grassland area, much of which is prime agricultural land near the hamlets, this change in the social relations of production significantly influences economic differentiation in the village. In particular, in the future the cattle bosses can use the enclosed land for other commercial purposes, such as market gardening; their followers must first seek their permission before so doing. Such permission, which may depend on a variety of factors, will not necessarily be forthcoming. What is especially important is that the project boundary fences enclose a single large area,[5] whereas the plots in which other villagers have rights are much smaller and dispersed. If mechanization or large-scale coffee production is introduced into the village agricultural system in the future, cattle bosses or their descendants should have a decided advantage in employing new forms of technology because of the large size of their holdings.

Maintaining control over the use of land is essential for the continuation of the cattle projects and for the perpetuation of economic inequalities. According to the Clan Land Usage Agreement, the loan applicants have exclusive rights to the land only for their lifetime. However, the bosses want their sons to inherit the projects. It is difficult to forecast what will happen when all the leaders die and to what extent the competing claims of those who have traditional rights in the estate of the deceased will negate the intentions of the bosses. In the only case to date in which a cattle boss died, his son assumed the role of project leader and only 2 of 19 cattle in the project were killed to satisfy those who held traditional rights to the assets of the deceased. If the sons of other cattle bosses also inherit a similar position, the projects should continue to function. Such continuity in the estate would mean the inheritance of an unprecedented amount of wealth and control over resources.

CONCLUSION

The introduction of smallholder cattle projects has significantly increased rural economic differentiation. I have examined differentiation in relation to changing control over the production process. Preexisting social relations of production have been altered, with the cattle bosses being the clear beneficiaries. They have been successful in mobilizing labor without adequate reciprocation, in part because of support from and manipulation of links with government agencies, though there are clearly limits as to how much labor followers will provide without just compensation. However, bosses now have the potential to pay others for required labor with project revenues. Cattle bosses also exercise a degree of control over the enclosed land that is unprecedented in the village's history. In addition, they appropriate a disproportionate share of the surplus from the enterprises for themselves. Their control over a large amount of capital may be passed on to subsequent generations, thus reproducing patterns of inequality. Although a certain amount of variation exists in the organization of other highlands cattle projects, and some have ceased operating, the social patterns concerning differentiation in relation to these projects are nevertheless widespread. . . .

NOTES

1. I recorded only two cases in which land was sold, and these were very small plots.

2. Kina is the monetary unit of Papua New Guinea. In 1977, K1.00 = approximately U.S.$1.35.

3. Projects are "relatively large" in relation to arable land in villages. According to a 1978 Department of Primary Industry survey, the average area of a project in Papua New Guinea is approximately 30 ha and in the Eastern Highlands District, 50 ha. Roughly 50 percent of the projects in the country have from 11 to 60 head of cattle. Figures are based on data from projects with and without PNGDB loans. Projects with such loans are in most cases larger than self-financed enterprises.

4. Following Epstein (1969), several types of land rights can be recognized. Rights held by all members of the village community regardless of kin group affiliation are "rights of commonality"; for example, everyone may hunt and gather environmental resources throughout the territory. A "proprietary right" is the ultimate interest that an individual can have in property. It includes the right of beneficial use and administration, immunity from trespass, and in certain circumstances the power to permanently transfer these rights to other Kapanarans. A proprietary right is usually obtained by cultivating an area that has not been gardened within memory. "Rights of encumbrance" give an individual a claim on the land and assets of others by virtue of the person's relationship with the rightholder. For a more detailed consideration of land tenure, see Grossman (1979).

5. The mean area enclosed per project is 78 ha, with a range from 48 to 107 ha.

REFERENCES

Connell, John
  1979 The Emergence of a Peasantry in Papua New Guinea. Peasant Studies 8:103–137.

Epstein, A. L.
  1969 Matupit: Land, Politics, and Change among the Tolai of New Britain. Canberra: Australian National University.

Finney, Ben R.
   1973   Big-Men and Business: Entrepreneurship and Economic Growth in the
   New Guinea Highlands. Honolulu: University Press of Hawaii.

Fleckenstein, F. von
   1975   Ketarovo: Case Study of a Cattle Project. *In* Four Papers on the Papua New
   Guinea Cattle Industry. pp. 91–138. New Guinea Research Bulletin No. 63.
   Canberra: Australian National University.

Gerritsen, Rolf
   1975   Aspects of the Political Evolution of Rural Papua New Guinea: Towards a
   Political Economy of the Terminal Peasantry. Seminar paper. Department of
   Political Science, Australian National University.

Good, Kenneth
   1979   The Formation of the Peasantry. *In* Development and Dependency: The
   Political Economy of Papua New Guinea. Azeem Amarshi, Kenneth Good, and
   Rex Mortimer, eds. pp. 101–122. Melbourne: Oxford University Press.

Grossman, Larry
   1980   The Beef Cattle Industry in Papua New Guinea: The Implications of Past
   Programmes for Future Planning. *In* Cattle Ranches Are About People: Social
   Science Dimensions of a Commercial Feasibility Study. Michael A. H. B. Walter, ed. pp. 17–42. Boroko: Institute of Applied Social and Economic Research.

Gunton, R. J.
   1974   A Banker's Gamble. *In* Problem of Choice: Land in Papua New Guinea's
   Future. Peter G. Sack, ed. pp. 107–114. Canberra: Australian National University.

Howlett, Diana
   1980   When Is a Peasant Not a Peasant: Rural Proletarianisation in Papua New
   Guinea. *In* Of Time and Place. J. N. Jennings and G. J. R. Linge, eds. pp. 193–
   210. Canberra: Australian National University.

Howlett, Diana, R. Hide, and Elspeth Young
   1976   Chimbu: Issues in Development. Canberra: Australian National University.

McKillop, Bob
   1976a   Helping the People in Papua New Guinea? A Case Study of a Cattle
   Introduction Programme. Paper presented at the Conference of the Sociological Association of Australia and New Zealand, La Trobe University.
   1976b   A Brief History of Agricultural Extension in Papua New Guinea. Extension Bulletin No. 10. Port Moresby: Department of Primary Industry.

Sahlins, M.D.
   1963   Poor Man, Rich Man, Big Man, Chief: Political Types in Melanesia and
   Polynesia. Comparative Studies in Society and History 5:285–303.

Standish, Bill
   1978   The Big-man Model Reconsidered: Power and Stratification in Chimbu.
   IASER Discussion Paper, No. 22. Boroko: Institute of Applied Social and Economic Research.

Watson, James B.
   1967   Tairora: The Politics of Despotism in a Small Society. Anthropological
   Forum 2:53–104.

VII

Human Rights and Political Struggle

Many observers emphasize that the central issue of development and tribal peoples is one of politics and human rights. In this view tribals have been damaged by development programs because, as relatively powerless minorities within modern nations, they are being denied their basic human rights. The human rights issue is not new. Since the earliest period of European colonial expansion, authorities on international law have maintained that tribal peoples had legitimate rights to political sovereignty and land ownership that could only be extinguished by conquest or treaty. Even into the twentieth century treaties were still being negotiated between essentially sovereign tribal groups and national governments, but many countries ignored or abandoned such gestures. In the post–World War II period, with the rise of international organizations like the United Nations and an increase in general concern for human rights, there has been renewed interest in the unique rights of tribal peoples. For example, in 1957 the International Labour Organisation adopted Convention No. 107 that specified in great detail the rights of tribal peoples to retain their traditional cultures and lands. At the present time a U.N. work group on indigenous populations is drafting a comprehensive new declaration of human rights for indigenous or tribal peoples and plans to prepare a legally binding international convention of indigenous rights.

Historically, national development planners in many countries have found it easy to disregard the obvious rights of tribal peoples to maintain their own ways of life. Genuine respect for human rights is the best way to reduce the detrimental impact of development. There is nothing inevitable about the advance of frontiers and the absorption of tribals—not if their human and political rights are recognized. There is a major political context for development policy toward tribals that cannot be ignored.

In recent decades tribal peoples themselves have become very active in the political struggle for the recognition of their right to self-determination. Conferences of tribal peoples have been held at national and international levels, and associations have been formed, most notably, the World Council of Indigenous Peoples, organized in 1975. Much of the political struggle understandably involves control of land and resources. There have been some outstanding gains, for example, in Australia and Canada (see selection by Lee, part V), but the major issue remains the unwillingness of nation-states to grant full control over natural resources to tribal peoples. Without such control it is impossible for tribals to maintain any reasonable degree of economic autonomy or of balanced resource management.

The following selections can only suggest the complexity of these issues. Ovesen examines some of the factors contributing to the Naga struggle for independence from India. Bay makes an important argument for the recognition of cultural rights above and beyond individual human rights where tribal peoples are concerned. Nietschmann considers two Central American groups, the Miskito of Nicaragua and the Kuna of Panama, and shows how political factors in both cases have shaped their level of cultural autonomy. Hyndman examines some of the Melanesian social movements that have followed the development of large-scale mining projects in New Guinea.

24 Cultural "Imperialism" and the Nagas

JAN OVESEN

Jan Ovesen is a docent in cultural anthropology at the University of Uppsala in Sweden. He holds a masters degree in anthropology from the University of Copenhagen and has studied at Oxford University. He conducted fieldwork in Afghanistan in 1977–78 and in West Africa in 1984. The Naga case illustrates the dilemma of tribal peoples who seek to maintain their independent identities in the postcolonial world. It also demonstrates the fact that colonial administration, even when it has included pacification and missionization, can prepare the way for pantribal indigenous independence movements.

This abridged version of Ovesen's paper follows the Naga from the point at which Williams (part 4) left off, prior to World War II, through the formation of the Indian state of Nagaland in 1962, up to the peace agreement of 1975. Ovesen shows how the Naga conceived of their identity as a distinct people vis-à-vis the British and independent India and how the Naga view conflicted with Indian intentions. Since 1975 the Naga have continued to press for independence from India in spite of steady military oppression and human rights abuses. It is important to note that the Naga people, or the "federation of Naga nations," occupy a continuous area in the Indian states of Assam, Nagaland, Manipur, and Arunchal Pradesh and in adjacent Burma. A number of pan-Naga resistance organizations exist, including armed resistance movements. An account of the situation as of 1986 may be found in IWGIA Document 56, *The Naga Nation and Its Struggle Against Genocide*.

As the preparations for Indian independence began the Nagas were acutely aware that unless some special arrangement was made for them they would suffer what in their eyes was the worst possible fate, domination by the peoples of the plains. They consequently began to prepare for their own independence; already in 1929 they approached a group of British MPs visiting the area and stated their case. That had a certain effect; I shall quote a bit of a speech made by one Mr. Cadogan in the House of Commons six years after his meeting with the Nagas (i.e. 1935), also because it shows that while the British left the Nagas much to

Reprinted in abridged form with permission of the author and the publisher, from *Cultural Imperialism and Cultural Identity: Proceedings of the 8th Conference of Nordic Ethnographers/ Anthropologists. Transactions of the Finnish Anthropological Society*, no. 2 (1977): 49–60. Copyright © 1977 Finnish Anthropological Society.

themselves they had not learnt much about them either. Here is what passed for witty and progressive:

> I suppose I am one of the few hon. Members of this House who have had conversation with the head-hunters of Kohima in their own jungle. These little head-hunters met us and had a palaver. Presumably the District Commissioner had informed the tribal chieftain that my head was of no intrinsic value as he evinced no disposition to transfer it from my shoulders to his head-hunter's basket which was slung over his back and was, I think, the only garment he affected. I am telling this to the Committee in order to prove that these little tribesmen are more sophisticated in their own particular way than perhaps the Committee may imagine. They have a very shrewd suspicion that something is being done to take away from them their immemorial rights and customs (quoted in Elwin 1961:49).

In the following years several propositions for special arrangements for the Nagas were discussed but no decision was reached, and when the Indians took over in 1947 it was all theirs. The Nagas sent a delegation, led by Mr. Angami Phizo, to Delhi with the request that the Naga Hills be left outside the Indian Union. An agreement was made granting a certain amount of autonomy to the region, an agreement which, it was stated, should be taken up for revision after a period of ten years. The Nagas took that latter point to mean that they would then get total independence, whereas to the Indians it meant integration after ten years. These differences of interpretation soon became apparent and the Nagas felt that they had been cheated. In response they totally boycotted the general elections in 1952 and civil disobedience gradually grew into violent resistance. In 1956 a Naga Federal Government was formed, and Nagaland was declared a people's sovereign republic. However, the Nagas were again forced to compromise, and in 1960 Nagaland was made the 16th state within the Indian Union. But compromise rarely makes anybody happy; nationalist leader Mr. Phizo went into exile in London, and at least until 1975 Naga guerrillas were still fighting for independence.[1]

As the Nagas see it (Ao 1972, Horam 1975) the British administration had only had a slight effect on their traditional way of life compared with the changes brought about by the Christian missionaries and the Second World War. As for the latter, the Japanese invaded the area in 1944 and Naga Hills became a battlefield. The Nagas fought bravely with the Allied Forces, and Field-Marshal Slim said, "Many a British and Indian soldier owes his life to the naked head-hunting Nagas, and no soldier of the Fourteenth Army who met them will ever think of them but with admiration and affection" (quoted in Horam 1975:15–16).

There had been missionaries among the Nagas since the turn of the century, but it was not until the early 1940s that their success really began, but from then on the number of converts quickly rose, and today Nagaland has a Christian majority. I do not think that it is too far fetched to postulate that one reason for the Nagas' readiness to adopt Christianity then was that, facing the coming independence of India, it represented, from their point of view, the lesser of two evils, the alternative, of course, being Hinduism.

> The tribal communities in the hills of North East India seem to have some amount of inhibition in the matter of adoption of Hinduism. One of the factors responsible for this is that Hinduism in their eyes is identified with the domination of the people of the plains (Roy Burman 1972:80).

In other parts of India we have seen how easily Hinduism can incorporate so-called animist religions, and whether they realized it or not, the Nagas would probably not stand much of a chance of retaining the autonomy of their traditional religion vis-à-vis Hinduism. Adopting Christianity, however, enabled them to confront Hinduism on equal terms. And indeed, after Indian independence when the last six foreign missionaries had left the Naga Hills, there were strong associations between the local church leaders and the guerrillas fighting against "Hindu Government." However, even if Christianity was to be used in defence of Naga cultural identity, the price they had had to pay in the first place was high. The activities of the missionaries, mainly American Baptists, had devastating effects on traditional culture; they had prohibited the drinking of rice-beer, had banned the traditional Feasts of Merit, and had persuaded people to abandon the bachelors' dormitories. "The result was a conflict . . . of culture, a conflict between the interest of community and individual which caused cultural tension in the society" (Ao 1972:479).

Added to this, Indian independence entailed a partial opening of the frontiers of the Naga Hills to "other Indian citizens."

> In the initial stages . . . certain business-minded communities belonging to the north, west, and central India came in great numbers to settle in the Hills and to conduct business there. They brought with them a sudden flow of new ideas, beliefs, goods, and also the know-how of successful entrepreneurship; also a fair share of dishonesty and exploitation . . . The plainsman appropriated all business openings and the very first 'Indian' the Nagas met was the crafty and wily merchant . . . Along with the new and higher standard of living came liabilities which were to destroy some of the finest aspects of Naga life and society (Horam 1975:128).

When the British left India they abandoned the White Man's Burden, and the new Government of India was faced with a "Naga problem." For a number of reasons this problem could not be left the way the British had left it. Firstly, any new state tends to be touchy about its frontiers, and the north-east region is obviously of some strategic importance. Secondly, the boundary problem is a cultural one as well as a political one; and in a culture which is dominated by distinctions between pure and impure we are not surprised that boundary problems are of central concern. So it was felt that the new Indian national identity should apply to the Nagas as well. But the Nagas were not interested in jumping into the Indian "melting pot," so they became "The Naga Problem." Various episodes (to use a euphemism) during the 1950s had made it abundantly clear that the problem was not to be solved by resort to armed force. The attitude of the general Indian public is clearly presented by Mr. Mankekar, an editor of The Times of India:

> This paper starts from the premises that the assimilation and integration of the north-eastern border tribes into the Indian nation is a paramount task before us not only because of national and strategic considerations but also for humanistic reasons (Mankekar 1972:110).

One obstacle to the integration, he says, is ignorance about the tribals, and he continues,

> The other, almost insuperable, barrier that has cut off these tribals from the rest of the country for 150 years, was raised by the British rulers of the period who pursued a deliberate policy of isolating the tribal people and sowing in their hearts distrust for the plainsmen (ibid:110–111).

This is pathetic. The paper is entitled "Understanding the tribals of the north-eastern border," and what he fails to understand is precisely the central point, viz., that as far as the Nagas are concerned they were never part of any country but their own hills, and the real trouble began only with the attempts of de-isolation of the last 30 years. However, our well-meaning journalist goes on,

> The isolation of the tribals was further accentuated by the advent of the Western Christian missionaries in the region. . . . [However,] as citizens of a secular and democratic India, we should not be concerned with the religious faith of the tribals or any section of the Indian people, but rather with their patriotism and loyalty to the Indian Union.
> Suspicion and distrust are however irrational passions which cannot be rooted out by external reasoning but have to be broken down through internal conversion and conviction. This can best be done not by outsiders but by the tribals' own kith and kin. To this end, therefore, we have to enlist the zealous cooperation of indigenous Christian missionaries. . . . The best way of enlisting the cooperation of the indigenous church leaders is therefore to convince them that these constitutional guarantees of freedom of religion and secularism of the State would be enforced honestly and sincerely by the present rulers of the country (ibid:111–113).

At this point, however, he nearly gives the whole game away by adding,

> Their efforts could of course be profitably supplemented by secular welfare organizations like the Shanti Sena or such reputable voluntary institutions as the Ramakrishna Mission whose disinterested ser-

vices and unobjectionable activities should be welcome to the tribals of the Assam Hills (ibid.)

In order to sum up the above description of the historical record let us first note that the Naga situation presents not so much an economic problem as a purely political one.[2] Earlier tribal uprisings in India had been caused by the British through economic deprivation; but the case of the Nagas does not fit that model. British imperialism in the economic sense of the word stopped at the foot of the Naga Hills, but even so it produced the foundation of a Naga cultural identity. The Christian missionaries started their work by attacking traditional cultural values, but later Christianity became part of the Naga identity. The Nagas fought alongside the British and the Indians in the war, but they refused to be governed by any of them. . . . cultural identity among the Nagas is not a result of prolonged colonization, it is rather a prophylactic against it.

Even if Christianity and the Second World War were felt by the Nagas to have had the most profound influences on their daily life, I think nevertheless that the British administration of the Naga Hills can be shown to have been of decisive importance; and we may well regard the Naga struggle for independence as a by-product of British imperialism. By way of conclusion we may present, in a schematic form, the various taxonomic spaces in which the parties operated. The British model of the taxonomic space would look like this:

British India	
Nontribals	Scheduled castes and tribes

FIGURE 1
British model

This model was essentially shared by the Nagas after they were brought under administration in 1881.

British rule		
Plainsmen	Nagas	Neighbouring hill tribes

FIGURE 2
Naga model before 1947

When the British withdrew, however, it appeared that the Indians and the Nagas were not in the same taxonomic space. For the Indians it was a question of replacing British India by the Indian Union, and of eventually "educating" the tribals as proper Indian citizens.

Indian Union	
Nontribals	Scheduled castes and tribes

FIGURE 3
Indian model

However, the Nagas' conception of the Indian model would rather look like this:

Indians	
Nagas	Neighbouring hill tribes

FIGURE 4
Naga conception of Indian model

The Nagas themselves were of the opinion that when the British left, the top section of their old model should just disappear:

Indians	Nagas	Neighbouring hill tribes

FIGURE 5
Naga model after 1947

Finally, let me point out that this last model is corroborated verbally by the Nagas themselves: "The main causes of the present movements are (1) Pride of ethnic identification; (2) Fear of exploitation; (3) Love of liberty and independence" (Ao 1972:484).

NOTES

An earlier version of this paper was presented at Mr. Edwin Ardener's seminar in social anthropology in Oxford, November 1976. I am grateful to Mr. Ardener and to members of the seminar for useful comments and suggestions.

In a previous paper (Ovesen, in press) I have analyzed some aspects of Naga cosmology in relation to the intertribal situation and to infrastructural conditions.

1. Following a couple of months' campaign against the guerrillas an "agreement" was made with the Government of India in November 1975. A sample of headlines which hit the front page of the Hindustan Times reads like this: 11.7. Surrendering Nagas assured better deal; 13.7. 20 Naga rebels arrested; 25.7 Naga "major" killed; 9.8. Pochuri cleared of rebel Nagas; 10.8. 200 rebel Nagas arrested; 12.8. Rebel Naga surrenders; 14.8. Naga "general" arrested; 8.9. Change in status of Nagaland ruled out; 18.9. Curfew in Naga areas; 23.9. 29 underground Nagas surrender; 26.9. Accord with Naga rebels in sight; 12.10. Naga rebels ready for settlement; 5.11. Talks with hostile Nagas continue; and finally, under the heading, ACCORD REACHED ON NAGA "ISSUES," the telegram starts, "Shillong, Nov. 11—The 20-year-old Naga problem has virtually been solved following an agreement between the Government of India and the Naga delegation representing underground organizations on 'basic issues' at a two-day Naga peace talks concluded here tonight."

2. In this paper I have been concerned only with the Nagas. It should be mentioned, however, that the example of the Nagas has spread to other tribes of Assam as well. The Naga National Council was duplicated in the Mizo National Front, the Garo National Council, and the Khasi Federation. As a result two more separate states of the Indian Union have been created out of Assam, namely Mizoram (formerly Lushai Hills) and Meghalaya (formerly Garo and Khasi Hills).

REFERENCES

Ao, M. A. Problems of Re-Adjustment to a new Situation (With Special Reference to the Naga Tribe). K. Suresh Singh (ed.), *Tribal Situation in India.* Indian Institute of Advanced Study. Simla 1972.

Elwin, V. *Nagaland.* Shillong 1961.

———. *The Nagas in the Nineteenth Century.* Bombay 1969.

Horam, M. *Naga Polity.* Delhi 1975.

Mankekar, D. R. Understanding the Tribals on the north-eastern Border. K. Suresh Singh (ed.) *Tribal Situation in India.* Indian Institute of Advanced Study. Simla 1972.

Ovesen, J. (in press) *Man or Beast? Lycanthropy in the Naga Hills.* E. Schwimmer (ed.), Yearbook of Symbolic Anthropology II. London.

Roy Burman, B. K. Integrated Area Approach to the Problems of the Hill Tribes of north-east India. K. Suresh Singh (ed.), *Tribal Situation in India.* Indian Institute of Advanced Study. Simla 1972.

25

Human Rights on the Periphery: No Room in the Ark for the Yanomami?

CHRISTIAN BAY

Christian Bay is a Norwegian-born political scientist who has been at the University of Toronto since 1972. His Ph.D. is from the University of Oslo (1959), and he helped establish the Institute for Social Research in Oslo after World War II. He has taught at Michigan State University, the University of California at Berkeley, Stanford University, and the University of Alberta. He is the author of well-known books and articles on freedom, human rights, and civil disobedience, most notably, *The Structure of Freedom* (1958, 1970), which won the Woodrow Wilson Award of the American Political Science Association.

In this selection Bay affirms the basic human right of relatively isolated tribal peoples to retain their traditional, communal way of life. Human rights are normally thought of as individual rights, but Bay recognizes that tribal or "indigenous" peoples constitute a special case in which "collective human rights" must apply. In opposition to Hippler and other writers who feel that culture is an abstraction, Bay believes that ethnocide is a reality and that it especially threatens relatively vulnerable isolated tribal groups when outside intrusion deprives them of the means of satisfying their basic human needs. There have been several proposals for the defense of the Yanomamo way of life in both Brazil and Venezuela, including a special Yanomamo Park and a biosphere reserve, but powerful development interests in both countries pose major obstacles to any such plan.

Important human rights issues arise whenever people are oppressed or victimized, as happens disproportionally to indigenous populations who have seldom or never been part of the new states, and whose habitats, both culturally and geographically, have tended to be far removed from the 'corridors of power'. In more than one sense, then, most of them may be considered peripheral peoples, reduced to subjection or dependency, whether the larger system surrounding them is mainly feudal or corporate-capitalist.

Some indigenous peoples are more peripheral than others, both geographically and culturally. In this paper I will discuss human rights and indigenous peoples in general, but with particular reference to one such

Reprinted in abridged form from *Development Dialogue* 1, no. 2 (1984): 23–41, by permission of the author and The Dag Hammarskjöld Foundation. Copyright © 1984 The Dag Hammarskjöld Foundation.

people, probably the largest forest-dwelling indigenous people in South America: the Yanomami,[1] a people whose survival is now in acute jeopardy. . . .

In this paper I cannot address the pressing practical issue of what can and must be done to influence the governments of the two nations, both (and especially Brazil) labouring under heavy pressures of external debts, to find honourable, practical and immediate ways to protect the survival prospects of the Yanomami. This struggle must be led from inside each country.

I will attempt something else: to make the case that the Yanomami's cause represents the most urgent category of all present day human rights issues anywhere in the world, since not only individual lives but the lives of whole peoples are almost immediately at stake. The specific issue is whether we can tolerate the prospects of a 'final solution' for the Yanomami. This is the moral issue. There is also the large existential issue: is a world without surviving indigenous peoples fit for survival for the rest of us?

.   .   .

'Human rights' surely must mean the rights of all humans, and it may at first seem awkward to speak of the human rights of indigenous peoples. But I shall argue that survival is the most basic of all human rights, and that the menace to survival, even collective survival, is particularly extreme in the case of the Yanomami and other largely unacculturated indigenous peoples.

To pursue this argument I must first explicate my conception of human rights, and of the basis for the 'natural' priorities that I find among categories of human rights. Next I develop my substantive case for insisting on the highest priority, as a human rights issue, for adequate protection of vulnerable peoples like the Yanomami against the mounting pressures that will soon destroy them, unless present trends can be reversed. In conclusion I go beyond the human rights argument to develop not only moral but practical grounds for the urgent need to defend vulnerable peoples who live close to nature. Our own civilization has for too long proceeded to pursue the 'conquest of nature', in heedless disregard for nature's limits; and it is time to confront and resist on a broad front the abuses of modern technology and the exploitive interests that these abuses serve. While for myself the moral grounds for defending indigenous rights come first, I mean to show that a viable future for our own 'developed' nations and peoples requires a viable future for the indigenous peoples also, for their right to determine their own cultural development, and above all for their self-preservation.

PRIORITIES IN HUMAN RIGHTS

Extrapolating from Maurice Cranston's classical discussion,[2] I shall assume that human rights are moral rights that are (1) universal, (2) paramount, and (3) practical. But I shall add two more definitional criteria: (4) human rights are entitlements that should (must) become incorporated in positive national and international law, as fully and as soon as possible; and (5) human rights cannot all be equally paramount; the ranking of relative urgency among categories of human rights must depend on (a) how basic is the level of *human need* which requires the enforcement of that right, and (b) how clearly and directly does a particular right bear on, and facilitate the meeting of, that kind of need? . . .

The conventional liberal wisdom asserts that the state exists for the sake of man, not man for the sake of the state. I mean to select and articulate a more precise interpretation of that affirmation: the highest-priority task of any legitimate state is to ensure, so far as possible, that all (universal) human needs are being met, with the *more* basic or urgent needs taking precedence over those that are less basic or less urgent. 'Human needs' is in principle an empirical concept, but on a high level of abstraction. I shall take the term to refer to any and all requirements for (1) human survival, (2) physical security, health protection, (3) dignity, mental health, and (4) freedom—that is, individual and collective freedom of choice, within the social constraint stipulating that choices are entitled to protection only to the extent that they do not jeopardize the survival, health, dignity, or equally basic freedoms of choice for others.

To facilitate the needed cooperation between social scientists and political and legal professionals it is necessary to switch from needs-language to rights-language. My position is that the universal and supreme task for legitimate politics and law (legislation, administration, and adjudication) is to struggle for a world of secure human rights for all, with the more basic human rights taking precedence over those less basic.

Why are priorities among human rights required? Because some categories of needs *are* more important than others: say, the need for protection against torture compared to the need for vacations with pay.[3]

Already in my definition of 'human needs' I have suggested what I take to be the right order of priorities among human rights categories: survival rights must come first; then the right to protection from physical injury and disease; then the right to dignity, identity, conditions compatible with mental health; and finally, freedom rights, rights to individual choice and free development, within the limits of social constraints.[4] . . .

It is easy enough to show that in the absence of an understanding and acceptance of priorities, tacitly at least, we should be doomed to maintaining a static pluralist society, in which even the superficial needs of the strong are routinely gratified at the expense of even the most dire needs of the weak. But how to determine more precisely (a) how basic is the human need that is at stake, if any, behind specific categories of human rights claims; and (b) how directly would the granting of a claim serve to meet that need, and how effectively, and how sure can we be about this?

These issues are far too complicated to be dealt with in a brief paper. They can be by-passed here, for I shall be concerned only with very elementary needs of manifestly endangered populations: the survival-related needs of indigenous peoples, and especially those of the still surviving forest-dwelling peoples in South America.

HUMAN RIGHTS AND THE PROTECTION OF INDIGENOUS PEOPLES

Human rights are by definition universal, I have asserted. Does it still make sense to speak of *indigenous* human rights? I think it does.

The rights at issue are crucial for the protection of the most basic and therefore universal human needs. My concern is first of all with the survival needs of persons and communities exposed to the same categories of threat: they are utterly defenseless and at the mercy of well-armed states and corporate interests and, what is often the worst part, of lawless individuals who covet their land and resources. Their own different heritage and views of the world, their vulnerability to diseases, their lack of cunning and of weaponry resources, and in general the fact that they have not been part of the national systems of influence and power, expose them to the most extreme neglect, once their land and resources have been invaded or destroyed or taken away from them. They may even, sometimes with impunity, be the victims of deliberate 'final solution'-type massacres.

Not because they are indigenous peoples, but because they are human beings with indigenous cultures, and with unique ways of being human, should their defense and protection be a matter of the highest-priority concern for all people the world over who care about human rights, and for the media that undertake to keep us informed about international news.

Human rights are the rights of individual human beings everywhere. Does it nonetheless make sense to speak of *collective* human rights for indigenous peoples? I shall argue that it does, and also that these collective human rights must be distinguished sharply from corporate rights, which may be legal rights but cannot be human rights.

Every individual's survival is at stake when the destruction of a people is in progress. Likewise, every individual's health and dignity are at stake when ethnocide, the destruction of a human culture, is in progress, by way of destroying the natural habitat or the religious faith or the needed privacy of an indigenous people, for purposes of imposed 'development', commercial exploitation, or 'civilizing' religious instruction and conversion. Forced acculturation is declared public policy today in several Latin American countries: even the more humane statutes, comparatively speaking, assert that 'integration' is the ultimate purpose of the state. In other words, the aim is the forced abandonment and destruction of ethnic and cultural identities, along with the 'freedom' to compete for individual survival in the jungles of the city slums.[5] This is not as bloody as outright genocide, but the result is the same: the extinction of yet another culturally distinct people. Ethnocide is like genocide on the instalment plan.

Short of omnicide, the killing of all human beings, which today can be and possibly will be accomplished with a nuclear world war, I shall assume that outright genocide must be considered the ultimate crime against humanity. This is not only because we must consider it a worse crime to kill many persons than it is to kill one. With genocide, you kill the future, too, with all the aspirations, hopes, dreams, and insights that countless generations have built up, within a given culture. To face individual death is one thing; to face death for all your kin and for all that you care for is a horror of an entirely different magnitude.[6]

Short of omnicide and short of genocide, ethnocide is also a monstrous crime, as it destroys the cultural dignity and identity of all members of a people, and very likely destroys their mental and physical health as well, as well as their unique world views and traditional knowledge, and it often terminates their ability or motivation to reproduce their own kind. The story has been repeated over and over again on the many 'frontiers of development', in South America and elsewhere: once proud, self-reliant peoples have been reduced to a state of dependency on handouts and on alcohol and other drugs, with many men becoming beggars and many women prostitutes, and all becoming available for cheap labour under conditions approximating slavery.

While some human rights are collective human rights, I have argued, none are corporate rights. Corporate rights may be legal rights, but they are never human rights. This is an important distinction to make, for I have argued that a legitimate state must be committed to making human rights, and especially the most basic human rights, prevail over (other) legal rights.

Corporations are coalitions of persons seeking to take continuous, accumulative advantage of their combined, well-organized resources of strength. Under capitalism, this is the most effective way to accumulate, with time, enormous economic and political power in a relatively few private hands. Under Marxist regimes, public corporations acquire enormous power, in alliance with the state; their behaviour may or may not differ significantly from that of private large corporations. Private corporations of the business world, in any event, are programmed to take advantage of their own strength against weaker competitors, and against weaker or less well-organized employees, consumers, and the general public. Clearly, a *legitimate*, human rights-oriented state would be on a collision course with most of the large commercial corporations. It is not surprising that most *actual* states in the liberal-capitalist world tend to be influenced, even infiltrated, by private corporate interests, with the result that most First World and many Third World governments routinely sacrifice human rights to corporate legal rights and interests. (I do not mean to imply that human rights tend to prevail over public corporate interests in the second world; that is a different matter.)

In this paper, I am concerned with only a relatively small part of the problem of collusion between private corporations and the state at the expense of human rights for the less privileged, but it is a crucial part of the problem in a number of countries, since those 'less privileged' who are most badly hurt are so vulnerable; their very existence is on the line, in either the near or the immediate future.

Can a collective human right to protection against ethnocide be in conflict with individual human rights to cultural choice? Do tribal elders, for example, have a moral right to forcibly prevent young members of their tribes from seeking outside contacts, or from moving away?

Undoubtedly, such conflicts frequently develop, and in principle I think the individual's right to choose how and where to live must prevail. But this requires that the choice must be possible—that a life within one's traditional community is still viable. If conditions of ethnocidal forced contact prevail, perhaps with the destruction of a people's means of subsistence to compound the crime, then neither the older traditionalists, nor the younger members of a given community will have retained their most basic right to choose, or preserve, a life with dignity among their own people.

Do indigenous individuals have a human right to reject certain traditional customs that they have come to find unacceptable, perhaps as a result of outside influence—for example, clitorectomy, as is still practiced in some African and Arab cultures; or infanticide? I should think yes, and perhaps even that they have a moral right to seek outside protection against such acts of violence if the community is effectively under a national jurisdiction for many other purposes; but I must stress that this poses an urgent challenge to anthropologists in collaboration with indigenous informants to account for the functions that such customs may have served, so that the possible damage from violations of traditions can be minimized.

There are many intricate theoretical issues involved in the analysis of human rights in the context of external threats to collective survival, once we take the position that genocide and ethnocide violate the most basic individual *and* collective human rights. Individuals singly *and* collectively have first of all a human right to life, to health, to dignity, and to freedom; as is well known in our society, too, individuals may suffer internal conflict, in that they may want to obey both personal inclinations and social responsibilities, even when the two would dictate opposite responses. People with such dilemmas may under some circumstances legitimately be ever so tenderly pushed, I should think, toward making the social choice. Perhaps elders in a community in danger of destruction are entitled to exert *some* pressure against youngsters taking off on their own, tempted by the anticipated glitter of far-away cities, in their perhaps media-influenced imagination.

But such pressures must stop short of physical violence and cannot legitimately be continued for more than a couple of years past reaching adulthood, in my view; or for more than a couple of years past initial contact with outsiders. It is proclaimed in the Universal Declaration of Human Rights that everyone 'has the right to leave any country . . .' (Article 13, 2); that must mean any reservation, or tribal territory, as well. However, I think this stipulation may be interpreted a bit more loosely in situations where an immediate choice to abandon a culture or a habitat could contribute to foreclosing the opportunity to make the opposite choice even only a few years later.

The same Article also affirms everyone's right to 'freedom of movement within the borders of each state . . .' (Article 13, 1). This is not to be understood as an unrestricted freedom, however. It is in fact restricted by private property rights. In many countries landowners have a right to forbid anyone access to or across their territories.

A more reasonable arrangement obtains in other countries, including the Scandinavian, where landowners have no right to bar innocent passage or harmless recreation on their lands, excepting private gardens and fields under cultivation during the growing season. The right to move about freely is deemed more important than the right to block passage (neither can other innocent uses be blocked, such as picking wild berries or common wildflowers). In countries with endangered indigenous populations, on the other hand, there should be strict enforcement of a total ban on passage through their territories, except by invitations issued at *their* initiative.

Eventually, I believe, most of the now isolated or semi-isolated indigenous peoples will choose to integrate in some ways and to a degree with the larger society. But adequate time must be allowed for each people to make that choice and to determine freely how it will adjust, if that is the choice, in order to come to terms with life in the larger society. Prematurely enforced contacts again and again have destroyed, culturally and often physically also, vulnerable communities and the people whose roots were within them.

One final theoretical problem must be touched on: since human rights by definition are universal, in the sense of being in principle generalizable to all human beings, would it not be contradictory to speak of indigenous claims to extensive traditional lands as a category of human rights? This would indeed be contradictory. Claims to large land areas, whether individual or collective, cannot be validated as a human right. But for indigenous forest-dwelling peoples like the Yanomami, these claims should nonetheless be given the status of a legal right as well as a moral right, for these principal reasons:

1. Indigenous peoples have a moral right to keep all the lands that they need for their survival as peoples, at least for as long as they choose to support themselves in the traditional ways.[7]

2. They have a human right to the means necessary to their survival.

3. They have a human right to exactly the same respect and legal protection for *their* property rights as any member of the larger society has for his or her property rights.

Moreover, as we shall see, there is much evidence that the indigenous peoples, for example in the Amazon Basin, have preserved their habitats as good custodians, while the people and interests that have driven so many of them out have been creating deserts where there were once healthy forests. But, whatever the force of this last justification for granting to indigenous peoples permanent title to their lands, this is a utilitarian justification, not a moral one rooted in their basic human needs, which is the end that, by my definition, human rights must serve.

THE DEFENCE OF VULNERABLE PEOPLES

One question remains: is it at all realistic today to engage in strenuous efforts to try to save the remaining, relatively unacculturated and unsubjugated, indigenous peoples from their destruction, in countries where they still exist? Or, as many would have us believe, is it impossible, too late, futile?

When conceived as a *general* principle there is in our civilization a wide agreement, I think, in support of the idea that all branches of the human family are equally human, and equally deserving of protection for their basic human rights; which means *more* deserving of assistance the more extreme their plight. Our mass media find it easier, to be sure, to empathize with well-known individual victims of human rights violations, for example with admirable persons like a Sakharov or a Walesa, but in my view a rational humanist must be even more deeply concerned when whole peoples are threatened with destruction. An analogy between politics and medicine may be useful: the medical staff in a good hospital do not worry equally about the health of every patient; instead, they provide for special care for those whose lives and health are in immediate or extreme danger.

The Kantian humanist premise is universal: each human life is to be treated as an end, never as a means. But are we today perhaps up against harsh historical realities that make the sanctity of human life a mere pipedream? Is the earth becoming too crowded, for one thing, to make universal human rights feasible; should we instead be struggling for the rights of Englishmen, or of Americans, or Canadians, or Latin Americans?

Garrett Hardin, the well-known Californian biologist, appears to think so: 'Cherishing individual lives in the short run diminishes the number of lives in the long run . . . *the concept of the sanctity of life is counterproductive.* To achieve its goal the concept of the sanctity of life must give precedence to the concept of the sanctity of carrying capacity.'[8] We must curtail food aid to Third World countries, Hardin has argued, unless they, or some of them, demonstrate that they can limit the growth of their populations. Otherwise, US aid programmes will lead to more mouths to feed, and over the coming decades the earth's soil and food resources will become progressively less and less adequate to feed the burgeoning Third World populations.[9]

As I have argued elsewhere, Hardin is right on one point: if we take for granted, as he does, the 'Free World's' almost limitless freedom for individuals and corporations to engage in the accumulation of private wealth, by way of helping themselves to natural resources, and dumping their wastes, then we will indeed soon be approaching the limits of the earth's carrying capacity, and rising populations in any part of the world will speed us along on our perilous course. But we are not yet anywhere near the end of available food resources, and I find it utterly obscene to advocate cutting famine relief to the most needy peoples today, instead of trying to do something about our world's present maldistribution and waste (including the stupendous military waste of human and natural resources). Moreover, with increasing social welfare, as has been demonstrated in many parts of the world, birth rates soon tend to go down. However, Hardin is evidently a dogmatic liberal, for he chooses to recommend the sacrifice of the most basic human rights in much of the Third World for the convenience of affluent North Americans, whose present system of private-corporate enterprise is to be preserved, he insists, whatever the cost to other, relatively poor and powerless nations.[10]

Let me pursue this issue one step further. While Hardin's argument about ecological limits is valid and important as a long-term projection, he is radically wrong, I have concluded, about our immediate situation, and his proposed inhumane policies are unnecessary. But suppose that his stark diagnosis in truth had applied to our present situation; might it not then have been necessary to seize sparsely populated indigenous lands, at the cost of genocide, in order to help meet the nutritional requirements of more numerous populations?

Even in such a desperate, fortunately hypothetical situation, the case for seizing indigenous lands, especially in the Amazon Basin, would be very weak, as it turns out, for the ecological system that supports the rain forests turns out to be very fragile. There is mounting evidence that the soil and climatic conditions have radically deteriorated in the large areas of Brazilian rain forests that have already been turned over to ranch and pasture lands (for the principal purpose of exporting beef to First World markets). While the indigenous peoples of the Amazon have lived for thousands of years in harmony with nature, the European invaders' civilization, and especially with the use of our present-day technologies (agricultural, road-building, manufacturing and mining technologies), has produced not only rather empty savannahs where there had been forests teeming with life, but as well has produced large areas of almost lifeless deserts. Writing in 1978, Kenneth I. Taylor states that in recent years 'the recognition seems to have been growing in Brazil that agricultural projects which involve heavy deforestation are doomed to failure.'[11]

Goodland and Irwin in a careful study published in 1975 conclude that, while indigenous forest clearings generally have been limited in space and time and have regenerated fresh forest growth, recent large-scale clearings for highways and ranches have wiped out whole species of fauna and flora in some cases, and as a rule have proved a non-reversible process.[12] In the preface to their monograph, Harold Sioli makes an impassioned plea to stop the process of destruction in Amazonia, and preserve 'her great natural and cultural heritage' for the generations to come.[13]

'In recent years', writes Shelton H. Davis, 'several ecologically minded scientists have made a strong case for the usage of indigenous, rather than imported, models for the development of the Amazon.' He quotes Paulo de Almeida Machado, then Director of Brazil's National Institute for Amazon Research, to the effect that the Indian is often regarded as inferior. 'But when you talk about living in the Amazon he is far superior because he harmonizes so perfectly with the whole ecological system.' Paraphrasing de Almeida Machado, Davis continues: 'The Indian, he said, has hundreds of crops that are not used by Western man, do not upset the ecological system, and could be exploited commercially. The Indian also possesses vast stores of cultural knowledge about medicines and other remedies, and in his natural condition is free from malaria and other Western diseases. Finally, the Indian has learned to balance population with resources, and for centuries has lived in the Amazon without poisoning its waters and lands. "The tragedy", Machado concluded, "is that the Indian is one of the main keys to the successful occupation of the Amazon, and as he disappears his vast wealth of knowledge goes with him".[14]

Must the Amerindians of South America disappear? If their basic human rights do not impress the governments in this part of the world as important enough to stem the tide of ethnocide and genocide, can the same authorities now be made to see that they *need* these peoples to continue to protect their traditional lands from destruction?

.   .   .

Of all the forces that the indigenous peoples of the Americas are up against, the constantly repeated and reaffirmed assumption, apparently shared by friend and foe and by the indifferent alike, to the effect that they are *doomed to disappear,* represents possibly the most intractable aspect of the massive menace to their future. It could become, even up to 'the final solution' for the last of the remaining native peoples, a cumulatively self-fulfilling prophecy.

The view that man's calling is to dominate nature, using the increasingly powerful tools of modern science and technology, has firm foundations in Western social and political thought of the last several centuries. 'Only let the human race recover that right over nature which belongs to it by divine bequest,' wrote Francis Bacon at the beginning of the 17th Century, 'and let power be given it; the exercise thereof will be governed by sound reason and true religion'.[15] With the notable exception of Rousseau, the French Enlightenment embraced this faith in modern science and this view of Nature as the principal adversary, destined to be subjugated for the good of Mankind; and subsequent generations of liberals as well as marxists have been following this lead.

Largely overlooked, until recent years, was the necessity of respecting nature's limits and nature's vulnerability. With so much 'empty' space in the Americas still available, nature seemed so abundant to Europeans; and before our present century, technology did not yet have as much destructive power as it has now. Even if we are spared another world war, present-day technology can alter, waste or even poison enormous acreages in a short time, and with our liberal-corporate system it is often very profitable to do so, and many corporations have a very wide latitude to do what is most profitable, in the Americas as in other parts of the 'Free World'. To be sure, in some countries a rising ecological consciousness has succeeded in establishing legal limits to private and public destruction of nature, but this is an uphill battle, in competition with other, more popular priorities such as employment opportunities in polluting industries. Apart from all the visible evidence of our technology's destructiveness, a fundamental problem with the concept of man's domination of nature, which has been articulated well by William Leiss, is that *human* nature, too, tends to be dominated. As the power of technology grows, and as the power over technology becomes concentrated in fewer corporate hands, to the same degree the thought and behaviour of most men and women tend to become dominated by the privileged few who possess knowledge, wealth, and power.[16]

In truth there is a massive war going on today between technology and nature, and nature keeps on losing ground. This means that the human species keeps on losing ground, too, for we are rooted in nature and are a part of nature, even if most of us are no longer as directly embedded in nature and are not as immediately vulnerable as the still surviving, still relatively unsubjugated peoples, peoples like the Yanomami, who have lived in and have cared so well for their forest habitats for so many centuries. In sharp contrast with the commercial exploiters of our own civilization, the Yanomami have been responsible trustees of nature, for their own future generations, and have known how to keep their own numbers limited. Are they now to be denied a future?

We desperately need to call a halt to our civilization's continuing war against nature, or the whole human species will lose irretrievably. And the lines of defense must include and accentuate the battle for survival for the remaining largely unacculturated peoples, like those of the Amazon Basin. If they are destroyed, chances are that the rest of us will share their fate, without a very long respite, even if we are fortunate enough to avoid nuclear war. Pat Roy Mooney has shown, for example, that our civilization's increasingly artificial agriculture (i.e., it has come to depend on increasingly gene-standardized, high-yield crops of wheat, rice, corn, etc., which are increasingly vulnerable to blights on a catastrophic scale) now acutely endangers the future nutrition of billions, and he calls for international emergency measures to retrieve and protect the earth's rapidly dwindling diversity of germ plasm from plants on the growing Endangered Species lists, and especially from the natural relatives and ancestors to our principal foodcrop-producing plants.[17] In this way, too, we have at our peril kept turning our back on nature. An anonymous North American Indian has formulated this warning to us all, but with particular address to our industrial, scientific, and technological establishments! 'When you have polluted the last river, when you have caught the very last fish, and when you have cut down the very last tree, it is too bad that then, and only then, will you realize that you can not eat all your money in the bank'.[18]

NOTES

1. William J. Smole uses the name Yanoama, and discusses various other designations, in his *The Yanoama Indians: A Cultural Geography*, Austin, TX, University of Texas Press, 1976, Note 1, p. 217. Smole cites one population estimate as high as 25,000 'or more', of course including the Yanomami on both sides of the border. Ramos reports that a 1977 FUNAI (the National Indian Foundation) aerial survey indicated a Brazilian population of at least 8,300 Yanomami. Chagnon in 1968 estimated a total Yanomami population of close to 10,000, but indicated that he was merely guessing. Alcida R. Ramos, 'Yanoama Indians in Northern Brazil Threatened by Highway' in Alcida R. Ramos and Kenneth I. Taylor, *The Yanoama in Brazil 1979*, Copenhagen, IWGIA (International Work Group on Indigenous Affairs), 1979, p. 1–41, at p. 31; and Napoleon A. Chagnon, *Yanomamo: The Fierce People*, New York, Holt, Rinehart and Winston, 1977 (1968), at p. 1.—A press release from Survival International, London, 'Tin Mines Threaten Yanomami', dated March 1, 1984, refers to 'the 13,500 Yanoama Indians of South Venezuela' (note the two spellings in the same document).

2. Cranston, Maurice, *What Are Human Rights?* London, Bodley Head, 1973, pp. 4–7, 21–24, and 66–67.

3. Articles 5 and 24 in the Universal Declaration of Human Rights.

4. Cf. my *Strategies of Political Emancipation*, Notre Dame, Ind., University of Notre Dame Press, 1981, Chapter 4.

5. 'All through Brazilian history, from the most distant colonial times to the present day, the efforts for the "integration" of the Indian constituted the essential and almost the sole object of the official Indian policy.' Dostal, W. (ed.), *The Situation of the Indian in South America*. Geneva: World Council of Churches, 1972, p. 340.

6. Jonathan Schell conveys this conception of 'the second death' with unforgettable poignancy in his recent book about nuclear war: *The Fate of the Earth*, New York, Knopf, 1982. I suppose that the quality of grief at the contemplation of the death of one's entire people, which has been and is experienced in the context of ongoing genocidal destruction in parts of South America, whether intended or not (it is often caused by epidemics which could with a modest concern and effort have been averted), is not on the same level with contemplating the impending death of the entire human race; it is more as if a whole nation is about to become extinct.

7. This refers to such peoples, like the Yanomami, whose survival prospects are in jeopardy, because their cultural traditions and economic self-sufficiency, as well as their health, is gravely threatened by incursions of outsiders onto their lands. Unsubjugated, still largely unacculturated peoples require, and should be entitled to, a lot of time before even *choices* are forced upon them, let alone dictates from outsiders. While I believe that acculturated indigenous peoples, too, should have legal title to their traditional lands, these peoples should allow to outsiders the right of innocent passage and freedom of movement on their territories, as stipulated in the Universal Declaration of Human Rights, referred to above on p. 13. These rights should yield only when the more basic rights of biological and cultural survival are at stake.

8. Hardin, Garrett, 'An Ecolate View of the Human Predicament', in McRostie, Clair N., (ed.), *Global Resources: Perspectives and Alternatives*, Baltimore, University Park Press, 1980, pp. 49–71, at p. 57. (Hardin's italics).

9. See Hardin, 'Lifeboat Ethics: The Case Against Helping the Poor', in *Psychology Today*, Vol. 8, (September, 1974), pp. 38–43 and 123–126. Also see his excellent and important essay, 'The Tragedy of the Commons', in his *Exploring New Ethics for Survival: The Voyage of the Spaceship Beagle*. Baltimore: Penguin, 1973, pp. 250–264 (first published in 1968).

10. See my 'On Ecolagy Sans Humanism', in *Alternatives*, Vol. 7, No. 3 (1981–82), pp. 395–402. Also see the papers by Raini Kothari, 'On Ecoimperialism', and by Richard Falk, 'On Advice to the Imperial Prince', in the same issue.

11. Taylor, Kenneth I., 'Development Against the Yanoama: The Case of Mining and Agriculture', in Ramos and Taylor, *op. cit.* (above, Note 2), pp. 85–86.

12. Goodland, R. J. A., and Irwin, H. S., *Amazon Jungle: Green Hell to Red Desert? An Ecological Discussion of the Environmental Impact of the Highway Construction Program in the Amazon Basin*, Amsterdam, Elsevier, 1975.

13. *Ibid.*, p. VII.

14. Davis, Shelton H., *Victims of the Miracle: Development and the Indians of Brazil*, Cambridge, Cambridge University Press, 1977, pp. 156–157.

15. Quoted by William Leiss from Francis Bacon's *The New Organon*. See Leiss, *The Domination of Nature*, New York, Braziller, 1972, p. 50.

16. Cf. *ibid.*, and also Leiss, *The Limits to Satisfaction: An Essay on the Problem of Needs and Commodities*, Toronto, University of Toronto Press, 1976.

17. Mooney, Pat Roy, 'The Law of the Seed: Another Development and Plant Genetic Resources', whole issue of *Development Dialogue*, 1983: 1–2, published by the Dag Hammarskjöld Foundation in Uppsala, Sweden.

18. This is an inscription on an Indian blanket, a photograph of which appears on the front page of the Mohawk Indians' publication, *Akwesasne Notes*. Vol. 14, No. 1 (Early Spring, 1982). Source of the saying is not indicated.

26 Miskito and Kuna Struggle for Nation Autonomy

BERNARD NIETSCHMANN

This selection was originally a paper presented at the 150th Annual Meeting of the American Association for the Advancement of Science held in New York in 1984 in a symposium entitled "The Position of Small-Scale Autonomous Cultures in Latin America." The purpose of the symposium was to explore both the desirability and the feasibility of tribal autonomy as a human rights objective for indigenous people in opposition to the dominant policy of national integration. Like Bay, Nietschmann takes the position that indigenous peoples have a legitimate human right to maintain political control over the resources they need to sustain their traditional ways of life. In this selection he presents two case studies from Central America in which tribal nations made direct efforts to retain their political independence. The Kuna are a model example of a successful self-defense movement. They resorted to a brief armed rebellion in 1925 against the newly formed and still weak nation of Panama and were granted an autonomous status within the Panamanian State. They are now attempting further to safeguard their territory by establishing an internationally sanctioned biosphere reserve conservation area along their frontier (see Wright, et al. part VIII).

The Miskito have been less fortunate. Their human rights struggle is now entangled with the armed conflict between the newly created socialist state of Nicaragua and the United States. Neither of the principals in the larger conflict seem genuinely supportive of Miskito autonomy. The ramifications of the international political-military context do not bode well for the Miskito. Those who oppose the Contras, as they are called, and support the Nicaraguan Sandinista government on humanitarian grounds might not condone the Sandinista military opposition to the Miskito. It is clear that the Miskito have suffered military oppression under the Sandinistas, but it is not clear that a victory by the Contra forces would guarantee the Miskito their human rights.

STATES VERSUS NATIONS

On every continent, throughout the Americas, in almost every country in Latin America, conflicts exist between states and indigenous nations over control of land, resources, and people. The interests of the state and indigenous nations are in fundamental opposition. States seek to exert centralized control over claimed national territory and inhabitants through introduced legal, economic, and bureaucratic means, backed by the threat or use of

Paper presented at the Annual Meeting of the American Association for the Advancement of Science, New York, 1984. Reprinted by permission of the author.

military force. Under the mantle of manifest destiny, national consolidation, resource procurement, economic development, and military security, states have subjugated or threatened indigenous nations with imposed external government policies ranging from extermination to integration. Indigenous peoples, on the other hand, maintain decentralized authority over their territories through locally recognized group rights to area and resource based on customary ownership, often centuries of occupation, and shared cultural identity, residence, and kinship.

Most international states are not nations. Nations are geographically bounded territories of a common people who share a sense of homogeneity and identify themselves as "one people" on the basis of common ancestry, history, society, institutions, ideology, often religion, and language. The existence of nations is ancient. Today there are between 3000 and 5000 nations; some have small populations and areas, and some have populations reaching into the millions and territories larger than many states. Most people could not name even ten of the world's nations.

A state is a centralized political system, recognized by other states, that uses a civilian and military bureaucracy to enforce one set of institutions and laws, and sometimes a single language and religion within its claimed boundaries. This is done regardless of the presence of nations that have preexisting and different laws and institutions and who may not accept imposed state sovereignty. Although most state governments assert that their state is made up of one common people (a nation), more than 95 percent of the international states are multinational, that is, composed of many nations, some unconsenting. In 1945 there were 72 states, and today there are 168, most of which are represented in the United Nations. Of these, very few are "nation-states" (Iceland, Western Samoa, East Germany, Poland, Denmark, and a few others).

The world's indigenous peoples are nation peoples whose territories and resources are claimed by state peoples. Much of the development and expansion of states has been accomplished by the takeover and absorption of nations. Over 400 years of colonialism have stripped indigenous peoples of land, resources, and rights. Wars of independence, wars of liberation, and decolonization have led to the creation of new states from overdeveloped colonial powers, mostly in the Third World—the developing countries.

Most persisting indigenous peoples are part of the Fourth World, which comprises indigenous nations colonized and dominated by First, Second, and Third World states that do not recognize separate indigenous sovereignty and rights of self-determination. Because states make the rules that determine international law, people of unrecognized indigenous nations have only very weak international "rights." Since many First, Second and Third World states have Fourth World peoples and nations within their claimed territories, it is in the interests of each state to ignore "internal colonialism" against indigenous peoples perpetrated by any other state. The Third World is doing to the Fourth World what used to be done to them.

Of the world's current 50 wars, fully 60 percent are between states and nations. State-versus-state conflicts (for example, Iran and Iraq) are few in number, usually last but a few years, and often are not over territory. State-versus-nation conflicts, however, are the most common type of war (32 of 50), last many years (for example, Burma versus Kawthoolei, 38 years; Ethiopia versus Eritrea, 26 years), and are always over territory. State-versus-nation conflicts are responsible not only for the majority of wars but also for over 60 percent of the world's refugees, for almost all of the genocide, and for the existence of most of the groups accused of being "terrorists."

Latin America is also Indian America, but there are no Indian states. There are only non-Indian states that call Indian peoples "Mexican," "Guatemalan," "Nicaraguan," "Panamanian," "Brazilian," and so on, in order to gain control over indigenous land and resources. The central issue for nation peoples is retention of autonomous control over indigenous land, resources, and communities. States seek to incorporate indigenous nations by unilateral decree, by force, by "development," and by "annexation by occupation"—the spread of non-Indian state populations (Ladino/Mestizo/Criollo agriculturalists, ranchers, loggers, miners) into the land of indigenous nations.

The problem for indigenous peoples is how to maintain or regain control over their own nations. The goal of almost every indigenous people and every indigenous movement is autonomy. Autonomy means self-determination within the boundaries of the indigenous nation. Autonomy means indigenous control over land, resources, culture, economics, and aspirations. Autonomy means continued existence of indigenous leaders and government. Autonomy is geographic democracy. Autonomy is the common goal of every one of the nations involved in military resistance against state takeover. And autonomy is the main subject of four state-nation negotiations now taking place: the Philippines and the Kalinga and Bontoc Alliance; the Philippines and the Moro National Liberation Front; India and the Nagas and the Mizos; and Sri Lanka and Tamil Eelan.

Fourth World nations increasingly are in contact with each other to share and seek solutions to attempted takeover by states. But some tactics may not be appropriate in different situations. Legal redress for indigenous land rights has made some gains in Canada and Australia, but it has no meaning in Guatemala, Nicaragua, Colombia, or Argentina. Mobilization of support for international recognition of autonomous indigenous nations and group rights for indigenous peoples has been making some progress. But international law follows state interests, not the interests of nations. Indigenous nations have had to seek other alternatives to halt and reverse expanding state takeover.

The Miskito, Sumo, and Rama nations have taken up arms against the Nicaraguan state to regain rights to their lands and to establish territorial and cultural autonomy. The San Blas Kuna, who achieved autonomous control over their territory by winning a 1925 war against Panamanian gov-

ernment forces, are now establishing national park and conservation programs further to protect their lands from invasions of non-Indian
agriculturalists. Presented here are two situations in which indigenous peoples are resisting politically and militarily. Given the pressures exerted
against autonomous peoples elsewhere in Latin America, the Miskito, the
Sumo, the Rama, and the San Blas Kuna might not represent isolated cases.

MISKITO ARMED RESISTANCE FOR AUTONOMY

Like most states, Nicaragua is a colonial creation outlined by artificial
boundaries imposed on preexisting and unconsenting indigenous nations.
Recognized internationally by other states, Nicaragua is really two countries: the west coast with its Ladino, Spanish-speaking, Catholic population,
densely settled on state and private lands with good soils, and the east coast
with its Indian and black, Miskito-Sumo-English-speaking, largely Protestant population, spread over communally owned thin-soil lands of three
nations. Different countries, different peoples, different histories, different
geographies, different identities, but claimed and dominated by one state.

Miskitos resisted with varying degrees of success more than four centuries of foreign intrusion. The Spanish who tried to invade to take resources
and slaves were stopped militarily at Miskito territorial borders. English,
French, and Dutch buccaneers and pirates were accepted through trade
alliances. Great Britain established a 200-year, mutually beneficial trade
alliance that did not interfere with Miskito sovereignty over their territory.
The Spanish again tried to impose control but were ousted in 1800 by the
Miskito, who liberated their territory 20 years before other anti-Spanish wars
of independence led to the creation of new independent countries from
former colonies. The 1860 Treaty of Managua recognized Indian autonomy
over a portion of their nation but was brushed aside in 1894 when a Nicaraguan military force—with U.S. support—invaded to "reincorporate" the
area into the nation.

Miskito, Sumo, and Rama peoples have long occupied their own territo-
rially distinct nations. Generations of extended relations have been born
and buried on their lands. Indian society, culture, and economy and communal land and life have evolved into indivisible, seamless wholes. In Indian communal life every economic activity has a social context, and every
relationship is reinforced through obligatory exchange of goods and labor.
Mutual social responsibilities that unite individual and community form a
moral economy through which goods, labor, and obligations circulate. The
moral economy is intimately tied to communally owned and used lands,
waters, and resources. Sustainable exploitation is maintained by circulating
pressure over large areas and limiting production to socially regulated, common levels. Thus in indigenous society land, resources, identity, and responsibilities are inseparable.

During the 43 years of the Somoza dictatorships, international and

Nicaraguan commercial interests expanded operations in the three east coast nations using Indian and Creole (black) labor to extract gold, lumber, and marine resources such as shrimp, lobster, and green turtles. This economic invasion took place in the years following the Nicaraguan government's 1894 territorial invasion. The imposed self-interest market economy conflicted with the Indians' moral economy, but participation in both was possible by extending labor to meet alternative demands: food and money. Capitalism threatened indigenous societies and their resource base, but the Miskito, Sumo, and Rama did not take up arms against the territorial and economic invasion of the Somoza dictatorships. This was because they still had the security of most of their lands for subsistence production and abundant labor and resources for market production. Things were bad, but the contradictions between Indian economy and capitalism had not yet reached critical mass.

The Nicaraguan revolution took place in the "Spanish interior," as it is considered by the east coast nations—in another country far away from Indian lands and peoples. Achieved by the revolt of west coast urban people, the 1979 victory over the Somoza dictatorship brought the Sandinistas (Sandinista National Liberation Front—FSLN) to power and to the east coast.

The new Sandinista government asserted that the Miskito, Sumo, and Rama nations and peoples were part of the Nicaraguan state and therefore should be "integrated" into the revolution and country. The Sandinistas saw the Indian peoples as a "politically and culturally backward" minority made into an exploited class by years of colonialism, capitalism, and discrimination. The Sandinistas believed that the Indian peoples' identity should be as poor campesinos with an allegiance to the revolution and to the FSLN "vanguard." To achieve this, the Sandinistas attempted to create what they called a "new Indian" with class consciousness through participation in mass organizations and state programs that were to transform all of Nicaragua. The Sandinistas wanted to erase what was Indian and substitute what was Ladino and Sandinista by trying to take over control of Indian land, resources, economy, society, identity, leaders, and government. The Indian peoples wanted to work with the Sandinistas to pursue recovery of Indian land lost during the Somoza takeover and to develop Indian human and natural resources. However, instead of liberation from the Somoza state commercial occupation of Indian nations, the new Sandinista state began to impose what was seen as total non-Indian control.

Miskito, Sumo, and Rama land and resources were transferred to state ownership in August 1980. Economic production was to be "rationalized" through state-run stores, state development programs, and redirected Indian labor. State control of Indian land, resources, and production threatened to tear to shreds kinship-based communal village life and the moral economy.

The Miskito, Sumo, and Rama see themselves as distinct peoples with inalienable rights to their national territories and to land and sea resources.

They do not consider themselves to be "minorities" or "ethnic groups" of Nicaragua, subservient to imposed Nicaraguan authority and sovereignty. The Indian rights organization MISURASATA told Sandinista leaders in 1980 that Nicaragua had no bill of sale for Indian nations, no treaty or vote from Indian peoples, and no east coast consent to transfer sovereignty.

In an effort to persuade the FSLN to recognize Indian land rights, MISURASATA initiated a land tenure and land use study in October 1980. The purpose was to map the boundaries of village lands that made up each of the three indigenous nations. Just before the mapping project was to be made public, February 18–20, 1981, the entire MISURASATA leadership was arrested by Sandinista State Security for "contradictory political development" and "separatist, racist, and counterrevolutionary activities," meaning the Indian peoples didn't accept the new invader's ideology and control.

The attempted arrest of a MISURASATA leader at a Moravian church ceremony in Prinsapolka on February 20, 1981, provoked a bare-handed defense against armed Sandinistas and left four dead on each side. Mass Indian demonstrations forced the release of MISURASATA leaders, some of whom sought exile in Honduras where many Miskitos and Sumos had fled in the wake of the crackdown by FSLN State Security.

To the Indian peoples the Sandinista state is a superpower that has invaded and taken over their nations. To speak of autonomy in 1981 was to be accused and arrested as a "separatist." With no other recourse, the Miskitos, Sumos, and Ramas were the first to confront the Sandinistas militarily. In November 1981 a group of 66 Miskitos returned from Honduras to oust the Sandinistas from their nation (Wan Tasbaia), village by village, gaining recruits as they moved south. They began with only ten weapons. They attacked and defeated many Sandinista military garrisons along the Wangki (Rio Coco), the international Honduras-Nicaragua border that cuts across the 400-mile-long Miskito nation with its population of 150,000. The Wangki is the most densely settled part of the Miskito nation. When the FSLN saw that the Indian people did not support Managua rule, they decided forcibly to relocate Indian villagers into what came to be 13 state camps in order to cut off the support base to the Indian combatants (shelter, food, information, recruits). Starting in late 1981 FSLN security and military forces burned down Miskito and Sumo villages and herded Indian peoples into the camps. Many people escaped into Honduras.

Now in its sixth year, the Indian-Sandinista war over control of the Indian nations has generated a serious refugee problem. Almost 35,000 Miskito and Sumo refugees are in Honduras, and another 5000 east coast refugees are in Costa Rica (Miskito, Rama, Creole). In addition, some Sandinista state relocation camps are still operating in Mategalpa and Jinotega where 4000 to 6000 Miskitos and Sumos are held.

The Indian war for self-determination can be understood either as a separate war against the FSLN or as one side of a triangle war involving the FSLN, the "Contras" (U.S.-backed Ladino "counterrevolutionaries"), and the Indians. The Contras and the Sandinistas are fighting over control of the Nicaraguan state. The two Indian forces, MISURASATA and KISAN (formerly MISURA), are fighting for Indian territorial autonomy and self-determination. Even though they are fighting each other, the Contras and the Sandinistas agree on suppression of Indian rights. The rights permitted to Indians in Articles 89–91 of Sandinista Nicaragua's new constitution (January 9, 1987) are indistinguishable from those described by the Contras in the 1986 United Nicaraguan Opposition's "National Democratic Project." The Sandinistas and the Contras both say that Indian peoples can keep their language, their culture, and their identity, but Indian territory and resources belong to the Nicaraguan state.

The largely Miskito forces fighting the Sandinistas comprise the only Indian army in the Americas. They have had major successes against Sandinista forces and are acknowledged to be the best fighters in Central America. Considerable efforts are being made to divert the Indian armed resistance from Indian goals to those of the FSLN or the Contras. After peace negotiations between the FSLN and MISURASATA failed in 1984–85, the Sandinistas began a "hearts and minds" campaign to gain support from Miskito, Sumo, and Rama villagers. The Sandinistas began their own "autonomy process" aimed at installing FSLN-controlled political and economic autonomy for "the Atlantic Coast." Although it falls far short of Indian demands for territorial autonomy, it is nevertheless a gain for the armed Indian self-determination forces whose leaders were jailed in 1981 for promoting autonomy. At the same time, the Contra leadership is trying to suppress the exiled Indian movement in Honduras and Costa Rica. The best fighters are the worst armed. The Contras don't want to face a well-armed Indian army if they should take over Managua and continue Nicaraguan claims to the three Indian nations.

The collective goals for the Indian peoples in arms are the following:

1. Recognition of the Miskito, Sumo, and Rama as indigenous sovereign peoples who have the natural right to determine freely their own political, economic, social, and cultural development.

2. Recognition of the inalienable right to an indigenous territory (land, river, lagoon, and sea) with natural resources for the Miskito, Sumo, and Rama peoples.

3. End to institutional repression of Indian peoples and FSLN military pullback from Indian nations. Indian resistance forces will then defend their nations against any aggressor, Contras included.

Indian plans for autonomy include the establishment of an autonomous territory to be internally governed by elected village councils and regional committees. The people are to be free to determine their own cultural and resource policies and the course of their own development. Indigenous methods of sustainable resource management will be maintained with resource exports controlled to ensure long-term use. As it is now, almost no resources are taken from the Indian nations because of the Indian-Sandinista war. Indian leaders want the assistance of international conservation and rational development organizations.

The war has meant the recovery of wildlife and environments once heavily sacked during the Somoza dictatorship. Indian conservation and protection plans are the most advanced this writer has seen for any region in the world. This is because Miskito revolutionary ideology (called *Indian Lukanka*) is based on communal ties and responsibilities to a finite land and resource base.

SAN BLAS KUNA REVOLUTION, AUTONOMY, AND CONSERVATION

The San Blas Kuna achieved Panamanian government recognition and support of their island-mainland territory by means of a 1925 revolution and of 1945 legislation. The Kuna are currently working to establish a forest preserve as a buffer against the intrusion of non-Indian Panamanian agriculturalists.

Like the Miskito, the Kuna resisted the Spanish—who raided villages and enslaved Indians—and made amicable trading ties with English buccaneers. During the early eighteenth century the Kuna attacked many Spanish settlements in Darien, culminating in a widespread war in 1725–26 that forced the Spanish from the area. A 1741 peace treaty between the Kuna and Spanish did not last. The Spanish tried to pacify the Indians with missionaries, forced relocations, and military operations against villages. Beginning in 1786 the Spanish built several forts along the San Blas coast, and in 1789 another treaty was signed. But by then the riches of Panama and the silver mines of South America were reduced and the buccaneers had departed. The need for Spanish forts on the Caribbean coast was over. The Spanish abandoned the San Blas Coast and left the Kuna's territory.

During the early 1800s the Kuna began to move to the coast to trade with the British, and then they gradually began to settle the islands. In 1831 some ten years after its independence from Spain, Colombia claimed all of the San Blas Coast as part of its national territory, but internal political problems diverted attention from this isolated area and the Kuna were again left pretty much to themselves.

When Panama seceded from Colombia in 1903 Kuna international support was divided between those who proposed political affiliation with the new country and those who wanted to maintain relationships with Colombia. Following the seventeenth- and eighteenth-century policies of the Spanish, the Panamanian government passed a law in 1908 aimed at "achieving, by all peaceful means, the reduction to a civilized life of all the savage tribes in the land." By 1919 Kuna factions gave tacit allegiance to Panama, but strong anti–Panamanian government feelings were fed by the presence of Panamanian government police on some of the islands, a forced policy of assimilation, Creole (black) encroachment onto Kuna lands, fishing, and turtling waters, and government grants of 25,000 and 30,000 hectares to two foreigners for banana plantations. In 1925 the Kuna staged a revolution, defeating the Panamanian government police force and driving out the Creoles. They created the independent Tule Republic that lasted until 1930, when the Panamanian government passed a law guaranteeing the integrity of Kuna territory. In 1945 the government and the Kuna agreed on the Carta Organica, which gave formal rights to the existing indirect rule, and in 1953 another law was passed that provided the Kuna with Panamanian assistance for agricultural development and public works. The Comarca de San Blas became a Kuna-controlled political division along the northeastern Caribbean coast of Panama, from the crest of the continental divide to the offshore islands. Within the Comarca Kunas run their own affairs through a highly organized political system of island and regional leaders, and Kuna representatives are part of the Panamanian National Assembly.

The Kunas control access by outsiders to all but a few tourist islands. No property can be owned by non-Kuna, and Kuna enjoy freedom from imposed cultural change from the outside.

Despite the Panamanian government laws and agreements, Kuna territory is still threatened. The government recently built a road from El Llano to Carti, opening up access to the edge of Kuna lands. And non-Indian Panamanian squatter farmers are spreading toward Kuna territory.

To help protect their autonomous territory, the Kuna are creating the first of several planned national parks, with financial assistance from U.S. AID, the World Wildlife Fund, and the Inter-American Foundation and technical assistance from the Centro Agronómico Tropical de Investigación y Ensenanza (CATIE) in Costa Rica. They now administer the 20-square-kilometer Udirbi Forest Preserve Park. The goals of the project are to add further weight to the Kuna's territorial boundary, to protect the watershed from damage from squatter farmers, to control terrestrial access to San Blas via the road, to provide assistance for scientific research, and to develop a model of how indigenous people can use such projects for cultural and ecological conservation. Eventually, the Kuna plan to establish a series of parks along the entire length of their terrestrial boundary and to extend their sea zone with marine parks.

MISKITO BATTLES AND KUNA PARKS

The Kuna have what the Miskito, Sumo, and Rama are fighting for. Like the Miskito, the Kuna resisted for centuries and then rose against state-imposed policies and threats to their land. However, the Kuna war lasted only a few days, but the Indian war against Nicaragua is now into its sixth year and is embroiled in complex global politics.

Other indigenous peoples have recognized autonomous status—for example, the Naga in Nagaland (India) and the Inuit in Greenland. Like the Miskito, the Sumo, the Rama, and the Kuna, the Naga had to use armed resistance.

If armed conflict between states and indigenous peoples is to be avoided, greater international attention and stronger laws must be focused on the cultural and territorial rights of what are now Fourth World peoples. National parks, biosphere reserves, and other types of protected areas offer attractive solutions for the conservation of nature and the rights of indigenous peoples.

Without land the only future for Indian peoples in Central America is to be cheap labor. Demands for territorial autonomy are demands for a democracy based on geography. Rights have to be tied to land, which guarantees what no central non-Indian government can: the survival of indigenous peoples. Latin America is also Indian America, but there are no Indian central governments even in states where Indians comprise the majority of the claimed population. Instead of taking over the state, indigenous movements seek only to defend their peoples' national territories. Autonomous Indian nations could be a stabilizing counterweight to the revolving doors of totalitarian state regimes.

Worldwide, the self-determination genie is out of the bottle and can't be restrained by state-sanctifying rules that shut out Fourth World indigenous nations. In Central America seven states claim sovereign control over almost 50 indigenous nations that have some 6 million people and 40 percent of the region's area. Internationally, 168 states assert hegemony over more than 3000 nations.

A second wave of self-determination is encircling the globe. The first broke the back of overseas white colonialism and led to the proliferation of Third World states. Many of these became brown and black colonial powers that invaded or continued the occupation of unconsenting indigenous nations. Now, scores of internationally unrecognized nations—the Fourth World—are at war as a result and must base their self-determination on ambushes rather than treaties. Some, such as the Kuna, are able to employ other means to guarantee control of indigenous land.

27

Melanesian Resistance to Ecocide and Ethnocide: Transnational Mining Projects and the Fourth World on the Island of New Guinea

DAVID HYNDMAN

David C. Hyndman received his Ph.D. in anthropology from the University of Queensland in 1979 based on his cultural ecological research in Papua New Guinea. In this selection he describes how large-scale mining developments in three areas of New Guinea have resulted in drastic social and environmental damage. Responses by the native peoples have included armed resistance and socioreligious movements. This material provides a valuable complement and update to the accounts in part V by De'Ath and Michalenko of lumbering development in Papua New Guinea and by Nietschmann of Indonesia's transmigration program in West Papua (West Irian). The extent to which large corporations can cause dangerous chemical pollution and ecocide in "remote" corners of the world while largely escaping media attention is truly remarkable. It should perhaps not be surprising that the native armed resistance movements, such as the Free Papua Movement, are not widely recognized or understood either. Hyndman's discussion of events in the Amungme territory of West Papua also shows how conservation programs may support the dispossession of peoples and mask serious environmental problems. The selections in part VIII demonstrate that this need not be the case.

INTRODUCTION

Three of the world's largest gold and copper mining projects were started on the island of New Guinea in the 1960s, and operations are continuing into the 1980s. The Bougainville and Ok Tedi projects are located in Papua New Guinea, and the Freeport project is located in West Papua (Fig. 1). As Fourth World Melanesians in the vicinity of the projects experienced ecocide, incorporation into larger regional, national, and international socioeconomic networks, and conversion of their natural resources into national and transnational resources, they responded with social protest. The continuing appearance of such social movements (May 1982) in Melanesia reflects differing scales of political and economic interrelationships among members of the Fourth World, colonizers, states, and transnationals in New Guinea.

This selection was written for this volume and appears here in print for the first time.

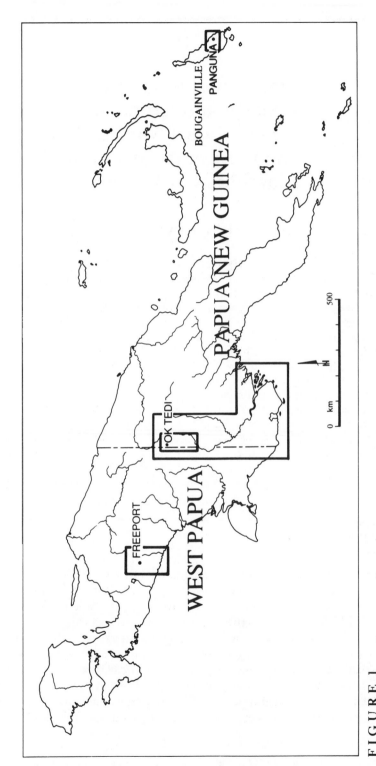

FIGURE 1
Transnational mining projects on the island of New Guinea.

THE FREEPORT PROJECT

The Amungme

The Amungme, who number about 12,000 (Pogolamun 1985:45), are the original landowners surrounding the Freeport project. The habitats encompassed in their homeland range from equatorial glacial through alpine, subalpine, and montane to lowland rainforest and swamp forest (Fig. 2). In the 1950s some Amungme took up the *hai*, a social movement whose focus was the search for eternal life, and started moving to the southern lowlands of their territory. Other Amungme were attracted to the Catholic missions, schools, and clinics opened in Tsinga and Noemba in 1955. The Dutch established a colonial administration post and rubber resettlement scheme at Kiliarama in the extreme south of Amungme territory in 1958. Resettlement started between 1961 and 1963 and continued until 1970 when West Papua became another province of Indonesia. Approximately 2500 Amungme eventually established a string of villages named Akimuga, but

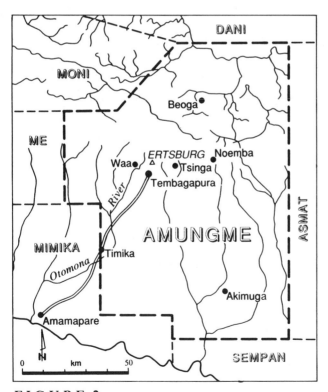

FIGURE 2
Amungme and the Freeport project.

they had no resistance to the endemic malaria of the lowlands and many died. The majority of the Amungme remained in the mountains (Pogolamun 1985:46–47).

Transnational Mining and the State

Copper on Amungme land was first reported internationally in 1936 by the Dutch geologist J. Dozy, who gave the name Ertsberg to the ore mountain of 33 million tonnes of 2.5 percent copper. Decades later, in 1959, without consulting the Amungme, J. van Gruisen, managing director of Oost Boreno Maatschappilj, took out a 100,000-hectare mining exploration concession based on the Dozy report (White 1983:49) and then passed it on to the U.S. transnational Freeport (Osborne 1985:118). Freeport waited until the Dutch withdrew and then started negotiating a prospecting authority with the Indonesians in 1963. According to a speech to the Indonesia Council by R. Hopper, a former geologist from Standard Oil, Freeport "had been waiting for the right time to enter Indonesia for the development of a long-known deposit of copper ore in a remote part of West Irian" (Hook n.d.:4), the right time apparently being after West Papua became part of Indonesia.

Sukarno's nationalism was a stumbling block for U.S. transnational intervention; furthermore, Indonesia was nationalizing Dutch transnationals between 1957 and 1958 because Holland refused to yield West Papua. From 1958 to 1962 a "neutral" United States mediated the dispute over West Papuan independence. The U.S. position was highly critical of West Papuan aspirations for self-determination, based on the claim that the Melanesians were straight out of the Stone Age and that the region was grossly lacking in natural resources. U.S. sponsorship of anthropological projects through Rockefeller and natural history projects through Archbold widely publicized and denigrated the West Papuans as Stone Age peoples. The Dani, north of the Amungme (see Fig. 2), became immortalized as warring primitives through the film *Dead Birds* and through books by Matthiessen (1962) and Heider (1970, 1979). The Me, east of the Amungme (see Fig. 2), well known ethnographically as the Kapauku, are portrayed by Pospisil as primitive capitalist natives (1978). Yet the West Papuan school teachers and university graduates espousing independence in 1963 were probably more competent than their Melanesian counterparts in Australian colonial New Guinea who enjoyed their own House of Assembly by 1964 and independence by 1975.

Freeport signed a "contract of work" on 7 April, 1967, soon after Indonesia enacted its Foreign Investment Law, thus becoming the first transnational to enter Indonesia under the new law. Infrastructure was contracted out to Bechtel, the U.S. construction transnational, in 1970, and the first shipment of copper concentrate went out in late 1972. A tax holiday over the first three years saved Freeport U.S.$15 to 25 million (Osborne 1985:119). Not until after the 1969 Act of Free Choice that annexed West Papua to Indonesia did the transnational localize as Freeport Indonesia, Inc. (FII).

Mining and Amungme Social Protest

Indonesia maintains a policy of oppression and ethnocide against Fourth World nations within the domestic boundaries of the state. All rural communities are categorized into an antiquated nineteenth-century evolutionary progression ranging from traditional (*swadaya*) villages, to transitional (*swakarya*) villages, to developed (*swasembada*) villages truly integrated into the Indonesian state, with Java at the top (Colchester 1986a:89). But an estimated 800,000 of the some 1.2 million West Papuans are denigrated as previllagers and classified as isolated and alien peoples (*suka suka terasing*); they are without legal provisions to safeguard their resource rights and sociocultural differences (Colchester 1986a:91). In order to confiscate land and resources from Fourth World nations within state borders, Indonesia utilizes article 33, section 3 of the 1945 constitution, which states that "land and water and natural riches therein shall be controlled by the State as the highest authority to manage their utilization for the maximum well-being of the whole people." Also used is the Agrarian Law, which only permits shifting cultivators rights to land currently under cultivation (Colchester 1986b:104–5).

For the Amungme, state and transnational collusion to mine gold and copper on their land is nothing short of economic development by invasion. Waa villagers (see Fig. 2) residing close to the mining complex at Tembagapura were the only Amungme to receive compensation, and it was a one-time payment for direct disruption of current gardens (Mitton 1977:367). Bechtel paid several hundred Amungme and other local Melanesians U.S. $.10 per hour for unskilled construction work, but once the mine was operational only 40 continued to be employed. FII is exempted from paying land rent or royalties to the Amungme or assisting the Amungme or the province in economic development (Osborne 1985:119). FII was not obliged to carry out an environmental impact statement (EIS) (Mitton 1977:367). Not only is the mining causing surface degradation and sediment and water pollution of the Otomona River, but employees are abusing wildlife (Petocz 1984:136).

A massive Indonesian military and police presence paralleled the buildup of the mining operation. According to a civilian pilot named T. Doyle who flew for eight years between Australia and Freeport, when an FII employee named J. Hansen encouraged the Amungme to start growing vegetables for sale to the mine,

> he fell foul of the Indonesians because they didn't like anyone having contact with the natives. They felt outsiders might promote the "false" idea of their owning the land—for which they'd received little or no compensation. They dealt with Hansen by firing bullets around his feet, like a cowboy movie. Get out of town or else! We had to fly him out in a bit of a hurry (Osborne 1985:71).

The Free Papua Movement, or Organisasi Papua Merdeka (OPM), is fighting a Fourth World resistance movement against Indonesia for West

Papuan self-determination. Major OPM and Indonesian military clashes occurred in 1977 among the nearby Me and Dani peoples (see Fig. 2). After Amungme in the southern Akimuga villages ejected two Indonesian policemen, the Indonesian military retaliated by strafing the area on the 22nd of July, 1977, from two Bronko OV-10s until they ran out of ammunition (Osborne 1985:69). After years of resentment, the attack provoked the Amungme into a major social protest culminating in sabotage against FII. The Amungme wanted the Indonesians and FII out, and they were aided by a group of OPM fighters under Otto Ondowame. With explosives stolen from FII, they blew up the copper slurry pipe running from the mine down to the port site of Amamapare. (The maintenance officer and his wife indicate that the pipe was only damaged by hacksaw blades—Carolyn Cook, personal communication.) They also burned fuel installations, blockaded airstrips, destroyed bridges, and attacked electricity lines (Osborne 1985:69–70). The Amungme and the OPM remained in control for several days.

The cost to FII for civil disturbance and property damage was U.S.$11 million; the cost to the Amungme was a massive military sweep code-named *Operasi Tumpas* ("annihilation"). The Indonesian military destroyed Amungme gardens, burned down houses and churches, and tortured and killed men, women, and children. The OPM believes thousands of Me, Dani, and Amungme were killed in 1977, although Indonesia claims it was far less, only about 900 (Osborne 1985:72). Petitions and letters of complaint from the Amungme were routinely ignored by the Indonesian authorities (Osborne 1985:122). Amungme living near Tembagapura addressed a long list of grievances and a request for assistance to the governor in May 1980 (Tapol 1984:43–44). The official response four months later was forced resettlement to the lowlands airstrip at Timika where, according to FII (n.d.:12), the Amungme could become farmers. Timika, with over 15,000 settlers in 1984, is the largest resettlement program of its kind in West Papua. During the move 20 percent of the Amungme infants died because of their lack of resistance to malaria (Osborne 1985:123), and all residents are threatened by metal oxide pollution of the Otomona River (Petocz 1984:135).

An agreement signed by the Amungme, FII, and the state on 8 January, 1984, placed Tembagapura and all other FII facilities within the 100,000-hectare mining concession completely off limits to the Amungme in exchange for construction of a school in Waa, which was not used, clinics in Waa and Tsinga, and markets used once a week in Waa and Timika (Pogolamun 1985:48). In 1980 the FII underground mine came into production (White 1983:46), which further reduced land available to the Amungme for gardening, travel, and hunting (Pogolamun 1985:49–50).

Not only is the FII 100,000-hectare mining concession effectively off limits to the Amungme, but 2,150,000 hectares of their territory were gazetted in 1978 as the Lorentz Strict Nature Reserve. Half of the reserve is under a petroleum exploration concession and 20 percent is under the FII mining concession. It has been proposed to the International Union for the Conservation of Nature for World Heritage listing as a national park of 1,560,000 hectares (Petocz 1984:79). Fourth World ownership and sustained-yield management of protected areas is not a priority of Indonesian conservation management, which only considers (1) biological importance, (2) relationship to ongoing development projects, (3) threats to integrity of reserves, and (4) location (Petocz 1984:78). Indigenous peoples are usually not informed if their land becomes a protected area. If they are informed, it is only after their land has been gazetted; their participation in future management planning is thus rendered negligible (Petocz 1984:77). FII's lack of a social or environmental conscience as well as the scale of ecocide, ethnocide, and transnational-state abuse of Amungme human rights are major condemnations of the mining project. These offenses cast grave doubts on the long-term feasibility of combining conservation and development in the region.

THE OK TEDI PROJECT

The Wopkaimin

The Wopkaimin are one of several Mountain Ok peoples of central New Guinea (Fig. 3). There are about 700 Wopkaimin; they are the original landowners surrounding the Ok Tedi project (Fig. 4). Wopkaimin culture was founded by the "great mother" ancestress Afek. She erected the sacred Futmanam cult house in Bultem (see Fig. 4). The Futmanam symbolizes Wopkaimin identity and sociality. It integrates the men into an initiatory cult and excludes women, validating the separation of the sexes. Hamlet sociality is divided by gender and residentially segregated into women's houses and the men's house. To Wopkaimin men ancestral land is a sacred geography collectively experienced and understood through religion and ritual. Land and resource use are perceived through the cultural filter of the men's house/cult complex. The state and the Ok Tedi Mining Limited (OTML) consortium do not seriously appreciate that intrusion of the transnational mining project means far more than loss of hunting, fishing, and gardening.

Transnational Mining and the State

Australian colonial presence in this area began with Patrol Officer Booth's expedition from Telefomin in 1957. Within a decade, and without consulting the Wopkaimin, the U.S. transnational Kennecott took out a prospecting authority on their land in 1968. In 1969 Kennecott started test drilling at Mt. Fubilan, the location now commonly referred to as the "pot of gold" (Jackson 1982). At the peak of their exploration activities in 1971 Kennecott employed over 45 whites and 500 Melanesians, but few of the latter were Wopkaimin or other Mountain Ok men. In 1970 negotiations were started

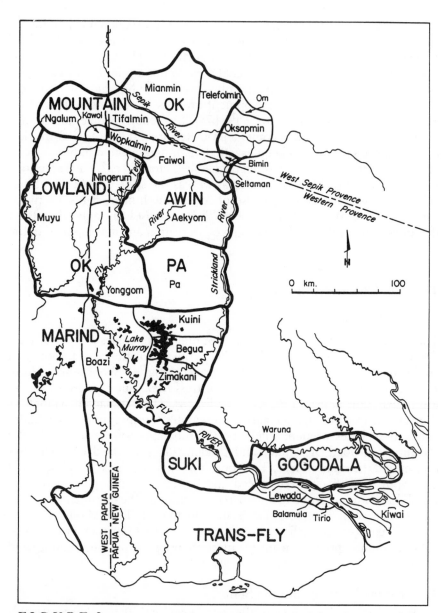

FIGURE 3
Indigenous peoples of the Fly and Ok Tedi rivers.

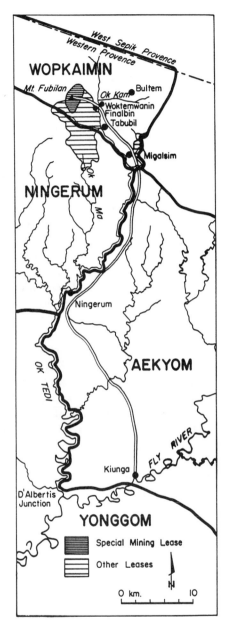

FIGURE 4
Wopkaimin and the Ok Tedi project.

between Kennecott and the interim colonial Australian administration for an agreement to mine at Ok Tedi. In March 1975 Kennecott abandoned the Ok Tedi project. Negotiations had failed because of disagreements over tax and arbitration provisions, not over environmental concerns or the issue of landowner protection (Jackson 1982:42–70; Pintz 1984:32–49).

Papua New Guinea established an interim Ok Tedi Development Company in 1975 and after the 1976 agreement pushed for the Ok Tedi project to proceed relatively quickly. In 1979 soaring gold prices accelerated the push to make the mine operational. The OTML consortium was finally formed in 1981, with the state taking a 20 percent share, BHP and Amoco taking 30 percent each, and a German industrial consortium taking 20 percent (Pintz 1984:14).

The Ok Tedi project is exempted from the Environmental Protection Act of 1978 because the 1982 *Ok Tedi Environmental Study* (OTES) is considered to be more environmentally appropriate. The fifth volume of the OTES outlines the resource base of indigenous peoples impacted by the project (Hyndman 1982; Pernetta and Hyndman 1982; Frodin and Hyndman 1982). The OTES predicted some 200 million tonnes of sediment would enter the Fly River system from waste dumps, and dissolved copper would increase up to 200 parts per billion (ppb) at Ningerum, over 100 kilometres below the mine (Fig. 4). The state initially insisted upon 50 ppb of peak soluble copper at Ningerum. Acute and chronic effects of soluble copper may be felt at as little as 5 ppb (Chambers 1985:181,182). It was hoped that pollution would be confined to the Ok Tedi River and peoples.

After a long series of ecocide disasters beginning in 1984, the Ok Tedi project now endangers aquatic resources sustaining over 50,000 indigenous peoples of the Ok Tedi and Fly rivers (Hyndman in press; see Fig. 3). In January 1984 a 50-million-tonne, one-kilometre-long landslide on the Ok Ma destroyed all prospects of a permanent tailings dam as a solution to pollution problems and threatened closure of the project. In June 1984 a barge overturned in the Fly River estuary, loosing 2700 sixty-litre drums of cyanide, and a bypass valve left open at the mine released 1000 cubic metres of highly concentrated cyanide waste into the Ok Tedi. The project has been plagued by renegotiations, but the sixth supplemental agreement allowed the second stage of mining to be launched in September 1986. Unbelievably, the project goes ahead without a permanent tailings dam, a hydroelectric scheme, or an ocean port. Mining releases undesirably large quantities of sediment, tailings, and chemical wastes with concentrations of copper exceeding 2400–4400 ppb (Chambers 1985:182), making a complete mockery of the 1982 OTES.

Mining and Wopkaimin Social Protest

Total land leases appropriated for the Ok Tedi project amount to 16,530 hectares. The Wopkaimin alone lose 7000 hectares (see Fig. 4), for which they receive compensation of about U.S.$25 per hectare annually. Although their compensation amounts to about U.S.$320,000 per year, half goes into a trust account for social inconvenience. The daily cash payment per person amounts to less than U.S.$ .65, which is not even enough to purchase a can of fish or meat in the trade store.

Previous lack of cash-earning activities among the Wopkaimin relegates them to a peripheral, unskilled wage-earner role in the Ok Tedi project. As with the Freeport project, construction of the infrastructure was contracted to Bechtel. Half the Wopkaimin men worked during the construction phase (Jackson and Ilave 1983:26), but once Bechtel departed in 1984, Ok Tedi became known to the Wopkaimin as the "place without work." In early 1981 the Wopkaimin went on strike, and OTML shut down the project and provided an emergency airlift out for all white women and children. The strike was a social protest against the loss of semiskilled jobs, they had performed themselves to foreigners and other nationals and against the Tabubil town plan (see Fig. 4), which forced their families off the land to make room for whites and other nationals who were moving in with their families. The Wopkaimin started expanding former sago groves at Woktemwanin and Finalbin (see Fig. 4) into small hamlets in 1980. They grew rapidly once Wopkaimin families were forced out of Tabubil in 1981, and by 1985 both were major roadside villages of over 350 residents.

These roadside squatter villages are extremely congested by Wopkaimin standards. Residents do not interact as a socially viable community, and established patterns of domesticity and sociality are completely altered. Families live together in coresident commensality, and all food prohibitions have been abandoned. Although gender restrictions exclude women from beer drinking, excessive drunken behaviour, black-marketing of beer, and fighting and adultery associated with heavy drinking threaten family life.

Northern Mountain Ok peoples initiated the first regional social protest movement. They abandoned the men's house/cult complex founded by the cultural ancestress Afek and replaced it with *rebaibal* (their Papua New Guinea Tok Pisin term for revival movement). The Baptists opened the first mission among the Telefomin (see Fig. 3), but their threat to the cult system did not reach a crisis point until 1974 (Frankel 1976; Jorgensen 1981). By 1977 Duranmin became the centre of mass ecstatic activities, and by 1983 *rebaibal*, with over 3000 followers, represented the most popular indigenous acceptance of Christianity among the northern Mountain Ok (Barr 1983). The ecstatic outbreaks of *rebaibal* are an innovation and adjustment to culture change, representing a major social protest/critique of an alien cultural system.

Since *rebaibal* completely rejects established cultural patterns, it is not simply another reworking of a traditional cult system to form a distinctly Melanesian Christianity (Guiart 1970). Gender roles are altered, with women acquiring more equal status. Food prohibitions and reciprocity of the men's house/cult complex are abandoned for a new coresident nuclear family domesticity and commensality. Emphasis is placed on spontaneity of worship, especially among women, and on contact with the supernatural through mass seizures (Barr and Trompf 1983).

The Wopkaimin never experienced missionary proselytizing until they started living in the new roadside squatter villages. Now Finalbin has Telefolmin rebaibalists, and Woktemwanin has Enkaiakmin Catholic catechists. When the rebaibalists burned down the Tifalmin cult house in 1979, the Futmanam ritual leader was appalled; he and the Wopkaimin have since found little appeal in the *rebaibal*, especially as it jeopardizes the status they exert among indigenous peoples as landowners of the project. Rather than follow *rebaibal*, many Wopkaimin are decentralizing to Bombakan hamlet at the confluence of the Ok Tedi and Ok Kam (see Fig. 4) and establishing new subsistence gardens. The Futmanam was refurbished in 1981 and was used to host a major initiation ceremony in 1983. Continuing their commitment to the Futmanam provides the Wopkaimin with cultural identity as a people.

As social movements, *rebaibal* and decentralization are mutually exclusive, because the former socially rejects past conditions and the latter socially rejects present conditions. By decentralizing, the Wopkaimin are constructing relationships with the transnational intruders into patterns comprehensible to them in terms of the established men's house/cult complex obligations underlying their own social relationships. They are continuing a presence in and proprietorship over their land and demonstrating that their culture has a capacity, albeit limited, for exercising social control, especially in the confines of the new roadside squatter villages. Decentralization is more than an atavistic retreat to tradition; rather, it is evolving with tradition. Many Wopkaimin are continuing their commitment to the Futmanam and have not lost the cultural skills and appreciation of their homeland necessary to carry the past forward.

THE BOUGAINVILLE PROJECT

The Nasioi

There are some 14,000 Nasioi (Wurm 1982:237); they are the original landowners surrounding the Bougainville project (Fig. 5), having settled as foothill and mountain dwellers in southern Bougainville in about 1911 (Ogan 1972:13). Following World War II an important economic innovation occurred; cash-cropping of coconuts and cocoa among the men and market vegetables among the women. Cash-cropping by the Nasioi (Ogan 1972:122,183) and the neighboring Nagovisi (Mitchell 1976:1) was disastrous because it created increasingly acute land shortages at the expense of subsistence production, at the same time providing low returns for the labour input. Big-men exchange among the Nasioi is conducted among kin or facilitated by putative kinship relations and is primarily a social activity. After cash-cropping, big-men competed for prestige in *bisnis* (Papua New

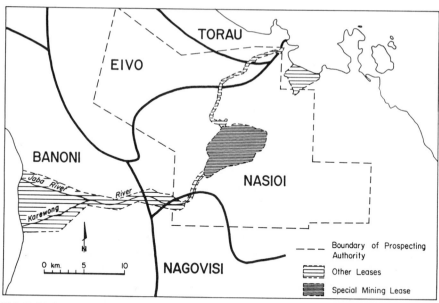

FIGURE 5
Nasioi and the Bougainville project

Guinea Tok Pisin term for cash earning by virtually any means other than wages) (Moulik 1977:73).

Cash-cropping and *bisnis* precipitated an acute crisis in established socioeconomic patterns among the indigenous peoples of southern Bougainville. They responded to the crisis with *kago* (Papua New Guinea Tok Pisin term for cargo cult belief that spiritual and material benefits are obtainable through ritual activity). *Kago* competed with *bisnis* and was used as a form of social protest against the cheapness of their labour and the expropriation of their land by the rich German and Australian colonizers. *Kago* was the first major critique of an alien cultural system and the first social protest for self-determination (Guiart 1951).

Transnational Mining and the State

Copper mineralization on Nasioi land was confirmed in 1960 by a geologist of the colonial Australian administration. The transnational Bougainville Copper Limited (BCL), an amalgamation of the Australian-based companies Conzinc Rio Tinto and Broken Hill Corporation, began prospecting in 1963. As BCL started test-drilling in 1964 the Nasioi reacted to the prospectors as trespassers (Bedford and Mamak 1977:7–10). From 1969 to 1972 the colonial Australian administration granted BCL leases for over 12,500 hectares for a mine site, access roads, and waste disposal (Bedford and Mamak 1977:27; see Fig. 5). The Nasioi and their neighbors vigorously opposed all land acquisition.

Environmental destruction caused by mining seriously disrupted subsistence and cash-cropping. Expansion of cash-cropping became feasible only at the expense of subsistence production (Mitchell 1976:1; Moulik 1977:44–45; Ogan 1972:122–83; Ward 1975:97–101), which placed an ever-greater reliance on *bisnis* as a source of cash earning. Compensation provides cash, but it is a very contentious issue because of the severe consequences of land appropriation and environmental degradation. The 1970 colonial Australian administration decision to flush all waste rock, silt, and chemical residue down the Karewong and Jaba rivers (see Fig. 5) continues to be socially and ecologically disastrous. In the decade 1973–1983 some 768 million tonnes of ore and waste were processed, half being deposited as waste into the Karewong and the other half as tailings into the Jaba, with half of the latter amount flowing into Empress Augusta Bay (see Fig. 5). Tailings are chemically contaminated with 800–1000 ppb of copper, the Jaba has risen 30 metres, and the entire valley is under 60 metres of sediment. All aquatic life has been killed, and remobilization of heavy metals ensures that ecocide will continue long after the mining is completed (Chambers 1985:180). Compensation was not standardized until 1980. As with the Ok Tedi project, payment is based on approximately U.S.$25 per hectare, but since there are many more Nasioi than Wopkaimin and the lease is smaller, the cash payment per person amounts to only a few cents per day.

Mining and Nasioi Social Protest

The Nasioi were hostile and active in their resistance to the state and to BCL exploration, construction, and operation phases because their rights as landowners were ignored (Dove *et al* 1974:184). Although 55 percent of the work force were Papua New Guineans when the construction phase peaked at 10,500 workers, only 2300 Bougainvilleans worked for BCL (Treadgold 1978:22). Among the landowners only 8 percent of the adult Nasioi men worked at the mine (Moulik 1977:47). The Nasioi and their neighbors largely refused to accept mining employment or compensation (Bedford and Mamak 1977:8–11; Stent 1970:7–8). Personal financial gain was rejected as an exchange for self-determination and autonomous control of land and resources (Moulik 1977:83). The post–World War II pattern of social protest characterized by rejection of plantation wage labour and competition among cash-cropping, *bisnis*, and *kago* was replicated when dissatisfaction with mining culminated in another major social protest movement.

Napidokae Navitu became the Nasioi social protest movement for autonomy and identity. It had its inception as a protest meeting against resumption of the Arawa plantation in 1969. The Nasioi used Napidokae Navitu as a militant protest movement for autonomy in land and resources. By 1972 the movement had attracted 8000 followers and become the social protest focus for Bougainvillean secession and nationalism (Bedford and Mamak 1977:22; Griffin 1982; Mamak *et al* 1974:9). The pay-back killing of two Bougainvillean civil servants after a motor accident in the Highlands in

1973 (Griffin 1982:135) accelerated social protest for secession and repatriation of mainlanders (Hannet 1975:290). Labour unrest and interethnic hostilities culminated in 1975 in a violent strike against BCL that caused damage to infrastructure and production. The self-governing Papua New Guinea administration punitively withheld Bougainville investment royalties. Bougainville officially seceded only days before Papua New Guinea became a new state. Bougainville affiliation was accomplished with restoration of their royalties and creation of provincial government autonomy (Bedford and Mamak 1977:88–89; 1979:74–85). During these developments Napidokae Navitu continued as a Bougainvillean focus for development, education, and autonomy (Griffin 1982; Oliver 1973:172–76).

Griffin (1982:138) concludes that by the mid-1970s Napidokae Navitu followers had achieved their social protest objectives:

> . . . land disputes of 1969 and other compensatory issues were adequately settled; a moral victory was scored over the colonial Administration; the mining agreement was drastically renegotiated to the chagrin of the intrusive transnational company (another moral victory); the full one-and-a-quarter percent royalties were paid to the provincial government; the North Solomons was united under a provincial government with real powers; local government councils were abolished and traditional authority sanctioned through village government; attempts were being made to foster traditional culture in schools and through provincial agencies; education came under substantial provincial control and North Solomonese maintained a high level of access to positions throughout Papua New Guinea in tertiary institutions, public service, church and business, and privileged access on the North Solomons itself; the elections of 1977 and 1982 saw Mola and Lapun eliminated and all four MPs committed to the one party, the radical Melanesian alliance, led by John Momis.

The Nasioi responded to cash-cropping with *kago* and to mining with Napidokae Navitu, a more successful protest movement that achieved compromise, modified the power of BCL, and provided a degree of local autonomy.

CONCLUSION

Fourth World Melanesians are not Stone Age primitives or passive recipients of social and ecological change. Determined, collective social protest has been the response to grave ecocide and ethnocide problems caused by transnational mining projects. The Nasioi had a long history of fragmentation caused by German and Australian colonialism. Colonialism, cash-cropping, *bisnis*, and *kago* differentiated interests among the Nasioi, but the people retained their autonomy in land, resources, culture, and language. They perceived the Bougainville project as a common threat, and Napidokae Navitu stimulated Bougainvillean unification for self-determination.

The Amungme and the Wopkaimin experienced the colonization frontier only in the late 1950s; the intrusion of transnational mining brought about social movements for self-determination. The Wopkaimin are struggling to maintain their identity; for the Amungme the struggle may already be lost. The Freeport project is by far the worst threat to an indigenous people and their environment. It is in fact a classic example of the Third World using transnationals for economic invasion of the Fourth World.

REFERENCES

Barr, J. 1983. A survey of ecstatic phenomena and "holy spirit movements" in Melanesia. *Oceania* 54:109–32.

———, and G. Trompf. 1983. Independent churches and recent ecstatic phenomena in Melanesia: A survey of materials. *Oceania* 54:48–50.

Bedford, R., and A. Mamak. 1977. *Compensating for development*. Bougainville Special Publication No. 2. Christchurch: University of Canterbury.

———. 1979. Bougainville. In *Race, class, and rebellion in the South Pacific*, ed. A. Mamak and A. Ali, 69–85. Sydney: George Allen and Unwin.

Chambers, M. 1985. Environmental management problems in Papua New Guinea. *The Environmental Professional* 7:178–85.

Colchester, M. 1986a. Unity and diversity: Indonesia's policy towards tribal peoples. *Ecologist* 16:89–98.

———. 1986b. The struggle for land: Tribal peoples in the face of the transmigration programme. *Ecologist* 16:99–110.

Dove, J., T. Miriung, and M. Togolo. 1974. Mining bitterness. In *Problems of choice: Land in Papua New Guinea's future*, ed. P. Sack. Canberra: Australian National University Press.

Frankel, S. 1976. Mass hysteria in the New Guinea highlands. *Oceania* 48:106–33.

Freeport Indonesia, Inc. n.d. *Tantangan Pertambangan mining challenge.*

Frodin, D., and D. Hyndman. 1982. Ethnobotany of the Ok Tedi drainage. Working Paper No. 14. In *Ok Tedi environmental study*, 209–340. Melbourne: Maunsell and Partners.

Griffin, J. 1982. Napidakoe Navitu. In *Micronational movements in Papua New Guinea*, ed. R. May. Canberra: Australian National University, Department of Political and Social Change.

Guiart, J. 1951. Forerunners of Melanesian nationalism. *Oceania* 22:81–90.

———. 1970. The millenarian aspect of conversion to Christianity in the South Pacific. In *Millennial dreams in action*, ed. S. Thrupp. New York: Schocken.

Hannett, L. 1975. The case for Bougainville secession. *Meangin Quarterly* 34, no. 3.

Heider, K. 1970. *The Dugum Dani: A Papuan culture in the highlands of West New Guinea*. Chicago: Aldine.

———. 1979. *Grand Valley Dani: Peaceful warriors*. New York: Holt, Rinehart and Winston.

Hook, C. n.d. *Treachery in West Papua*. Deventer, Neth.: Foundation Workgroup New Guinea.

Hyndman, D. 1982. Population, settlement, and resource use. Working Paper No. 12. In *Ok Tedi environmental study*, 1–71. Melbourne: Maunsell and Partners.

———. In press. Mining, modernization and movements of social protest in Papua New Guinea. *Social Analysis* 6, no. 21.

Jackson, R. 1982. *Ok Tedi: The pot of gold*. Waigani: University of Papua New Guinea, Word Publishing.

———, and T. Ilave. 1983. *The Progress and impact of the Ok Tedi project*. Report No. 1. Waigani, PNG: Institute of Applied Social and Economic Research.

Jorgensen, D. 1981. Life on the fringe: History and society in Telefolmin. In *The plight of peripheral peoples in Papua New Guinea*, ed. R. Gordon. Occasional Paper No. 7. Cambridge: Cultural Survival.

Mamak, A., and R. Bedford, with L. Hannett and M. Havini. 1974. *Bougainville nationalism: Aspects of unity and discord*. Special Publication No. 1. Christchurch: University of Canterbury.

Matthiessen, P. 1962. *Under the mountain wall: A chronicle of two seasons in the Stone Age*. New York: Viking.

May, R. 1982. *Micronationalist movements in Papua New Guinea*. Canberra: Australian National University, Department of Political and Social Change.

Mitchell, D. 1976. *Land and agriculture in Nagovisi, Papua New Guinea*. Monograph No. 3. Boroko, PNG: Institute of Applied Social and Economic Research.

Mitton, R. 1975. Development of the Freeport copper mine. In *The Melanesian environment*, ed. J. Winslow, 365–72. Canberra: Australian National University.

Moulik, T. 1977. *Bougainville in transition*. Monograph No. 7. Canberra: Australian National University, Development Studies Centre.

Ogan, E. 1972. *Business and cargo: Socio-economic change among the Nasioi of Bougainville*. New Guinea Research Bulletin No. 44. Canberra: Australian National University.

Oliver, D. 1973. *Bougainville: A personal history*. Melbourne: Melbourne University Press.

Osborne, R. 1985. *Indonesia's secret war: The guerrilla struggle in Irian Jaya*. Sydney: George Allen and Unwin.

Pernetta, J., and D. Hyndman. 1982. Ethnozoology of the Ok Tedi drainage. Working Paper No. 13. In *Ok Tedi environmental study*, 73–207. Melbourne: Maunsell and Partners.

Petocz, R. 1984. *Conservation and development in Irian Jaya: A strategy for rational resource utilization*. Gland, Switz.: WWF/IUCN.

Pintz, W. 1984. *Ok Tedi: Evolution of a Third World mining project*. London: Mining Journal Books.

Pogolamun, M. 1985. Akimuga to Timika: All that glitters is not copper. *Kabar Dari Kampung* 1, no. 3/4:45–50.

Pospisil, L. 1978. *The Kapauku Papuans of West New Guinea*. (1st ed., 1963.) New York: Holt, Rinehart and Winston.

Stent, W. 1970. What is truth? *New Guinea and Australia, the Pacific and South-east Asia* 5:6–12.

Tapol. 1984. *West Papua: The obliteration of a people.* London: Tapol.

Treadgold, M. 1978. *The regional economy of Bougainville: Growth and structural change.* Occasional Paper No. 10. Canberra: Australian National University, Development Studies Centre.

Ward, M. 1975. *Roads and development in Southwest Bougainville.* New Guinea Research Bulletin No. 62. Canberra: Australian National University.

White, L. 1983. Freeport Indonesia's Ertsberg Project sets sights on expanded concentrate production. *Engineering and Mining Journal*, September:46–55.

Wurm, S. 1982. *Papuan languages of Oceania.* Tübingen, W. Ger.: Gunter Narr Verlag.

VIII

Parks, Conservation, and Tribals

There is still debate over the extent to which tribal peoples maintained traditional balances with their natural resource base, but it is clear that throughout the world environments still controlled by tribals are often less degraded than surrounding territories under other forms of management. Today, tribal lands are often prime areas for a special form of development: the creation of national parks and wildlife refuges. Tribal areas are also a concern for conservationists because ordinary development of these territories has frequently been accompanied by resource depletion and accelerated environmental deterioration. When parks have been created on tribal lands, tribals have sometimes been removed, as was the case with the Ik described by Turnbull in his book *The Mountain People*. In some cases exotic tribals have themselves been seen as valuable tourist attractions along with the wildlife. In other cases tribals have been encouraged to remain in place and participate in park management.

The articles in this section were written largely by wildlife biologists, ecologists, and professional conservationists. They represent an important emerging alliance between tribal peoples and conservationists that began as an outgrowth of the global environmental movement of the early 1970s. By contrasting what he calls "ecosystem people" with "biosphere people," Dasmann, in the first selection, argues for incorporating tribals into conservation planning. In the second selection Homewood and Rodgers use data from east Africa to show that traditional cattle herding by tribal pastoralists can be quite compatible with the maintenance of large herds of wild game. Clad explores in detail the possibilities for alliances between tribals and conservationists. Gardner and Nelson review specific American, Canadian, and Australian policies toward native peoples in national parks. Wright et al. describe the efforts of the Kuna Indians of Panama to establish their own conservation zone in order to protect their environment and keep potential invaders out of their territory.

28 National Parks, Nature Conservation, and "Future Primitive"

RAYMOND DASMANN

As originally conceived, conservation parks were designed to prohibit any direct human exploitation of natural resources, and resident tribal peoples have sometimes been forcibly removed from their traditional lands to make way for parks. This selection, a paper originally published in 1976 by internationally respected ecologist and conservationist Raymond Dasmann, highlights a significant turning point in the thinking of resource planners in regard to tribal peoples. Dasmann argues that tribal, or "ecosystem," peoples are far more attuned to environmental conservation than industrialized, or "biosphere," peoples. Tribals rely solely on local ecosystems and must take care of them; biosphere peoples, on the other hand, draw on ecosystems from all over the globe and are less concerned with the condition of any given local ecosystem. As a result the nature preserves that tribals normally live in must now be artificially created by biosphere people as parks. Dasmann advocates full support for the rights of tribal peoples to maintain control over their traditional lands and resources within specially protected areas where necessary. He recommends that conservation parks be cooperative ventures with local tribal peoples.

Dasmann (b. 1919) holds a Ph.D. from Berkeley (1954). He has taught at the University of Minnesota, Humboldt State University, and the University of California at Berkeley. Since 1977 he has been a professor of ecology at the University of California at Santa Cruz, where he is now a provost and the chairman of Environmental Studies. He has written several books on environmental themes, including a widely used basic text, *Environmental Conservation* (first edition, 1959), and *Planet in Peril* (1972).

Those who have grown up in Europe or North America, and have assimilated the view of history proclaimed in those civilizations, know that once there was a paradise on earth and it was called the South Pacific. For more than two centuries, adherents of western technological culture have been fleeing from the supposed benefits of their culture in search of that paradise or its remnants. The more they have searched, the farther it has receded from their vision. Finally, in desperation, they have

Reprinted with permission from *The Ecologist* 6, no. 5 (1976): 164–78. (Originally presented at the South Pacific Conference on National Parks, Wellington, New Zealand, 1975, sponsored by the International Union for Conservation of Nature and Natural Resources.) Copyright © 1976 Ecosystems Ltd., Camelford, Cornwall, U.K.

attempted to recreate it in the tourist lands of Hawaii or Tahiti. But the new model has not been pleasing to the soul.

THE SEARCH FOR PARADISE

More than a century ago, the European invaders of North America were pushing into what they called the wilderness of the West. Most were concerned only with the problems and perils of each day, but a few could see the realities about them with a vision that transcended the purely utilitarian. George Catlin, the artist, was one of these who was greatly disturbed by the destruction of the North American bison and its consequences for the future of the Plains Indian people. He had a proposal that he hoped might save both wildlife and people:

> And what a splendid contemplation too, when one . . . imagines them as they might in the future be seen . . . preserved in their pristine beauty and wildness, in a *magnificent park*, where the world could see for ages to come, the native Indian in his classic attire, galloping his wild horse, with sinewy bow, and shield and lance, amid the fleeting herds of elks and buffaloes. What a beautiful and thrilling specimen for America to preserve and hold up to the view of her refined citizens and the world, in future ages! A *nation's Park*, containing man and beast, in all the wild and freshness of their nature's beauty! (Nash, 1968).

This proposal made in 1832 is commonly regarded as being the first request that a large area of wild America be set aside as a national park. Let us ignore for the moment the obvious chauvinism, since this characterized most 19th century Europeans. Catlin's was no modest proposal, for he wanted the entire Great Plains from Mexico to Canada set aside for the protection and use of those people and animals to whom it rightfully belonged.

At the time there was no receptive audience. The West was being won by those to whom, in Catlin's words *"power is right and voracity a virtue."* Viewed from the other side, however, the howling wilderness that these narrow men were trying to subdue looked quite different. In the words of Chief Standing Bear of the Oglala Sioux Indians (McLuhan, 1971):

> We did not think of the great open plains, the beautiful rolling hills, and winding streams with tangled growth as 'wild'. Only to the white man was nature a 'wilderness' and only to him was the land 'infested' with 'wild' animals and 'savage' people. To us it was tame. Earth was bountiful and we were surrounded with the blessings of the Great Mystery. Not until the hairy man from the east came and with brutal frenzy heaped injustices upon us and the families we loved was it 'wild' for us. When the very animals of the forest began fleeing from his approach, then it was for us the 'Wild West' began.

THE NATIONAL PARKS MOVEMENT

Forty years after Catlin's time, in 1872, the Congress of the United States proclaimed the world's first national park in the Yellowstone region of the territory of Wyoming. Eighteen years after that, shortly after Christmas in 1890, the Army of the United States surrounded and massacred most of the last independent band of the Sioux Indians at a place called Wounded Knee in South Dakota. A survivor, Black Elk, stated:

> . . . something else died there in the bloody mud, and was buried in the blizzard. A people's dream died there. It was a beautiful dream . . . the nation's hoop is broken and scattered. There is no center any longer, and the sacred tree is dead (Brown, 1971).

Later, half of Catlin's dream was realized. The animals were given the first national park. The Indians had a different appointment with destiny.

The national park movement, started at Yellowstone, has been generally regarded as a great success. When many of us met at Grand Teton and Yellowstone, in 1972, we noted that there were more than 1200 national parks or their equivalents throughout the world that met the high standards of the United Nations' List (IUCN, 1974). The centennial of the national parks movement was a stirring occasion for those of us who favour conservation. But I wonder how many noted that in the following year, 1973, a band of Oglala Sioux and other Indians seized and held the town of Wounded Knee, South Dakota, for many months, in a dramatic protest against treaty violations. They were asking, among other things, that the lands that had been guaranteed to them by solemn treaties with the United States government, be in fact given back to them. Some of these lands are in national parks (Burnette and Koster, 1974).

These things are mentioned because I believe that this is a good time to re-examine the entire concept of national parks and all equivalent protected areas. To begin with, those who were responsible for the creation of the system of protected areas in the United States, including national parks, national forests, wildlife refuges and many other categories, were attempting to establish buffers against the greed and rapacity of their fellow citizens. In the 1850s Henry David Thoreau had proclaimed the necessity for protecting at least some areas in which nature could remain intact against the destructive forces of civilization. In the 1860s George Perkins Marsh wrote about the devastation being created by deforestation and the misuse of lands (Nash, 1968). During the decades before Yellowstone was set aside, and until the first national forests were reserved in the 1890s, it was not only the Indians who were being massacred. In the 1860s, because of heavy use by domestic grazing animals, virtually the entire native grassland area of California was knocked out, and the grasslands that developed in its place were dominated by exotics from Europe and Asia. A good share of the hardwood forests of eastern America had been cut down and similar destruction was starting in the West. Farming lands, particularly in the American South, were misused and abandoned in an eroded, infertile state. Wildlife was being slaughtered everywhere.

It is little wonder that those concerned with conservation of nature attempted to set some areas aside, and it is remarkable that they were as successful as they were in doing so. But is there not cause to wonder that it was accepted that those lands outside the national parks were going to be beaten and battered, or used in such a way that any hope for the survival of wildlife in their vicinity was to be considered an idle dream? Is it not strange that it was taken for granted that people and nature were somehow incompatible, and that the drive for profit or power must take precedence over any concern for the kind of world in which people live? People were not always that way. Perhaps it would be well to listen once more to Chief Standing Bear of the Oglala Sioux (known in his day as the Lakotas) (McLuhan, 1971):

> Kinship with all creatures of the earth, sky and water was a real and active principle. For the animal and bird world there existed a brotherly feeling that kept the Lakota safe among them and so close did some of the Lakotas come to their feathered and furred friends that in true brotherhood they spoke a common tongue.
>
> The old Lakota was wise. He knew that man's heart away from nature becomes hard; he knew that lack of respect for growing, living things soon led to lack of respect for humans too. So he kept his youth close to its softening influence.

Here in the Pacific, if one is to judge from the writings of the early European visitors and invaders, much of the same attitude toward nature must have prevailed. Sir Joseph Banks, who accompanied Captain Cook in his explorations of the Pacific, grew quite ecstatic about the ways of life of the island people and the balance that existed between humanity and the natural world. All who visited the islands before the traders, the raiders, and the missionaries did their evil work, seemed to share that opinion. Among the Australian aboriginal people was a sense of responsibility that was continually renewed by the visions of Dreamtime through which people were restored to unity with heaven and earth (Meggitt, 1974).

ECOSYSTEM PEOPLE vs BIOSPHERE PEOPLE

In an earlier paper (Dasmann, 1974), I have postulated that there are two types of people in the world, *ecosystem people* and *biosphere people*. In the former category are all of the members of indigenous traditional cultures and some who have seceded from, or have been pushed out of, technological society; in the latter are those who are tied in with the global technological civilization. Ecosystem people live within a single ecosystem, or at most two or three adjacent and closely related ecosystems. They are dependent upon that ecosystem for their survival. If they persistently violate its ecological rules, they must necessarily perish. Thus a hunting people who continually kill more wild game than can be produced by the normal reproduction of wild animal populations must run out of food and starve. A fishing people who persist in overfishing will destroy their base of support. Those who practice subsistence agriculture must develop some means for keeping the soil in place and for restoring its fertility. Island people have lived under particularly strong restraints, and could not tolerate any great increase in their own numbers, since the resources of islands are not only limited but tend to make their limitations obvious. Only continental people can develop myths of unlimited resources.

Biosphere people draw their support, not from the resources of any one ecosystem, but from the entire biosphere. Any large modern city is the focus for a network of transportation and communication that reaches throughout the globe—drawing perhaps beef from Argentina, lamb from New Zealand, wheat from Canada, tea from Ceylon, coffee from Brazil, herring from the North Atlantic, and so on. Local catastrophes that would wipe out people dependent on a single ecosystem may create only minor perturbations among the biosphere people, since they can simply draw more heavily on a different ecosystem. Consequently, biosphere people can exert incredible pressure upon an ecosystem that they wish to exploit, and create great devastation—something that would be impossible or unthinkable for people who were dependent upon that particular ecosystem. The impact of biosphere people upon ecosystem people has usually been destructive. Even if the intentions of the biosphere invaders are the best, and they seldom are, their effect is to break down the local constraints, the traditional practices that have held the delicate balances between humanity and nature, and thus allow ecosystem destruction to take place.

INDIGENOUS SOCIETIES DISPLACED

Here in the Pacific we see some glaring examples of what happens when ecosystem peoples are brought into the biosphere network. The people of Nauru would never have thought of mining their island out from under themselves, until they were tied into the trade and transportation of the biosphere network. The same applies to other phosphate islands. No ecosystem person would have thought of taking the top off New Caledonia to get at the nickel, until he was sucked into the biosphere network. In Australia there is an enormous uranium deposit, an estimated 1 per cent of the world's known supply, on aboriginal land at a place called Gabo Djang. According to Robert Allen, this is known to the Aborigines as the Dreaming Place of the Green Ant, and if it is desecrated, the Great Green Ant, one of the powerful spirits, will come down and ravage the world. Queensland Mines Limited offered the Aborigines the munificent sum of $7,425 in 1971 for the right to mine this 300-million-dollar ore supply, but later raised the offer to $891,000 along with more than 13 million dollars in royalties. The offer was for a long time refused, but in December 1974 it was reported that the people had agreed to sell. The biosphere people have again triumphed and that much more uranium will be turned loose to do the work of the Great Green Ant in ravaging the world (Allen, 1974). Admittedly, some of the ecosystem people who sell out to the biosphere network become very rich, which permits them to go somewhere else to live—*so long as there is a somewhere else that the biosphere people have not destroyed.*

Biosphere people *create* national parks. Ecosystem people have *always* lived in the equivalent of a national park. It is the kind of country that ecosystem people have always protected that biosphere people want to have formally reserved and safeguarded. But, of course, first the ecosystem people must be removed—or at least that has been the prevailing custom. The consequences are almost always destructive to the people affected. Colin Turnbull's book *The Mountain People* is a particularly disturbing account of what happened to a hunting-subsistence-agriculture people when they were pushed out of Uganda's Kidepo Valley National Park (Turnbull, 1972). A similar, but perhaps less severe, disintegration took place among the elephant-hunting Waliangulu who were displaced by Tsavo National Park—a park that has subsequently suffered from a plague of elephants (Gomm, 1974). As Tururin, chief of the Pataxo Indians of Brazil, has put it, "We Indians are like plants: when changed from one place to another we don't die but we never fully recover. We will not leave here because even before the reservation existed we already lived on this land. It may be bad, it may be good but it's our land." But in Brazil the previously isolated ecosystem people are being threatened or destroyed by the massive drive for the exploitation of Amazonia—a process far less benign than any effort to create national parks (Supysáua, 1974).

It is characteristic of wealthier biosphere people that they do not want to stay at home. They wander the globe always searching—searching for something they seem to have lost along the way in their rush to capture the resources of the world and accumulate its wealth. Thus they give rise to the tourist industry, and this in turn provides a financial justification for creating and maintaining national parks. In these parks the wanderers can see some of the wonders that they left behind, and can pretend for a while that they have not really destroyed the natural world—at least not all of it. They will pay highly for this experience. But for some reason the money nearly always tends to be channelled back into the biosphere network. It does not go to those who were once ecosystem people and who have the strange idea that what is now called a national park is really just the land that was home.

This situation must not continue. National parks must not serve as a means for displacing the members of traditional societies who have always cared for the land and its biota. Nor can national parks survive as islands surrounded by hostile people who have lost the land that was once their home. Parks cannot survive in a natural state if they are surrounded by lands that are degraded or devastated by failure to obey the simplest ecological rules. Today, with the increase in human numbers and the enormous pressure being exerted on all ecosystems, one of the distinctions between ecosystem and total biosphere is being broken down. No longer can biosphere people remain buffered against the breakdown of particular ecosystems. A drought in India or North America now has global repercussions. The entire biosphere is now becoming as closely interconnected through human endeavour as the most delicately balanced ecosystem within it. Not just national parks but nature conservation in its fullest sense are now becoming absolutely vital.

Few anywhere would argue with the concept of national parks, but many would argue with the way the concept has been applied—too often at the cost of displacement of traditional cultures, and nearly always with insufficient consideration for the practices and policies affecting the lands outside of the park.

ESTABLISHING NATIONAL PARKS IN THE SOUTH PACIFIC

Here in the South Pacific there is no doubt that more national parks, or something equivalent to them, are badly needed. There is some question, however, about what kind of national park, and how it is to fit in with the patterns of life, and the necessities of life, for those people who inhabit the Pacific. I would suggest that the ideal national park for the Pacific islands would be fairly close to what existed here before the invaders from Europe and Asia took over. I do not propose, however, that we attempt to turn back the clock. I am suggesting, however, that in going forward we take into account some rules that should be mandatory for those agencies, national or international, responsible for advocating or creating new national parks.

1. The rights of members of indigenous cultures to the lands they have traditionally occupied must be recognized, and any plans for establishing parks or reserves in these lands must be developed in consultation with, and in agreement with, the people involved. Papua/New Guinea has been taking some noteworthy initiatives in this direction, and I trust that their government will continue along this course. Furthermore, the Australian government has now fully recognized the rights of its Aborigines to their lands, including full control of mineral rights.

2. Recognizing the long-prevailing balances that have existed between people and nature in areas where traditional societies have remained isolated from the influence of biosphere cultures, the establishment of fully protected areas in which these people can maintain their isolation *for as long as they wish to do so* should be encouraged. Such areas will do much to further the conservation of nature, and equally important, will protect ways-of-life that are in balance with nature.

We all have much to learn from these traditional cultures. In this respect there are some examples to follow. The Manu National Park in Peru shelters an isolated Indian tribe which, for the present at least, remains undisturbed. The Odzala National Park in the Congo provides a home for Pygmy peoples. In Botswana and South Africa the 6 million hectares of the Central Kalahari Game Reserve and Kalahari Gemsbok National Parks permit the Bushmen to continue their traditional hunting life. There were once some good examples in Brazil also, but I am afraid that these are being brushed aside in the sacred name of "development" (Supysáua, 1974).

3. Wherever national parks are created, their protection needs to be co-ordinated with the people who occupy the surrounding lands. Those who are most affected by the presence of a national park must fully share in its benefits, financial or other. They must become the protectors of the park, whether they are directly employed by the park, receive a share of park receipts, or are in other ways brought to appreciate its value. Without this, we will find that we are entering a waiting game, at best. The people outside the park will await the change in government or the relaxation of vigilance that will permit them to invade the park.

4. Land use in areas surrounding parks must be compatible with the protection of nature inside the park. This too will require negotiation and understanding among the people who own or occupy these lands. It cannot be effectively accomplished by some sweeping government decree unless the lands are unoccupied.

This is not a comprehensive list of rules, but only an attempt to emphasize those rules which have been far too generally ignored in the establishment of national parks in the past. However, if national parks are really to survive, and if they are going to accomplish their objectives, then we must have more than just a set of rules concerning the parks and their surroundings. I cannot see much hope for the future of either parks or people, unless some of the old sense of belonging to the natural world, of being a part of nature, and not hostile to it, is restored. In an article prepared for *Planet Drum*, Jerry Gorsline and Linn House have made this comparison:

We have been awakened to the richness and complexity of the primitive mind which merges sanctity, food, life and death—where culture is integrated with nature at the level of the *particular ecosystem* and employs for its cognition a body of metaphor drawn from and structured in relation to that ecosystem. We have found therein a mode of thinking parallel to modern science but operating at the entirely different level of sensible intuition, a tradition that prepared the ground for the neolithic revolution; a science of the *concrete*, where nature is the model for culture because the mind has been nourished and weaned on nature; a *logic* that recognizes soil fertility, the magic of animals, the continuum of mind between species. Successful culture is a semi-permeable membrane between man and nature. We are witnessing North America's post-industrial phase right now, during which human society strives to remain predominant over nature. No mere extrapolation from present to future seems possible. We are in transition from one condition of symbiotic balance—the primitive— to another which we will call the *future primitive* . . . a condition having the attributes of a mature ecosystem: stable, diverse, in symbiotic balance again. . . . If we wish to integrate our cultures with nature we do so at the *level of the ecosystem* which everywhere has a common structure and progression but everywhere varies specifically in composition and function according to time and place (Gorsline and House, 1974).

I would propose that the answer for nature conservation in the South Pacific, as elsewhere, will be found to lie in the direction of "Future Primitive." This does not mean the rejection of the best of modern technology, but it does mean the avoidance of the worst. It does mean using the tools and energy that are still available to create something permanent, to create a way of life that can be *sustained*. In such a way of life, nature conservation would necessarily be taken for granted, since people will recognize that their future depends on the health and diversity of the natural world.

Already some of the handwriting is beginning to appear on the wall. The airlines are in serious trouble; the tourist industry is struggling to survive. No future can be built around a national park system that depends on the big jets arriving around the clock and pouring their loads of wealthy Asians and Europeans into the island scene. Unless some miracle fuels are invented soon, the big jets will be increasingly empty and some day they may not come at all. The economies of the technological biosphere society are in a chaotic state—and no two economists can agree about their future direction. Those who live in the Pacific and who have any sense of prudence would be wise to look to their own resources, their own levels of population, and to turn back to examine some of the old skills and ways of life that have been left behind. Not too long ago most people in the Pacific were ecosystem people. Now I would propose that the future belongs to those who can regain, at a higher level, the old sense of balance and belonging between man and nature.

REFERENCES

Allen, Robert, 1974. Hunting peoples: harmony between community and environment. *Ecologist/Resurgence*, Vol. 4. 9.

Brown, Dee, 1971. *Bury My Heart at Wounded Knee*, Bantam Books, New York.

Burnette, Robert & John Koster, 1974. *The Road to Wounded Knee*, Bantam Books, New York.

Dasmann, R. F., 1974. Ecosystems. Symposium on the Future of Traditional 'Primitive' Societies. Cambridge, England, December, 1974. To be published.

Gomm, Roger, 1974. The elephant men. *Ecologist*, 4: 53–57.

Gorsline, Jerry & Linn House, 1974. Future Primitive. *Planet Drum*, San Francisco, Issue 3.

I.U.C.N. *1974 United Nations List of National Parks and Equivalent Reserves.* IUCN Publications New Series. No. 29, IUCN, Morges.

McLuhan, T. C., 1971. *Touch the earth. A self-portrait of Indian existence.* Pocket Books, New York.

Meggitt, M. J., 1974. The Australian Aborigines. Symposium on the Future of Traditional 'Primitive' Societies. Cambridge, England, December, 1974. To be published.

Nash, Roderick, 1968. *The American environment: readings in the history of conservation.* Addison-Wesley, Reading, Massachusetts.

Supysáua. A documentary report on the conditions of the Indian peoples in Brazil. 1974. *Indigena* and American Friends of Brazil, Berkeley, California.

Turnbull, Colin, 1972. *The Mountain People.* Simon and Schuster, New York.

29   Pastoralism and Conservation

K. M. HOMEWOOD

W. A. RODGERS

African wildlife figure prominently in worldwide conservation programs. The East African game parks with their elephants and vast herds of zebra and wildebeest are conservation showpieces as well as tourist attractions. K. M. Homewood and W. A. Rodgers point out that traditional cattle herders are caught between the conservationists who feel they are threatening the wildlife and the ranch developers who feel they are wasting valuable commercial rangeland. Most dramatically, tribal herders may be accused of fostering desertification as a result of overstocking. The authors present a review of the data from East Africa on game and livestock numbers, overgrazing, and environmental deterioration; they conclude that there is no clear evidence that traditional herding is incompatible with conservation interests. More detailed evidence from the Maasai herders within the

Reprinted from *Human Ecology* 12, no. 4 (1984): 431–41, by permission of Plenum Publishing Corporation.

Ngorongoro Conservation Area of Tanzania provides further support for their argument.

K. M. Homewood obtained her Ph.D. from the University of London in 1976; her dissertation was based on field studies of primates in East Africa. She is currently with the Department of Anthropology, University College London, and has frequently collaborated with W. A. Rodgers on projects dealing with East African ecology. Rodgers has worked extensively as a zoologist in Tanzania and is currently with the Wildlife Institute of India.

INTRODUCTION

Is pastoralism compatible with conservation? What are the conflicts, and where do possible compromises lie? In this paper, we look at some general ideas and then go on to discuss in detail one particular case study.

Conflicts between pastoralism and conservation might arise as a result of direct extermination of wildlife by pastoralists, or livestock by wildlife, competition for resources, disease interaction, or finally, through potential long-term environmental degradation by overgrazing. There are no recorded cases where pastoralists are responsible for the direct extermination of an endangered species. Competition for resources is a more real problem. Pastoralists coexist with wildlife populations throughout the rangelands of East Africa, and there are clear similarities between pastoralist livestock and a range of wild ungulate species, in terms of their ecological needs and patterns of exploitation of these environments (Jewell, 1980). The obvious example is perhaps that of the Serengeti wildebeest and the Maasai zebu cattle with which they overlap: similar body weights, similar diets, similar constraints on daily travel distance (Pennycuick, 1979), similar shift from resident/altitudinal transhumant to long-distance migratory/nomadic ranging patterns with increasing aridity (Homewood and Rodgers, 1984). One would expect direct competition to ensue from such close overlap. Jewell (1980) suggests that the relative paucity of large wild mammals in West Africa is a product of the spread of pastoralists from the north over the last 6500 years. This competitive exclusion may not always be the case. In some areas, for example, the toich grasslands of the Sudd and the Amboseli ecosystem (Western, 1975) stock are seen as complementary with as well as overlapping wildlife niches. They are felt to be an integral part of the grazing succession, a temporal sequence of species both wild and domesticated that in turn exploit different layers of the same rangeland. Factors other than competition have a major effect. The work of ecologists, historians, and wildlife and livestock scientists has established that the rinderpest epidemic of the 1890s wiped out up to 90% of cattle populations and several wild ungulate species in East Africa and probably elsewhere. For the last hundred years, numbers have been increasing for both wild and domesticated ungulates (Sinclair and Norton-Griffiths, 1979; Kjekshus, 1977). Over the last 20 years, Serengeti wildlife numbers (particularly wildebeest) have grown far more rapidly than livestock populations and are now displacing them even in the surrounding buffer zones (e.g., in 1970–1980, there was a four-fold increase in wildebeest in adjacent, primary livestock-oriented Kajiado District). The major factor here is disease interaction. The wildebeest carry and are resistant to malignant catarrhal fever, a disease fatal to the cattle, and as a result, pastoralists must avoid areas used by wildlife during the infectious period. Wildebeest are also thought to be a major factor in the maintenance and spread of disease-bearing tick populations, and both pastoralists and ranchers are showing a trend toward increasing small stock holdings, which are less affected. There is now a recrudescence of rinderpest in the Serengeti. Surrounding cattle populations are protected by inoculation, but wildebeest are susceptible. This seesaw of disease interaction may well have enabled coexistence without severe competition over the last few thousand years and could continue to do so in the future.

There is a more fundamental level of potential conflict, in terms not of immediate resource use but of long-term effects on those resources, and long-term policies concerning their exploitation. Areas occupied by pastoralists almost inevitably attract the attention of conservationists on the one hand and livestock and agricultural development groups on the other. Despite the fact that pastoralist communities usually have some traditional system of resource control, and unlike many commercial ranching concerns, tolerate the continued existence of nonproductive plants and animals, they are often accused of environmental degradation by both livestock development and conservation experts. This pastoralist-induced habitat deterioration is a widely accepted view of the historical origin of present-day Mediterranean landscapes, and has now become conventional wisdom for Subsaharan Africa. African rangelands are commonly thought of as undergoing desertification largely as a result of the "tragedy of the commons" (Hardin, 1968). According to this idea, individuals would have nothing to gain from limiting the numbers of their own stock grazing communally owned land—any environmental benefit from restraint would be exploited by others—and, as a result, common land is systematically overgrazed. With the advent of modern veterinary care and the erosion of any traditional controls through social and ecological changes, this is commonly said to have led to progressive desertification. This widely held view has only recently begun to be questioned. Sandford (1984) points out the lack of real data on desertification, overstocking, actual livestock numbers, their meaning in terms of densities, the actual impact of veterinary care on stock populations, and the efficacy of imported range management techniques:

1. There are many different definitions of desertification. Those that refer to serious, long-term, or irreversible degradation are hard to demonstrate as occurring in practice, as annual variation in productivity as a function of rainfall variation is usually greater than any decline due to degradation. The other definitions describe processes only undesirable if

seen from a narrow viewpoint, e.g., by reference to vegetation in the absence of man and livestock (Conant, 1982).

2. There is no consistent consensus on appropriate stocking levels; this invalidates many if not most estimates of overstocking. Many estimates imply serious overstocking hardly consistent with the simultaneous accusation of rapid growth. The whole concept of stabilizing stock densities may be inappropriate for arid and semi-arid rangelands. Sandford has modeled the effects of conservative, stable stocking levels vs. those of tracking environmental variation and suggests the greater efficiency of the latter method under the unpredictable and widely fluctuating conditions prevailing in arid and semi-arid rangelands (Sandford, 1982).

3. Although published figures indicate unprecedented increases of livestock populations over the last 30 years, the methods used to arrive at these estimates are so inaccurate and imprecise, and the distribution of stock so subject to rapid change, that all suggested increases lie well within the margin of error. Actual increases have probably taken place; there is, however, no firm evidence from counts *per se*, and not infrequently, results are at least partly generated by fudge factors introduced to rectify what is thought to be underenumeration.

4. Changes in density are more important than changes in numbers. In some countries, new areas have become available through water development and/or declining wildlife populations (in others, the reverse is true).

5. Part of the conviction that stock numbers have grown comes from the feeling that modern veterinary care must have made a difference. Veterinary care has conquered rinderpest but no other arid area stock diseases in Africa. Has this really opened the way for an unprecedented stock increase? Rinderpest only arrived in Africa in the 1890s. What controlled stock populations prior to that?

6. Techniques for prevention and repair of desertification have been developed elsewhere (United States, Israel, etc.) and imported to Subsaharan Africa. Although these methods have been tested and found successful in their countries of origin, there is little or no evidence that, for example, stocking rates, rests, and rotations recommended for African rangelands produce better results than traditional transhumance and seminomadism. Nyerges (1982) stresses the idea of local co-evolution of rangeland, herbivores, and husbandry methods and warns against importing techniques from one area to attack superficially similar problems in another.

Sanford suggests that the twin ideas of overgrazing and desertification have become not only entrenched but self-reinforcing despite the inadequacy of the evidence for either, and quotes cases where data disagreeing with conventional wisdom have been not only suppressed but distorted to give it new support in the context of, for example, the 1977 United Nations

Conference on Desertification. This is not to suggest that overgrazing and desertification do not occur; rather, it is to point out that so far they are not well substantiated.

We have outlined potential conflicts between pastoralism and conservation in terms of immediate competition, of disease interaction, and of environmental degradation by pastoralist stock. We now go on to look at one particular case study that illustrates some of the general points raised above, to propose some possible solutions and contrast them with management policies proposed elsewhere.

Ngorongoro Conservation Area (NCA) is a joint land use area in northern Tanzania. As well as supporting some 18,000 resident Maasai pastoralists and their stock, it is a UNESCO World Heritage site combining world-famous archaeological and paleontological sites with extraordinary geological, ecological, and wildlife diversity; and, together with the adjacent Serengeti, it has enormous tourist potential. Maasai in NCA are forbidden cultivation and access to key conservation sites; the NCA has recently considered excluding them altogether. Past management decisions have been influenced by the enormous and internationally recognized body of knowledge accumulated on Serengeti and NCA wildlife biology. By contrast, nothing beyond rough estimates of numbers was known of the ecology of resident pastoralists. They were assumed to have a generally negative effect on environment, wildlife, and other conservation values of the area. Our study aimed to investigate potential ecological problems and management possibilities. It involved aerial surveys of wildlife, livestock and pastoral settlement numbers, distribution, and relation to erosion, as well as ground studies of livestock management, production, and human consumption of products. Three different intensive study sites allowed us to cover the range of environmental variation in NCA in our ground studies. Several aspects, particularly milk production and changes in herd size through birth, death, sale, exchange, and transfer were monitored over a 2-year period with the help of NCA staff, who were also locally resident Maasai.

The detailed results of our study have been presented elsewhere (Homewood and Rodgers, 1984). Our general findings, together with those of related studies in the area, are relevant to the whole issue of pastoralism and conservation. What is the evidence for uncontrolled stock population growth leading to increased competition with wildlife, overgrazing, and environmental deterioration? First, there is no indication of significant stock increases. To the extent that they can be trusted, the figures over the last 20 years indicate fluctuations rather than any rising trend. For example, cattle numbers fluctuated from around 160,000 in 1960 to 70,000 in 1970 and back to 140,000 in 1980 (Arhem, 1981). This is partly because NCA is neither a social nor an ecological unit but rather an administrative one, unresponsive to local short-term variation in rainfall and production. However, while there is no doubt whatsoever that stock populations have increased over the last 100 years since the rinderpest epidemic, there is no reason to think they are any greater or smaller on average than before 1890. Unlike the herds, the human population of NCA has shown a marked increase from around 10,500 in 1960, falling to 6,000 in 1970, but rising to over 18,000 in 1984. As a result, stock per capita figures have fallen consistently over the last 20 years. This, together with overall low calving (0.6 calves/yr), survival (adult and calf survivorship 0.9 to 0.7, respectively), milk production figures (mean yield 0.42 kg/day), and an annual offtake of around 8% (Homewood and Rodgers, 1984), has meant a steadily declining standard of living for NCA pastoralists (Arhem, 1981).

What is the evidence for immediate competition for resources between wildlife and pastoralists in NCA? The area has been used by pastoralists over the last 2,000 years or more (the Maasai themselves have only used NCA for the last 200 years), so there is a long history not only of coexistence but also of pastoralist activities shaping the present highly valued landscape through grazing and burning. However, have conditions changed so as to preclude continued existence? Within NCA, wildlife populations are concentrated in such areas as the central Caldera, from which Maasai stock are excluded except for occasional brief access to natural salt licks. Aerial surveys with Ecosystems Ltd. showed that the 82% of Arusha Region, which has no cultivation (including NCA), supports 56% of its total stock and 98% of its total wildlife populations. However, a finer-grained analysis shows that, on a more local scale, 95% of all wildlife overlap with only 9% of cattle, and, conversely, 91% cattle with 5% of wildlife. This is partly determined by law excluding cattle from conservation areas, rather than by ecology. However, certain wildlife species showed higher degrees of overlap with cattle (91% impala with 38% cattle, 94% zebra with 26% cattle). As far as species like wildebeest are concerned, mutual competitive exclusion on a local scale is the most likely conclusion. Recent historical trends in the course of this process are neatly illustrated by traces of shifting settlement patterns, as old bomas leave characteristic marks. The Ecosystems report presented evidence that the distribution of Maasai settlements along the western boundary of NCA, among other areas, has changed over the last 15 years, receding from the Serengeti in response to a change in the migratory movements of the Serengeti wildebeest. This is substantiated by current complaints from NCA Maasai about ever-further encroaching wildebeest migrations depleting grazing and forcing the cattle herds to move because of the danger of wildlife-borne disease. Because of the susceptibility of their cattle to malignant catarrhal fever (to which wildebeest are relatively resistant) Maasai have to avoid contact with wildebeest herds and the areas they graze during critical infectious periods. As a result, the pastoralists forfeit access to the most nutritious grazing at the start of the rains, a period thought to be critical in reestablishing condition and determining survival and fertility in the ensuing year (Swift, 1983). As Sandford has pointed out, livestock densities are presumably more important than overall numbers in assessing levels of exploitation. The gradual shift away from Serengeti borders may contribute to the apparent overconcentration of stock elsewhere in NCA (50–100% greater than theoretical biomass levels derived from rainfall and production figures, no allowance made for seasonal transhumant absence; Homewood and Rodgers, 1984).

Is there evidence for overgrazing? Whereas Western range management experts use range condition as an indication to move stock on, pastoralists assess the condition of their stock and base their decision on the animals' welfare, of which milk production is one immediate and conspicuous indicator. While initial indications of overgrazing in the short term will be lack of grass cover and poor stock condition, which will both be observed in a bad dry season and be rapidly reversed with the onset of adequate rain, indications of longer-term overgrazing are held by Western scientists to be, first, adverse changes in vegetation composition, and eventually loss of ground cover with erosion and desertification. Despite the high stock densities throughout NCA and the shortage of dry season pasture in many areas, actual overgrazing in terms of a deteriorating trend in vegetation composition was only suggested in one of our study areas: Sendui, a high altitude site at 2,800 m with >1,000 mm annual rainfall. Here it is suggested that the tussock grass *Eleusine jaegeri*, which is coarse and too tough for cattle except as very new growth, may be spreading at the expense of more palatable species, which are more heavily grazed. This suggestion originated in a report by Fosbrooke (personal communication) in the early 1940s and has been invoked several times since. A number of people have set out to investigate the idea through exclosure studies, but none of these studies has ever been completed. Perhaps the best indication of a likely answer comes from the Olmoti crater near Sendui, from which pastoralist stock have now been excluded for well over 10 years on the grounds of overgrazing and *Eleusine* spread. Although no actual measurements have been taken, neither utilization nor, more recently, exclusion have had any noticeable impact on the vegetation since the first observation was made. The impact on stock of losing this as a dry season grazing area is felt to have been serious.

Erosion is generally taken as a strong indication of adverse human impact on the environment. The Ecosystems Ltd. aerial survey of Arusha Region as a whole allows some overall assessment of the importance of erosion within NCA, compared with surrounding areas, and indicates the association of erosion with particular types of human land use. The most severe erosion was associated with Arumeru (Arusha itself) and Monduli District, immediately adjacent to but outside NCA. In NCA as in Mbulu and Hanang Districts to the immediate south, erosion was primarily associated with topographic features of the Gol mountains and the Rift wall, and on recent unconsolidated ash from active volcanoes, e.g., Salei Plains, and was mainly due to eroding trails caused by both cattle and wildlife. Gully and sheet erosion were associated with districts other than NCA. The Ecosystems survey found erosion to be primarily associated with agropastoral and cultivator settlement outside NCA; there was no significant association with pastoral settlement. Overall, the problem of erosion appears negligible in NCA, although on a completely different scale, concern over potential trampling of archaeological sites has led to exclusion of pastoralists from previously important dry season grazing and watering in Olduvai.

To sum up, the NCA livestock population does not show signs of unprecedented or even steady growth. Possible local overstocking, diagnosed on the basis of theoretical figures, is not borne out by other evidence. There is no single definition of overgrazing. Pastures such as those of NCA may well be overgrazed from the point of view of commercial yield but not in terms of environmental degradation. There is no clear erosion problem. The speculative nature of both theoretical stock levels and actual counts, as well as the flexible deployment of the herds, make the idea of an overstocking problem even more dubious. By contrast, there is both direct and circumstantial evidence that wildlife populations, in particular the migratory wildebeest, have been expanding steadily. In theory, some balance of competitive interaction between livestock and wildlife could continue indefinitely. In practice, disease interaction, together with current conservation measures which allow wildlife to trespass on human land-use areas (but not vice versa) and policies against poaching, hunting, and game cropping tip the balance in favor of wildlife (particularly wildebeest). Declining stock-per-person ratios make a continued purely pastoral economy impossible in the long run, unless water development enables better use of range resources, and grain becomes more readily available and accessible in exchange for livestock. An unsympathetic administration, as might result for example from the proposed amalgamation of NCA Authority with National Parks, could make continued joint land use in NCA increasingly untenable and in the long run impossible.

Would the pastoralists be better off outside NCA altogether? The Ecosystems survey presented evidence that one third of Arusha Region pastoralist settlement is concentrated in 4% of its area—that 4% representing the overlap zone between pure pastoralist and pure cultivator settlement, and being indicative both of sedentarization and strong competition with cultivators. Judging by historical precedent elsewhere in Subsaharan Africa (Swift, 1982) as well as Arusha Region distribution patterns, cultivation is responsible for displacing both pastoralist and wildlife land use. In our view, displacing NCA pastoralists in favor of wildlife would be not only ecologically unnecessary and an injustice but would so exacerbate popular feeling against conservation that ultimately areas such as the Serengeti could suffer seriously.

Is there any solution which would work to the long-term benefit both of wildlife and of pastoralists? Western (1982) describes the compromise achieved for Amboseli National Park, where local Maasai receive compensation in terms of park revenue and employment possibilities, as well as proposed water development, in return for ceding part of their traditional dry season swampland grazing to wildlife conservation and tourism. The areas surrounding the park make up the wet season dispersal area of the wildlife populations. This land is now registered as group ranches on which traditional pastoralism continues largely unchanged and, importantly, this arrangement allows wet season wildlife utilization. Landowners are paid a fee for the use of such land by wildlife. The situation in NCA is different. First, the current revenue from tourism does not even allow hotels and administration to break even, let alone pay dividends. Second, while the main wildlife values and tourist attractions in Amboseli are in the swamp area, the prime dry season resource itself, the attractions in NCA, are the Caldera and other craters as well as the archaeological sites. Pastoralists are already excluded from these areas, which represent potentially useful but not critical resources for stock.

In our view, joint land use is the best option in the long run for both pastoralists and wildlife, and a more robust solution than exclusive use for either alone. However, we have pointed out that both stock per capita and standards of living in general are declining for NCA Maasai, and that a purely pastoral economy cannot continue indefinitely under prevailing conditions. Our study (Homewood and Rodgers, 1984) and the revised management plan (IRA, 1983) suggest simple measures to alleviate immediate problems revealed by Arhem (1981) and other studies. The main suggestions, which are currently being implemented, are, first to substitute low-maintenance windmill pumps for the perennially broken diesel machines (proposal before the EEC), and second, to improve an access track to Sendui, which will facilitate trade for grain in this remote and impoverished area (under construction in Oxfam). More reliable provision of acaricide may alleviate the problem of tick-borne disease, which causes high calf and adult mortality in Ilmesigio area (proposal before the EEC). As well as these immediate measures, the revised management plan recommended northward extension of NCA boundaries to cover the wet season dispersal area of the majority of livestock, greater Maasai participation in NCA management, and eventual dividends from conservation. These ideas have not been enthusiastically received by the current NCA Authority and there are renewed suggestions to amalgamate NCA with National Parks. We hope that the immediate measures will show sufficiently rapid success for the NCA to reconsider long-term policy and the likely outcome of a one-sided view of the interaction of pastoralism and conservation.

Our findings have wider implications. Although some of the best examples come from East Africa, e.g., Kenya Maasai (Hjort, 1982; Campbell, 1984; Little, 1984), many pastoralist peoples elsewhere in Subsaharan Africa, central Asia, and India have lost considerable areas of rangeland to other forms of land use since the turn of the century.

This alienation of land, particularly in the case of its transfer to conservation estate, has been justified on the grounds of alleged actual or potential misuse with degradation of both habitat and wildlife populations (Campbell, 1983). It continues today with currently consolidating conservation interests in Somalia, India, and Outer Mongolia, to name but a few examples outside our case study. Our results from NCA emphasize the importance of evaluating each individual case as to whether accusations of environmental damage are well founded and as serious as they seem, and the need for careful consideration of a joint land use compromise as a solution that may be ecologically, socioeconomically, and politically preferable to exclusive conservation use.

REFERENCES

Arhem, K. (1981). Maasai pastoralism in the Ngorongoro Conservation Area: Sociological and ecological issues. BRALUP Research Paper No. 69, University of Dar es Salaam, Tanzania.

Campbell, B. (1983). *Human Ecology* (Chap. 8). *Pastoralism*. Heinemann, London.

Campbell, D. (1984). Response to drought among farmers and herders in Southern Kajiado District, Kenya. *Human Ecology* 12: 35–64.

Conant, F. (1982). Thorns paired, sharply recurved: Cultural controls and rangeland quality in East Africa. In Spooner, B., and Mann, H. (eds.), *Desertification and Development; Dryland Ecology in Social Perspective*. Academic Press, London.

Ecosystems Ltd. (1980). (i). Livestock, wildlife and land use survey of Arusha Region, Tanzania; (ii). The status and utilisation of wildlife in Arusha Region, Tanzania, USAID Contract no. AID/AFR-C-1556, Ecosystems Ltd., P.O. 30239, Nairobi, Kenya.

Hardin, G. (1968). The tragedy of the Commons. *Science* 162: 1243–1248.

Hjort, A. (1982). A critique of "ecological" models of pastoral land use. *Nomadic Peoples* 10: 11–27.

Homewood K., and Rodgers, W. (1984). Pastoralist ecology in Ngorongoro Conservation Area, Tanzania. ODI Pastoral Network Paper 17d, London.

Institute for Resource Assessment. (1983). *A Revised Management Plan for the Ngorongoro Conservation Area*, University of Dar es Salaam, Tanzania.

Jewell, P. (1980). Ecology and management of game animals and domestic livestock in African savannahs. In Harris, D. (ed.), *Human Ecology in Savannah Environments*. Academic Press, London, pp. 353–382.

Kjekshus, H. (1977). *Ecology, Control and Economic Development on East African History: The Case of Tanzania 1850–1950*. Heinemann, London.

Little, P. (1984). Critical socio-economic variables in African pastoral livestock development. In Simpson, J., and Evangelou, P. (eds.), *Livestock Development in Subsaharan Africa*, Westview Press, Boulder, Colorado, pp. 201–214.

Nyerges, A. (1982). Pastoralists, flocks and vegetation: Processes of coadaptation. In Spooner, B., and Mann, H. (eds.), *Desertification and Development: Dryland Ecology in Social Perspective*. Academic Press, London.

Pennycuick, C. (1979). Energy costs of locomotion and the concept of a foraging radius. In Sinclair, A., and Norton-Griffiths, M. (eds.), *Serengeti: Dynamics of an Ecosystem*. University of Chicago Press, Chicago, pp. 164–182.

Sandford, S. (1982). Pastoral strategies and desertification: Opportunism and con-
servatism in dry lands. In Spooner, B., and Mann, H. (eds.), *Desertification and
Development: Dryland Ecology in Social Perspective.* Academic Press, London.

Sandford, S. (1984). *Management of Pastoral Development in the Third World.* ODI,
London; John Wiley and Sons, Chichester and New York.

Sinclair, A., and Norton-Griffiths, M. (1979). *Serengeti: Dynamics of an Ecosystem.*
University of Chicago Press, Chicago.

Swift, J. (1982). The future of African hunter gatherer and pastoralist peoples.
Development and Change 13: 159–181.

Swift, J. (1983). The start of the rains. Research memo, Institute for Development
Studies, Sussex University.

Western, D. (1975). Water availability and its influence on the structure and dynamics of a savannah large mammal community. *East African Wildlife Journal*
13: 265–286.

Western, D. (1982). Amboseli National Park: Enlisting landowners to conserve migratory wildlife. *Ambio* 11(5): 302–308.

---

30   Conservation and Indigenous Peoples: A Study of Convergent Interests

JAMES C. CLAD

From the viewpoint of a conservationist James C. Clad ex-
amines the possibilities for cooperation between conservationists and tribal peoples
for the protection of natural resources within areas traditionally claimed by tribal
groups. He stresses that, assuming the harmonious existence of tribals with their
environment, there is an obvious basis for alliance between the two interest groups.
However, the situation is more complex because not all tribal groups may actually be
in balance with their resource base at the present time. Furthermore, tribals may
reject any imposed conservation effort as a form of external control. Clad discusses
examples of apparently successful cooperative ventures between conservation interests and the Maori in New Zealand and the Sherpas in Nepal. He also outlines the

Reprinted with permission from *Culture and Conservation: The Human Dimension in Environmental Planning*, ed. Jeffrey A. McNeely and David Pitt, 45–62. Copyright © 1985 International Union for Conservation of Nature and Natural Resources.

issues that international conservation groups such as the International Union for the Conservation of Nature and Natural Resources (IUCN) are now considering.

INTRODUCTION

The prevailing temperament in the world today of "development at all costs" requires advocates of indigenous peoples' welfare—particularly of the integrity of isolated tribal groups—to marshal arguments available to best effect and to choose both remedies and advocates with care.

The renewed political assertiveness by (and on behalf of) the world's estimated 200 million indigenous peoples has three broad dimensions.[1] The first concerns itself with "remedies", with quasi-legal efforts to protect and enhance the welfare of indigenous peoples. Both international law and national law remedies fall into the first category. The second dimension follows from the first: how best to use these (often quite insubstantial) remedies to best effort—in other words, the choice of "tactics". The final dimension develops from the first two: a search for new allies and leverage.

A crucial issue before tribal societies (at the national political level) and lobbyists on their behalf (at the level of international pressure and advocacy) is therefore to find strategies that will enlist the energies of others to act on their behalf. This task involves a search for convergent interests, for pairing indigenous objectives with other matters on the international agenda. Many sympathetic human rights groups at the international level have begun to lobby for better aboriginal entitlement, and in other political struggles arising out of resource exploitation projects, national linguistic policies, mass tourism proposals or improved social services, there is also much interest and relevance to the movement for improved aboriginal entitlement.

Of all these concerns, none approaches as close a coincidence of interests as the conservation movement.

In common with much of the environmental lobby, indigenous or tribal peoples have battled to overcome the lack of receptive constituencies—either within or outside the home country—that are capable of exerting pressure (financial, electoral or moral) on decision-makers. Indigenous peoples not only lack this basic political capital, but they also (unlike conservationists) have the misfortune of carrying demands—e.g. calls for greater self-determination—that run counter to the mainstream of political development for the last 30 years, a period witnessing a trebling of nation-states, each jealous of its prerogatives.

"Self-determination", "inviolability of indigenous territory" or "freedom to the use of mother tongues": these and other demands represent an attack on the prevailing political consensus, all the more so in countries where loyalties are uncertain and governments promote assimilationist nationalisms. Moreover, because many issues crucial to indigenous peoples arise from large-scale economic activities (e.g. resource exploitation and extraction, hydro-power schemes or transportation improvements), governments see indigenous resistance as obduracy—or worse, as a challenge to the very legitimacy of economic development fostered under government patronage.

The coincidence of interests characterizing the indigenous peoples' movement and the international lobby for better management of natural resources has been apparent for some time. Since 1975, for example, the International Union for Conservation of Nature and Natural Resources (IUCN) has had a "Task Force on Traditional Lifestyles" examining the interplay of traditional peoples and the natural environment. For the purposes of the Task Force, "traditional lifestyles" have been defined as:

> The ways of life (cultures) of indigenous people which have evolved locally and are based on sustainable use of local ecosystems; such lifestyles are often at subsistence levels of production and are seldom a part of the mainstream culture of their country, though they do contribute to its cultural wealth.

One of the best recent formulations of this convergence of objectives appears in a paper entitled "Native Cultures and Protected Areas: Management Options" (Brownrigg, 1981). "Native populations and national resource managers are appropriate allies," Brownrigg writes, "Given . . . the close union of the goals of native people to preserve the environment in perpetuity with the goals of the advocates of protected areas, alliance is a logical step."

In the same paper, Brownrigg delineates the common goals more explicitly:

> *For resource managers*, the benefits of working with native peoples include gaining an additional constituency, recruiting personnel with profound knowledge of local areas and learning about long-term resource strategies which have proven their adaptability for thousands of years. *For native peoples*, the benefits include legal recognition of ecologically-sound traditional land-use practices, appropriate employment of their traditional lands, and new advocates at the national level.

The argument that indigenous peoples and conservationists are "natural allies" is made with particular force when strategies to preserve tropical forests (traditional homeland to a variety of isolated forest-dwellers) are discussed. The clash between what might be called the "resource-extractive dynamic" and hitherto isolated or uncontacted peoples seems most acute in regions of dwindling tropical forest cover. The January 1980 issue of *The Ecologist*, for example, argued that, ". . . maintenance of primary forest and its use in traditional ways preserving it for millenia in balance with indigenous lifestyles might well be consistent with the local people's aspirations for an improved subsistence lifestyle based firmly on their own culture, their own society and on local self-determination".

This is not the only area where co-operative possibilities between conservationists and indigenous peoples exist: similar management objectives for mangrove forests, coral atolls or upriver watershed protection may be better served by links with appropriate indigenes.[2]

The remaining pages of this paper examine these propositions, looking at obstacles impeding a genuine working alliance, either internationally (as a coalition of compatible viewpoints) or nationally (as a concerted response to particular development issues).

INDIGENOUS LIFESTYLES OR INDIGENOUS PEOPLES?

If one merely asserts that certain indigenous ways of living deal more gently with an ecosystem's carrying capacity than resource-extractive policies, then the point is unexceptional. Indeed, one writer states that the conservation movement can only "deal with traditional *lifestyles* and patterns, rather than with traditionally *living peoples*" (emphasis added) (Schultze-Westrum M.S.). If nothing more than "lifestyle patterns" or "practices" disassociated from living cultures receive conservationist endorsement, the convergence of indigenous peoples' and conservationists' interests will remain at the level of principle only. If mutual support in the field is the objective, however, the "natural alliance" posited above needs to be looked at more closely.

The proposition that both movements gain by cooperation stands or falls on their compatibility of views. In a number of respects they differ markedly.

One perspective (the indigenes') sees unceasing encroachment penetrating inwards to the core of separate cultures. Danger resides in a restive external dynamic that deliberately (or even with the best of intentions) administers the fatal elixir to the aboriginal status. The other view (that of the conservationists) sees an agrandissement rolling outwards from the metropoles in which they most often reside, a complex combination of "development", land hunger and movement in commodity markets that threatens generic diversity and specific species. Conservationists therefore seek local indigenous support for (or, at the very least, acquiescence in) protection of remaining wild lands. Indigenes seek relief from encroachment, either by a lessening of external pressure or by a strengthening of tribal position vis-à-vis national authorities.

In principle, a comfortable convergence exists. Pragmatically, however, considerable difficulties belie an easy assumption that interests are automatically shared. The following pages focus on what may be the blind spots in this argument and suggest ways to marshal conservation's "natural constituency" to better effect.

The key principles of the conservation movement originate (as a recent IUCN working group paper notes) "from the urban society of highly developed countries". These principles promote "a system of mainly restrictive control patterns upon the ecosystems that are set up by national governments". The paper also notes that "correlations with traditional cultures that inhabit resource management areas" have not been well studied (Schultze-Westrum, 1980).

Any restriction on the use of territory has as its essence the principle of *exclusion*. To protect, one must exclude certain categories of outsiders or specific activities judged to be harmful. Because the power to exclude is so inescapably political, national governments not surprisingly reserve this power for themselves. Indigenous peoples almost never initiate this exclusion (legitimized by the national authorities on grounds of "national development", "national security" or "resource conservation".

To this extent, therefore, protected areas (of whatever description and for whatever purpose) continue to be, for indigenes, paternalistically devolved and implemented. Precisely for this reason, a national park in areas of traditional settlement is more likely to be feared as "taking something away" rather than welcomed for the protection it bestows. Useful contrasts between indigene reactions to national park creation in Canada, the USA and Australia have been described recently (Gardner and Nelson, 1981), and it appears that even active involvement of indigenous peoples in protected area planning and administration yields uneven results, largely because most resource management agencies are still perceived as "taking something away"—if only in an intangible sense. A history of unequal dealing with dominant "settler cultures" supports indigenes' suspicions. In those areas where indigenous peoples have become politicized and seek self-determination, the "foreclosure of opportunity" effected by prohibition of development within indigene territory may be deeply resented. Development *per se* is not always resisted by indigenes; what troubles (and rallies) them is their powerlessness vis-à-vis the outsider.

Just as indigenes misunderstand conservation trade-offs, so also may conservation planners misjudge the extent to which aboriginal groups living within or adjacent to proposed protected areas actually wish to work for (or guard) the attainment of conservation objectives. For example, assumptions that traditional lifestyles practised by the indigenes necessarily complement conservation objectives often turn out to be wide of the mark. Some commentators acknowledge this; for example, Brownrigg (1981) writes that, "the social and behavioural patterns of native population have been integrated with natural environment variables in a way which usually, *though not always*, results in ecologically sound long-term use of an area (emphasis added)".

To illustrate how choice of new technology poses awkward problems to conservationists, the following indicative examples might be noted:

Some Inuit whale hunters now favour using explosive harpoons and other contemporary technology.

Petrol-powered chain saws accelerate land clearing by slash and burn agriculturalists.

Occasionally explosives are used to stun-kill fish in traditional Maori hunting and fishing areas of New Zealand.

These examples suggest that some contemporary manifestations of traditional "lifestyles" can no longer be assumed to conform to a harmonious prototype.

In part, many of these misapprehensions result from protestations from the fledgling international indigenous peoples movement which attributes all the disruptive ecological consequences of possessive individualism to western colonizers. The following extract from a report to the International NGO Conference on Indigenous Peoples and the Land, held from 15–18 September 1981 in Geneva, illustrates the point:

> In the world of today there are two systems, two different irreconcilable "ways of life". The Indian world—collective, communal, human, respectful of nature and wise—and the western world—greedy, destructive, individualist, and enemy of mother nature.

Similar views embellish pronouncements from the World Council of Indigenous Peoples. While the sincerity of such statements cannot be disputed, the likelihood of their being true is open to question. Such formulations by the indigenes themselves consolidate the view that indigenous lifestyles are, almost by definition, compatible with conservationist goals. Such statements not only ignore past adoption of biologically disruptive technology by aboriginal peoples but also in a curious way buttress the fallacy of the "noble savage", a uniquely European conceit.

The same misconception lies buried in the automatic assumption that indigenous peoples will accept or even welcome cultural status as a condition of their involvement in conservation management. The specialist literature shows many examples of national parks or protected reserves having, as one objective of a multiple-use design, the goal of retaining traditional technologies, settlement patterns and food gathering. While this is a worthy objective, incorporation of endangered tribal cultures into conservation areas must be subject to the caveat that these peoples may maintain their isolation only for as long as they desire to do so.

The World Bank makes a similar point:

> Enforced "primitivism" is a disruptive policy occasionally practised on a reservation. This policy is often followed either to promote tourism . . . or it is defended as a means of preserving the tribe's cultural identity. However, whereas enforced "primitivism" is always damaging, elective "primitivism" can be beneficial as in the case of the Cunas of Panama. Minority culture never has been a static entity which must be preserved exactly as it is found or as it is believed to have been. Rather it is a dynamic reality which should be provided with conditions adequate for development in a natural and progressive manner. Cultural continuity should be encouraged in all spheres, but the choice of whether to continue to modify old ways should be left

to the tribal people themselves and not imposed upon them (IBRD, 1980).

To act otherwise leads to results as coercive and contrived as the disruptive development which "anthropological reserves" are designed to prevent. During their occupation of Taiwan, for example, the Japanese turned the small island of Lan Yu (ancestral home to the Yami people) into a private botanical/anthropological museum with living exhibits and severely limited admission. Until defeated in 1945, Japan restricted access into Lan Yu to officials and anthropologists, making no effort to raise material living standards or to intervene with medical or educational services. This achievement was as paternalist as the imposition of government-initiated economic development in tribal territories.

While the idea of creating coterminous nature/anthropological reserves is not new, the concept has gained renewed support in recent years. In June 1979, for example, a group of Brazilian and foreign anthropologists formally urged the Federal Government in Brasilia to create a national park for the Yanomamo Indians, an indigenous group of around 20,000 persons living in north-western Brazil and Venezuela. The proposal's sponsors fear that Brazil's readiness to allow mining concessions in Yanomamo territory will lead to cultural extinction. One sponsor—the London-based Survival International group—reports that twenty-six distinct tribes have been culturally destroyed in Brazil during the past decade. The "ethnocide" has been accompanied by extensive disruption to local ecosystems from mining, forestry or land settlement projects.

Dasmann (1975), Jungius (1976), Gardner and Nelson (1981), Gorio (1978) and many others have written about protecting indigenes' habitat and local ecosystems by creating multi-purpose national parks. The countries choosing to do so are as disparate as the Congo (Odzala National Park), Botswana (Kalahari Reserves), Peru (Manu Park), USA (Gates of the Arctic Monument), Canada (the Yukon's Kluane Park), Australia (Kakadu National Park in the Northern Territory), Papua New Guinea (Varirata National Park) and Honduras (Rio Platano Biosphere Reserve). Other examples include a proposed reserve at Siberut (an Indonesian island near Sumatra where traditional Mentawai lifestyles are threatened by timber concessions), Tanzania's Ngorongoro Crater (where the Maasai have the right to graze their cattle), the Ghin forest reserve in India (which permits traditional gathering by the Maldhari people), and several of Sweden's National Parks (where the Laps still graze reindeer). Nearly all of these areas have been established in the last decade (the list above is indicative only).

At the levels of principle and practice, therefore, conservationists have become increasingly aware of the "close interrelationship between ecological factors, rural traditions . . . and cultural patterns (like sustained self-reliant land-use, intimate knowledge and adaptation, self-restriction and conservation) that offers tangible direct benefits, including reserve guardianship and ranger functions, field knowledge of local fauna and flora and long-term resource strategies which have proven their adaptability for thousands of years" (Dasmann, 1975). What is needed is a more balanced view of the opportunities present in this co-operation.

INDIGENOUS PEOPLE AND CONSERVATION AREAS: SOME LESSER OPTIONS

While attention focuses primarily on national parks as safe havens for endangered cultures (or, vice versa, on tribal *lifestyles* as intrinsically supportive of conservationist ethic), one should not assume that the convergence of interests starts and ends there. Indeed, just as IUCN (1978) acknowledges that "the National Park can be complemented by other distinct categories which . . . can provide land managers and decision-makers with a broad set of legal and managerial options for conservation land management", so too is there an intermediate range of options available to indigenous groups and resource managers desirous of collaboration. In other words, the territory inhabited by indigenous peoples *need not be* co-extensive with the protected conservation area. Just as there is a recognition that hitherto neglected parts of the human habitat (which traditionally have not been included in national park activities) now need urgent attention, so also is there a significant range of opportunities to involve indigenous peoples at any place along the "spectrum" of acculturation to the national society—from the virtually uncontacted to the almost entirely acculturated. The World Bank, for example, distinguishes four successive phases of acculturation or integration into the national society: completely uncontacted tribes; semi-isolated groups in intermittent contact; groups in permanent contact; and integrated groups retaining a residual sense of tribal identification (IBRD, 1981).

Indeed there may be good reasons why tribal groups (or national governments) do not welcome tribal incorporation into entirely "conservation-specific" entities like national parks: tribes find this may compromise their land claims to the same or adjacent areas; inclusion in a park may constrict customary livelihood activity; or the park design may restrict too severely the territory's future resource-extraction possibilities. In addition, national governments may not welcome parks with an "anthropological" element because inclusion of affected tribes in park planning may "tribalize" them (i.e. politicize them to the extent their tribal solidarity is enhanced by reaction to outside pressure).

At this juncture it might be salient to explore New Zealand's experience in developing "half-way house" possibilities, which (although they fall well short of creating extensive nature/anthropological reserves or parks) illustrate a variety of collaborative possibilities with indigenous peoples.

New Zealand protects over 2.6 million hectares of national parks and special purpose reserves, much of it gifted directly to the nation by Maori tribes. For example, elders of the Ngati Tuwharetoa gave land for the country's first national park at Tongariro in 1889; other examples include the gifting of scenic reserves at Lakes Rotoiti and Okataina to the nation and more recently a grant of land at Taranaki to comprise Egmont National Park.

New Zealand's legislation (the National Park Act 1952 and the Reserves Act 1977) now promotes gifting of land for conservation purposes, and the management of "multiple use reserves" (which includes indigenous use) permits interesting alternatives to public ownership of land. Some of the indigenous uses which reserves and national parks in New Zealand quietly accommodate include food and herb gathering (usually done on horseback) in the North Island's Urerewa National Park, mutton-bird hunting on Kaitoreti Spit and active assertion of traditional fishing rights on Lake Waikeremoana by the local tribe (which also rents the lake to the surrounding national park).

Conservation objectives are also being enlisted to deal with difficulties inherent in the Maoris' communal tenure. Although 75% of New Zealand's 300,000 Maoris (approximately 10% of the total population) now live in urban areas, 1.3 million hectares of rural Maori land remain. By custom, Maori communal landowners share the land in equal portion with all progeny so that each generation tends to add to the total number of owners of each communally-held block. This leads to two difficulties; the land is not able to support all the owners, and special arrangements are necessary to enable land-owners to make binding decisions about future land use. Up to now, Maori land has been leased—often to European new Zealanders—but new responses to indigenous tenure have evolved. One quarter of Maori land is unoccupied, and considerable areas are still in primary or secondary bush. Much of this is administered as Maori Reserve Land under the relevant legislation, and one option being investigated by the New Zealand Government is the creation—with full tribal support—of "tribal reserves", entry to which will be restricted to owners whose usage will conform to specific conservation objectives.

Some of this experience has guided New Zealand's assistance to the fledgling Sagarmatha National Park in Nepal. Some 2,500 of Nepal's estimated 20,000 Sherpa people live in the 124,000 hectares of the Park (which also includes the Khumbu area, famous for Mount Everest).

The treks and mountaineering following the opening of the area to outsiders in 1950 has led to worrying changes in traditional Sherpa life, associated with the depletion of manpower (for porters) and firewood (it is estimated that each mountaineering expedition needs 30,000 kilogrammes of wood for fuel).

In association with New Zealand rangers, the Park's managers have determined upon the following objectives, directed specifically at the inclusion of the indigenous Sherpas in the Park's activities:

Constant liaison with monastery lamas

Restoration of religious structures within the Park

Retention and protection of all monastery buildings

Maintenance of traditional village water supply schemes

Active encouragement of the traditional character and architectural styles of villages within the Park

Prohibition of all trekking within sacred areas (including whole mountains) where guardian spirits reside

Employment of Sherpas as rangers on a preferential basis

Retention as far as possible of firewood as the Sherpas' fuel (rather than displacement by kerosene or other new—and imported—fuel technology)

Internal modification where possible of traditional Sherpa houses to minimize heat losses and consequently reduce firewood consumption

Revival of Sherpas' traditional forest-use control system, i.e. the *Shing-i Nawas* ("protectors of the forests") who are empowered to allocate wood for families.

These objectives demonstrate an active involvement of a partially-acculturated indigenous people in a Park which is *not* co-extensive with the indigene territory. Briefly, the conservation objectives of Sagarmatha are to arrest a situation where over half of the forest cover within the park territory has disappeared and to revive, within a system catering also to outsiders' mountaineering expeditions, a pattern of traditional usage in which prior to the influx of tourism and mountaineering, the Sherpas were managing a partly modified landscape under a system of social and community controls which ensured wisest use of forest resources and minimized long-term forest degradation.

CONCLUSIONS

The launching in March 1981 of the *World Conservation Strategy* (IUCN, 1980) brought the convergence of indigene and conservation interests into sharp focus: the strategy deals with global problems such as deforestation, desertification, depletion of fisheries, soil erosion and misuse of crop lands—all matters of direct concern to aboriginal populations. The logic behind this compatibility of interests has already occurred to the World Council of Indigenous Peoples which was invited by the United Nations Environment Programme in 1980 to prepare a study on "environmental degradation in indigenous areas". The WCIP is following closely the operation of the international agreements such as the 1972 Convention for the Protection of World Cultural and Natural Heritage. This Convention was followed by the Man and the Biosphere Programme, resulting in a number of "biosphere reserves" created in various parts of the world, many with a direct effect on the indigenous peoples *in situ*. The Rio Platano Biosphere

Reserve in Honduras is a case in point; the reserve is designed, *inter alia*, to protect two indigenous tribes.

As suggested above, outright conflict between conservationist and indigenous objectives has occurred in the past. Tribes have been expelled from national parks or denied the use of resources within the Park: e.g. the Shakilla were driven from Lake Rukana Park in Kenya and the Ik expelled from Kidepo National Park in Uganda. Understanding of conservation objectives by aboriginal peoples remains low (battles erupt in Ethiopia's Simien Park over wood-cutting rights, for example). Some conflict even has an international dimension; enforcing the Migratory Birds Convention and accommodating native Indian demands have caused headaches for governments in Canada and the USA. Another example: International Whaling Commission sessions grapple with Inuits who oppose bow-head whale-hunting prohibitions, and argument still revolves around Inuit rights to use modern whaling technology.

Several commentators have advanced suggestions for successful involvement of indigenous groups with an interest in territories in which restrictive land-use policies are tied to conservation objectives. Brownrigg (1980) offers four management options for resource managers contemplating cooperation with indigenes:

1. *Reserves*, where a protected natural area corresponds with the territory of a particular native population
2. *Native-owned lands*, where the protection of the area is by native peoples
3. *Buffer zones*, where a protected area serves as a physical or ecological barrier between native lands and the lands of others
4. *Research stations*, where certain areas under native management are organized as agricultural or ecological research stations

Brownrigg concludes that, "Each option of relations between native cultures and protected areas will fit only in certain circumstances. The appropriateness of a particular option and its details must be determined on a case by case basis, and certain elements for different options can be combined to form new models."

Discussing Peru's Manu Park, Jungius (1976) urges incorporation of indigene-inhabited territories into a national park and creation of a buffer zone. Indigenes are to practise traditional hunting patterns, except where species are endangered. The objective is to provide for "gradual social and economic development on the basis of (the peoples') own culture and traditions".

Dasmann (1975) argues that national parks should "permit indigenous people to maintain their isolation for as long as they wish to do so", and to allow them "to become the protectors of the parks, to receive a share of park receipts and in other ways to be brought to appreciate its value".

Gardner and Nelson (1981) analyse national park agencies, paying close attention to institutional character, extent of management control, extent of indigenous or park agency control of land and links between the agencies and indigenes in three parks in the USA, Canada and Australia respectively. They find that the best indigene/conservationist relations occur when:

Indigenes see national parks as assisting to maintain their culture (and to provide employment)

Indigenous organizations have strong bargaining positions (related to unambiguous title to their lands)

Permitted land use in the Park is well-defined

In addition to these guidelines, the following issues should be addressed by conservationists:

The suspicions of indigenous peoples (many of whom—such as New Zealand's Maoris—are substantially acculturated into the national society) need to be directly countered with arguments that demonstrate clear advantages from supporting conservation aims.

National parks, reserves or even restrictive land-use policies in general should not be seen as foreclosing indigenous economic or self-development opportunities. Indeed, in some parts of the world, argument often centres on the "retention of resource-extraction possibilities" by indigenous populations—e.g., the Inuits in Canada's Northwest Territory—who prefer to exploit their own natural resources, albeit at a different pace.

Conservation areas of whatever description should not be seen as predetermining title to the lands in question; however, the creation of conservation reserves co-extensive with areas inhabited by indigenous peoples can be a first step towards acknowledgement of native title to the area in question; i.e., there are "gifting back" possibilities (available, for example, in New Zealand where the Crown may return lands to Maori tenure with conservation-inspired restrictive land-use covenants).

Whatever indigene/conservation deal is struck, the terms of the agreement should be beyond reach of upset by other, separately empowered bureaucracies of the national authority (e.g., tax agencies or defence authorities).

If fully restrictive nature/anthropological reserves are created (or established in all but name) some hard decisions must be faced. Intrusions by census-takers, missionaries, tourists, security forces or even medical personnel must be kept to a minimum if the integrity of the reserve is to last.

At the country or field level, conservation lobbies (particularly at the international pressure-group level) should become conversant with the following areas of direct concern to threatened indigenes:

1. The economics of import-dependent agricultural projects, extractive silviculture or mass resettlement schemes (such as Amazonian small holdings or Indonesia's "transmigration" programmes). These endeavours are often poorly reasoned. By analogy to well-founded second thoughts about the advantages of mass tourism, opportunities exist to take pressure off nonrenewable resources (and the indigenes who may live among them) especially if feasible alternatives in the form of intensive/improved productivity techniques (such as new rubber-tapping methods or quicker regeneration of exotic trees) can be offered to national planners.

2. The creative use of existing legal remedies. For example, recognition by national authorities of indigenes' animist religions can yield unexpected results; in most states, places of religious significance invariably enjoy legal protection from all development. Australian aboriginals, for example, have large tracts of land declared reserves because they are sacred sites.

3. Intimate local knowledge of local fauna and flora is frequently acknowledged but inventories of such knowledge (e.g., pharmaceutical benefits from tropical biota) are lacking. The material advantages of such knowledge (which in the dominant national societies is protected by copyright or other "intellectual property" statutes) wait to be quantified.

4. Tribal lands include not only those areas inhabited at any given time, but other tracts which are used only intermittently. There are two possibilities here: first, many countries permit acquisition of rights to land by prescription, i.e. continuous and uncontested use of the land for a determined number of years. A wider definition of particular indigene land "uses" can lead to successful tribal land claims (and therefore to more lands put outside the reach of "development"). The second possibility concerns the systematic, nondamaging land use practised by intermittent users such as hunter-gatherers (the Kalahari or Australian bushmen) or pastoralists (Fulani or Masai of Africa, the Gujjars of India or the Bedouins). The advantages of these practices need to be demonstrated quantitatively to national authorities.

Together with a summary of some other analyses of convergent indigene/conservation interests, I have tried to suggest guidelines and areas of further research that should make genuine collaboration more likely at the national, or "field", level as well as at the level of principle. The essence of the task seems to be in the choice of strategies to enlist the support of indigenous peoples themselves for conservation objectives (whether in the form of reserves or mere practices) while retaining the confidence of the national authorities. Tribal peoples have suffered for centuries under the impact of exogenous expansion into areas that once supported greatly larger numbers of indigenes, and the process has led to decimation and even extinction of many tribal populations. Some indigenes have proved to be demographically resilient, retaining tribal identities while acculturating to the national (or "settler") society. Some—the Surui or Parakanans in Brazil, the Andaman islanders, the Semang and Sakai in Malaysia, the Todas in India or the Mbuti in Zaire—live precariously close to cultural or even physical extinction. The starting point, it seems to me, for co-operation with tribal peoples or their advocates is to recognize that national society *and* the indigenes need to be persuaded that conservation objectives can be married to the quest for better aboriginal entitlement, to the lasting benefit of all parties. It is not an easy task but it is one worth doing, and worth doing well.

NOTES

1. It is estimated that nearly 4% of the world's population are "tribal peoples" (IBRD, 1981). The term "indigenous peoples" is applied to a wider population; the World Council of Indigenous Peoples uses the following definition:

> The term indigenous people refers to people living in countries which have a population composed of differing ethnic or racial groups who are descendants of the earliest populations living in the area and who do not, as a group, control the national government of the countries within which they live.

A Sub-Commission of the UN Human Rights Commission has commissioned a report which adopts the following "working definition" of the term "indigenous peoples":

> . . . the existing descendants of the people who inhabited the present territory of a country wholly or partially at the time when persons of a different culture or ethnic origin arrived from other parts of the world, overcame them and, by conquest, settlement or other means reduced them to a non-dominant or colonial condition; who today live more in conformity with their particular social, economic and cultural customs or traditions than with the institutions of the country of which they now form part, under a State structure which incorporates mainly the national, social and cultural characteristics of other segments of the populations which are predominant.

In a paper entitled "Law, Politics and Indigenous Peoples: A Study of Convergent Interests" (prepared for Cultural Survival Inc., Cambridge, Mass. (1981), the author reviewed historical and contemporary doctrines of international law as they apply to the status of indigenous peoples, including international conventions and declaratory pronouncements with direct or tangential bearing on the protection of indigenous peoples and national laws in various countries where indigenous questions, mostly concerning land disputes, are being litigated.

2. The potential for liaising with indigenous peoples in island, estuary or tidal flats environments is often neglected. Traditional fisheries and marine lifestyles depend closely on the retention of basic character of these particular ecosystems; and co-operative possibilities between indigenes and conservation managers exist. See, for example, an IUCN paper prepared for the Second Regional South Pacific Symposium on the Conservation of Nature by G. Carleton Ray (SPC-IUCN/2 RSCN/WP.5: 1975) which envisages incorporating traditional us-

ages into the management of marine reserves. See also: Auburn, F.M., "Convention for the Preservation of Man's Cultural Heritage in the Ocean," *Science*, 185 (4153) 1974, and Kearney, R.E., "Some Problems of Developing and Managing Fisheries in Small Island States", in *Island States of the Pacific and Indian Oceans* (edited by R. Shand), Australian National University, 1980.

31   National Parks and Native Peoples in Northern Canada, Alaska, and Northern Australia

J. E. GARDNER

J. G. NELSON

In this selection the authors present a detailed comparison of national park management vis-à-vis native peoples in the Canadian Yukon, in arctic Alaska, and in Arnhem Land in the Northern Territory of Australia. There are striking parallels among the cases, some of which were discussed in an earlier selection by Lee (see part V). All three areas are in remote "hinterlands" that have recently become the focus of mineral development activity, and all three contain relatively large, traditionally oriented native populations who are actively attempting to retain control over their land and resources in order to safeguard traditional lifestyles. The authors show that motivations differ considerably in the three areas, on the part of both park officials and natives. Historical and cultural factors account for some of the differences, but policies and constraints at national and state or territorial levels are also involved. This analysis suggests that successful cooperation between native peoples and park administrators is certainly possible.

J. E. Gardner holds a Ph.D. from the University of Canterbury. She has taught geography at McGill University and is currently a free-lance environmental consultant. J. G. Nelson is a professor of geography and urban regional planning and dean of the faculty of Environmental Studies at the University of Waterloo.

Reprinted with permission from *Environmental Conservation* 8, no. 3 (Autumn 1981): 207–15. Copyright © 1981 The Foundation for Environmental Conservation, Geneva, Switzerland.

INTRODUCTION

Aims, Background, and Approach

At the general level, the aim of this paper is to compare the interaction between national parks and native people in Northern Canada (in Yukon Territory), Alaska, and the Northern Territory of Australia. All three of these 'hinterland areas' are vast and sparsely populated. The Yukon Territory comprises 536,325 km² of land and water and has a population of 23,306 (1978), of whom about 5,000 are considered to be of native descent. Alaska has an area of 1,524,640 km² and a population of 330,000, of whom 63,615 were classified as non-white in 1973. The Northern Territory of Australia covers 1,346,200 km²; its 1977 population was 105,500, of whom 28,200 are considered to be of aboriginal descent.

Governmentally, with the exception of Alaska, these outlying areas or 'hinterlands' have yet to receive the fuller political powers of their more developed provincial and state counterparts in Canada, the United States, and Australia. In reaction to mining and industrial development pressures, the governments of the three countries are intensifying efforts to protect wildlife, wildlife habitat, and other biophysical features, through various kinds of conservation arrangements. These include such land-use ordinances and more general laws and legislation as apply, for example, to hunting and fishing. They also include national parks and other reserves. Northern Canada, Alaska, and Northern Australia are also the homes of small populations of native peoples who are attempting to adapt themselves to these conservation, mining, industrial, and associated changes. These native peoples in Northern Canada, Alaska, and Northern Australia helps Inuit (Eskimo) in northern North America, and 'Aboriginals' in Australia.

The combination of land-use interests described above holds potential for problems and conflicts that are peculiar to large, sparsely populated outlying areas. An examination of interaction between national parks and native peoples in Northern Canada, Alaska, and Northern Australia helps to shed light on the management of some of the issues and problems involved, and provides learning that could be of benefit to a number of countries (Armstrong, 1977; Gardner & Nelson, 1980).

The study begins by describing native land-use issues in each 'hinterland'. The national parks agencies are then described in terms of a four-parts framework. The first part, 'Institutional Character', covers such aspects as legislated mandate, objectives, and hierarchies of responsibility. The section, entitled 'Fields of Management', is a brief description of the reserves controlled by the national parks agencies. 'Control of Land' includes types of tenure, policy, and legislation, on areas of native land-use. The fourth part, 'External Links', refers to the means by which the agencies maintain contact with other interest-groups, such as the native people.

After this general analysis, case-studies of a national park in each 'hinterland' are undertaken to provide more details on national park interaction with native people. The sample parks are 'Gates of the Arctic' in Alaska, 'Kluane' in Yukon Territory, and 'Kakadu' in the Australian Northern Territory. These areas are chosen because, as relatively new parks or park reserves, they are thought to illustrate problems very well; moreover, information about them is available.

Sources of Information

Most of the documentary sources were traced through academic individuals or corporate sources, public servants, or representatives of various interest-groups. Gardner visited Ottawa, Washington, Winnipeg, Seattle, Anchorage, Whitehorse, and Kluane National Park. Postal correspondence had to suffice for the more inaccessible locations such as Gates of the Arctic in Alaska and the Northern Territory of Australia. Nelson obtained information on Australian parks while travelling in New South Wales and Queensland and attending the second South Pacific Conference on National Parks and Related Reserves in Sydney, Australia, in May 1979. At that Conference, reports (as yet unpublished) were presented by informed persons on national parks and related reserves in all Australian states and territories.

NATIVE LAND ISSUES

One major response to the recent surge of mining development in the three 'hinterlands' has been native demand for recognition of aboriginal rights and settlement of land claims. The current status of these claims varies widely among the three areas.

Yukon Territory

In the early 1970s, the Yukon Native Brotherhood was formed to represent registered Indians of the Territory on land-claims issues, while the Yukon Association of Non-Status Indians (YANSI) was formed to represent those natives who were not recognized as Indian people under the *Indian Act*. In 1973 the Yukon Native Brotherhood, supported by YANSI, presented to the Canadian Federal Government a brief, entitled *Together Today For Our Children Tomorrow*, stating grievances and suggesting an approach to a land-claims settlement. The philosophy behind this brief is rooted in the land:

> A just settlement will permit Yukon Indian people to control our future, both politically and economically, and the basis of that control is land (Council for Yukon Indians, undated).

The Indians are fearful that, without a settlement, their access to development benefits will be less, and nonrenewable resource development will erode the 'traditional' livelihood of hunting, fishing, and trapping.

The Government of Canada has responded with a general policy on

Indian rights, stating that it would recognize grievances and 'the existence of a native interest in those areas where it had not been extinguished by treaty or superceded by law' (Redpath, 1979). The Council for Yukon Indians was then formed to negotiate claims with the Federal Government on the part of both the above-mentioned Yukon native groups. At least three rounds of negotiations have since been undertaken, and work is continuing on an agreement-in-principle, although the priority which the Government places on these negotiations is uncertain.

Northern Territory of Australia

The underlying themes of the *Aboriginal Land Rights (Northern Territory) Act* of 1976 are: respect for the Aboriginals' relationship with the land, and due recognition of Aboriginal title, 'allowing Aboriginals to use and occupy land in accordance with traditional customs'. Under the Act, all Aboriginal reserve land in the Northern Territory, totalling 18.4% of the Territory, has been granted to about twenty Aboriginal Land Trusts (Department of Aboriginal Affairs, 1979). The trusts hold title to reserve lands, but three Land Councils administer them.

Claims for vacant Crown lands, traditionally used by the Aboriginals but not part of the reserves, can be lodged with the Aboriginal Land Commissioner. He will take other interests into account and decide whether strong traditional links with the land have been proven before making a recommendation to the Minister for Aboriginal Affairs. Thus the Act does not extinguish native rights to Crown lands that have not yet been claimed by the people.

Alaska

The *Alaska Native Claims Settlement Act* (ANCSA) was passed in 1971:

> In essence, the Act granted Alaska Natives title to 44 million acres ($1,087,000$ km^2) of land plus a cash settlement of nearly a billion dollars, in return for which all further claims to Native lands in Alaska were extinguished (Kresge *et al.*, 1977).

Twelve regional corporations and 220 village corporations were established to hold title to native lands in Alaska. The land selection process is proving to be long and involved but, unlike the Australian one, it has limits in terms of ultimate area to be granted to native people. While the corporations have full rights to the land they own, including mineral development, they have no special privileges for activities such as subsistence hunting on other lands—unless their activities are specifically exempted from general regulations. Culture and tradition appear to be smaller concerns in the Alaska legislation than in the *Aboriginal Land Rights (Northern Territory) Act* or the Council for Yukon Indians proposal. Thus, 'the Act was intended to grant Alaska Natives the ability to participate fully in American life, but on the same basis as other citizens' (Hunt, 1978).

COMPARATIVE ASPECTS OF NATIONAL PARK
AGENCIES IN THE THREE HINTERLANDS

Institutional Character

The national park agencies involved in the three 'hinterlands' all aim to protect or preserve certain lands for their biophysical and cultural or heritage values. Parks Canada (PC), the Australian National Parks and Wildlife Service (ANPWS), and the United States National Park Service (NPS), are also mandated to provide for public enjoyment of these lands. All of the agencies intend to establish a network of national parks representing the various biomes or landscapes composing the agency's area of concern. However, only Parks Canada and the NPS have so far begun to work within actual systems-planning frameworks which guide the selection of new parksites (Gardner & Nelson, 1980). In all three 'hinterlands', federal and state agencies other than those above-named also have responsibility for a variety of park, wildlife, and other, reserve interests.

National parks in Australia have traditionally been a responsibility of state governments, unlike the situation in the United States and Canada. As a result, the Northern Territory Reserves Board, constituted as the Territory Parks and Wildlife Commission (TPWC) in 1978, has responsibility for a system of national parks in Northern Australia. In recent years, however, the Federal Government has taken a stronger role in the Territory, in part because of issues involving uranium mining and the welfare of the Aboriginals. The federal Australian National Park and Wildlife Service (ANPWS) was formed in 1975 and has assumed responsibility for certain new national parks in the Northern Territory, one of which, Kakadu, will be discussed in more detail later.

Fields of Management

The fields of management of national park agencies are currently in a state of transition, as planning continues for more parks in Northern Canada, Alaska, and Northern Australia. Recent acquisitions to each system generally involve lands that are used and/or claimed by natives. They increase the pressure for greater interaction between natives and the responsible government agencies.

Until late in 1978, the National Park Service controlled five units in Alaska: Mount McKinley National Park, Glacier Bay and Katmai National Monuments, and Sitka and Klondike National Historic Parks. In 1977, under Section 17(d)(2) of the *Alaska Native Claims Settlement Act*, the Secretary of the Interior was directed to withdraw, from all forms of appropriation, up to 323,000 km^2 of Alaska federal lands and to report to Congress his recommendations for administering them as units of the national park, national forest, national wildlife refuge, and national wild and scenic river systems. Subsequently the United States House of Representatives (HR) passed *The Alaska National Interest Lands Conservation Act* or

HR 39 for the allocation of these so-called 'd-2 lands', but the Senate could not reach an agreement on this and other proposals. In the absence of Senate action, President Carter proclaimed 17 national monuments totalling 250,000 km^2 to protect many of the proposed reserve lands. Thirteen of the monuments, covering 165,000 km^2, have been allocated to the national parks system. Bills are currently before the U.S. Congress to obtain approval for funds for the administration of the monuments, and to resolve the issues posed in HR 39.

Parks Canada now has in the Yukon Territory one national park reserve (Kluane), one historic park (the Klondike Gold-Rush International Historic Park), and a number of historic sites. Thirty-nine thousand square kilometres of land north of the Porcupine River were withdrawn for national park and other conservation purposes in 1978. Kluane (26,237 km^2) was established in 1972, along with Nahanni (4,765 km^2) and Auyuittuq (21,470 km^2) in the Northwest Territories. Official designation of all three areas as national parks depends on settlement of native land-claims.

In the late 1970s, the newly-formed federal Australian National Parks and Wildlife Service (ANPWS) acquired two parks in the Northern Territory. Uluru (1,262 km^2) and Kakadu (6,450 km^2); these are still the only North Australia parks under its control. In contrast, the Northern Territory Parks and Wildlife Commission controls forty-eight parks, reserves, and sanctuaries, totalling 51,725 km^2, in the Northern Territory.

Control of Land

Control of land is defined in legislation and policy statements and varies from country to country. Of the three federal agencies involved, only Parks Canada requires outright public ownership of national park land. The Australian and U.S. federal agencies are willing to enter into cooperative management arrangements with other owners such as native people.

Sports hunting is generally prohibited by federal agencies in all three countries, except in United States NPS National Preserves, but policy on native hunting rights is ambiguous in all three countries. Traditional native hunting, fishing, and trapping, are allowed for people of native origin in the Yukon and Northwest Territories under a 1974 amendment to the *National Parks Act*. In certain circumstances, Parks Canada policy acknowledges the rights of traditional subsistence resource users, and of people recognized in treaties and land-claims. The 'traditional subsistence user' is, however, difficult to define for management purposes. The Parks Canada Draft Policy (Parks Canada, 1978) suggested a number of aspects of such use that required clarification:

1. What traditional subsistence-resource uses have taken place and in what areas;
2. Who would qualify to continue traditional subsistence-resource uses;
3. What level of traditional subsistence-resource use would be appropriate;

4. What methods of transportation, harvesting, etc., would be appropriate;

5. What research would be essential to manage the continuing traditional use of renewable resources; and

6. Under what circumstances could local people live temporarily within a national (wilderness) park?

The 1979 final Parks Canada Policy did not include the foregoing statements but did specify certain general conditions for traditional subsistence use, as follows:

> In new national parks, guarantees will be provided so that certain traditional subsistence resource uses by local people will be permitted to continue in parts of national parks for one or more generations when such uses are an essential part of the local way of life and when no alternatives exist outside the park boundaries (Parks Canada, 1979).

The United States NPS has developed relatively detailed guidelines on who may extract wildlife resources from a national park and the limits of this use. HR 39 defined 'subsistence uses' as:

> the customary and traditional uses by rural Alaska residents of wild, renewable resources for direct personal or family use or consumption as food, shelter, fuel, clothing, tools, or transportation, and for the making and selling of handicraft articles out of the nonedible by-products of fish and wildlife resources taken for personal or family consumption; and for customary noncommercial trade (*Alaska National Interest Lands Conservation Act* of 1979).

The regulations for the new Alaska National Monuments define a 'local rural resident' (who may engage in subsistence uses within the Monuments) according to geographic, economic, and historical, criteria. Degree of dependence and availability of alternative resources may also be deciding factors.

Identical sections in Australian Federal (*National Parks and Wildlife Conservation Act* of 1975) and Northern Territory (*Territory Parks and Wildlife Conservation Ordinance* of 1976) legislation, address aboriginal use of park land:

> (1) Subject to sub-section (2), and to the operation of this Act in relation to parks, reserves, and conservation zones, nothing in this Act prevents Aboriginals from continuing, in accordance with law, the traditional use of any area of land or water for hunting or food-gathering (otherwise than for purposes of sale) and for ceremonial and religious purposes.
> (2) The operation of sub-section (1), is subject to regulations made for the purpose of conserving wildlife in any area and expressly affecting the traditional use of the area by Aboriginals.

In summary, in none of the three countries have the terms of native use of national parks been specifically defined, though the United States NPS appears to be closest to a detailed definition. Some flexibility is desired, allowing for variability of circumstances among parks. In all cases, legislation provides that the protection of park values can override aboriginal hunting arrangements.

External Links

National Park agencies in all three study areas are required to consult the public on establishing and planning for new parks. Recent planning exercises in each case have provided opportunities for public input. In Australia, Justice Fox conducted the Ranger Uranium Environmental Inquiry, which made recommendations on the establishment of Kakadu, a national park, on native land. In Canada the Mackenzie Valley Pipeline Inquiry led by Justice Berger gave high priority to the native interest, and promoted the idea of a national wilderness area in northern Yukon. Various groups provided forums for public input in the 'd-2 lands' (*see* above 'Fields of Management' section) debates in Alaska and the mainland United States. These included the Federal State Land Use Planning Commission, the Department of the Interior's Alaska Planning Group, and the Sieberling hearings conducted for the House of Representatives Committee on Interior and Insular Affairs.

Consultation with Aboriginals is required in Australian Northern Territory legislation for park agency management of:

(a) Land vested in an Aboriginal or Aboriginals, or in a body corporate that is wholly owned by Aboriginals; (b) Land held upon trust for the benefit of Aboriginals, or (c) Any other land occupied by Aboriginals (*Territory Parks and Wildlife Conservation Ordinance* of 1976 and *National Parks and Wildlife Conservation Act* of 1975).

Canadian policy states that:

Where new national parks are established in conjunction with the settlement of land claims of native people, an agreement will be negotiated between Parks Canada and representatives of local native communities prior to formal establishment of the national park, creating a joint management régime for the planning and management of the national park (Parks Canada, 1979).

In Alaska, as well, specific native consultation is only imperative when native land interests are legally at stake, as for example when areas claimed by native corporations are included within a national monument.

For ongoing park-native coordination, the United States NPS office in Anchorage has a Native Liaison Officer and the Parks Canada Prairie Regional Office has a Native Involvement Coordinator. A new Parks Canada office in Yellowknife provides a base for northern consultation, though it is more central to the interests of the Northwest Territory than to those of the Yukon.

THREE HINTERLAND PARKS: KLUANE, KAKADU, AND GATES OF THE ARCTIC

Kluane National Park in the Yukon Territory, Kakadu National Park in Australia's Northern Territory, and Gates of the Arctic National Monument in Alaska are all vast—covering, respectively, 26,237, 6,450, and 33,184 km². While the biophysical aspects of the parks vary widely, they each possess outstanding landscape features and a wide variety of animal wildlife and vegetation.

Conservation History

Conservation efforts in the areas of Kakadu and Gates of the Arctic began in the early 1960s, but measures for the protection of land in Kluane were proposed two decades earlier (cf. Theberge, 1978). The establishment of the Kluane Game Sanctuary and Park Reserve was in response to threats to wildlife that were associated with the construction of the Alaska Highway in the 1940s. The area later became a park reserve under the control of Parks Canada, but it still awaits full national park status.

Kakadu was also first protected as a sanctuary, but the Ranger Uranium Environmental Inquiry finally promoted national park designation for it. Serious consideration of park potential for Gates of the Arctic began as a component of the much broader planning exercise for the 'd-2 lands'. Gates of the Arctic is classified as a national monument and the NPS eventually hopes to redesignate it a national park. Thus in all three areas, interim protection as a reserve other than a national park has been provided, pending any granting of full national park status.

Boundary delineation has been a continuous exercise in each of the three areas. Thus boundary changes have been made in response to regional land-use interests, to national park agency objectives, and to practical and political considerations, while adjustments continue to be made to Gates of the Arctic boundaries as land-trades are arranged with state and native interests. The boundaries of Kakadu are being established in two stages, the first of which is already complete. Further changes may occur in the boundaries of Kluane, given that conservation organizations would like to see certain other areas included in the park, and native land-claim negotiations are incomplete.

The evolution of management proposals for Kakadu and Gates of the Arctic is not well documented, and indeed management plans are not yet available for these areas. Regulations for new NPS units in Alaska apply to Gates of the Arctic, and guidelines for managing the monument have been proposed, with minimal staffing envisaged for on-site park management. General arrangements for Kakadu suggested by the Ranger Inquiry have been approved by the Australian government, and the federal and territorial agencies involved appear to be implementing them. About five TPWC wildlife rangers are now stationed in the Park. A detailed management planning programme for Kluane began in 1977; for it a final plan has been proposed and is now undergoing public and agency review. At present there are approximately twenty-five full-time park employees in Kluane.

Native Involvement

Native peoples made extensive use of all three park areas before the arrival of the white man. The exact patterns of early use are most obscure in Kluane, where native resource-use has been virtually non-existent for over thirty years (owing to management policies). In Kakadu, some natives continue to live off the land, while most local natives still hunt and trap in Gates of the Arctic.

The parts played by the native peoples in the creation and management of Kluane, Kakadu, and Gates of the Arctic, vary very widely. Their role tends to be strongest where they secured land-tenure and organizational advantages at an early stage in the development of national park issues. In both Gates of the Arctic and Kakadu, the settlement of native land-claims prior to, or in conjunction with, park planning, gave natives the legal rights to participate in parks and related reserve issues. Legislation also created native corporations and aboriginal land-councils to represent the native people. Thus there were vehicles in place to ensure that the natives would maintain some control over the land, and some input into planning. Involvement was most intense in Kakadu, where the natives own the parkland. In Gates of the Arctic, native corporations made land-trades and agreements with the NPS, but the areas under the control of the two groups do not overlap.

Early conservation arrangements for Kluane were made with comparatively little consideration for the local natives, the park having been established in the absence of a land-claim settlement. National park interaction with native people has not been without conflict in any of the three cases, but there was more opposition to the national park from the Kluane natives, when they finally became involved, than from the other two native groups. A problem for both the Kluane and Kakadu natives has been their lack of experience in presenting their views through the channels available to them, such as public inquiries and committee hearings.

Provisions for native land-use in the parks to date are made in the terms of the lease for the native-owned lands composing Kakadu, in the National Monument regulations for Gates of the Arctic, and in federal legislation and policy for Kluane. In order to maintain a unified front, Kluane natives now decline to take a public stand on the land-use issue until a native land-claim settlement is reached. Similar reasoning may be keeping proposed management plans for Kakadu from being made public.

Kluane area natives have, nevertheless, had some input into management planning for the park, facilitated by a contract provided by Parks Canada: this input included the development of an alternative plan. Gates of the Arctic natives submitted a park proposal to a Department of the Interior planning group and to Congress. Both the Kluane and Gates of the

Arctic proposals stressed increased native involvement in park management—especially wildlife management—and increased opportunity for natives to derive economic benefit from the parks. Programmes are currently under way to train natives for park management positions in Kakadu and Kluane.

The ANPWS hopes to benefit from the Aboriginals' knowledge of Kakadu's resources in managing the Park. The United States NPS sees the local natives as an asset to Gates of the Arctic, in their portrayal of a unique relationship with the land; but Parks Canada does not appear to recognize as fully as the NPS the advantages to be gained from increased interaction with the native people in the area.

CONCLUSIONS

The major findings of this study can be classified into four groups: (1) motivation for interaction, (2) mechanisms for policy definition and implementation, (3) facilitators of native involvement, and (4) native use of parkland. Under these headings, the problems and issues surrounding interaction between national parks and native peoples can be summarized. A matrix (Table 1) facilitates comparative evaluation of policies and institutional arrangements relating to native peoples for national parks in each hinterland.

Motivation for Interaction

Motivation for interaction is the most value-laden component of the study. National park agencies and native people must interact as long as they are interested in the same land-area. However, the extent and intensity of interaction is largely determined by motivation. This is in turn affected by the perceptions, attitudes, and values or ideology, of each group. The ideology of the national park agencies is largely reflected in their goals and objectives, and native ideology is a product of native history, life-styles, and aspirations.

Among the national parks agencies, the Canadian agency shows the lowest motivation to interact. Parks Canada does not explicitly recognize as many values of national park—native interaction as do the United States and Australian agencies. These values include helping the natives to preserve their culture, and employing native skills and knowledge in park management. Yukon Territory natives also show less motivation to interact with national park agencies than the natives of the other 'hinterlands'. Their outlook could create impediments to the establishment of national park programmes in the Yukon—especially as they attain more control over land through land-claims settlements. A change in the public ownership policy for Canadian National Parks could, however, create opportunities for more Parks Canada—native people cooperation in the creation of national parks in the Yukon.

TABLE 1

Comparative Evaluation of Policies and Institutional Arrangements: National Parks and Native People

Components	Yukon Territory	Alaska	Northern Territory of Australia
1. Motivation for interaction			
National park agency motivation	Low indication of motivation in benefits to the visitor or experience from traditional cultures.	High motivation due to factors related to both native interests and national park values.	High motivation —see national park and native objectives as overlapping, compatible; —also practical management advantages.
Native motivation	Low motivation —see national parks as threatening to lifestyle and land claim but desire share of economic benefit.	Moderate motivation —see national parks as assisting in maintenance of native culture and traditions, also for employment.	Low, then high motivation —see national parks as assistance in managing places of value to natives and employment opportunities.
2. Mechanisms for policy definition and implementation			
Federal level	Few mechanisms at federal level preclude non-federal ownership; special arrangements for northern parks abandoned.	Federal legislation gives native rights priority. NPS regulations for Alaska national monuments stress role of certain land-users including natives (*see* (4)).	Federal legislation recognizes Aboriginal rights in the Northern Territory, with specific provisions for national parks on native land.
State/territorial level	No specifically northern arrangements to date.	Anchorage office has heavy input into federal regulations.	Northern Territory national parks legislation recognizes important role of Aboriginals.
Park level (based on case-studies)	Mechanisms for interaction at park level implemented in reaction to problems or federal requirements.	Detailed agreements resulting from application of ANCSA land allotment requirements.	Terms of lease of Aboriginal land to ANPWS clearly define native role in Kakadu.
3. Facilitators of native involvement			
Native initiative	Native organizations without legislative backing. Low input through briefs, testimony at hearings, and meetings on park planning and management.	Native organizations with legislative backing in strong bargaining position. High input through negotiations over land allotments.	Native organizations with legislative backing and ownership rights to land in near-controlling position. High input through terms of lease and 2 members on TPWC.
National park initiative	Moderate to high initiative through native involvement coordinator, employment policy, and public consultation in the park planning process.	Moderate to high initiative through native liaison officer, employment policy, park research, and interpretive programmes.	High initiative through consultation; training programmes for eventual native management of park.

(continued)

T A B L E 1 (*continued*)

Components	Yukon Territory	Alaska	Northern Territory of Australia
Other initiatives	Interested individuals have played a moderate role in assessing native interests for Parks Canada. A federal pipeline inquiry has helped to represent the natives.	An extensive planning process for Alaska national interest lands has played a major role in facilitating native input prior to park establishment.	Federal inquiries related to native rights and uranium development have played major roles in facilitating native input in planning for park.
4. Native use of parkland			
Type of use provided for (general terms)	Various terms used: 'traditional subsistence resource use' dominates. Inconsistent.	Various terms used: 'local subsistence resource-use' dominates. Moderately consistent.	'Traditional use by Aboriginals' is only term used. Very consistent.
Definitions—use	Many qualifications, restrictions. Potentially severe limitations. Imprecisely defined.	Several qualifications, restrictions. Moderate potential limitations. More precisely defined.	Few qualifications, restrictions. Potentially severe limitations. Imprecisely defined.
—user	Often defined racially, as Natives; Indians.	Rarely defined racially.	Always defined racially, as Aboriginals.
Regulation	Enforcement and surveillance by wardens, good staffing. 'Gentleman's agreement' not to use Kluane for native hunting. Indefinite.	Superintendant will issue permits, low staffing. Monitoring and environmental statements to be undertaken. Regulations define methods. Evolving in detail.	Patrolling by wildlife rangers, moderate staffing. Indefinite.

Mechanisms for Policy Definition and Implementation

Many mechanisms for policy definition and implementation exist in each 'hinterland'. They range from national to local levels of operation, from policy statements through legislation and federal inquiry recommendations, to the terms of a lease. The *Alaska Native Claims Settlement Act*, and the *Aboriginal Land Rights (Northern Territory) Act*, provide strong assurance that native interests will be considered by national park agencies. Several modes of interaction between native peoples and national parks in the Canadian North will probably not be possible unless native rights are established in similar federal legislation.

Regional national park offices in Alaska and the Northern Territory of Australia are reportedly improving interaction between native people and national parks. The growing importance of the Alaskan national park system to the NPS is reflected in the growth of its Anchorage office. The lack of arrangements for interaction in the Yukon may be partly related to the Territory's remoteness from the regional office in Winnipeg, and the situation may not be much improved by the new northern office in Yellowknife, NWT.

Agreements made at the individual park level are a mechanism for policy definition and implementation that is used in all three 'hinterlands'. They have the advantage of maximum park-to-park flexibility, but their formulation may take years. Moreover, concessions to native land-use interests in such agreements conceivably could erode what some interest-groups may perceive as key wildlife and other national park values, and set undesirable precedents. Nevertheless, such agreements are preferable to the *ad hoc* approach to decision-making concerning the interaction of native people with Kluane National Park, where neither natives nor park managers are certain of the native role in the Park.

Problems could be encountered in policy definition and implementation, as all three state/territorial governments become more responsible for resource management in the 'hinterlands'. State–territorial competition with federal agencies for wildlife management in particular complicates national park interaction with native peoples. Overlapping interests of the TPWC and the ANPWS in the Northern Territory of Australia could lead to rivalries which would hinder coordination with the Aboriginals.

Facilitators of Native Involvement

The roles that native people can play in national parks are categorized in the matrix (Table 1) by the term 'facilitators of native involvement'. Native input depends at least in part on the presence, and strength, of native organizations. Legislative provisions and other support for native organizations in Alaska and the Australian Northern Territory have ensured the natives of a means of representation in the park planning process. Land-claim settlements provided the Alaska and Northern Territory natives with additional control over input into national park planning and management, through native ownership of parkland or land desired for park purposes. Comprehensive land-use planning, as in Alaska and the Kakadu National Park area, also appears to provide an avenue for native input.

Native people encounter difficulty in contributing to national park planning and management through standard channels such as public hearings. Native organizations are, however, gaining participatory experience; even so, national park agencies should continue to attempt to provide for more native involvement in the public consultation process—through research financing and special participatory mechanisms for native input.

The relatively new United States NPS position of native liaison officer or coordinator is effectively facilitating native involvement. However, native employment by the park agency, or contractual or research participation, may not as effectively represent the native interest as significant native involvement in the upper policy-making and management levels of the park agency itself. The Northern Territory Parks and Wildlife Commission has set an interesting precedent in this respect, in that two members of the Commission must be Aboriginals living in the Northern Territory.

Native Use of Parkland

Native use of national parkland is the most complex element of interaction in each 'hinterland'. Table 1 showed that there is considerable variation in the terminology and conceptualization of this type of use. Parks Canada describes native use in different ways in its policy statements, none of which agrees with legislative terminology. The United States NPS almost always discusses 'local subsistence resource-use' in its policy and regulations, even though the latter are largely the result of legislated 'native' rights. Consistency in terminology in Australian policy and legislation should aid in policy implementation.

Table 1 also refers to native use in terms of the definition of the user and the use. Definitions vary in content and detail. Parks Canada and the Northern Territory national park agencies have not yet clearly defined the types of allowable native or related use. The situation is accordingly confusing. United States NPS policy is leading to a non-racial definition of users that would include natives, while the Australian agencies use racial criteria in the definition of park users. The Canadian position here is not clear, with some apparent shifts occurring during the formulation of a Parks Canada Policy in 1978 and 1979.

Problems of terminology and definition are, like the motivation component, partly based on perceptions, attitudes, and values. Before these problems can be solved, decisions must be made on issues such as the credibility of native land-rights as well as 'subsistence' and associated cultural values. There is also a conservational aspect to native use of wildlife which has implications for the regulation of the use. It involves questions of biological carrying-capacity, wildlife population-cycles, and habitat, which are not examined here. It also concerns methods, technology, and numbers of native users and their possible impact on wildlife.

All these factors must be allowed for in regulations and other management arrangements for native use of national parks. Other considerations include monitoring of use, surveillance, and enforcement of regulations. Low levels of staffing for the 'hinterland' parks hardly seem adequate to manage effectively the land involved—so that users are, in a sense, largely free to do as they choose.

In conclusion, a number of aids to a more productive interaction of national park and native interest in the 'hinterlands' can be identified. One is better motivation, or recognition by both parties that there are advantages to consultation and cooperation. Another is a land-claims settlement, stating the legislated rights of native peoples in the 'hinterlands' and giving them a land-holding and bargaining status that is comparable with that of the park agencies. The third is a more comprehensive systems and regional planning effort involving opportunities for informed input from all affected parties.

Such planning would provide a forum for a greater variety of land-use interests, including national parks and native people (Theberge *et al.*, 1980). Finally, satisfactory interaction on the park site could be assisted by clear yet flexible means of deciding the nature of native use of parkland, the conservation of wildlife, and associated economic and cultural issues.

Further research in a variety of directions would help to clarify and resolve problems in the interaction of national parks and native peoples. Land-use objectives and land values of the two groups should be carefully compared, to identify areas of convergence and divergence. Details of the impacts of native use on parks should be gathered, so that this use can be regulated appropriately. Other interests, such as the park visitor, the non-native 'hinterland' resident, and non-renewable resource developers, must also be considered, for their effects on national parks and native peoples will influence the interaction of the two groups.

SUMMARY

At the very general level, the aim of this paper is to compare the interaction of national parks and native peoples in Northern Canada (Yukon Territory), Alaska, and the Northern Territory of Australia. Currently these areas are subject to increasing land-use pressures from mining, industrial development, the creation of national parks and related reserves, and native attempts to maintain traditional wildlife and renewable resource use. The study focuses on the interactions between national parks and native peoples on the premise that experiences can be compared and problems encountered in one area but possibly avoided in another.

The study begins by briefly describing native land-use issues, land-rights arrangements, and organizations, in the Yukon Territory, central Alaska, and Northern Australia. The national park agencies are described, compared, and shown to differ considerably in institutional character, field of management, control of land, and external links with interest groups such as native peoples. Case-studies of the national parks, etc., named Kluane (Yukon), Gates of the Arctic (Alaska), and Kakadu (Northern Territory of Australia), are presented to provide more details on similarities and differences in planning, types of tenure, native subsistence activities, and other factors.

In the Yukon Territory, neither the national parks agency nor the native people are highly motivated to interact. In contrast, the park agencies and native people in Alaska and the Northern Territory of Australia recognize mutual benefits from interaction, largely as a result of legislation and policies which encourage cooperation. Native involvement officers now facilitate coordination in the Yukon and Alaska. Park agency native employment programmes are proceeding in all three 'hinterlands', while native people can own land on which national parks are established in Alaska and the Australian Northern Territory. Only in Australia are native people known to be directly involved in upper-level national park management. Potential limitations on native subsistence and associated use of national parks range from moderate to severe, and are only defined clearly in Alaska. Lack of definition leads to confusion in deciding upon native use, while exceedingly precise definition precludes flexibility at the park level.

A number of aids to a more mutually satisfactory interaction can be identified. One is motivation, or recognition by both parties that there are advantages to consultation and cooperation. Another, not yet achieved in the Yukon, is a land-claims settlement, stating the legislated rights of native peoples in the 'hinterlands' and giving them a land-holding and bargaining status which is comparable with that of government agencies. A third aid is comprehensive systematic and regional planning efforts involving opportunities for informed input from all affected parties. Such planning would provide a forum for consideration of a variety of interests, including national parks and native peoples. Finally, satisfactory interaction on the park site could be assisted by clear yet flexible means of deciding upon acceptable native use of parkland, the conservation of wildlife, and associated economic and cultural factors.

REFERENCES

Armstrong, G. (1977). A comparison of Australian and Canadian approaches to national park planning. Pp. 220–8 in *Leisure and Recreation in Australia* (Ed. D. Mercer), Sorrett Publishing, Malvern, Australia: 264 pp.

Council for Yukon Indians (undated). *Together Today for Our Children Tomorrow*. Carters Publishing Company, Brampton, Ontario: 140 pp.

Department of Aboriginal Affairs (1979). *Background Notes: Aboriginal Land Rights (Northern Territory) Act 1976*, No. 1 (Revised). Department of Indian and Northern Affairs, Canberra, Australia: 8 pp.

Gardner, J. E. (1979). *National Parks and Native People in Northern Canada*. M.A. thesis, Department of Geography, University of Waterloo, Waterloo, Ontario: viii + 223 pp., illustr.

Gardner, J. E. & Nelson, J. G. (1980). Comparing national park and related reserve policy in hinterland areas: Alaska, Northern Canada, and Northern Australia. *Environmental Conservation*, 7(1), pp. 43—50, 3 maps.

Hunt, C. D. (1978). Approaches to native land settlements and implications for northern land-use and resource management policies. Pp. 5–41 in *Northern Transitions*, Vol. 2 (Ed. R. T. Keith & J. B. Wright). Canadian Arctic Resources Committee, Ottawa, Ontario: xiv + 470 pp., illustr.

Kresge, D. T., Morehouse, T. A. & Rogers, G. W. (1977). *Issues in Alaska Development*. University of Washington Press, Seattle, Washington: 223 pp., illustr.

Parks Canada (1978). *Parks Canada Draft Policy*. Parks Canada Department of Indian and Northern Affairs, Ottawa, Ontario: 118 pp.

Parks Canada (1979). *Parks Canada Policy*. Parks Canada Department of Indian and Northern Affairs, Ottawa, Ontario: 79 pp.

Redpath, D. K. (1979). *Land Use Programs in Canada: Yukon Territory.* Minister of Supply and Services Canada, Hull, Quebec: 303 pp., illustr.

Theberge, J. B. (1978). Kluane National Park. Pp. 151–89 in *Northern Transitions,* Vol. 1 (Ed. E. B. Peterson & J. B. Wright). Canadian Arctic Resources Committee, Ottawa, Ontario: xv + 320 pp., illustr.

Theberge, J. B., Nelson, J. G. & Fenge, T. (Ed.) (1980). *Environmentally Significant Areas of the Yukon Territory.* Canadian Arctic Resources Committee, Ottawa: xiv + 134 pp., illustr.

LEGISLATION CITED

Australia

Aboriginal Land Rights (Northern Territory) Act of 1976.
National Parks and Wildlife Conservation Act of 1975.
Territory Parks and Wildlife Ordinance of 1976.

Canada

National Parks Act of 1930, Amended 1974.

United States

Alaska Native Claims Settlement Act of 1971.
Alaska National Interest Lands Conservation Act of 1978, passed by House of Representatives (HR. 39) but not by Senate.

32   Kuna Yala: Indigenous Biosphere Reserve in the Making?

R. MICHAEL WRIGHT

BRIAN HOUSEAL

CEBALDO DE LEON

The project described in this selection seems in many respects to be an ideal blend in which indigenous people and conservationists worked together to preserve a threatened ecosystem. In this case the Kuna themselves (see Nietschmann, part VII), have proposed the establishment of a biosphere reserve to protect lands they traditionally control in order to prevent them from being invaded and destroyed by settlers. The Kuna are one of the most independent tribal groups in the world and provide an encouraging model of how tribals can direct their own development. R. Michael Wright, project officer for the Kuna project, is vice president of the World Wildlife Fund—U.S., based in Washington, D.C. Brian Houseal, technical consultant for the Kuna project, is with the Tropical Agriculture Center for Instruction and Research (CATIE), Turrialba, Costa Rica. Cebaldo De Leon is a Kuna anthropologist who is assisting with the drafting of the management plan for the Kuna Pemasky project, Comarca de Kuna Yala, Panama.

When a Kuna Indian awakens on one of the small coral islands off the Panamanian coast where most of his people live, his gaze wanders past the thatched houses of his neighbors, out over the low-riding canoes of farmers heading for their mainland plots, and then across a mile or so of shimmering water to a mass of green rest rising, virgin and luxuriant, to the ridge of the San Blas mountains. At his back, the sun climbs above the calm Caribbean, and its first rays strike the tufts of mists snagged like fleece in the clefts of the hills. For generations, this dawn panorama, serene and unchanging, has greeted the Kuna People.

But if he were standing atop the 2,400 foot high San Blas Range, the view down the other slope would be less reassuring. Large swaths of thick vegetation have fallen victim to the machete and the torch. Ash-grey tree trunks stand above the denuded landscape, skeletal remnants of the once towering jungle. (*Breslin and Chapin*)

Reprinted from *Parks* 10, no. 3 (1985): 25–27 by permission of R. Michael Wright.

During the last decade concern for disappearing tropical forests has grown increasingly acute for the conservationists and protected area managers of the world. The earth's tropical forests, both representative and exceptional, are being cut at an alarming rate. Deforestation in Panama is currently 50,000 ha (123,550 ac) per year and the wet tropical forest of the Kuna reservation, with its astonishing diversity of plant and animal life, is one of only a half dozen large tracts of original forest left in all of Central America.

A convergence of interests—the conservationists' concern for threatened biological and natural resources and the determination of the Kuna Indians to resist a threat to their cultural survival—may result in a unique biosphere reserve. The IUCN report *The Biosphere Reserve and its Relationship to other Protected Areas* states "To be successful [a biospheres reserve] must preserve areas of undisturbed nature as genetic reservoirs and as standards against which change outside can be measured and judged. It must equally include man and his works. If handled imaginatively it should provide an excellent opportunity of increasing understanding of the problems of the biosphere and involving people, especially local people, in conservation and research having a vital bearing on their own future." In the Pemasky (Proyecto de Estudio para el Manejo de Areas Silvestres de Kuna Yala) project the Kuna are beyond participation, they are in charge (see Figure 1). The biosphere reserve, if it is so designated, will be established, managed and integrated into the local society by the Kuna themselves.

The Comarca de Kuna Yala (reservation of the Kuna Indian established in 1938) is an isolated stretch of lush tropical jungle 124 miles (200 km) long and averaging 16 miles (26.7 km) wide, extending from the Continental Divide to the coast on the Caribbean side of Panama (see Figure 1, inset). Thirty thousand Kuna Indians reside in 60 villages on some of the 350 tiny, offshore coral islands, their tightly packed thatched houses seeming to float inches above the bright Caribbean sea, supporting themselves with fishing and complex multi-crop agriculture on the flat alluvial soils of the coast.

Traditionally the forested mountain divide has proven to be a valuable buffer to protect the reservation from the ravages of the slash and burn and cattle economies of Panama's interior. As the abode of spirits and a source of medicinal plants, the maintenance of tracts of primary forest serves essential cultural needs. Less well recognized, even on the islands themselves, is the ecological link between the forest hydrological system and rivers which provide the Kuna access into the interior; erosion from deforestation of these mountains, with their 2,500–3,500 mm (100–140 in) of rain per year, could also jeopardize the coral reefs and marine system which provide the Kuna their primary source of protein.

Yet the forest which prevents encroachment means the Kuna themselves can only leave the reservation by boat or plane, and with increasing fuel costs these expenses are becoming prohibitive. Thus the Kuna were intrigued by the proposal of US/AID in the early 1970s to put a road into the western end of the reservation from El Lano on the Pan-American Highway

PEMASKY

PROYECTO DE ESTUDIO PARA EL MANEJO
DE AREAS SILVESTRES DE KUNA YALA

CARIBBEAN SEA

SAN BLAS ISLANDS

Cartí

Rio Mandinga

CHAGRES
NATIONAL
PARK

1

Nusagandi

2

4

3

2

2

BAYANO
INDIGENOUS
RESERVE
(PROPOSED)

Continental Divide and
Border of Comarca de Kuna Yala

El Llano-Cartí Road

PAN-AMERICAN HIGHWAY

El Llano

POTENTIAL MANAGEMENT AREAS

1 **Natural or Core Area: Pemasky**
   (scientific research and tourism)

2 **Manipulative Area**
   (traditional Kuna agriculture)

3 **Stable Cultural Area**
   (Kuna villages on islands, fisheries
   and coastal zone)

4 **Reclamation or Restoration Area**
   (outside reserve borders)

COSTA RICA

COMARCA DE
KUNA YALA

PANAMA

CANAL

N
↑

COLOMBIA

FIGURE 1
Area covered in the Pemasky project

to the tiny airstrip at Carti. However, as construction proceeded apace concern mounted among some Kuna who recognized that, unless a permanent presence could be established where the road penetrated the reserve, squatters would quickly flow into the reservation. In 1975 an enthusiastic and committed group of young Kuna began to establish an agriculture community at the vulnerable point, but the attempt failed when coastal techniques proved inappropriate to the ecological zones of the mountains and the Kuna elders, with their traditional knowledge, were not effectively brought into the effort. After a frustrating five years, the young Kuna decided to join tourism, scientific research and a protected area (modeled on traditional Kuna spirit reserves) in order to enlist the support of the outside conservation and scientific community in their cultural preservation goals. Advice was sought from CATIE (Centro Agronómico Tropical de Investigación y Ensénanza) in Costa Rica and the Smithsonian Tropical Research Institute in Panama with the bulk of the financial resources provided by the Interamerica Foundation as well as World Wildlife Fund-U.S. and the Kuna themselves.

The conservation success of the project depends, as does its ecological aspects, on the link between the mountains and the coast, the young defenders of the reservation and the traditional knowledge base of the islands, the balance of scientific tourism and the cattle culture of the interior. The project has now received the blessing of the Kuna General Congress and every other week volunteers from the island communities come to Pemasky to help demarcate the border of the reservation, returning with an awareness of the devastated landscape beyond the mountains. The Pemasky—or Kuna Wildlands—Project also provides a link between the populations of Kuna at both ends of the reservation and is seen as a model for resource management and defense of the Comarca as a whole. The goals of the protected area complex have now grown beyond merely holding the line along the border of the 60,000 ha (148,260 ac) study area in the western sector of the reserve to the possibility of including the entire Comarca and perhaps some adjacent protected areas in subsequent phases of the project. As a result, the Kuna have begun to seek a classification appropriate to the mixed objectives of their initiative. The protected area designation should not threaten the Kuna culture by injecting national institutions into the Comarca, but, instead, should recognize the unique legal protection provided by the Kuna's land title (by law non-Kuna are prohibited from holding land in the reservation).

For the moment the biosphere reserve is the only category of protected area that seems appropriate to this project. Interestingly enough, the concept of the biosphere reserve, which seeks to conserve representative samples of the world's biogeographical regions and man's traditional relationships to them, coincides directly with the Kuna Indian concept of "Kuna Yala" (Kuna place, or territory) being an integral part of "Abia Yala" (the mother earth, biosphere) and thereby worthy of conservation for cultural and spiritual reasons.

Scientific research and tourism, as well as a core protected area, would be included in the Pemasky complex in the mountains of Nusagandi. Terrestrial and marine systems important to Kuna life ways will be maintained. Their traditional multi-crop agricultural system will continue on the coastal fringe (a recent study edited by Moreno and McKay of one small area identified 72 agroforestry combinations, utilizing 48 species of trees and 16 crop plants), and the islands will retain their status as centers of the Kuna culture. Ironically, the one management area missing within the reservation is a rehabilitation or restoration area, and the objective of the project is to keep it so. However, already serious degradation is taking place on the portion of the Panamanian side of the Continental Divide which could be incorporated into a biosphere reserve. Ideally such an area under Kuna control could provide an additional buffer and a legal basis for Kuna management beyond the reservation proper.

The biosphere reserve designation needs exploration at both the international and national level but, like every aspect of this project, the ultimate decision will rest firmly with the Kuna themselves as perhaps the most socially and culturally cohesive indigenous society in the hemisphere. The Pemasky project demonstrates the potential of the biosphere reserve concept to provide an international linkage between projects whose uniqueness would otherwise have to be compromised if not destroyed to make them fit into more traditional protected area classification systems.

REFERENCES

Patrick Breslin and Mac Chapin "Conservation Kuna-Style" 8:2 Grassroots Development: *Journal of the Inter-American Foundation* (1984)

Catherine Caufield, *In the Rainforest*, Alfred Knopf (1985); Adrian Forsyth and Kenneth Miyata, *Tropical Nature*, Charles Scribner & Sons (1984)

Norman Myers, *The Primary Source: Tropical Forests and Our Future*. W.W. Norton (1984)

Brian Houseal, Craig MacFarland, Guillermo Archibold and Aurelio Chiari, "Indigenous Cultures and Protected Areas in Central America" 9:1 *Cultural Survival Quarterly* (Parks and People), (Feb 1985)

CNPPA, *The Biosphere Reserve and its Relationship to other Protected Areas* IUCN, (1979)

Stanley Heckadon Moreno and Alberto McKay (eds) *Colonizacion y Destruccion de Basques en Panama*, Panamanian Anthropology Asso. 1982

IX

Policy Alternatives

This final section offers a diverse range of policy critiques and recommendations concerning development issues. The selections are well-informed attempts to outline responsible, just, humane policies toward tribal peoples, either with a global perspective or with particular regions in mind. In some respects this part represents a continuation of the policy debate initiated in part IV on intervention philosophy, but these selections are less concerned with the issue of intervention itself or the need to identify "positive" and "negative" traits of tribal cultures. All of these writers assume that the standard approach to development has been detrimental to tribal peoples and that tribal cultures have an inherent value of their own. Given this common perspective, a variety of policy alternatives is explored in these selections, ranging from the possibility of leaving certain tribal groups totally undisturbed through various levels of tribal participation in development decision making.

At one extreme Wollaston and Lambert recommend permanent nonintervention in tribal societies as a policy approach under very special circumstances. This approach would involve leaving tribals alone and preventing outside intrusion into their territories, which would not be available for any type of development by outsiders. It resembles the biosphere reserve approach but differs from most of the conservationist approaches discussed in part VIII. It would be the ultimate in self-determination and would not require political struggle by tribal peoples. Few advocates of tribal rights would be prepared to go this far.

Other writers recognize the desirability of tribal peoples' making their own development decisions, as in the "ethnodevelopment" approach discussed by Talalla, but there is less agreement over precisely what self-determination or cultural autonomy might mean or how they might be actualized. Maybury-Lewis discusses the complexity of the issues confronting organizations that attempt to support tribal peoples in the defense of their human rights and culture. Goodland argues from the perspective of the World Bank, one of the most important sources of development funds in the world, that large-scale development projects can be made compatible with the interests of tribal peoples. Bodley critiques Goodland's position in detail and argues that it contains serious shortcomings. The final selection presents an alternative proposed by the Cordillera People's Alliance, a recently formed intertribal political organization in the Philippines. This formal resolution leaves little doubt about how some tribal peoples view these issues.

33 Remarks on "The Opening of New Territories in Papua"

A. F. R. Wollaston

Alexander Frederick Richmond Wollaston (1875–1930) was Honorary Secretary of the Royal Geographical Society of London and Fellow and Tutor at King's College, Cambridge, at the time of his death. He was widely respected for his exploration and his mountain-climbing activities in New Guinea, East Africa, and the Himalayas. In 1910–11 his expedition to totally unknown country in Dutch New Guinea made contact with many tribes who had never before encountered Europeans. He developed a respect for tribal peoples and their culture that was unusual even among anthropologists of the time. His bold public comments following a lecture by E. W. Chinnery to the Royal Geographical Society must have surprised everyone, for they questioned the basic assumptions underlying even the enlightened policy of colonial administration in New Guinea. Chinnery had presented an enthusiastic endorsement of the official program of extending government control into independent tribal areas in order to open them for development. Wollaston recognized that such conquest might not be welcomed by the natives, that it might not be doing them a favor, and that it was unjust. He recommended that a large block of the still-undisturbed New Guinea interior be left entirely under tribal control—forever.

This was an unthinkable idea, given prevailing policies, but it was indeed quite reasonable. At that time no Europeans knew that a vast interconnecting network of tribes consisting of perhaps half a million people controlled the highlands. They were well protected by the rugged topography and surely would have continued to thrive as they had for millenia if the invading colonial government had chosen to halt its piecemeal conquest. As it was, in 1920 no one was prepared to take Wollaston's recommendations seriously. The president of the Royal Society brushed them aside by suggesting that Britain really needed all the land, labor, and natural resources that it could get.

I am very glad to add to the congratulations of the other speakers. At the risk of appearing reactionary and giving unasked advice to Government officials, I will make a few remarks with which you will profoundly disagree. The paper is called the opening up of new territory in Papua. It is very nice to see the world opened up: we like to see new lines of railways on our maps and to see Africa dotted with aerodromes and such things, but I do not think we sufficiently consider the point of view of the

Reprinted with permission from *The Geographical Journal* (June 1920): 457–58. Copyright © 1920 *The Geographical Journal*.

people whose countries are opened up. Mr. Chinnery objects to inter-tribal warfare. Well, we have spent years in killing each other, at great expense, to make the world free for democracy. Now and again the Papuans kill one or two people to celebrate a festival, or perhaps because the country does not produce beef and mutton. I do not think really it is quite fair of us to inflict what we are pleased to call our Western civilization on these people. You call them "savages." Many of these people—not those you have seen photographs of to-night, but their cousins who live a few hundred miles to the west—are personal friends of mine. I have always found them to be a happy and cheerful people, sufficiently fed and suitably clad. So far as I know they are as truthful as most of us, and in many months I have spent with them, though they have had endless opportunities and unspeakable temptation, I have never known one of them to steal. The lecturer says we must alter—modify—their traditions ("institutions," I think, is the word) so that they may "fall into line with the needs of progress." I hope they will go very slowly about this modifying of institutions. You have in New Guinea the last people, I believe, who have not yet been contaminated, if that is not an unkind word, by association with the white races. They have an extraordinarily interesting culture of which we know very little, and we have much to learn from them. I suppose it is too much to expect that the whole of the interior of New Guinea should be kept as a vast ethnological museum, but I should like to believe that the Australian Government will set apart a really large area—there is plenty of room—to be kept as a native reserve where these people can live their own life, work out their own destiny, whatever it may be. And into that country no traders, no missionaries, no exploiters, not even Government police themselves should be allowed to go. There are, of course, difficulties, but they are not insuperable. The inland regions are invariably difficult of access, so that it should be easy to prevent an invasion of undesirable outsiders. The mountain tribes wander very little from their own valleys, and if approach from the coast were cut off, they would live undisturbing and undisturbed by their more sophisticated neighbours. Perhaps it is an impossible dream, but I am looking ahead through two or three or more centuries, and the example of the fate of the Tasmanians and the present condition of the aboriginal Australian natives ought to be a sufficient warning.

34 Health Survey of Rennell and Bellona Islands

S. M. LAMBERT

This brief selection is drawn from a larger report describing the basically good living conditions of the last genuinely traditional and fully autonomous Polynesian society. Rennell and Bellona islands lie some 200 kilometers south of Guadalcanal in the British Solomon Islands. Treacherous currents as well as the remoteness of the islands and their lack of major resources except phosphates meant that they were very rarely visited. At the time of Lambert's health survey in 1930 the culture was quite self-sufficient. His policy recommendation that the islanders officially be left undisturbed made good sense and no doubt would have pleased Wollaston, but such a policy was still out of step with prevailing anthropological advice and administrative practice in the South Pacific. Remarkably, in this case, where there was no economic justification for intervention, the Rennell and Bellona islanders were left largely to their own devices. Eventually, Christian missionaries gained a foothold and converted the entire population, but there were no other serious threats to the basic independence of the islanders until 1975, when outsiders proposed extracting the phosphate. This case deserves careful study as a possible model for policy approaches in similar situations, which will unfortunately be very rare.

Dr. Sylvester M. Lambert (1880–1947) worked for the Commonwealth Health Service in the western Pacific beginning in 1919. He helped establish an anti-hookworm campaign in Papua and Queensland and served as health adviser in Fiji, Tonga, Samoa, and Rarotonga. In addition to his many technical medical studies, he was well known for his book *A Doctor in Paradise*. Lambert's health survey of Rennell and Bellona was conducted at the suggestion of the Resident Commissioner of the British Solomon Islands and was carried out in conjunction with the Whitney South Sea Expedition from the American Museum of Natural History.

Rennell Island (Mungava) should be kept as a native reserve, in order to preserve in its entirety a culture possessing characteristics that have, or may have, great value to western civilization. The Rennell Islanders are probably the only group of people in the world in which the paterfamilias is retained in a pure state, unblemished by the influence of group culture.

There are two great causes for the maladjustment which exists in all societies to-day: first, an improper land-man ratio; second, the clash of cultures, which usually means the overpowering of a weaker race by a stronger. This has been the history of all the weaker cultures in the South Seas.

Reprinted in abridged form with permission from *Oceania* 2, no. 2 (1931): 136–73. Copyright © 1931 University of Sydney.

In Rennell, the land-man ratio seems to be excellent, and the second cause of maladjustment could easily be eliminated by making the island a strictly native reserve, so that cultures other than its own could not be impressed upon it. Here we have an opportunity to allow nature to follow its course of social evolution without outside interference and without harm to the native people or to economic values.

Rennell Island is an ideal testing ground for social theories. It is almost untouched by outside cultural forces except for the fact that iron implements have been brought in. The religion of the people, their family relationships, and their arts have remained unchanged; their sustenance is well adjusted to their physical requirements, and there is a favourable sex balance in population, commensurate with the birth-rate. By leaving these people alone as much as possible, except for health administration, I believe it may be shown that it is interference with customs, religion, marriage, the family, and property, and particularly the infiltration of new customs, which are the causes of the decline of primitive cultures and the ultimate destruction of population.

The island offers no conceivable economic advantages for the white man; its produce could be converted into profit for a trader only by robbing the people of needed sustenance. The total amount of copra and shell that could be obtained annually would not support a single trader, and the geographic location would make trade more expensive than results would warrant.

The people have a religion perfectly adjusted to their mental outlook. The basic morality of the island is proved by the favourable balance of population; general health is excellent. Any introduction of Christian missions would only be followed by social maladjustment and its attendant disasters. Isolation from western culture and the ways of the white man removes the most important and principal benefit of the missionary to such a society, that is, the people do not need the protection of the mission against the white man. No one knows how many ages it has taken to bring this primitive culture to its present bloom, and this can be destroyed permanently by white settlement, or the introduction of missions, or both, in a very short time. In most places, white culture has destroyed or obliterated native culture before the anthropologist could study it. Here we have the complete records of past ages to be read as a living page. Some one should go to Mungava and make a complete record of these people while the opportunity is available.

35

Ethnodevelopment and the Orang Asli of Malaysia: A Case Study of the Betau Settlement for Semai-Senoi

ROHINI TALALLA

The policy of "ethnodevelopment," or tribal development from within, is here proposed as an alternative to the outside development programs that so frequently destroy tribal cultures. Ethnodevelopment would allow tribal people to retain significant degrees of economic and political autonomy so they could adapt to the dominant society in their own way. Although retaining control over resources is a critical requirement for the well-being of any tribal people, adapting to an intruding dominant society is perhaps not something that everyone should be required to do. The built-in contradiction of ethnodevelopment is that tribals are forced to engage in it in response to outside interests, and thus they do not have real autonomy. Likewise, *conscientizacion*, or political mobilization, may be an important component of ethnodevelopment, but many tribal groups may be too small or dispersed effectively to use such an approach, and it may be quite incompatible with traditional cultural patterns. The Malaysian resettlement program described by Rohini Talalla for the Semai-Senoi may appear to be a culturally sensitive ethnodevelopment program, but closer analysis reveals that in the long run it is unlikely to contribute to tribal independence.

TENTATIVE GUIDELINES FOR ETHNODEVELOPMENT

Horvath and Jensen's (1976) application of the dependency and underdevelopment paradigm (Frank 1966) to an analysis of the Eskimo experience provides a characteristic profile of the historical effects of outside intervention on indigenous minorities. The effects include the growth of the materially more powerful and expansive dominant society and its encroachment on traditional territories and spatial needs; displacement from resource rich lands to marginal land at the peripheries; the destruction of traditional means of livelihood and disruption of traditional interactions with the ecological habitat; maladjustment to alien work-patterns; trade debts leading to indentured status; a decline in communal cooperation and economic redistribution as a means of collective survival; the value of goods being deter-

Reprinted with permission from *Antipode* 16, no. 2 (1984): 27–32. Copyright © 1984 Richard Peet, editor.

mined by outsiders; a decline in self-governance, through domination by a totally alien political, legal, and educational system; the deterioration of highly evolved traditional religious and cultural values; and psychological and social dislocation. In extreme cases, this pattern has included geno-cide—in nearly every case ethnocide. By these means formerly self-reliant and independent groups have become 'vulnerable societies' (van Arkadie, 1978).

There have been a few spirited responses: adaptive strategies such as urban transhumance (Wulff, 1974) and political militancy (Roberts, 1978; de Silva, 1979); and the representation of international activist organizations such as Survival International. But the most prevalent responses have been retreat, piecemeal assimilation, and apathy. The groups experience extreme poverty, dependency on welfare, social dislocation, and disintegration. In-migration to small towns or urban centers often leads to alcoholism and prostitution. The fate of these minority groups requires finding alternatives within the 'interstices of deviance' (Goulet, 1979) in the dominant social structure and system.

Ethnodevelopment is explored here as a means to this end, i.e., making indigenous minorities less vulnerable to surrounding dominant societies through programs that are culture-sensitive and produce a degree of eco-nomic, social, and political autonomy; allowing these groups to work out their own adaptations, their own forms of social, cultural, and economic synthesis. This approach is suggested as part of the normative movement toward development alternatives in Third World planning (e.g., Ghai, 1977; Friedmann, 1979a; publications of the International Foundation for Devel-opment Alternatives and of the Dag Hammarskjold Foundation).

Culturally inappropriate programs, even when well-intentioned, tend to reinforce rather than remedy patterns of dependency and underdevelop-ment (van Arkadie, 1978). A first step in reversing this trend involves over-coming Eurocentric assumptions, notions that Western development models are universal, and recognizing the viability of traditional cultures, their unique social, political, economic, and cultural practices, their per-ceptions and values (Diamond, 1960; Firth, 1965; Sahlins, 1971; Mair, 1977). These provide the cultural context for change, determining the kinds of developmental variations that might occur, and the values that will motivate change from within the community. This perspective does not uncondition-ally embrace all traditional culture, or assume that these groups are neces-sarily resistant to change, integration or assimilation. The issue is not cultural incompatibility, but how cultural bias expresses itself as economic exploitiveness and unequal access to social power. There is a need to deter-mine what kinds of adaptations and innovative social organizations are pos-sible, how they emerge, and how they settle into the social matrix of a given society. This requires a process of planning and social change which in-volves a synthesis of traditional institutions and values with exogenous influ-ences and structures.

The following are suggested as tentative guidelines for ethnodevelopment:

1. There must be autonomy of experience: groups must have time to work out conflicts and feelings of ambivalence toward change, evolving their own forms of adaptation, so that a continuity is maintained in the structure of meaning (Marris, 1975, p. 166). Change should represent their interests, preferences, special needs, and abilities, permitting them to evolve gradually and with minimum disruption into bi-culturality, full or partial integration.

2. There must be a degree of autonomy and control over resources and some development of an 'indigenous economy' (Marris, 1978). This provides a secure livelihood, renews traditions of self-reliance, reduces dependency on the dominant system, and provides a basis for development from within. It expedites access to social power through productive assets and financial resources; these provide a foundation from which to gain further bases for social power: social and political organization, social networks, appropriate knowledge and skills (Friedmann, 1979b, p. 101).

3. There must be an evolving *conscientizacion*, 'the process in which men, not as recipients, but as knowing subjects, achieve a deepening awareness both of the socio-cultural reality which shapes their lives and of their capacity to transform that reality' (Freire, 1970, p. 452). This should manifest itself as a politics of cultural identity to provide motivation and social cohesion in dealing with the dominant society, and produce concrete gains in the political arena.

4. These factors should continuously interact, yielding new adaptations, new forms of social, cultural, economic, and political synthesis. Through the gradual synthesis of indigenous and exogenous factors, indigenous minorities may experience ethnodevelopment.

This research explores these principles with reference to the Orang Asli, the Betau plan for Semai in the Tititwangsa Region in particular, and identifies some of the processes by which these effects might occur.

HISTORICAL RELATIONS BETWEEN THE ORANG ASLI AND THE DOMINANT SOCIETY

The historical relations between the dominant society and the Orang Asli can be described in terms of characteristic interactions during several periods:

1. The Sultanate governance of the States of Malaya (1400's to 1919, when British administration took complete control): the Orang Asli, living mostly in the deep jungles, had limited contact with the dominant society, though some did carry on limited trade with Malays

and later with Chinese living in remote areas. The Orang Asli were called *sakai* (Malay for slaves or dependents), and were often hunted, captured, and sold to ruling Sultans as objects of curiosity (Carey, 1976, pp. 283–288).

2. The British Colonial Period (beginning in 1786, total domination from 1919 to 1957): the Orang Asli remained largely independent. The British regarded them as uncivilized, but also romanticized them as noble savages with whom they shared some intuitive rapport. This led to an attitude of patronizing benevolence, the Orang Asli being regarded as museum pieces, to be studied and protected from the ill effects of modernity (and from slavery, the last traces of which were eliminated in the 1930's). There was no official policy or administration up to World War II. During the Japanese occupation (1942–1945) the Orang Asli had friendly relations with the Malayan People's Anti-Japanese Army, a force made up largely of Chinese Communist guerillas.

After World War II, re-establishment of the British administration was followed by the Emergency (1948–1960), a guerilla war being waged by the Malayan Communist Party (MCP). This was the turning point toward formal administration, sedentarization, planned projects and swiftly changing cultural images. The Communist insurgents elicited the help of the Orang Asli to supply food, porters, intelligence, and tribal communication networks in exchange for simple medical aid, and gestures of friendship. The Orang Asli were no longer museum pieces; they were now a security threat (Carey, 1976, pp. 288–291). In the early 1950's thousands were resettled into camps hastily built outside the jungle and surrounded by barbed wire. Over 8,000 Orang Asli died in these camps because of psychological shock, inability to adjust to removal from their normal environment, confinement, and drastic change in diet (Voon and Khoo, 1977, p. 14). But hundreds also escaped and returned to the deep jungle, seeking protection of the terrorists and collaborating more closely with them. The MCP called them *asal* (Malay for aboriginal); the British still used the term *sakai* (Carey, 1976, pp. 305–308).

In 1954 the British enacted a new policy under the Aboriginal People's Ordinance, allowing them to return to the jungles, setting up jungle forts, and offering medical aid, supplies, and airstrips for flying out the extremely ill (Short, 1975, p. 450). Gradually the British gained increasing cooperation from the Orang Asli. However, their unauthorized departures from the detention camps and their pragmatic ploys of giving both British and Terrorists false or stale information (to deter fighting in their village areas) suggest a sense of independence and a capacity for justifiable guile in dealing with outsiders (Short, 1975, p. 451). These traits are reflected in their present tendency to regard settlement schemes, including Betau, with considerable skepticism.

3. The Post-Independence Period (1957 to the present): in this pe-

riod the Orang Asli program was expanded from its Emergency beginnings (the forts, or *pos*) into formal land settlement schemes. In 1963, the same year as the establishment of Malaysia, the Department of Aboriginal Affairs was renamed in Malay (*Jabatan Hal Ehwal Orang Asli*, or JHEOA), reorganized, and given total responsibility for administration, education, medical, and economic development.

The official Statement of Policy Regarding the Administration of the Orang Asli states that the sedentarization programs and plans are intended to (a) protect national security by preventing their future collaboration with the MCP; while (b) at the same time 'integrating' them with the rest of the national community (particularly the Malay sector) through medical, educational, and economic development programs designed to restructure Orang Asli society. Integration and national security are purportedly to be achieved through 'resettlement' or 'regroupment' into permanent agriculture schemes (Ministry of Interior, 1961).

Minor experimental schemes for economic advancement of the Orang Asli have included pattern settlements (i.e., models for new Orang Asli farming villages), agricultural assistance, and animal husbandry schemes. Each pattern settlement has dwelling houses, a community hall and, in some settlements, a school, clinic, and transmitter-receiver set. Land in these projects is cleared for planting rubber, coconuts and fruit trees in an attempt to provide each family with a few acres of long-term cash crop (Voon and Khoo, 1977, p. 10).

Prior to the Tititwangsa Development Scheme (of which Betau is one project) started two years ago, these pattern settlement programs constituted the basic strategy of JHEOA's socio-economic development division. It should be noted that not all Orang Asli are involved in these programs. Some of the groups inhabiting highly inaccessible regions are allowed to live in their traditional habitats and follow their normal living routines.

Despite the outward appearance of increasingly enlightened policy regarding the Orang Asli, their development experience has close parallels with that described in regard to the Eskimos by Horvath and Jensen (1976). These effects, described earlier, resulted from innovations introduced to the Eskimos by the State (through the Royal Canadian Mounted Police), the Church (missionaries) and the Market Economy (whalers and traders), resulting in a firmly entrenched dependency and underdevelopment, rather than evolution toward an improved quality of life. There have been similar results among the Orang Asli from intervention of the State (JHEOA and the military), the Church (Islamic missionaries and educators) and the Market Economy (Malay and Chinese middlemen, plantation owners, small farm sedentarization schemes). Among the less isolated groups the economy has become clearly transitional: traditional subsistence activities, such as hunting, fishing and shifting cultivation, are continued while more remunerative activities, such as agricultural labor, mining labor, logging and the gathering of rattan or other jungle products, are pursued. A few examples evidencing increasing dependency and underdevelopment from various interventions are: decline in traditional means of production (resulting from resettlement on small farms which provide insufficient land) which has increased dependency on the JHEOA for welfare support (Sharpe, 1976, p. 82); the Orang Asli are not provided with as much credit and marketing assistance as are Malay small holders, and are thus often in debt to Malay and Chinese middlemen, lack union or legal representation in dealing with estate owners, and are therefore exploited (Sharpe, 1976, pp. 80, 101); the introduction to cash crops has created a demand for consumer goods (radios, phonographs, motorcycles, wristwatches), but communities can often only earn enough for subsistence, and their feeling of poverty is aggravated by an awareness of commodities that other ethnic groups can purchase (Tan, 1973, p. 137); at the same time, welfare, free diesel oil, and other supplies often heighten dependency and stifle initiative (Tan, 1973, p. 138); many JHEOA settlements have been deserted, the community members have returned to traditional forest habitats, and use the settlement as a mere way-station (Endicott, 1977, p. 2); crops often die because watering and fertilizing methods are unfamiliar to former swidden farmers (Endicott, 1977, p. 25); severe epidemics sometimes result during resettlement (JHEOA, 1976, pp. 25–26); some studies indicate that the general health and protein intake of non-sedentarized groups, such as some Temuan, is higher than among the sedentarized Orang Asli and even higher than the national recommended totals (Rambo, 1977, p. 18); migration to logging camps and small towns has been accompanied by a rise in alcoholism and prostitution (Means, 1978).

Further evidence of underdevelopment would include the following: the Orang Asli do not hold title to settlement or traditional lands, and land is rarely gazetted to guaranty security of occupancy—they are thus frequently displaced to make way for tin mining operations (Sharpe, 1976, p. 87) or dams (Endicott, 1977, pp. 32–34); much of the settlement land is marginal, and there is little incentive to develop it (or for the JHEOA to invest money in it) since it may be taken away at any time; some land is so remote that increased production would not pay, since markets are too far away and transportation poor (Sharpe, 1976, p. 85); statements by public officials regarding Orang Asli education raise unrealistic expectations for upward mobility of offspring, since opportunities are not commensurate with these hopes (Endicott, 1977, p. 80); conversely, parents often refuse to send children to school because they disapprove of Malay teachers preaching Islamic dietary and religious doctrines in spite of government policy requiring that the Orang Asli be free to continue their traditional beliefs (Endicott, 1977, p. 16); there is harassment from non-Orang Asli teachers and students in schools outside the villages (Ayampillar, 1976, pp. 163–165); the Orang Asli are often cheated in business dealings because they have not learned weights and measures, and they are held in low regard by many non-Orang Asli who still call them *sakai* (Jones, 1968, pp. 189–90); education is also producing young Orang Asli who are insufficiently trained to obtain employment in the modern economy, but are no longer willing to live in isolated jungle regions, and have lost interest in agriculture (Carey, 1976, pp. 334–335); the alien quality of education leads to learning problems, since they have no formal learning or written language in their tradition (Ayampillar, 1976, pp. 163–165).

There are numerous contradictions between policy, Orang Asli culture, and the realities of the dominant socio-economic structure. Policy places an independent, subsistence oriented, non-capitalistic and non-competitive, culturally distinct group of peoples into a milieu of market dependency, competition, consumerism and alien values. Forced into this new context, they are limited by lack of capital and essential skills, remote locations, discrimination of other races against them, low self-confidence and, as yet, a lack of aggressive leaders (Sharpe, 1976, p. 101). This perspective must be tempered, however, by the realization that traditional modes of life and culture have also continued among various groups: cooperation and communal sharing remains widespread, traditional modes of subsistence and jungle produce collection for cash sale are continued not only to supplement low earnings from settlement crops, but also because these modes of economic activity are preferred among certain groups (Endicott, 1977, pp. 9, 22). Moreover, in addition to continued cultural viability, there have also been successes and positive effects from JHEOA efforts. For example, the medical program has been very successful, not only in terms of delivering health care to the people but in producing a culturally hybrid system of healing in which traditional shamanistic ritual and herbal treatments are combined with western medication (thus retaining an important psychic element of traditional healing; communal support and responsibility for the sick) (Bolton, 1973, p. 1). The medical program does not impose the structural changes implicit in socio-economic and resettlement programs, and is thus less likely to create problems. But the success is nevertheless a positive effect of policy. The JHEOA structure has also inadvertently created a new communal feeling among the Orang Asli despite their widely varying cultural and linguistic traditions. This feeling is reflected in the opinion expressed by some observers that the Orang Asli thinks of himself first as a member of a particular tribe, second as a member of the aboriginal group, and only third as a Malaysian (Carey, 1976, p. 335).

THE BETAU PROJECT

The improvement of Orang Asli conditions requires new programs which will guarantee them land, a financial cushion through continuance of jungle produce collection for local markets while becoming skilled in sedentarized farming or other occupation, and some degree of protection in dealings with outsiders. This hope may find its beginnings in the Tititwangsa Development Scheme in central peninsular Malaysia (including portions of the States Pahang, Kelantan, and Perak), of which Betau is one of the 25 proposed settlements. The leverage which fostered these ostensibly improved programs stems in part from the JHEOA's concern over past failures and also from the Federal Government's increasing concern with jungle security. The case study of Betau is intended to determine what gains are being made, whether patterns of dependency and underdevelopment are diminishing or recurring and whether the project may produce some initial insights into the principles of ethnodevelopment. Horvath and Jensen (1975) would doubtless argue that the structural causes of Orang Asli underdevelopment, rooted in capitalistic market structures, make reform unlikely. But the unique role of the Orang Asli in jungle security, and the strong influence of anthropologists among the JHEOA leaders, provide levers which may produce policies to overcome at least some of the structural forces within the interstices of the dominant social order.

The group being resettled at Betau are Semai, a subgroup of the Senoi, the largest of the three main groups. The 30,000 Senoi are divided into five major groups of which the Semai and the Temuan are the most numerous (15,000 and 8,500 respectively). They are primarily hill people, living in settlements between 4,000 and 7,000 feet above sea level. Settlements are typically comprised of 50 to 200 inhabitants, and are composed of long houses usually along high ground near rivers (Idris, 1972, pp. 3–4). The traditional Semai pattern is one of politically autonomous settlements. Each village exploits a defined territory and subsists by swidden cultivation of manioc and hill rice, supplemented by hunting, fishing, gathering, and trapping. They are a nonaggressive people, with a strong aversion to interpersonal violence of any kind. Conflict resolution occurs through verbal persuasion and a talking out of the problem at communal meetings (*bcaaras*); the process is structured along complex relationships between disputants and their various cognatic kindreds (*waris*) (Robarchek, 1979, pp. 104–105). Leadership is through the traditional headman (*batin*) who leads solely by verbal persuasion (which is a deep cultural value in this group). He is assisted by the *tandir* and *juru kerah* in seeing that tasks are carried out. The shaman (*halak*) and the Semai midwives also carry social influence.

The 1159 Semai being regrouped into Betau constitute 22.8% of the total Semai in the State of Pahang. Their twenty traditional villages, each containing approximately 10 to 20 families (of approximately 5 or 6 members each), and formerly scattered within a nine-mile radius of Betau. Six of the previous villages already within the new radius have been allowed to remain in their previous locations. The economy in the Betau area is based primarily on subsistence agriculture (hill padi, maize, tapioca, banana, tobacco, vegetables). Among and within communities the exchange of food, services and commodities is by sharing or trade. The society is close-knit. In addition to farming, hunting and fishing are also employed.

It is anticipated that the 7,539-acre scheme will develop into a rural settlement with its own economic base and central facilities, linked with other Malaysian rural and urban settlements. The center presently includes a small administrative office with wireless radio communications, a small medical facility, a cooperative shop, a mosque (primarily for Moslem staff), a one room school (staffed by non-professional teachers; JHEOA Field Officers), a small guest-house, staff quarters, a community hall and open spaces for games, film screenings, and other cultural activities. There are two helipads (one for the project and the other for the Police Field Force). Even prior to the project, this area had (since the 1950's) been used as a center for meetings, entertainment, medical aid, purchase of goods, and socializing by Semai from the surrounding area.

The ideal planning guidelines include the following: the project is said to encourage the existing sense of community service, communal farming, communal ownership and self help; those dwelling in the six settlements which were not relocated are to be permitted to continue working land already developed by them ('whenever possible'); where possible, villages close to rivers will be allowed to occupy locations close to the same river within the reserve area; villages will be located so as not to lose their existing groupings; each shall retain its identity, headman, and social organization; villages will be close to their agricultural land, and near a water course; dwellings will reflect indigenous styles and groupings (but be built with timber instead of bamboo frames; and use treated bamboo for wall and floor slats); each family will have 8.5 acres with an option of 2 further acres later, plus an additional half an acre of grazing land; all land is to be owned communally by the Betau Branch Kigan Mas Cooperation, and is to be developed communally; the environment is to be conserved, logging and clearing of jungle severely limited; existing facilities at the center are to be improved and expanded; education is to be improved, with increasing emphasis on vocational training (but there is no provision for adult education); joining the scheme is wholly voluntary. The Plan acknowledges the suspicion and uncertainty felt by the Semai toward resettlement and suggests gradualism, attentiveness to their wishes, and involvement of the Semai in carrying out the Plan.

Although the Project appears to represent a considerable advance toward more culture-sensitive and self-reliant development, there are structural issues which may signify a hidden agenda of further dependency and underdevelopment that has occurred in the pattern settlements. For example, sedentarization and increasing participation in the regional market economy diminishes the remaining autonomy that traditional subsistence methods and freedom of movement provide. There is thus the possibility that the Semai may be placed at the lowest end of the regional market, living as a society of underdeveloped, lower-class, rural Malay peasants. Likewise increasing reliance on government bureaucracy for problem solving could have the same effect as it has in many of the pattern settlements: a reduction in the self-reliance that is supposedly fostered by the program, and an increasing reliance on welfare for support.

Further contradictions are raised by the two primary policy reasons for resettlement: jungle security and the integration of the Orang Asli into the mainstream society of Malaysia. First, since jungle security is the most urgent concern of the government, the benefits offered the Semai must be perceived primarily as the carrot which is to attract their cooperation; the stick is provided by the constant threat of displacement as the dominant society increasingly impinges on their territory and resource base. The notion of voluntary resettlement is therefore questionable; ultimately there is no real choice. To cooperate may be to subvert their own interests, but to ignore or subvert the project may have an even worse effect in the long run. The Semai must therefore choose between these pressures to cooperate and the desire to stay in their present surroundings, where they are not regimented and can pursue a diversified, self-generated way of life. They are distrustful of the program, yet it has persuasive benefits: it offers an ostensibly secure resource base in their shrinking territory, and the potential for more cash, consumer goods, and conveniences—which are attractive and useful, whatever their disbenefits and hidden costs. The Semai's strategic role in jungle security may provide them with some bargaining powers; but it is not clear what they are getting from the bargain. Second, the Plan restates the government policy of providing for integration (and eventual assimilation) into Malaysian society while also allowing the Semai to continue with their traditional values and way of life. This contradiction will be either through a process of integration/assimilation which destroys their culture and economic base, or through a process which allows them to evolve their own form of bi-culturality. Thus, the lessons for ethnodevelopment may derive from negative rather than from positive inference, but both tendencies are likely to be manifested.

REFERENCES

Ayampillay, S.D. (1976), "Kampung Tanjung Sepat: A Besese (Mah Meri) Community of Coastal Selangor," Report No. 6, ed. A.R. Walker, Social Anthropology Section, School of Comparative Social Sciences, Universiti Sains Malaysia, Pulau Penang.

Bolton, J.M. (1973), "A Training-Oriented Medical Programme in West Malaysian Aboriginals," *The Medical Journal of Australia*, Vol. 2:1–3.

Brokensha, P. and McGuigan, C. (1977), "Listen to the Dreaming: The Aboriginal Homelands Movement," *Australian Natural History*, Vol. 19, No. 4, Oct./Dec., pp. 118–123.

Bruyn, S.T. (1970), "The New Empiricists: The Participant Observer and Phenomenologist" and "The Methodology of Participant Observation," *Qualitative Methodology*, Filstead, W.J. (ed.), Chicago: Markham Publishing Co., pp. 283–327.

Carey, I. (1976), *Orang Asli: The Aboriginal Tribes of Peninsular Malaysia*, Kuala Lumpur. Oxford University Press.

de Silva, G.V.S., Mehta, N., Rahman, A., and Wignaraja, P. (1979), "Bhoomi Sena—A Struggle for Peoples Power," *IFDA Dossier*, March, pp. 1–16.

Diamond, S. (1960), *Primitive Views of the World*, New York: Columbia University Press.

Filstead, W.J., ed. (1970), *Qualitative Methodology*, Chicago: Markham Publishing Co.

Firth, R. (1965), *Primitive Polynesian Economy*, New York: W.W. Norton & Co.

Frank, A.G. (1966), "The Development of Underdevelopment," *Monthly Review*, Vol. XVII, pp. 17–31.

Freire, P. (1970), "The Adult Literacy Process as Cultural Action for Freedom," *Harvard Educational Review*, Vol. 40, No. 2, pp. 205–225.

Friedmann, J. (1979a), "Basic Needs, Agropolitan Development, and Planning from Below," *World Development*, Vol. 7, pp. 607–613.

——— (1979b), "Urban Poverty in Latin America," *Development Dialogue*, No. 1, pp. 98–114.

Garfinkel, H. (1968), "The Origins of the Term Ethnomethodology," in Turner, R. (ed.) *Ethnomethodology: Selected Readings*, England: Penguin Books.

Ghai, D.P. *et al.* (1977), *The Basic Needs Approach to Development: Some Issues Regarding Concepts and Methodology*, Geneva: ILO.

Goulet, D. (1979), "Development as Liberation: Policy Lessons from Case Studies," *IFDA Dossier*, January, pp. 1–17.

Horvath, R.J. and Jensen, K.D. (1976), "The Underdevelopment of the Eskimo in Canada," manuscript.

Idris, J.B. (1972), "A Brief Note on the Orang Asli of West Malaysia and their Administration," JHEOA. Ministry of National and Rural Development, Kuala Lumpur, March.

JHEOA (1976), "Proposals for the Regrouping and Socio-Economic Development of the Orang Asli in the Kemar Area of Perak."

Jones, A. (1968), "The Orang Asli: An Outline of Their Progress in Modern Malaya," *Journal of South East Asian History*, Vol. IX, No. 2. Sept., pp. 286–305.

Lonner, W.I. (1979), "Issues in Cross-Cultural Psychology," in Marsella, *et al.* (eds.), *Perspectives in Cross-Cultural Psychology*, New York: Academic Press, pp. 17–45.

Mair, L. (1977), *Primitive Government: A Study of Traditional Political Systems in Eastern Africa*, Bloomington, Indiana: Indiana University Press.

Marris, P. (1975), *Loss and Change*, New York: Anchor Books.

Morauta, L. (1979), "Indigenous Anthropology in Papua New Guinea," *Current Anthropology*, Vol. 20, No. 3, Sept. pp. 77-98.

——— (1978), "The Meaning of Slums and Patterns of Change," SAUP Paper, May.

Pelto, P. (1970), *Anthropological Research: The Structure of Inquiry*, New York: Harper & Row.

Pollner, M. (1974), "Sociological and Common Sense Models of the Labelling Process," *Ethnomethodology: Selected Readings*, Turner, R. (ed.), England: Penguin Books, pp. 27–40.

Pollner, M. and Emerson, R.M. (1978), "Ethnographic Field Work," Monograph.

Price-Williams, D.R. (1975), *Explorations in Cross-Cultural Psychology*, San Francisco: Chandler and Sharp, Inc.

Rambo, T. (1977), "Orang Asli Ecology: A Review of Research Environmental Relations of the Aborigines of Peninsular Malaysia," Paper presented at the Malaysian Society for Asian Studies Seminar on Orang Asli Ethnography, Kuala Lumpur, March.

Robarchek, C.A. (1979), "Conflict, Emotion and Abreaction: Resolution of Conflict Among the Semai Senoi," *Ethos*, Vol. 7, No. 2, Summer, pp. 104–123.

Roberts, J. (1978), *From Massacres to Mining, the Colonization of Aboriginal Australia*, London: Colonialism and Indigenous Minorities Research and Action.

Sahlins, M. (1971), "Tribal Economics," *Economic Development and Social Change*, Dalton, G. (ed.) New York: The Natural History Press.

Salamone, F.A. (1977), "The Methodological Significance of the Lying Informant," *Anthropological Quarterly*, Vol. 50, No. 3, July, pp. 117–121.

Sharpe, B.P. (1976), "Interim Report on the Economic Conditions and Prospects of the Orang Asli of Southeast Pahang," Lembaga Kemajuan Pahang Tenggara, Dec.

Short, A. (1975), *The Communist Insurrection in Malaya, 1948–1960*, London: Frederick Muller Ltd.

Smelser, N.J. (1971), "Mechanisms of Change and Adjustments to Change," *Economic Development and Social Change*, Dalton, G. (ed.), New York: Natural History Press.

Spradley, J.P. (1980), *Participant Observation*, New York: Holt, Rinehart & Winston.

Stea, D. (1979), "Native American Reservation Planning: Four Case Studies," Abstract.

——— (1980a), "Proposal for a Project to Study Adjustment of Egyptian Bedouin to Sedentary Agriculture," Prospectus.

——— (1980b), "Cultural Adjustment to New Patterns of Settlement Among the New Zealand Maori," Erickson, N. (ed.) New Zealand: UNESCO.

Tan, S.H. (1973), "Regional Planning, The Malaysian Experience: An Appraisal," paper presented to Joint Meeting of UNCRD and EAROPII Planning Commission, Nagora, Dec. 2–7.

Turner, R. (ed.) (1974), *Ethnomethodology: Selected Readings*, England: Penguin Books.

van Arkadie, B. (1978), "The Future of Vulnerable Societies," *Development and Change*, Vol. 9, pp. 161–174.

Voon, P.K. and Khoo, S.H. (1977), "A Perspective of Orang Asli Settlement and Resettlement in Peninsular Malaysia," Seminar Ethnographi Orang Asli,

Malaysian Society for Asian Studies, University of Malaya, Kuala Lumpur, Oct. 1–2.

Webb, *et al.* (1966), *Unobtrusive Measures: Nonreactive Research in the Social Sciences*, Chicago: Rand McNally & Co.

Wulff, R.M. (1974), "Industrial Transhumance and the Urban Field: The Papago Case," Paper presented for Settling Nomads, Conference on Psychological Consequences of Sedentarization, UCLA, Dec. 12–14.

---

36   A Special Sort of Pleading: Anthropology at the Service of Ethnic Groups

DAVID MAYBURY-LEWIS

In recent years many organizations have been formed to lend support to tribal peoples who are being overwhelmed by national development programs. One of the most prominent, Cultural Survival, was founded in 1972 by Harvard anthropologist David Maybury-Lewis (Ph.D. Oxford 1960), who also serves as the organization's president. Maybury-Lewis conducted extensive fieldwork among the Sherente and Shavante Indians of central Brazil beginning in 1955 when they were still independent. Over the years he was able to monitor the impact of the expanding frontier on the Indians and their reaction to it. Cultural Survival was founded for the specific purpose of helping groups like the Sherente and Shavante defend their interests and maintain themselves as successful ethnic minorities within the national society. In this selection Maybury-Lewis discusses the complex issues that face anyone who would be an advocate for the rights of tribal peoples. Advocacy of this sort is an important role, but it requires great sensitivity and involves difficult moral and political judgments. Specific examples of the advocacy stance taken by Cultural Survival demonstrate the issues at stake and the possibilities for positive intervention.

COMMON MISCONCEPTIONS

Advocacy has a distinctly dubious reputation in the United States and, I suspect, elsewhere. It conjures up images of lobbyists and lawyers and of

Reprinted with permission of the author and the publisher from *Advocacy and Anthropology*, ed. Robert Paine, 130–49. Copyright © 1985 Institute of Social and Economic Research, Memorial University of Newfoundland, St. John's.

people whose ethics leave much to be desired. So, if anthropologists are to be cast in the role of advocates, it is important to emphasize the peculiar nature of their advocacy. It has little in common with the hallowed tradition of Anglo-American jurisprudence, according to which truth emerges from the efforts of skilled pleaders who make themselves available to argue the cases of any who can afford their fees. By contrast, anthropologists normally do not possess special skills in advocacy which they can put at the disposal of the peoples they try to assist. In the case of tribal societies and underpriviledged ethnic groups, anthropologists usually try to help because of their conviction that such societies are being wronged, often with no very clear idea of how to set about righting the wrong.

The ethical stance is important. It is what impels us to get involved in this work in the first place: but it is not enough. It needs to be supplemented by a rigorous analysis of the nature of the injustices against which we inveigh and the possible strategies for fighting them. Such issues may not be part of the usual anthropological curriculum, although they are increasingly being included in it: but they are directly related to what I consider to be fundamental anthropological precepts. I shall demonstrate this by referring to data from the Americas, but the argument is applicable to other parts of the world as well.

It is well known that the original conquest of the Americas by European invaders had traumatic consequences for the autochthonous inhabitants of the New World. Many indigenous societies with low population densities were annihilated altogether. Others were driven into remote areas or survived as small pockets of population in regions dominated by aliens. The larger Indian populations of Central and Andean America were decimated, then enslaved, and survive today in a state of virtual peonage in countries which they can hardly call their own.

The conquerors offered justifications for this terrible history. They suggested at first that the indigenous peoples were perhaps not fully human. They did not possess souls. Their barbarous customs placed them beyond the pale. At the very least there were circumstances which made it legitimate to wage just wars on them and to enslave them.[1] Later the mission of conquest tended to be justified in the name of a higher civilization, which would impart peace, scientific thinking and rational institutions to the warlike and illogical natives (Merivale 1861).

These old arguments may seem preposterous, but I repeat them here in order to show their relationship to the modern versions of them that still persist in our conventional wisdom and in much contemporary theorizing. There is something like a second conquest taking place in the Americas today, powered by the world-wide search for resources. This new conquest threatens the Indians with the expropriation of their remaining lands and the total destruction of their way of life. This conquest too has its justification. It is carried out in the name of development. Indigenous peoples are thus stigmatized for clinging to a backward way of life and thereby "standing in the way of development." To the extent that they are reluctant or unable to abandon their separate identities and disappear into the mainstream of the states in which they live, they are also condemned as obstacles to nation-building and therefore to modernization. Hence, the argument runs, they should give up their archaic cultures and join the mainstream. This would not only make development much easier for all concerned but would conveniently remove "ethnic cysts" (to borrow the phrase once used by a Brazilian minister to refer to his country's Indians) from lands which they occupy and which other people covet. Meanwhile the world is assured that this doubtless regrettable disappearance of Indian cultures is inevitable and therefore should not be artificially or sentimentally delayed. This corresponds to the neo-Darwinian view which permeates the thinking of much of what we are pleased to call the developed world, according to which stronger societies are bound to extinguish weaker ones; this is coupled with the implication that there is not much that can be done about this, since it is some sort of natural law.

Such arguments are, of course, the direct descendants of those used by the conquistadors. They are self-serving justifications for the convenient use of power against the relatively powerless and they obscure the fact that indigenous cultures are not extinguished by natural laws so much as by political choices. Moreover, since such arguments make the destruction of indigenous cultures seem not only natural but even beneficial, they preempt any discussion of possible alternatives and thus contribute to the inevitability of that destruction.

Any advocacy of indigenous rights must therefore begin by countering such arguments and reopening the discussion of possible futures for indigenous cultures. We need to remember that it was seriously argued until recently that slavery was a natural part of the human condition. Scholars based their arguments on Aristotle, the Justinian codes and the writings of the French *philosophes* of the eighteenth century as they maintained that the differences in the natural endowments of individuals and races, coupled with the unavoidable differences of power in human affairs, rendered slavery inevitable.[2] We have seen this contention demonstrated as false and we no longer take seriously the nineteenth and even twentieth century arguments about the natural superiority or inferiority of certain races. Pro-indigenous advocates must work to create a similar climate of opinion in which we can look back with bemusement at the plausible falsehoods that were generally and conveniently believed by those who condemned indigenous cultures to extinction.

That is why I have elsewhere (Maybury-Lewis 1984) criticized the mesmeric fascination with which the modern world regards the nation-state. I showed that the divisive effects of ethnic attachments have been systematically over-emphasized and contrasted with the hypothetical benefits of the idealized nation-state. This is done equally by high-minded reformers trying to better the lot of the Indians and by oligarchs trying to break up their communities. The one thing that Simon Bolivar and General Pinochet have in common is the belief that Indians should abandon their traditional ways, should in effect abandon their Indianness, and become solid (preferably property-owing) citizens of their states. For quite different reasons both leaders concluded the persistence of Indian cultures was undesirable, since they weakened the state. If, however, we re-examine the role of ethnic subcultures, particularly in Third World countries, we find that allegations of ethnic divisiveness, backwardness or separatism are often used by governments as cloaks for exploitation, authoritarianism and hegemonic privilege. The cry of "One nation, indivisible" with perhaps added imprecations hurled against tribalists and separatists is all too often used as an ideological weapon against those who wish to alter the *status quo* and to share fully and equally the privileges of citizenship. This is particularly ironic, since our modern fascination with the needs of the state derives from the French revolutionary idea of the state, based on equality and fraternity. Nowadays, in many parts of the world, people are resorting to their ethnicity as a sort of civil rights movement, to achieve the equality of treatment which had previously been denied them in the name of modernization. Yet people do not cling to their cultures merely to use them as inter-ethnic strategies. They cling to them because it is through them that they make sense of the world and have a sense of themselves. We know that when people are forced to give up their culture or when they give it up too rapidly, the consequences are normally social breakdown and personal disorientation and despair. The right of a people to its own culture is therefore derived from a fundamental human need, yet it receives less protection, even in theory, than other human rights because it concerns groups rather than individuals.

The United Nations, for example, has declared its intent to protect the rights of individuals and in practice is most solicitous of the rights of states. But it skirts the issue of the rights of peoples, preferring to assume that peoples who are not part of the mainstream culture of their state should assimilate to it (Claude 1955 and Kuper 1984). There is in fact a world-wide tendency to deny the rights and sometimes even the very existence of ethnic minorities, in order to protect the nation-states. Advocacy of indigenous rights must therefore expose this tendency and develop the arguments for the desirability and viability of multi-ethnic polities.

The right of a people to its own culture is however a complex matter and insistence on it is frequently misunderstood. Let me dispose quickly of two common misunderstandings. The first of these is that the advocacy of the right of peoples to their own cultures entails a total moral and cultural relativism. Anthropologists are sometimes accused of such a relativism, according to which we are supposed to defend the right of any people to engage in any practice, however reprehensible, simply because it is "part of their culture." The charge is absurd but it serves to distract attention from the comfortable and unreasoning ethnocentrism and prejudice of those who make it. It needs therefore to be stressed that what is taken for anthropological relativism is in reality an anthropological insistence on suspending judgment on other peoples' practices; not forever, but only until those practices have been understood in their own cultural terms. This injunction sounds simple enough, but most people (and that includes the majority of the world's planners) find it extremely hard to follow. They tend to pass judgment on other cultures and their practices long before they have any understanding of them and in fact those often unthinking judgments frequently prevent understanding of other cultures in their own terms. An important part of the discipline of an anthropological training is to teach people to recognize and avoid premature judgment on other cultures. It is only where this is done systematically that we can hope to incorporate other peoples' values into our own thinking, or at least to mediate between our values and theirs. This is a critical matter when our thinking is about the life or death of their cultures. The anthropological stance then is that one does not avoid making judgments, but rather postpones them in order to make informed judgments later.

Another common misconception is that those who defend the right of a people to its own culture are arguing that other societies should remain true to their own traditions. Anthropologists are accused, for good measure, of wanting to keep traditional societies in their backward state in order to study them. The second suggestion is merely a malicious variation on the first, which implies that cultural survival is an antiquarian matter of clinging to tradition and resisting change. It is important to stress therefore that both of these perceptions are quite false. For instance, Cultural Survival, the organization of which I am president, defends the right of tribal societies and ethnic groups to maintain their own cultures, but we do not see this as a matter of maintaining folkways, but rather as a question of a society's having a say in its own affairs and its own future. Our advocacy and our projects therefore aim to create the conditions under which such societies can retain the largest measure of autonomy and power of decision over their own affairs. Ideally we believe that this is best achieved through the creation of appropriate mechanisms in multi-ethnic states. Furthermore, the advocacy of self-determination for indigenous peoples within such states is often a politically more viable strategy, for it cannot be opposed on the usual grounds that any recognition of the rights of ethnic groups leads inevitably to separatism and the undermining of the state. Nevertheless, we understand the pessimism about multi-ethnic solutions which has led many native peoples to demand that they be recognized internationally as sovereign nations. Independence and separation may be the only solution where justice is denied within the state, which is why it is particularly important to make multi-ethnic solutions work.

It is worth stressing that the sort of cultural survival for which we work is defined in the last analysis by the societies which we assist. We do not urge them to be true to their traditions; partly because such a stance would be intolerably paternalistic, but also because we assume that all societies are constantly changing and some are abandoning their traditions of their own accord. We therefore offer our help to tribal societies and ethnic groups who need it to maintain those aspects of their culture which they consider important.

This brings me at last from theory to the practicalities of advocacy in action. I make no apology for spending so much of this short paper on theoretical questions, for I am convinced that useful action must flow logically from a clear understanding of theoretical issues. Much project action, in the Americas and elsewhere, revolves around land and access to material resources. These issues are particularly acute in the Americas since it was the invading Europeans who set up the systems of law and land titling which everywhere form the basis of valid claims to land ownership. The indigenous inhabitants were outside these systems, which were then manipulated to their detriment; so that they have been engaged in a constant struggle to force or persuade their unsympathetic conquerors to grant them title to any part of the lands which they originally considered theirs.

This continues to be extremely difficult for most indigenous peoples. Although most nations in the Americas recognize in theory that their aboriginal inhabitants have some rights to land, the gap between that theoretical recognition and actual granting of title is wide and all too often permanent. Most native land claims are disputed by interests with the power to block them. Even when they are not, the process of demarcating, registering and titling lands has often proved impossible for indigenous groups to complete.

Such a situation recently posed a cruel dilemma for pro-Indian organizations in Paraguay. In the late 1970s few Indian societies in Paraguay had legal title to the lands they occupied and Paraguayan law did not recognize collective title to land, even for indigenous peoples. The two major organizations working for the Indians in Paraguay responded to this problem in different, even conflicting ways. AIP (the Paraguayan Indigenist Association) insisted that Indians had inherent rights of ownership in their lands and was lobbying to persuade the government to recognize this, by passing a law enabling Indian societies to hold lands collectively, and by putting this law into effect. Meanwhile, API (the Association of Indian Peoples) also insisted on Indian rights to land; but it had concluded that the situation of many Indian groups was so desperate that it had begun to buy lands for them from Paraguayans. AIP complained that their campaign to get the government to recognize Indian land rights was being undercut by the willingness of their sister organization to buy lands for the Indians. API responded that it was trying to help groups which would starve or disband or both if they waited for the success of AIP's strategy (see Maybury-Lewis and Howe 1980).

PROBLEMS OF LAND

Land is the key to the cultural and often even the physical survival of indigenous peoples. Tribal societies that have traditionally supplied their own wants from their own environment can be physically annihilated if forced off their land. Cast adrift, with no marketable skills, to fend for themselves in an alien society, whose language they do not speak and whose economy they do not understand, such peoples face a grim future or no future at all. It is their plight, as the nations of the Americas have stepped up their efforts to explore and exploit their own hinterlands, that has recently been arousing world-wide concern. Yet peoples who are long settled and have centuries of contact with settler society are still traumatically threatened by the prospect of losing their lands.

Such losses are a constant threat, because the indigenous society's title is usually unclear and because it is usually unable to protect its holdings against powerful interests in settler society. Meanwhile there is constant pressure on indigenous societies to break up their communal lands and to treat them as individual (and saleable) holdings. A variety of factors combine to produce this pressure. The laws of most American countries do not recognize communal land holdings or make it extremely difficult to register them. Meanwhile, even liberal reformers have traditionally thought that the individual ownership of land was the means by which indigenous peoples could modernize and join the mainstream. At the same time, those who wish to eliminate Indian societies altogether find that insistence on individual landholding is an effective way to do it and one which does not incur the opprobrium which is occasionally visited nowadays on nations that resort to genocide. So Chile's new land law, making it obligatory to subdivide the lands left to the Mapuche Indians if only one person living on them requests such subdivision, may achieve the final elimination of Mapuche society and culture which has survived incredible pressures for more than four hundred years.[3] Meanwhile, in an entirely different spirit, the Alaskan Native Claims Settlement Act, which is regarded as a reasonably generous settlement of indigenous land-claims, may have similar results. In the 1990s Alaskan native communities will legally become joint stock corporations, in which individuals who received shares at the time of the act will hold stock. This is an entirely different notion of community from the one the indigenous peoples are accustomed to and the one which most of them still live by. It is becoming clear that the majority of them have not realized the implications of what is likely to happen in ten years time when individuals can sell their stock in the 'community,' and shares in the 'community' can be bought on the open market (see Arnold 1976).

Here then is one of the critically important aspects of pro-indigenous advocacy. The advocate can help native communities to analyze not only the consequences of their own actions, but also the possible effects of processes which affect them. This is a vital matter in the negotiation of land rights. A normal and natural reaction on the part of tribal communities whose land is threatened for the first time is to insist that they should be left alone to enjoy what has traditionally been theirs. Advocacy in such a case involves helping the indigenous community realize that it is unlikely to be left alone, that it will have to fight (but not physically) for its lands and that it is unlikely to be able to hold onto all of them. At the same time it involves persuading the powers-that-be that native rights should be taken seriously and, if necessary, creating administrative or public pressure to see that this is done. In the Pichis-Palcazu area of Amazonian Peru, for example, advocacy involved persuading the Peruvian government which was sponsoring a scheme of massive colonization for the area and US AID (Agency for International Development) which was about to finance it, that the valleys were already occupied by native peoples and that the project would be a disaster. Cultural Survival took a leading role in this campaign, which ultimately succeeded in changing the original colonization scheme into the Central Selva Resource Management project. The new project is more sensibly designed to protect not only the Indian inhabitants of the area but also the local environment and the interests of the future occupants, both Indian and non-Indian, of the region as a whole. As a preliminary to the implementation of the project, survey teams were sent out and they enabled the Amuesha Indians to gain formal title to their lands for the first time. This is no more than a reprieve, however. The project as originally designed has yet to be put into effect and it is not clear whether it will be, now that the economic and political climate in Peru is becoming more and more uncertain.[4]

Ideally, native lands should be titled and guaranteed before development projects are planned for their areas but, as we have seen, the native land situation in the Americas is far from ideal. There are therefore twin strategies which should be followed by pro-Indian organizations. One is to exert constant pressure for the regularization of all native land titles. The other is to try and turn the threat posed to native peoples by development projects into an opportunity to create pressure for the protection of indigenous lands. Cultural Survival used the latter strategy when the Brazilian government asked the World Bank for a loan to improve the road system in its northwestern region and thus encourage colonization of a vast area where scores of small Indian tribes are known to live. Cultural Survival urged the bank to make the demarcation of Indian lands and the protection of their cultures a condition of the loan. In response to years of pressure the bank finally adopted, prior to the signing of the loan agreement, its own policy guidelines making it mandatory in the future to insist on guarantees for tribal peoples and ethnic minorities in areas where loans are contemplated (World Bank 1981). I believe that these are the only such guidelines at present contained in the policies of any international lending agency. Naturally the policies are only as effective as their enforcement and the preliminary reports from Brazil indicate that this leaves much to be desired, but having such policies and laws on the books is not unimportant as I shall argue in a moment.[5]

The defence of native land rights is a complex matter, even when they are not threatened by ruthless and unscrupulous interests. The view that native peoples have a dubious claim to land if other people can make better (i.e., more productive) use of it is very common in developmental circles. The moral and legal absurdity of such a view is readily exposed if one asks the earnest planner whether he or she would be willing to apply the same precepts to his or her own piece of property. Does another person have a superior claim to that property to plant vegetables on it, if the present owner manages only flowers and crab-grass? Yet governments regularly use such arguments when moving to take native lands by eminent domain. They act, they insist, for the greater good of the greatest number, to make better use of the land and they imply that it is somehow selfish of native peoples to want to sit on resources which should rightfully be distributed throughout the entire populace. Such arguments can usually be exposed as flimsy justifications for exploitation.

PROBLEMS OF DEVELOPMENT

In Brazil, for example, this type of argument has regularly been used by successive military governments, all claiming to give development the highest priority and insisting that small Indian tribes should not be allowed to stand in the way of it. The argument only holds, however, if development promotes equity and Indian peoples are obstacles to it. Yet neither contention is true. The Brazilian model of development, which was so highly touted in the sixties and seventies (though not by those of us who were working at the grass roots) is no longer regarded as a miracle. In fact it is closer to being regarded as a disaster for the entire Western banking system. This is not due to bad luck, like the rise in the price of oil, which Brazil has still been unable to find within her own capacious land, but rather to a policy which has paid insufficient attention to structural change and modernization within Brazilian society. The years of the "miracle" produced enormous profits for some but they did little to solve the problems of Northeastern Brazil (the largest pocket of poverty in the western hemisphere) or of the increasing numbers of urban poor or of the landless rural labourers. The latter are constantly moved off their patches of land in much the same way as the state has intermittently sought to move the Indians off theirs. The arguments from equity thus break down.[6] Hypothetically, such an argument could be made in other places, but it would in any case come down to a question of what compensation should be made to native peoples (or others) who are asked to give up a resource for the common good.

At the same time it is important to insist that native peoples are not inherently "obstacles to development." This is only true if 'development' is defined in such a way as to exclude their participation. There are innumerable examples to show that indigenous peoples whose land base and cultural survival are guaranteed, can make productive contributions to the local economy. Advocacy here becomes a matter of persuading the powers-that-be that this is so, and getting them to include indigenous representatives in the development planning for a given region. Cultural Survival has recently succeeded in doing this, for example, in Ecuador. There the Ecuadorian government established a commission consisting of representatives from Cultural Survival, the National Agrarian Reform Institute, the Forestry and National Parks Department, a regional development agency and 22 Indians representing three groups. The commission studied the land needs of Ecuador's most seriously threatened Indian groups, the Siona-Secoya, Cofan and Huaorani. It documented their land requirements and recommended specific borders to satisfy their needs. It also recommended that Indian lands should be titled at the borders of national parks. The Indians would have access to the parks for subsistence hunting and fishing and their lands would act as buffers to protect the parks from settler incursion. Meanwhile these newly titled Indian lands were incorporated into a large forestry development and management project (see Macdonald 1980 and in press, and Uquillas 1982).

Another dramatic example of such a project is one which I have recently been observing in Brazil. This is the project sponsored in the midst of bitter controversy by the Brazilian Indian Agency (FUNAI) and which has transformed many communities of Shavante Indians into extensive, tractor-driven rice farmers. The project was put into effect over the violent protests of the local landowners who complained to the President of the Republic that FUNAI was trying to turn the State of Mato Grosso into a vast Indian reserve. This was hyperbole, even by settler standards, considering that Mato Grosso was so large—larger than Bolivia or Colombia and only slightly smaller than Peru—that it has now been divided into two states; moreover its population is still tiny. The project was finally put into effect because the Shavante were tough enough to threaten the local landowners and force them off Indian lands and astute enough to visit Brasilia regularly to present their demands to the government. These visits also served to rally their supporters among anthropologists and the Brazilian public at large and received great publicity. The publicity reached its peak when a delegation of Shavante chiefs threatened to defenestrate the general in charge of FUNAI, and escaped reprisals since the threat was carried out with the cameras of the major TV networks waiting to record the consequences (Maybury-Lewis 1983a and 1985).

PROBLEMS OF REPRESENTATION

The Shavante affair highlights another dilemma of pro-Indian advocacy. Whom do pro-Indian advocates represent and how do they relate to the Indians who are being their own advocates? Initially of course, such advocates may not represent any more than their own consciences. They are people who are willing to speak out to denounce what they perceive as injustice. The pro-Indian commissions which were formed all over Brazil at the end of the 1970s came into existence because of the outcry raised by anthropologists over the government's proposal to "emancipate" the Indians. It was concerned anthropologists who pointed out that such emancipation would abolish the FUNAI and its tutelary role towards the Indians. It would thus do away with the legal requirement to demarcate and defend Indian lands and the agency which was supposed to carry it out. The newly "emancipated" Indians would then be able to take their chances on their own and as individuals against whichever interests happened to be threatening them in their part of the country. When these consequences were pointed out to the Indians, they themselves opposed emancipation unreservedly and, backed by the newly formed pro-Indian commissions, insisted that the government, rather than abolish FUNAI, should press it to do its job on behalf of the Indians (see Maybury-Lewis 1979 and Comissão Pro-Indio 1979).

Later the pressure and publicity generated by such commissions were instrumental in helping the Shavante gain their objectives. The campaign on behalf of the Shavante launched one of their number into national prominence. Mario Juruna, the chief of a small Shavante community, had spent years in his youth travelling and working his way around Brazil and learning the ways of the white man. He endeared himself to the Brazilian media as "the Indian with the tape recorder," because he carried around his own recording machine and insisted on recording the promises made to him and his people, so that they could not later be blandly forgotten or denied. In 1982 he was elected to Congress as the first Indian ever to become a federal deputy. Needless to say he was elected to represent Rio de Janeiro, not his native Mato Grosso, a state which is hardly ripe yet for an Indian candidacy. It is not even clear that he would have been elected in a solely Shavante constituency, if such a one were to exist. He has nevertheless become a leader who speaks for Brazilian Indians in general and is recognized by most of them as their spokesman (Maybury-Lewis 1983b).

The question of who really represents indigenous peoples has led to some confusion among those who deal with them or seek to assist them. It is of course a question which is often debated with reference to other societies as well. When the representative of a nation state speaks on behalf of its people, we know that he or she is unlikely to represent the views of all of them; but we also know how he or she came by his or her credentials and we normally have a good deal of information about which groups are represented by the official view and which groups are not. It is precisely this kind of information which is usually lacking for indigenous societies. The world at large does not normally know much about their internal politics, nor does it know whom their representatives do and do not speak for, nor how the representatives came to be chosen in the first place. Indeed, the situation is so fluid that individuals can and do appear at international gatherings and claim to represent indigenous societies, without those societies being aware that they are being so represented and in some cases without those societies even knowing the individuals who claim to represent them. Obviously this makes for considerable misunderstanding and political manipulation (see Richard Chase Smith 1982).

Even when there are no such uncertainties concerning the leaders or representatives of an indigenous group, there is no guarantee that its leadership will speak with a single voice. It is a form of naïve romanticism to believe that political disagreements do not exist among indigenous peoples or to suppose that they always achieve consensus on every issue, even though such claims are sometimes made on their behalf, especially when their way is being contrasted with the white man's way. Both the record and ordinary common sense would lead us instead to expect a certain amount of politicking in indigenous societies. One deals with this in much the same way as one does with politicking in any other society, by being as well informed as possible about the divisive issues and how people stand on them. Cultural Survival, for example, tries hard to get opinions from its own network of contacts on the politics of indigenous societies in order to discover which leaders enjoy a sufficient base of support for them to represent their peoples with some legitimacy. Where a people or a community is so badly divided that they cannot be so represented, then Cultural Survival would not normally consider collaborating with them on a project. Since all of our field projects are designed and carried out in collaboration with the people they are intended to help, this means in effect that we would not consider a project to assist these people until the political situation was clarified.

PROBLEMS OF DISAGREEMENT

A more difficult question is what to do when the indigenous society and its recognized leaders insist on pursuing a course of action which we, as advocates, believe to be disastrous. Let me give two examples to illustrate this sort of dilemma. In southern Brazil an Indian society was offered what seemed to them to be a vast sum of money by lumber companies in return for the right to cut down trees on Indian land. The Indians, who had no idea of the ecological devastation which uncontrolled lumbering can cause, felt that they were being offered a small fortune for the depletion of an essentially inexhaustible resource. They were anxious to accept. Anthropologists from the University of Santa Catarina, who have been very active in the pro-Indian cause, tried hard to dissuade them. In the meantime they also worked to prevent the start of the lumbering operation. Eventually however they failed to convince the Indians, abandoned their active opposition to the lumbering project and withdrew as advisers to these particular Indians. It seems to me that this was the correct thing to do. The lumbering project was being carried out with the informed consent of the Indians and the anthropologists had done what they could to make the harmful consequences of it known to the people it was going to harm. It would have been the worst sort of paternalism to try to prevent the project from being put into effect over the wishes of the Indians themselves.

Even more difficult is the issue of what to do when indigenous leaders espouse what we consider to be the harmful rhetoric of settler society. Mario Juruna, the Shavante deputy in the Brazilian congress, learned for example that Brazilian farmers could raise money by mortgaging their land. He therefore argued at one time that Indians should be allowed to do the same. They are normally unable to do so because their land (when it is legally theirs at all) is held in trust for their communities by FUNAI. Juruna wanted the government to get off the backs of the Indians by making it possible for them to own their own land individually and to do what they like with it. Here again there is only one course of action open to an advocate who believes, as I do, that such a policy would be disastrous for the Indians. That is to try and persuade both Juruna himself and the Indians in general of the reasons why this is so and to encourage them to support a different point of view. This may not be so difficult. I have heard many Indian leaders lecture me eloquently about their people's attitude to land as a common and sacred good and their revulsion against the white man's insistence on treating it as a commodity that may be individually owned, bought and sold. The Mapuche, for example, are desperately aware of what individual land holding is likely to do to their way of life and have requested help to try and hold their society together in what they see as a last do or die effort. Yet if it came to the point that an Indian people was fully aware of the likely consequences of dividing up the land and still wanted to do it, then it should have the right to do so.

ADVOCACY IN A SUPPORTING ROLE

It follows from this that I see no particular problem posed for pro-Indian groups by the fact that Indians are increasingly doing their own advocacy. On the contrary, it should be the desired aim of such groups to assist indigenous peoples to conduct their own advocacy. The form of this assistance will change as a function of the relations between the Indians being assisted and the outside world. A tribal society which has had little contact with settler society needs advocates to speak for it in the nation at large. It also needs people who are able to help its members understand the national and regional forces with which it must henceforward cope. Eventually, one hopes, such a society will be able to negotiate on its own behalf or at least to join with others in indigenous associations which can do such negotiating. Even at this stage, however, indigenous associations which speak for their own people can be well served by friendly advocates in the world at large. Such advocates can provide them with expertise which it is difficult and unnecessary for them to acquire on their own. Cultural Survival can, for example, document what happens to Indian societies whose land is divided into individually owned parcels and make this information available to the Indians themselves. We can tell Indians in Brazil about the techniques used in successful projects that have benefitted Indians in, say, Ecuador. We can put Indian societies in touch with each other both at a national and international level. Above all, indigenous advocacy normally depends for its success on a favourable or at least not resolutely hostile climate of opinion in the country concerned. The role of national and international advocates of the indigenous cause, in creating this climate and keeping up the pressure to maintain it, should not be underestimated.

This brings me back to the point I made earlier about the importance of good laws and policies, even when they are ineffectively enforced. Settler societies are everywhere unscrupulous about the rights of the autochthonous peoples whom they dispossess. The frontiersmen and their supporters in the metropolis can always be relied upon to be resolutely anti-Indian or anti any other native people. It is when these elements receive the wholehearted support of the metropolis that indigenous peoples suffer most. It is no accident that the tribal Indians of Brazil suffered most acutely in the late sixties, at a time when the military regime in power was at its most repressive and was insisting on development without regard to human costs. When liberal elements gain a hearing in the metropolis, they are unlikely ever to eliminate the anti-Indian factions and are certainly unlikely to change the minds of the frontiersmen. But they can and do provide a counterweight to the sentiments of the frontiersmen, and it is this tension that provides indigenous peoples with the opportunity to have their rights respected and to establish themselves in the wider society. It is thus critical to keep up the pressure for good laws. They represent the conscience of the society and can thus be appealed to when they are not being properly enforced. The link between good laws and effective enforcement has to be the focus of advocacy efforts on behalf of indigenous peoples.

UNUSUAL ADVOCACY: ORDINARY ANTHROPOLOGY

I hope these comments have served to show that although work on behalf of tribal peoples and ethnic groups may be a peculiar form of advocacy it is not a very strange sort of anthropology. It only seems strange at times because it abandons old anthropological habits that were once so much part of anthropological practice that they acquired ritual, if not actually canonical status. Anthropologists used to see themselves as lone scientists who dissected exotic cultures and presented the truth of their systems to a scholarly audience. They now know that they are not alone in their work, that the truth of another culture is never monolithic, that better and better approximations to it emerge from rigorous analysis and vigorous debate, in which the members of the cultures studied increasingly participate. Anthropologists used to think that advocacy was "unscientific" and would undermine their scholarly credibility. Many of us now believe that it is precisely the most rigorous anthropological analysis which impels us toward advocacy and provides us with the tools to engage in it. Indeed the credibility of anthropologists and their work in many parts of the world is nowadays more threatened by an unwillingness to engage in any form of advocacy than the reverse.

The kind of advocacy discussed in this paper requires the classic skills of anthropology. It requires the ability to suspend judgment while analyzing societies very unlike our own. It also requires the ability to study our own society (or other "modern industrial societies") with a detachment similar to that we strive for in studying the exotic. It requires the ability to analyze national policies, developmental ideologies and the workings of bureaucracies with a detachment that enables us to see beyond their familiar obfuscations and self-deceptions. It then requires the advocate to combine these analyses dialectically in order to understand and eventually influence the complex processes which affect underprivileged ethnic groups. The rest is politics and the extent to which the advocate is willing or effectively able to get involved in that depends very much on temperament, circumstance and opportunity. Even at the political stage of advocacy an anthropological training is not a bad preparation, though an anthropological temperament may well be. Above all, this type of advocacy is intimately related to what I consider to be perhaps the most important impulse behind anthropology itself—the interest in social theory and moral philosophy. Boas and Durkheim, to mention the apical ancestors of what used to be thought of as the American and British styles of anthropology, did not devote themselves to their professions just to do science. This misreading of their efforts was a distortion introduced by their disciples; one that reduced anthropology to a kind of functionalist trick which was soon proclaimed not to work. In fact, Boas and Durkheim, while extremely concerned that their work should be properly scientific, both felt strongly that they were engaged in researches which would help to improve the human conditions. They practised, as Boas once put it, "science in the service of a higher tolerance." Boas devoted his science to the fight against racism. We could do worse than to devote ours to the battle against ethnocentrism in the struggle to shape a world where people can live together in multi-ethnic societies on the basis of mutual tolerance and respect.

NOTES

1. See Hanke 1959 for a discussion of the famous debates on these issues at the Spanish court between Las Casas and Sepulveda.

2. For a discussion of these ideas, see D. B. Davis 1966.

3. See the report of the Interchurch Committee on Human Rights in Latin America (1980) and Barreiro and Wright (1982:60–63).

4. See Cultural Survival 1981a and Richard Chase Smith 1979, 1982.

5. For a discussion of the World Bank project in northwestern Brazil, see Cultural Survival 1981b.

6. There is voluminous literature on the Brazilian "miracle," but especially relevant to the points made here are Furtado 1982, Fishlow 1973, Foweraker 1981 and Velho 1976.

REFERENCES

Barreiro, Jose and Robin Wright (eds.). 1982. *Native Peoples in Struggle: Russell Tribunal and Other International Forums*. Boston: Anthropology Resource Center, Inc.

Cultural Survival. 1981a. "Development Planning in Peru's Amazon—the Palcazu." *Cultural Survival Newsletter*. 5(3).

———. 1981b. *In the Path of Polonoroeste: Endangered Peoples of Western Brazil*. Cambridge: Cultural Survival Occasional Paper No. 6.

Davis, David Brion. 1966. *The Problem of Slavery in Western Culture*. Ithaca: Cornell University Press.

Fishlow, Albert. 1973. "Some Reflections on Post-1964 Brazilian Economic Policy." In Alfred Stepan (ed.), *Authoritarian Brazil*. New Haven: Yale University Press.

Foweraker, Joe. 1981. *The Struggle for Land: A Political Economy of the Pioneer Frontier in Brazil from 1930 to the Present Day*. Cambridge: Cambridge Latin American Studies No. 39.

Furtado, Celso. 1982. *Analise do "Modelo" Brasileiro*. Rio de Janeiro: Civilizaçao Brasileira.

Hanke, Lewis. 1959. *Aristotle and the American Indians: A Study in Race Prejudice in the Modern World*. Bloomington: University of Indiana Press.

Interchurch Committee on Human Rights in Latin America. 1980. *Mapuches: People of the Land*. Toronto: ICCHRLA.

Smith, Richard Chase. 1979. *The Multinational Squeeze on the Amuesha People of Central Peru*. Copenhagen: International Work Group for Indigenous Affairs. Document No. 35.

———. 1982. *The Dialectics of Domination in Peru: Native Communities and the Myth of the Vast Amazonian Emptiness*. Cambridge: Cultural Survival Occasional Paper No. 8.

Velho, Otavio. 1976. *Capitalismo Autoritário e Campesinato*. São Paulo, Brazil: DIFEL.

37

Tribal Peoples and Economic Development: The Human Ecological Dimension

ROBERT GOODLAND

The rising political awareness of tribal peoples and the energetic efforts of the support organizations have made it difficult for development agencies to ignore the legitimate interests of tribal people. As noted earlier (Drucker, part V), World Bank–supported Philippine hydroelectric projects encountered major tribal resistance, and parts of the program had to be abandoned at great expense. No doubt in response to such problems, the World Bank in 1982 issued a background paper by Robert Goodland on tribal peoples and development. This selection is a synopsis of that paper. It clearly acknowledges the serious threat to tribal welfare imposed by development projects and recommends positive action along the lines of a "cultural autonomy" approach. The emphasis on protection of tribal land and resources and on the right of tribal peoples to set their own development objectives are certainly appropriate. However, "cultural autonomy" as defined here stresses "ethnicity" rather than tribal political independence and appears to be a temporary objective. The possibility that there may be serious incompatibilities between national development objectives and the interests of tribal peoples receives little attention. The emphasis is still on tribals' adjusting to the intruders. Although the maintenance of a modified "traditional way of life" is seen as desirable, there is little attempt to specify what unique features of tribal culture might be indispensable.

Goodland is an ecologist for the World Bank Office of Scientific and Environmental Affairs. He has previously researched the impact of development projects in Brazil, and together with H.S. Irwin in 1975 he published *Amazon Jungle: Green Hell to Red Desert?*, which examined the environmental impact of the Trans-Amazon Highway.

It is estimated that, at present, there are approximately 200 million tribal people, roughly 4% of the global population. They are found in all regions of the world and number among the poorest of the poor. Development projects, assisted by the World Bank, are increasingly

Reprinted with permission from *Culture and Conservation: The Human Dimension in Environmental Planning*, ed. Jeffrey A. McNeely and David Pitt, 13–31. Copyright © 1985 International Union for Conservation of Nature and Natural Resources. Condensed from *Tribal Peoples and Economic Development: Human Ecological Considerations* by Robert Goodland. Copyright © 1982 The International Bank for Reconstruction and Development/The World Bank. The views and interpretations presented in this article are the author's and do not necessarily reflect the policy of the World Bank.

directed to remote, marginal areas of the rural environment and, without special precautions, will affect these peoples. It is frequently difficult to anticipate the nature and dimension of the impact that a development project may have on tribal people living in these areas, especially when this is their first contact with the dominant society. Without precautions, the ensuing acculturation process proves prejudicial to such people. Until relatively recently, development planning had not adequately addressed the human, economic, and social aspects of the acculturation process.

Certain basic needs must be acknowledged and accommodated if tribal groups are to benefit from—rather than being harmed by—development projects. These fundamental needs are equally important, and each must be met for continued physical, socioeconomic, and cultural survival in the face of development.

INTRODUCTION: FUNDAMENTAL NEEDS

The four fundamental needs of tribal societies relate to autonomy and participation, to conditions that will maintain their culture and their ethnic identity to the extent they desire: (a) recognition of territorial rights, (b) protection from introduced disease, (c) time to adapt to the national society, and (d) self-determination. Clearly, freedom of choice is worthless without understanding the implications of the given alternatives and the ability to choose between them. That is why tribal people must be allowed time to make their own adjustments at their own pace, and must be given the opportunity to learn about the wider society and to gain a place for themselves within it.

The needs of tribal groups, outlined in this chapter, differ critically from those of other rural and urban populations for whom Bank-assisted projects are usually designed, and from the experience of most development and project planners. Further, social needs differ also among tribal groups themselves. For this reason, each project affecting such peoples must be designed to meet the specific needs of the tribal groups within or near the project area.

EFFECTS OF CONTACT

Particular problems occur and needs are evident in cases of uncontacted tribal groups. While there are only a few such groups remaining in the world today, special action is necessary if they are in the area of influence of any project considered by the Bank. These special measures do not apply to the more acculturated peoples who are more frequently affected by development projects. The contacting process, also known euphemistically as "pacification" or "attraction," poses serious risks for the survival of such tribal groups. In some cases, their physical flight from a contact team can so disrupt the normal economic and social life of the group as to leave them underfed, weakened both physically and psychologically, and highly vulnerable to disease particularly when newly introduced to different circumstances. Whether or not actual flight occurs, the risk from introduced disease is common and serious. This is in part because of the special difficulties of implementing preventive or curative health services for a group unaccustomed to such outside attention.

This situation becomes especially critical when the newly contacted group is brought into more or less immediate contact with nationals in addition to the original contact team. Records from various parts of the world document severe and rapid depopulation as an immediate, though not always direct, consequence of contact. Examples of this are the Kreenakrore, Surui, and Parakanan Amerindian groups in Brazil (Dostal, 1972; Seeger, 1981), all contacted in the last twenty years; the Semang and Sakai in Malaysia; the Andaman Islanders and the Todas and Kathodis in India; the Pygmies in Zaire; and the Igorottes in the Philippines. In fact, contact has inevitably resulted in a considerable loss of life among the tribal group involved. A number of precautions must, therefore, be taken if this risk is at least to be held to a minimum and appropriate procedures must be tailored to each specific case.

LAND

The first and fundamental need for tribal survival and cultural viability is continued habitation in and use of the traditional land areas. The tribe's economic resource management, socio-political organization, and belief systems are tightly woven into the particular land areas inhabited and used to obtain and produce all necessities. The members of a tribe are intimately familiar with locations of different game animals and their habits, as well as the vegetation within the traditional range. Maintaining the traditional land-based patterns of environmental adaptation is essential to the perpetuation of most aspects of the tribal way of life.

Large Land Areas

Tribal lands include not only areas which are obviously inhabited at a given time, but others that may be used or occupied only intermittently in supra-annual cycles. Hunter-gatherers—the Kalahari in Southern Africa and Australian Bushmen, for example—range over wide areas and exploit them systematically (Maybury-Lewis, 1968). Pastoralists, such as the Masai in Kenya and Tanzania, the Fulani in Nigeria, the Bedouins of Cyrenaica in north-eastern Libya, the Shah Saran of Iran, and the Gujjars of north-western India, require large areas of land which may seem to the casual visitor to be unoccupied. Shifting agriculturalists, like the Kalinga of the Philippines, also leave large fallow areas to recuperate before replanting.

To the extent that tribal groups inhabit marginal areas, much larger land areas may be required to support the population than would be the case in more fertile regions. When common shifting-agriculture methods are used, new areas are needed for clearance every two to five years when weeds encroach and yields decline. This method of tropical forest land use does not damage the environment when practised by an appropriate number of people, since exhausted soils have time to recuperate while other tracts are planted. The isolation and small size of the cleared areas avoid excessive erosion and accelerate regrowth of forest. Tribal societies practising such systems have traditionally developed population control which enables the society to stay within the techno-environmental carrying capacity of the land.

Tribal people have the knowledge to select more fertile areas and avoid less productive soils. Nontribal settlers without sophisticated agricultural extension lack such selective ability.

Inter-tribal exchanges are often carried out over long distances. Tribal people may travel weeks or even months on hunting or trading expeditions. Limitations on such routes used for such necessary travel and for transhumance will damage tribal viability.

Modern legal concepts of "private" property are inapplicable to tribal land-use patterns, since land is owned in common and parcels of land are used intermittently. The solution of corporate ownership is outlined later in this chapter. Governments have often acquired lands used by tribal people on the assumption that they were uninhabited wasteland. In the process, they have often disrupted the larger human-land equilibrium systems evolved by the tribal cultures (Bodley, 1975). When land-use patterns are radically altered, traditional tribal economic and social organizations, authority, and belief systems are inevitably impaired.

Symbolic Value of Land

Along with economic significance, the traditional land base holds important symbolic and emotional meaning for tribal people. It is the repository for ancestral remains, group origin sites, and other sacred features closely linked to tribal economic systems.

> The Kalinga and Bontoc tribes in the Philippines completely identify with their physical environment. They are part of a complex and well-balanced ecosystem. Their economic and social life is based on the old hand-built rice paddy terraces formed out of the steep mountain slopes along the Chico River. The economic forces tying people to their land also tie them to their traditions because the attachment to the land is more than economic and organizational. The particular land areas were constructed by their ancestors and are, they believe, where the sacred spirits dwell.

The relocation changes that now confront these Philippine tribal people are more devastating than changes in the sixteenth century when nomadic slash-and-burn farmers transformed themselves into settled rice cultivators.

Then, they were still able to inhabit lands that were the centre of their life, continuing their self-sufficiency. Now, they are under pressure to relinquish the territorial foundations that have been the basis of their cultural and economic survival (S.E. Asia Resource Center, 1979; Rocamore, 1975).

Similarly in Brazil, attempts by the National Indian Foundation (FUNAI) to transfer the Nambiquara out of the Guapore valley into an inappropriate reserve generally resulted in failure. The Nambiquara refusal to move involved not only the natural resource scarcity in the new area, which was savanna rather than forest, but also the fact that they would lose touch with the land where their dead had been buried (Price, 1977a).

Legalization of Tribal Land Rights

Land rights, access to traditional lands, and maintenance of transhumant routes are vital to the economic, social, and psychological well-being of individual tribal members, as well as for the maintenance of the group's cultural stability. Those national governments that are signatory to the UN charter and require Bank assistance can be guided by the UN Declaration of Human Rights, 1948 (Annexes 3 and 4) on tribal issues and land title. This is often difficult to accomplish because most tribal peoples hold land in common, demarcated only in the perception of their members. Land is regarded as a common good, to which individuals have rights of use, but which cannot be alienated. The tenure is in the nature of a trust in which all members—dead, living, and unborn—are co-sharers. Communal title, or group tenure, may need legislative innovation on the part of a nation; such innovations are neither unknown nor especially difficult. The Bank can discuss tribal policies with governments, which would act to implement agreed policies.

In India, the concept of Hindu joint family property, where each male member of a joint family had a fluctuating share in the property (and this included conceived, yet unborn, males) closely approximates the concept of communal tenure. This system has been recognized in law for several centuries and now has been incorporated into "modern" law. In 1946, it was proposed that group tenure in the U.S. Trust Territory of the Pacific Islands be recognized and controlled as a trust, by a Land Control Board. Similarly in Fiji, "native land" has been successfully controlled by the Native Land Trust Board. The exercise has provided a remarkable example of the careful use of tribal lands to promote development. As in the case of communal tenure among other tribal populations, native land in Fiji cannot be alienated; only limited leases can be created with the approval of the Board.

Further, many transhumant migrations are regular, their routes are well-defined and can be demarcated. It should not, therefore, be difficult to grant these tribal people rights of way or easements recognized by law. In most countries, rights of way resulting from continuous use are part of the general law available to all persons. These rights cover both private and public use of lands.

Creation of Reserves

In some cases, the creation of a tribal reserve may be the most feasible means of protecting a tribal group whose culture is endangered by national intrusion, or by a development project, mainly in order to provide time necessary for adaptation. Reserve creation may be vital for tribes in the early first and second phases of integration, and in special cases for societies in the third phase. Such a reserve should function as a secure base, providing the tribe with time and space to make its own adaptations; not a prison in which the tribe is confined. In many cases, land held in reserve status could quite simply be transformed into title held communally by the tribe or, in the early stages of contact, in trust by the national government. Most countries lack such legislative mechanisms, although they are not difficult to draw up. This is the spirit of the Peruvian law of Native Peoples, 1974. Recently contacted tribal groups, when their lands are protected as reserves, can receive some medical attention for introduced disease and some protection against encroachment by outsiders. In Brazil, the living conditions of tribal people on reserves are generally better than among those which have lost their lands. Health benefits, however meagre, derived from the establishment of reserves are critical to the physical well-being of tribal groups (Ramos, 1976a). Although the reserve becomes less necessary as the tribal society becomes able to tolerate or withstand the pressures of the national society, title to their lands remains fundamental.

A major drawback to the establishment of reserves is tribal exposé to the national authorities who, usually out of ignorance, may encourage or enforce possibly well-intentioned, though often detrimental, modifications to traditional practices. Disruption occurs when a government removes a tribe to a new area in order to resettle it on a reserve and then administers that reserve. The ecological setting is usually quite different on the reservation, movement is usually restricted, and nomadic groups are suddenly forced to become sedentary. Religious and cultural practices are usually modified. Even the type of crops planted may be determined beforehand by government representatives. The procedures for involuntary resettlement formulated by the Bank will alleviate these problems (see Appendix 1).

Enforced "primitivism" is also a disruptive policy occasionally practised on a reservation. This policy is often followed either to promote tourism, since "primitive" costumes, houses, and crafts are tourist attractions, or it is defended as a means of preserving the tribe's cultural identity. However, whereas enforced "primitivism" is always damaging, elective "primitivism" can be beneficial as in the case of the Cunas of Panama. Minority culture has never been a static entity which must be preserved exactly as it is found or as it is believed to have been. Rather it is a dynamic reality that should be provided with conditions adequate for development in a natural and progressive manner. Cultural continuity should be encouraged in all spheres, but the choice of whether to continue to modify old ways should be left to the tribal people themselves and not imposed upon them. Two examples of enforced "primitivism" are:

On the Matigsalug reservation in the Simod area of Bukidnon on Mindanao (Philippines) the Monobos are required to wear tribal costumes and build tulugan tribal houses without the use of nails.

The Higaunons in the Salug reservation in Agusan, Mindanao, had to consent to the bulldozing of their substantial houses, some made of concrete blocks, to qualify for assistance from the Office of the Presidential Assistant on National Minorities (PANAMIN) (Rocamora, 1979).

The reservation system easily accommodates these practices and systems of exploited labour, as the reservation is usually located in a remote area and its inhabitants have little legal recourse or representation at higher political levels. The administration of the reservation represents the government and enforces government policy; it may not be inclined, or even able, to respond to the interests of the inhabitants. If the tribal group has no channel through which to articulate its rights and needs, abuses are likely to occur. The major problem with the creation of reserves is that, as currently practised, control of the tribe and its lands is transferred to outsiders—be they government administrators or a specially appointed group. The role these administrators generally play is one of pacification, the resolution of disputes within the tribe, and the partial prevention of contact with the national society. Few administrators have readily moved from a traditional "law and order" concept of their role to one that is more development oriented. In these circumstances, the socio-economic gap widens between the tribe and the nationals. Bank emphasis on strengthening the tribal agency and tribal administrators in member governments is more appropriate than for the Bank to assume a leading role in tribal affairs.

The most successful means by which a reservation could form the basis of tribal development is, first, and as early as possible, to leave the governance of the tribe and its resources to the tribe itself as it was before the reserve was created. Second, administrators should act as facilitators, bringing to the tribe the protection, benefits, or specially designed education and health programmes it may request. Third, the administrators, and eventually the tribal leaders, should have the power to defend tribal lands against incursions by outsiders. It is only when tribal people are accorded equality under the law (either as individuals, families, or larger groupings—legal recognition of "pastoralist groups" was deemed an essential precondition to implementation of Bank-assisted livestock projects in Chad and Niger) and have the capability to choose their own destiny that they can contribute fully to the national society. All this will be difficult and time-consuming, and not amenable to acceleration. Tribal representatives capable of dealing with administrators, nationals, and the government, as well as with communal title are pivotal to survival. Though examples are few, it can be done: the

Gavioes in Amazonia (Brazil) requested the tribal agent to operate only outside the reservation gates in one year, bought and managed their own truck the next, and started hiring non-tribal day labourers the following year.

HEALTH

After recognition of title to land, the maintenance and protection of health standards is the second fundamental prerequisite to the tribe's survival (except in the rare cases of "first contact," in which health measures are initially most urgent). The process of development can so disrupt life that new and old health and disease problems develop. In normal circumstances, an individual can interact with disease-carrying agents without suffering ill effects. Health is a continuing property that can be measured by the individual's ability to rally from a wide range and amplitude of changes or disruption.

Indigenous medicine in tribal areas has usually controlled endemic diseases and met the needs of the tribal society in its traditional habitat. Therefore, the object of health measures within the context of development is to foster existing therapies, to introduce appropriate new repertoires, and to avoid the introduction of unfamiliar diseases and conditions that might disrupt existing standards of health. Three major factors impair indigenous health: first, transmission of disease; second, modification of diet and living conditions; and third, social change and stress. These factors disrupt the normal levels of community health of the tribal people compared with neighbouring peasants, as well as lower resistance and increase vulnerability to disease.

Introduction of Disease

First, health is jeopardized by the introduction, usually accidental, of diseases to which the tribal people have had little or no exposure, either individually or throughout the tribe's genetic history. In such exceptionally homozygous populations, severe and often fatal reactions to pathogens which are innocuous to the national society must be anticipated. The literature on tribal groups is filled with accounts of contracted illnesses and frequent deaths due to contact with outsiders. In fact, the staggering population losses among Amerindians in Brazil after the intrusion of European settlers—from 230 tribes in 1900 to about half that in 1980—were caused more by disease and starvation, than by conflict.

> In 1500, there were an estimated 6 million to 9 million Amerindians in Brazil. Today barely 200,000 survive—an attrition rate of two million people per century.
> In the 1930s, there were between 2,000 and 3,000 Nambiquara of the Guapore valley in Mato Grosso, Brazil. In the late 1960s, a road (Cuiaba-Porto Velho) cut through their territory and large-scale cattle

ranching operations were established. By 1972, more than 20 agribusiness projects were promoted in the region by fiscal incentives from SUDAM (Superintendency for the Development of Amazonia). Diseases almost completely exterminated the Nambiquara to the point that, in two of the Guapore valley groups, the entire population younger than 15 years was killed by influenza and measles (Ramos, 1979; Ribeiro, 1956).

Since disease can be transferred to the tribal group by any interchange with outsiders—such as project labourers and the use of their water, food, supplies, or clothing, or by other tribes who have been exposed to pathogens—protection or isolation is essential until a massive vaccination campaign can be implemented. Medical screening of all project workers is, therefore, imperative.

Alterations in Diet and Living Conditions

Clearly, health is significantly affected by diet and, particularly, by sudden changes in it. Frequently, tribal peoples are compelled to adjust to sharp dietary changes. This adaptation is often due to loss of land, with consequent changes in the traditional manner of its exploitation; to relocation to a different environment and, therefore, alterations in food availability; to an increase in wage or debt-bondage labour resulting in inadequate time to work their own lands; or to higher purchases of manufactured or processed foods. The changes are accompanied by malnutrition, dental decay, and lowered resistance to disease (particularly measles, for which no immunity has been developed, and the heightened action of malarial and other parasites). Caries and other dental abnormalities are conspicuously absent or rare among tribal people who have retained traditional diets (Bodley, 1975). Dietary changes also result from the disruption of traditional trade systems and routes.

> In the late 1950s and early 1960s, an increase in endemic cretinism, a birth defect, was noted among the people of the Jimi valley in Papua New Guinea. The first cases of endemic cretinism began to appear shortly after contact with government patrols, and the incidence of the disease increased rapidly with more contact.
> Investigations revealed that early government patrols rewarded with salt (deficient in elemental iodine) all services rendered by the indigenous inhabitants. The precontact era salt traded into the Jimi valley by neighbouring indigenous groups was a distillate extremely rich in iodine. Contact had disrupted the efficient trading arrangements. The deprivation of a significant iodine supplement manifested itself by the appearance of cases of endemic cretinism.

Contact with dominant groups also results in dietary damage among tribal people who desire to imitate the food habits of the dominant group and, thereby, seek to enhance their own status within the wider society.

Before the dominance of the more Hinduized groups in Nepal, tribal groups like the Kamang, Magar, and Sherpa consumed meat. Today, increasing numbers of these tribes are giving up meat with the result that their present diets do not provide the nutritional balance they formerly enjoyed. Further, as a result of the growing reluctance to slaughter animals, the number of livestock has far exceeded the carrying capacity of the land, which is fast deteriorating.

Whether the result of relocation or willing adoption of new modes of life, sudden change is usually detrimental to health. For example, influenza swept the Pacific Islands after the islanders were compelled to adopt clothes on the grounds of modesty. Clothes were worn, but no advice was tendered that they had to be changed and washed regularly. Colds and influenza were the consequence. Again, in relocation, tribal houses have been constructed to provide accommodation only for nuclear families (as in the unsuccessful attempt to settle the Shah Sevan of Iran), or they have been constructed of brick and mortar with galvanized metal roofs, as in Africa. Many tribal people do not live in nuclear families, but rather in extended families; and bricks and mortar do not provide acceptable living conditions. Breaking up families and providing unacceptable living conditions impair adjustment and lower resistance to disease.

The diet and health aspects of relocation have been recognized by the Bank, although until recently this was limited to involuntary relocation. These principles are now applied whenever tribal peoples are affected, whether or not there is relocation involved. Education in nutrition for both tribal people and nationals who are in regular contact with them is desirable.

Social Change

While all change involves some degree of social disruption, rapid change increases social tension and, ultimately, vulnerability to disease and emotional disorders, antisocial behaviour, and alcoholism. While societies are dynamic, the capacity to adapt to change is not infinite, especially in the case of tribal populations. The social resources that help tribal members manage and cope with change are limited. Unfamiliar concepts, values, and roles impose additional demands on the coping process of the tribal society. Unless introduced carefully, recognizing the absorptive capacity of the population, sudden demands decrease the capacity to adapt successfully. Major and rapid social changes are associated with:

1. Loss of self-esteem
2. Increase in actual and perceived role conflict and ambiguity
3. Increase in the perceived gap between aspiration and achievement

Loss of self-esteem   A tribal population confronted with development or modernization often experiences loss of self-esteem; its members feel a deprivation of their sense of personal worth and a devaluation of their social identity. Loss of self-esteem may result from explicit critical or negative evaluations of the tribal culture by the agents of change or members of the dominant society. Belittling the tribal population as ignorant, dirty, or backward is common, and may even be used to encourage the tribal society to change. Development itself may be phrased in terms that implicitly, if not explicitly, devalues the tribal culture and its members. Tribal traditions and knowledge are stigmatized and simply replaced by the dominant culture. Seldom are traditional tribal values acknowledged or are attempts made to perpetuate them.

Increased role conflict and ambiguity Rapid social change introduces new individual or group roles and modifies old ones. These modifications increase role conflict and ambiguity, which further erode the self-esteem and social identity of an individual or group. For example, people in a hunting and gathering society are trained to be independent and opportunistic, and to use initiative. These qualities become disadvantages when such people are forced to offer themselves as dependent and obedient wage or debt-bondage labourers. Tribal leaders suddenly find that their value has been downgraded and their power is usurped by the arrival of an appointed official or by the appointment of a new non-traditional tribal leader by nationals. From the position of managers, leaders are reduced to servants. This is traumatic for them personally but even more so for the people who benefited from or depended on their leadership. Even such fundamental matters as the relationship between the sexes may be radically altered.

The Nivakle in the Paraguayan Chaco adapted to settler intrusion into their traditional lands by raising their own herds of cattle, sheep, and goats. Mennonite settlers in the Central Chaco discouraged the Nivakle from maintaining these flocks, which were difficult to keep off the Mennonite farms. The Nivakle were, therefore, forced to rely on the Mennonites for wage labour, of which there was not enough for all. Meanwhile, the patriarchal Mennonites dealt only with male Nivakle and paid only the men, damaging what had traditionally been a very egalitarian relationship between men and women in Nivakle society.

The Nivakle had traditionally spaced their children through the practice of abortion. They also believed that a nursing mother who had sexual intercourse would harm the soul and, therefore, cripple the body of her baby. Mothers nursed as long as they had milk and refrained from sexual intercourse. Their husbands were expected to share sex with other women who were not bound by the same retribution. The Mennonites vigorously opposed these customs, moving to stamp out abortion and to promote sexual fidelity between husband and wife. This resulted in a population increase among Nivakle and considerable anxiety as to the fate of their children, reared under conditions that threatened both their souls and their bodies.

In 1962, there was a severe drought in the Chaco. The Mennonite settlers felt obliged to retrench and to lay off many of their Nivakle labourers. But many were now totally dependent on working for the Mennonites. In the case of the Nivakle, they had lost their livestock and had acquired a larger number of mouths to feed (Loewen, 1964).

Increase in the aspiration-achievement gap   Rapid social change widens the gap between the aspirations of an individual or group and the ability to achieve new goals, particularly since traditional ways to achieve goals are often disrupted. During disruption due to development, the normal resources for the support and maintenance of institutions with the tribal group cannot operate effectively, because the entire population must meet added demands for adjustment. At the same time, the social and maintenance mechanisms of the dominant society are largely inappropriate for the tribe's needs. Encouragement of achievements or goals that are unrealistic or unattainable within the traditional value system will further widen this aspiration-achievement gap.

CULTURAL AUTONOMY

The prerequisite for successful survival of a tribal group as an ethnic minority is the retention of autonomy: cultural, social, economic. This freedom of choice involves continued control by the tribal people over their own institutions: tribal customs, beliefs, language, and means of subsistence or production.

Economic development has often been promoted at the expense of tribal institutions. Development strategies often tacitly assumed that there were no viable institutions or practices existing in the tribal culture that could be used to foster development. This "vacuum ideology" has led to the large-scale transfer of national structures or practices to tribal cultures that were little understood (Colletta, 1977). The primary example of this is the spread of Western technology and schooling throughout the non-Western world by colonial warders. While contact with nationals will inevitably bring some change in tribal practices and attitudes, prevailing basic customs and traditions need not be drastically altered or eliminated. Furthermore, the tribe alone should choose which traditions should be altered. Retention of tribal customs enhances maintenance of ethnic identity, stability as a productive unit, and, more importantly, successful adaptation to new circumstances. One reason, for instance, why the Balinese have been relatively impervious to outside influence is that they have maintained their cultural integrity, will not admit non-Balinese as members of their communities, and have adopted changes that reinforce their culture.

Policy of Cultural Autonomy

The policies usually adopted concerning the degree of social change that is to occur within tribal groups range widely. The two extremes are: total enforced isolation of the tribal groups allowing no change, on the one hand, all the way through rapid and complete assimilation resulting in the loss of the tribe's identity, on the other. Isolation should be rejected as impossible: a zoo-like arrangement of an enforced primitive state. Complete assimilation into the national society denies, then extinguishes, ethnic diversity. Furthermore, as noted earlier, rapid change can separate tribal people from their cultural identity: a form of extinction.

An intermediate policy adopted by the Bank under the projects it finances is more humane, prudent and productive. This allows the retention of a large measure of tribal autonomy and cultural choice. Such a policy of self-determination emphasizes the choice of tribal groups to their own way of life and seeks, therefore, to minimize the imposition of different social or economic systems until such time as the tribal society is sufficiently robust and resilient to tolerate people so that they themselves can manage the pace and style of their own involvement with the national society. The following conditions are essential if this intermediate policy is to succeed:

1. National governments and international organizations must support rights to land used or occupied by tribal people, to their ethnic identity, and to cultural autonomy.
2. The tribe must be provided with interim safeguards that enable it to deal with unwelcome outside influences on its own land until the tribe adapts sufficiently.
3. Neither the nation nor the non-tribal neighbours should compete with the tribal society on its own lands for its resources.

The Bank adopts this intermediate policy, where appropriate, in order to assist these beleaguered societies. When these conditions are observed, not only does tribal culture survive, but the tribe becomes a productive contributor to the nation, rather than a ward of the state.

Cultural autonomy differs from the integrationist approach in several respects. First, cultural autonomy stresses the value of the tribal culture and the desirability of maintaining the culture rather than replacing it as quickly as possible with the customs and values of the dominant society. Second, cultural autonomy recognizes the potentially harmful effects of unrestrained contact between dominant culture and tribal culture, and seeks to moderate them. Third, cultural autonomy creates conditions under which the tribal members themselves control the pace and manner of their admustment to national society and culture. Finally, cultural autonomy does not preclude the training of selected tribal representatives in the dominant culture and their role as mediators with the latter—provided controls by the tribe are designed to prevent abuse of authority by the dominant society.

Desired Outcome

Action to guarantee the physical survival of tribal populations and encourage freedom of cultural choice is directed towards the following outcome:

1. A tribal population that forms a recognized and accepted ethnic minority—one component of an ethnically pluralistic national society.

2. As such, this ethnic minority maintains its traditional way of life, more or less modified in accordance with the preferences of the tribal population itself.

3. The tribal economic system progressively evolves from "precontact" subsistence to a sustained-yield agro-ecosystem with the production of a surplus on occasion.

Immediate integration of tribal populations can only swell the numbers of the rural and urban poor. Since developing countries already face enormous problems in their attempts to eliminate poverty, adding to the numbers of the poor by dispossessing tribal societies only worsens their situation. This is ameliorated by maintaining ethnic minorities as viable and productive societies, and by retaining their cultural autonomy. This policy will be facilitated by recognizing the need for a pluralistic view of national identity and an understanding that cultural or ethnic diversity is desirable. Then, tribal peoples will belong to societies as fully participatory and productive components.

Given the fundamental importance of economic patterns in all cultures, and considering the extreme contrasts between tribal and national economies, the economic interaction of tribal cultures with the national market economies is a critical one.

A tribal culture may surrender part of its political autonomy, but can still continue to be ethnically distinct if it is allowed to retain its economy and if it remains unexploited by outsiders (Bodley, 1975).

Appendix 1
The World Bank and
Involuntary Resettlement

The Bank tries to avoid involuntary resettlement whenever feasible. Where relocation is unavoidable (for instance, in the case of large construction projects, such as dams, irrigation schemes, ports and airports, new towns and highways), a well-prepared resettlement plan should be drawn up in accordance with principles that leave room for considerable flexibility in the solutions and implementation that are most suitable in any particular case. Where only a few people are to be relocated, appropriate compensation for assets, coupled with arrangements for removal and a relocation grant may suffice. In the case of large numbers of people, or whole communities, the resettlement plan would include compensation as one principal element, as well as relocation and establishment in a new area, or integration with existing communities in an already settled area. The major objective is to ensure that settlers are afforded opportunities to become established and economically self-sustaining in the shortest possible period at living standards that match those before resettlement; that the settlers' social and cultural institutions are supported and their own initiative is encouraged; and that the new areas should be those in which the skills and aptitudes of the involuntary settlers can be readily employed. Important considerations include access to land, markets, employment and the provision of needed services and infrastructure in the new area. Careful preparatory work with the involuntary settlers, the host community, and their respective leaders prior to the move is of primary importance.

REFERENCES

Bodley, J. 1975. *Victims of Progress*. Menlo Park, Calif.: Cummings.

Colletta, N. J. 1977. Folk Culture and Development. *International Journal of Adult Education* 10: (2).

Dostal, W. (Ed). 1972. *The Situation of the Indian in South America*. World Council of Churches, Geneva.

Maybury-Lewis, D. 1968. *The Savage and the Innocent*. Beacon, Boston.

Price, D. 1977. Acculturation, Social Assistance and Political Context. Proceedings, 42nd International Congress of Americanists (603–9).

Rocamora, J. 1975. *Rural Development Strategies*. Ateneo de Manila University, Institute of Philippine Culture.

Rocamora, J. 1979. The Political Uses of PANAMIN. S.E. Asia Chronicle 6–7: (11–21).

Seeger, A. 1981. *Nature and Society in Central Brazil*. Harvard University Press, Cambridge.

South East Asia Resource Center. 1979. *Tribal People and the Marcos Regime*. Berkeley, California.

38 The World Bank Tribal Policy: Criticisms and Recommendations

JOHN H. BODLEY

Recognition by the World Bank that large-scale development programs may harm tribal peoples is certainly a major step forward. However, acknowledging the existence of the problem and identifying its causes do not mean that it can be easily solved. The following selection is a detailed critique of the basic assumptions implied by the full-length background document *Tribal Peoples and Economic Development* prepared by Robert Goodland and published by the World Bank in 1982 (the preceding selection is condensed from the much longer original). According to World Bank officials, the document represents Goodland's views and interpretations and does not necessarily reflect World Bank policy. Actual policy is worked out in specific cases. The World Bank makes loans to governments; it cannot of course interfere directly in internal political affairs. Therefore, it cannot support the autonomy or "sovereignty" movements of tribal peoples in opposition to national governments. It is not surprising that the document appears to equivocate on the meaning of autonomy. Likewise, stressing essentially nonnegotiable cultural differences between tribals and national societies might suggest that development goals might not be attainable. Thus, there is no emphasis on the unique qualities of tribals, since the World Bank is clearly pro-"development."

In 1983 a draft of this paper was submitted to Goodland at the World Bank for his comments. Later in 1983 it was presented at special symposiums on tribal rights at the 53rd Annual Meeting of the Australia and New Zealand Association for the Advancement of Science in Perth, Australia, and at the 11th International Congress of Anthropological and Ethnological Sciences in Vancouver, Canada. The paper was also included with testimony on the World Bank presented by the National Congress of American Indians (NCAI) to the U.S. House of Representatives Committee on Banking, Finance, and Urban Affairs, Subcommittee on International Development, Institutions, and Finance, which held special hearings on the World Bank on June 29, 1983 (Congressional Record, Serial No. 98-37, pp. 515–21). In their testimony before the congressional committee, representatives of the NCAI emphasized that there was a "fundamental conflict over development goals" between the World Bank and indigenous peoples that was obscured by the tone of the "background paper" in question. The NCAI recommended that multilateral funding agents such as the World Bank not support projects that might adversely impact indigenous people unless the latter groups granted consent through "a process of internationally supervised negotiations to which all parties agree."

Paper prepared for the "Anthropology and Indigenous Movements" session sponsored by the International Work Group for Indigenous Affairs at the 11th International Congress of Anthropological and Ethnological Sciences, Vancouver, Canada, August 21, 1983.

Bodley obtained a Ph.D. in anthropology from the University of Oregon and has been a member of the Department of Anthropology at Washington State University since 1970. His primary fieldwork was in the Peruvian Amazon with the Campa (Ashaninka) and Shipibo Indians beginning in 1964.

The official policy statement of the World Bank "Tribal Peoples and Economic Development" (Goodland 1982) is intended to minimize the adverse impact on tribal peoples that might be caused by World Bank–funded development projects. However, this humanistic objective may actually not be so easily realized. The policy as it now stands contains serious contradictions and represents a single philosophical approach that may not always provide the best defense for tribal peoples. Furthermore, this policy would preclude alternative approaches that might in many cases be more appropriate. One of the most serious problems with the World Bank policy is that it does not allow tribal peoples the option of rejecting a threatening development project. At the same time the policy takes a dangerously optimistic view of the benefits of such projects for tribal peoples and of the feasibility of safeguarding tribal cultures after a project has been initiated.

The issues that the bank is addressing are extremely important because national development projects constitute one of the most serious threats to the continued survival and well-being of tribal peoples and cultures throughout the world. Although the bank's concern with these issues is certainly appropriate and timely, in my view the present policy statement is inadequate and in need of major revision. My specific criticisms and recommendations follow.

BASIC ASSUMPTIONS UNDERLYING BANK POLICY

The following questionable assumptions appear to provide the philosophical basis of the World Bank's tribal policy:

1. All tribals will inevitably be developed.
2. Development will benefit tribal peoples.
3. Tribals will be allowed a choice.
4. Tribals must become ethnic minorities.

Some of these assumptions represent nineteenth-century colonial approaches toward tribal peoples that conflict with both the spirit and the letter of U.N. declarations on human rights and various international resolutions. Other assumptions seriously misrepresent the complexity of the development process as it relates to tribal peoples and cultures. In the following sections I will examine each assumption, showing where the bank policy represents it and why it should be rejected or modified.

THE INEVITABILITY ARGUMENT

The first assumption of the World Bank policy is what I have elsewhere called the "inevitability argument" (Bodley 1977:34–36). It is expressed clearly on page 1 of the policy, as follows: "Assuming that tribal cultures will either acculturate or disappear . . ." This phrase is strikingly reminiscent of the words of Herman Merivale (1861:510), the English expert on colonial policy, who declared in the mid-nineteenth century, "Native races must in every instance either perish, or be amalgamated with the general population of their country." Implicit in this is the notion that industrial civilization is superior and has a moral right to incorporate what it considers to be obsolete cultural systems. The World Bank explicitly states that "tribal populations cannot continue to be left out of the mainstream of development" (Goodland 1982:3), but we are not told why this is the case.

There are many serious problems with this assumption. In the first place it confuses changes in general level of cultural complexity, such as from tribe to state, with the adaptation of specific cultures to specific environments. The first kind of change matches what Sahlins (1960) labeled general evolution. There does seem to be an inherent inevitability in the direction of general evolutionary changes, but there certainly is no inevitability that all cultures will go through these changes. Actually, the archaeological record provides ample evidence of great cultural stability for tribal cultures that have adapted to specific local environments (the specific evolution of Sahlins). Australian aborigines, for example, maintained a basically tribal way of life for 50,000 years or more before the British colonial intrusion in the late eighteenth century.

The point is that the incorporation of tribal peoples into national economies is the result of the expansionist policies of industrial states, not an inevitable process initiated by tribal cultures. The real danger is that if the inevitability assumption becomes the basis of World Bank policy it will be self-fulfilling and will preclude the possibility of tribal independence.

THE BENEFITS OF DEVELOPMENT

The World Bank clearly assumes that development projects can be designed to both protect tribal cultures and bring them the "benefits of civilization." The policy refuses to recognize that tribal cultures may be so different from national market societies that forced development will unavoidably destroy their most important features. The bank acknowledges that in the past national development projects have invariably harmed tribal peoples, but it prefers to blame these failures on inadequate planning (Goodland 1982:3).

The problem with this assumption is that it does not start with a clear concept of what tribal cultures are like. The bank describes tribals as ethnically distinct, small, isolated, nonliterate, unacculturated, cashless, impoverished ("the poorest of the poor") groups, dependent on local environments. The effects of development can be better evaluated if we emphasize that tribal cultures are economically self-sufficient, egalitarian systems that are designed to satisfy basic human needs on a sustained basis. They are politically sovereign, small-scale societies that control their natural resources on a local, communal basis and manage them for long-term sustained yield.

It must be emphasized that the kind of large-scale development projects that the World Bank would normally fund would take away the political autonomy of tribes and undermine their economic self-sufficiency by imposing national political authority and forcing them into the market economy. These changes would in turn undermine social equality and make local management of tribal resources for sustained yield difficult, if not impossible. In the end tribal peoples often do become impoverished by development while only a few benefit.

DEVELOPMENT CHOICES

The assumption that tribal peoples can make free and informed development choices is presented as a fundamental principle of bank policy. For example, the paper declares that the bank will not support a project unless "it is satisfied that best efforts have been made to obtain the voluntary, full, and conscionable agreement . . . . of the tribal people" (Goodland 1981:1).

The problem with this is that the actual procedures for obtaining consent are not outlined, and it is clear that there will actually be many cases in which the bank will fund projects that tribal peoples oppose. Furthermore, the bank refers to its procedures for "involuntary resettlement" (Goodland 1982:20) for those cases in which tribals resist development.

It should also be clear that while the bank officially endorses what it calls "cultural autonomy" (Goodland 1982:28) and "freedom of choice" (1982:27) for tribals, the bank's policy of cultural autonomy is very different from the "cultural autonomy alternative" that I have advocated earlier (Bodley 1975:168–169, 1977:43–46). The bank's version of cultural autonomy superficially resembles my own and even borrows some of my wording, but the bank deletes local political sovereignty of tribal peoples and would allow them only temporary control over access to tribal land. These are such critical issues for the future well-being of tribal peoples that the two versions of "cultural autonomy" deserve to be compared in detail; they are quoted below to highlight the differences:

World Bank

1. National governments and international organizations must support rights to land used or occupied by tribal people, to their ethnic identity, and to cultural autonomy.
2. The tribe must be provided with interim safeguards that enable it to deal with unwelcome outside influences on its own land until the tribe adapts sufficiently (Goodland 1982:28).

Bodley

1. National governments and international organizations must recognize and support tribal rights to their traditional land, cultural autonomy, and full local sovereignty.
2. The responsibility for initiating outside contacts must rest with the tribal peoples themselves: outside influences may not have free access to tribal areas (Bodley 1975:168–169, 1977:43–46).

Significantly, the form of cultural autonomy that I advocated corresponds closely to the position consistently taken by tribal political spokesmen over the past decade throughout the world.

A further difficulty with the World Bank policy of "free and informed" choice is that tribal peoples may not always be "informed" about the long-range consequences of projects. This is particularly the case when many consequences can not be adequately foreseen by the project planners themselves. This point is specifically acknowledged by the bank, but the policy suggests that careful planning will minimize unforeseen consequences. In my view this is dangerous optimism serving only the short-term interests of those who will immediately benefit from the implementation of development projects.

ETHNIC IDENTITY OR TRIBAL CULTURE?

The explicitly stated objective of the bank policy is for tribal peoples to become "recognized and accepted ethnic minorities" (Goodland 1982:28), and to "minimize the imposition of different social or economic systems until such time as the tribal society is sufficiently robust and resilient to tolerate the effects of change" (Goodland 1982:27). The substitution of "ethnicity" for an autonomous, self-sufficient tribal way of life is really at the very heart of the World Bank policy. It should be made very clear that although this approach may prevent large-scale depopulation as tribal areas are developed, and although some vestige of tribal identity may be maintained, unique cultural systems will still be destroyed. Replacing tribal culture with ethnic identity by forcing development on unwilling recipients is in direct opposition to Article 21 of the U.N. Declaration on Racism and Racial Discrimination of 1978, and it clearly opposes the spirit of the U.N. 1948 Declaration of Human Rights.

I must clearly disassociate myself from this approach because the bank policy concludes with a paraphrased quote attributed to me that suggests that I endorse the bank policy of turning tribal peoples into ethnic minorities, whereas I see this as one of the least desirable alternatives. Again, the two passages are placed side by side to highlight the differences. A tribal culture

> . . . can continue to be ethnically distinct if it is allowed to retain its economy and if it remains unexploited by outsiders (Goodland 1982:29).

. . . can still continue to be an essentially primitive culture if it is allowed to retain its self-sufficient, subsistence economy and if it remains unexploited by outsiders (Bodley 1975:125).

The difference between an "ethnically distinct" culture and a primitive or tribal culture is critical, as is the distinction between an economy and an economy that is a specifically tribal economy. The U.N. Declaration on Racism and Racial Discrimination of 1978 specifically endorses

the right of indigenous peoples to maintain their traditional structure of economy and culture . . . and stresses that their land, land rights and natural resources should not be taken away from them (Article 21).

The World Bank policy would grant tribal peoples an economy and an ethnic identity, but not necessarily their traditional tribal economy and traditional culture. This position has a certain logic, because the World Bank also rejects the retention of local political sovereignty by tribal peoples. Without local autonomy a traditional tribal economy and culture cannot be maintained in the face of an intruding national society because tribal lands and resources will not be secure.

ALTERNATIVE POLICY APPROACHES

The basic aim of the World Bank tribal policy is clearly to accommodate tribal peoples to national development goals while minimizing deleterious side effects. This is a reasonable objective where disruptive development programs are irrevocably underway, but it is certainly not the only approach. Furthermore, it is inappropriate for an organization such as the World Bank, which is in a position to shape development policies through its funding decisions, to take this approach exclusively. Other viable alternative policy approaches should not be precluded when projects are still in the planning stage. Alternative approaches would include helping tribal peoples who are already partially integrated with the national society to mobilize themselves politically in defense of their basic right to maintain their way of life. This would of course mean supporting local tribal political autonomy and tribal control of natural resources, and it could delay or divert specific development projects. This is no doubt the reason that the World Bank rejects such an alternative, but if there is no real intent to respect tribal rights, then the bank policy should not pretend otherwise.

CONCLUSION

In conclusion I will list my main arguments against the underlying assumptions of the World Bank policy, and I will include several specific recommendations for revisions in the policy.

1. *The inevitability of development*   The incorporation of tribal peoples into national economies with the loss of tribal self-sufficiency results from specific national development policies. It is not a "natural, inevitable process" that cannot be avoided.

2. *The benefits of development*   Development policies that weaken the political autonomy of tribal peoples and reduce tribal control over resources will almost certainly lead to detribalization and resource depletion.

3. *Development choices*   The World Bank policy does not ensure freedom of choice for tribal peoples, and they should not be asked to approve development projects when the long-range consequences for them cannot be adequately foreseen by project planners.

4. *Ethnic identity or tribal culture?*   The preservation of ethnic identity and the creation of "successful ethnic minorities" should not be equated with the defense of tribal cultures and may not always be the best alternative in a given development context.

Recommendations

1. The World Bank should not fund projects that would disturb or displace isolated, fully traditional tribal groups.

2. The World Bank tribal policy should include a full discussion of how the "choice" process can be implemented for partly integrated tribal peoples. There must be mechanisms that will allow tribal peoples to reject threatening projects and to negotiate specific details of projects as they affect them.

3. The World Bank should not fund projects that do not include specific provisions granting tribals a political voice in national decisions affecting them and retention of full communal control over their traditional resource base.

4. A revised World Bank tribal policy should be subjected to critical review by a panel of tribal political leaders from throughout the world and by other recognized authorities representing a wide range of viewpoints.

REFERENCES

Bodley, John H. 1975. *Victims of progress.* Menlo Park, Calif.: Cummings.

———. (1977). Alternatives to ethnocide: Human zoos, living museums, and real people. *Western expansion and indigenous peoples,* ed. Elias Sevilla-Casas, 31–50. The Hague and Paris: Mouton.

———. 1982. *Victims of progress.* 2d ed. Palo Alto, Calif: Mayfield.

Goodland, Robert. 1982. *Tribal peoples and economic development: Human ecologic considerations.* Washington, D.C.: World Bank.

Merivale, Herman. 1861. *Lectures on colonization and colonies*. London: Green, Longman & Roberts.

Sahlins, Marshall. 1960. Evolution: Specific and general. In *Evolution and culture*, ed. Marshall Sahlins and Elman Service, 12–44. Ann Arbor: University of Michigan Press.

39   Resolution for a Regional Autonomous Government in the Cordillera

CORDILLERA PEOPLE'S ALLIANCE

The following resolution calls for autonomy for the Igorot tribal areas of northern Luzon in the Philippines. It was written by the Cordillera People's Alliance in March 1986 immediately after the fall of the Marcos government and circulated in the tribal areas as a petition for popular endorsement. It is the autonomy position presented by tribal delegates to the Aquino-appointed commission for the new Philippine constitution. The Cordillera People's Alliance is a political organization of tribal Filipinos, formed in 1984 by more than 300 representatives of 23 local tribal organizations from throughout the mountains of Luzon. *Kaigorotan* means "united Igorot people."

We, the indigenous people of the Cordillera, assert our right as national minorities to genuine regional autonomy within a democratic and sovereign Filipino nation.

We welcome the new government of President Corazon Aquino—a President who governs with popular mandate, and who has committed herself to the goals of liberty and social justice for all Filipinos.

We are Filipinos. With all other Filipinos, we share the responsibility of keeping vigilant watch over the democratic gains made with the people's overthrow of the old, tyrannical regime. With all other Filipinos, we share the burden of laboring to build a nation fully independent from foreign domination, a society governed by a truly just order.

We are Filipinos, and claim the right to be heard in equality with all other Filipinos.

No previous government of the Philippines has treated us with fairness, or with proper regard for our human rights as individuals and as communities.

State laws and structures have denied us any real say in the management, disposition, and actual use of the land and resources within our native territories. Government consent and collaboration, even government initiative, have been responsible for the grabbing of thousands of hectares of our ancestral land. Now, big corporations plunder our mountains' mineral wealth. Now, logging concessionaires ravage our forests. Fields once productive are now submerged in the dammed waters of Ambuclao, Binga, and Magat, or are now lying idle in barely used resort parks and over-sized state installations.

Meanwhile, many of us who have been displaced remain unjustly compensated for our losses. Others among us are denied free access to our own forests and mineral land. In plains areas of our homeland there are those among us who have been reduced to the status of tenants. In the vegetable growing areas, there are those among us who are now mere hired workers. Those of us who have been pushed by marginalized conditions in the countryside are now regarded as squatters in the city.

Much of the wealth of our ancestral domain has been appropriated by a privileged few, most of whom are even outsiders. Meanwhile, the majority of us are regarded as illegal occupants of so called public land.

Yet, this entire Cordillera has been the home of our families, clans, communities, and tribes for generations—our territorial ownership.

Our indigenous system of organizing ourselves and administering our own affairs has likewise been disregarded. No government or constitution of the Philippines has yet recognized the structures and institutions that our various ethno-linguistic groups have evolved through generations of self-government. We have our own democratic systems of settling disputes, of judging and punishing wrongdoers, of communities, and tribes. In place of these are imposed on us systems that are alien, less democratic, and often ineffective.

It is no wonder, then, that we are unable to effectively protect our interests and assert our rights as persons and as a people. We are thus treated as second-class citizens in our own country. Past governments of the Philippines have made no secret of endorsing such policies as those which proclaim that we "the minority must sacrifice for the benefit of the majority."

Even our indigenous culture has been trampled upon. State and business enterprise have capitalized on our customs, rituals, and artistic skills and traditions to boost our dollar earnings. The institutions of mass media have been allowed to misinterpret us and spread discriminatory notions about our peoples. Worse, educational and religious institutions have taught our children to regard their ancestors' way of life as an oddity. By doing so, these institutions have contributed to our youth's gradual estrangement from their own people.

Unable to endure these conditions, we have time and again risen in protest. Resistance has taught us to develop new kinds of people's organizations, and strengthen our already existing organs of popular power. In the struggle to defend people and homeland, many among us have even taken up arms.

State response to our growing unrest has been standard: repression and militarization. Instead of heeding our demands, the past regime has tried to silence us. Hundreds of our people have been arrested, detained, even tortured; many have been executed. Villages, entire municipalities have been placed in a stage of seige. Up to now, many of our families remain hamletted in reconcentration areas far from their farms and homes.

Repression, however, has only succeeded in alienating more and more of us from government. It has failed to silence us; it has not broken our peoples' will.

Long years of suffering and struggle have, in fact, strengthened us. We are now conscious of the rights that have been denied us, and of the power that we, as one unified people, can wield.

As one kaigorotan, we the people of the Cordillera, are now more prepared to partake in the effort of restructuring Philippine society from the ruins of past regimes. As we do so, however, we cannot see to our own concerns as national minorities.

We, Kaigorotan, therefore resolve to work for the establishment of a regional autonomous government in our homeland. Only within the framework of genuine regional autonomy can we effectively assert and defend our rights as a distinct people.

We envision a regional autonomous government that shall, in general:

1. Have jurisdiction over our entire ancestral domain, which shall be defined to include all contiguous areas occupied and used by our people: the provinces of Kalinga-Apayao, Mountain Province, Ifugao, Benguet; the City of Baguio; the Tinggian Areas of Abra; all boundary areas which are occupied and used by our people, but which have been arbitrarily added or incorporated into adjacent lowland municipalities and/or provinces;

2. Be responsible for safeguarding our inalienable and primary right as an indigenous people to our ancestral domain, and thus our ancestral proprietary right to the management, disposition, and utilization of its land and resources;

3. Be our venue for asserting and defending our economic, social, cultural, and political rights as national minorities;

4. Be controlled by our own people, through such representative organs as may conform with or be evolved from our various existing indigenous sociopolitical structures and institutions;

5. Be governed, at the local level, according to existing custom law,

and, at the regional level, according to a Cordillera Charter drafted by a duly constituted Cordillera legislature and ratified by our people. This Charter shall define the relations of the Cordillera autonomous region with the national government of the Philippines;

6. Have the right to demand from the national government of the Philippine Republic rectification of and/or restitution for all past violations of our human rights as persons and as a people.

Additional Readings

GENERAL PERSPECTIVES

Bodley, John H. 1982. *Victims of Progress*. Palo Alto, Calif.: Mayfield.

Cultural Survival Quarterly. Cambridge, Mass.: Cultural Survival.

Fagan, Brian M. 1984. *Clash of Cultures*. New York: Freeman.

Goodland, Robert. 1982. *Tribal Peoples and Economic Development: Human Ecologic Considerations*. Washington, D.C.: World Bank.

IWGIA Newsletter. Copenhagen: International Work Group for Indigenous Affairs.

Wolf, Eric R. 1982. *Europe and the People without History*. Berkeley: University of California Press.

PART I
QUALITY OF TRIBAL LIFE

Altman, J.C. 1984. Hunter-gatherer subsistence production in Arnhem Land: The original affluence hypothesis reconsidered. *Mankind* 14, no. 3: 179–90.

Colchester, Marcus. 1984. Rethinking Stone Age economics: Some speculations concerning the pre-Columbian Yanoama economy. *Human Ecology* 12, no. 3, 291–314.

Colson, Elizabeth. 1979. In good years and in bad: Food strategies of self-reliant societies. *Journal of Anthropological Research* 35, no. 1: 18–29.

Dyson-Hudson, Rada and Neville. 1969. Subsistence herding in Uganda. *Scientific American* 220, no. 2: 76–89.

Guenther, Mathias Georg. 1980. From "brutal savages" to "harmless people": Notes on the changing Western image of the Bushman. *Paideuma* 26: 123–40.

Larrick, James W., et al. 1979. Patterns of health and disease among the Waorani Indians of eastern Ecuador. *Medical Anthropology* 3, no. 2: 147–89.

Polunin, Ivan. 1977. Some characteristics of tribal peoples. In *Health and Disease in tribal societies*, 5–20. Ciba Foundation Symposium 49.

Sahlins, Marhall. 1972. The original affluent society. In *Stone Age economics*, 1–39. Chicago: Aldine.

Woodburn, James. 1968. An introduction to Hadza ecology. In *Man the Hunter*, ed. R.B. Lee and I. Devoe, 49–55; 103–110. Chicago: Aldine.

PART II
FIRST CONTACTS: THE LOSS OF AUTONOMY

Jennes, Diamond. 1921. The cultural transformation of the Copper Eskimo. *Geographical Review* 11, no. 4: 541–50.

Fitzhugh, William W., ed. 1985. *Cultures in contact: The impact of European contact on Native American cultural institutions, A.D. 1000–1800.* Washington, D.C.: Smithsonian Institute Press.

Mann, R.S. 1973. Jarawas of Andaman: An analysis of hostility. *Man in India* 53, no. 2: 201–20.

Rodman, Margaret, and Matthew Cooper. 1979. The pacification of Melanesia. Monograph No. 7, Association for Social Anthropology in Oceania. Honolulu: University Press of Hawaii.

Stefansson, Vilhjalmur. 1912. The Eskimo and civilization. *The American Museum Journal* 12, no. 6: 195–203.

PART III
THE SHOCK PHASE: ASSESSING INITIAL IMPACT

Fagan, Brian M. 1984. *Clash of Cultures.* New York: Freeman.

Lewis, Norman. 1970. Brazil's dead Indians: The killing of an unwanted race. *Atlas* (January):22–29.

Ribeiro, Darcy. 1967. Indigenous cultures and languages of Brazil. In *Indians of Brazil in the twentieth century,* ed. Janice H. Hopper, 77–165. Washington, D.C.: Institute for Cross-Cultural Research.

Thurnwald, Richard C. 1936. The price of the white man's peace. *Pacific Affairs* 9, no. 3: 347–57.

PART IV
INTERVENTION PHILOSOPHY

Aaby, Peter. 1977. What are we fighting for? "Progress" or "cultural autonomy"? In *Cultural Imperialism and Cultural Identity,* ed. Carola Sandbacka, 61–76. Transactions of the Finnish Anthropological Society, no. 2, Helsinki.

Hanlon, David. 1984. God versus gods: The first years of the Micronesian mission on Ponape, 1852–1859. *The Journal of Pacific History* 19, no. 1: 41–59.

Hippler, Arthur E. 1977. Cultural evolution: Some hypotheses concerning the significance of cognitive and affective interpenetration during latency. *Journal of Psychohistory* 4, no. 4: 419–60.

———. 1979. Comments on 'Causality among cross-cultural correlations' by Janet Reis and 'Ideological bias' by Walter Precourt. *Behavior Science Research* 14, no. 4: 293–96.

Hvalkof, Soren, and Peter Aaby. 1981. No tobacco, no hallelujah. In *Is God An American?* 173–86. Copenhagen: IWGIA.

Nida, Eugene A. 1954. In defense of missionaries. In *Customs and Cultures,* 253–55. New York: Harper.

Stipe, Claude E. 1980. Anthropologists versus missionaries: The influence of presuppositions. *Current Anthropology* 21, no. 2: 165–80.

Turner, Terence S. 1979. Anthropology and the politics of indigenous peoples' struggles. *Cambridge Anthropology* 5, no. 1: 1–43.

Wise, Mary Ruth, Eugene E. Loos, and Patricia Davis. 1977. Filosofia y metodos del Instituto Linguistico de Verano. *Proceedings of the International Congress of Americanists* 42, no. 4: 499–525.

PART V
TRIBALS AND CONTEMPORARY DEVELOPMENT POLICY

America Indigena 44, no. 1. 1984. (Special issue, Misiones y pueblos indigenas/ Missions and indigenous peoples.)

Anti-Slavery Society. 1983. The Philippines: The power generation programme and the national minorities. *Indigenous Peoples and Development* Series 1:91–119.

Arhem, Kaj. 1985. The Maasai and the state: The impact of rural development policies on a pastoral people in Tanzania. Document 52. Copenhagen: IWGIA.

Cooke, H.J. 1985. The Kalahari today: A case of conflict over resource use. *Geographical Journal* 151, no. 1: 239–56.

Cultural Survival Newsletter. Cambridge, Mass.: Cultural Survival.

Davis, Shelton H. 1977. *Victims of the miracle: Development and the Indians of Brazil.* Cambridge: Cambridge University Press.

Franke, Richard W. 1984. Tuareg of West Africa: Five experiments in Fourth World development. *Antipode* 16, no. 2: 45–53.

Gross, Daniel R. 1982. The Indians and the Brazilian frontier. *Journal of International Affairs* 36, no. 1: 1–14.

Henningsgaard, William. 1981. The Akawaio, the Upper Mazaruni Hydroelectric Project and national development in Guyana. Occasional Paper 4. Cambridge, Mass.: Cultural Survival.

Howell, P. P. 1983. The impact of the Jonglei Canal in the Sudan. *Geographical Journal* 149, no. 3: 286–300.

Jojola, Theodore. 1984. The conflicting role of national governments in the tribal development process: Two case studies. *Antipode* 16, no. 2: 19–26.

Narby, Jeremy, and Shelton Davis. 1983. *Resource development and indigenous peoples: A comparative bibliography.* Boston, Mass.: Anthropology Resource Center.

Peterson, Nicolas, ed. 1981. *Aboriginal land rights: A handbook.* Canberra: Australian Institute of Aboriginal Studies.

Price, David. 1982. A reservation for the Nambiquara. In *Involuntary migration and resettlement*, ed. Art Hansen and Anthony Oliver Smith, 179–200. Boulder, Colo.: Westview Press.

Swift, Jeremy. 1982. The future of African hunter-gatherer and pastoral peoples. *Development and Change* 13, no. 2: 159–81.

PART VI
DEVELOPMENT, TRIBAL SOCIETY, AND HEALTH

Bijlmer, H.J.T. 1953a. The influence of Western contact on primitive peoples in Indonesia and the Pacific, more especially from a medical point of view. *Proceedings of the Seventh Pacific Science Congress*, 7, (1949): 118–31.

Brookfield, Harold. 1973. Full circle in Chimbu: A study of trends and cycles. In *The Pacific in Transition*, 127–60. New York: St. Martin's Press.

Kruse, John A., Judith Kleinfeld, and Robert Travis. 1982. Energy development on Alaska's North Slope: Effects on the Inupiat population. *Human Organization* 41, no. 2: 97–106.

Rode, A., and R.J. Shepard. 1984. Ten years of "civilization" and fitness of the Inuit. *Journal of Applied Physiology* 56:1472–77.

Rodman, Margaret. 1984. Masters of tradition: Customary land tenure and new forms of social inequality in a Vanuatu peasantry. *American Ethnologist* 11, no. 1: 42–60.

Sharp, Lauriston. 1965. Steel axes for Stone Age aborigines. In *Human Problems in Technological Change*, ed. Edward H. Spicer, 69–90. New York: Wiley.

Sorenson, E. Richard. 1972. Socio-ecological change among the Fore of New Guinea. *Current Anthropology* 13, nos. 3–4: 349–83.

Stoll, David. 1982. The Huaorani go to market. In *Fishers of men or founders of empire?* 278–318. Cambridge, Mass.: Cultural Survival.

Vickers, William T. 1983. Development and Amazonian Indians: The Aguarico case and some general principles. In *The Dilemma of Amazonian Development*, ed. Emilio F. Moran, 25–50. Boulder, Colo.: Westview Press.

Wirsing, Rolf L. 1985. The health of traditional societies and the effects of acculturation. *Current Anthropology* 26, no. 3: 303–18.

PART VII
HUMAN RIGHTS AND POLITICAL STRUGGLE

Antipode 16, no. 2. 1984. (Special issue, The Fourth World: A geography of indigenous struggles.)

Bennett, Gordon. 1978. Tribal and indigenous peoples' convention. Occasional Paper No. 37. London: Royal Anthropological Institute.

Berndt, Ronald M., ed. 1982. *Aboriginal sites, rights and resource development*. Perth: University of Western Australia.

Bort, John R., and Philip D. Young. 1984. Economic and political adaptations to national development among the Guaymi. *Anthropological Quarterly* 58, no. 1: 1–11.

Brosted, Jens, et al., eds. 1985. *Native power: The quest for autonomy and nationhood of indigenous peoples*. Bergen, Norway: Universitetsforlaget AS.

Dyck, Noel. 1985. *Indigenous peoples and the nation-state*. Social and Economic Paper No. 14. St. John's Newfoundland, Canada: Memorial University of Newfoundland, Institute of Social and Economic Research.

IWGIA Newsletter. Copenhagen: International Work Group for Indigenous Affairs.

Journal of International Affairs 36, no. 1. 1982. (Special issue, The human rights of indigenous peoples.

Junqueira, Carmen. 1984. The Brazilian Indian minority: Ethnocide and political consciousness. *Journal of the Anthropological Society of Oxford* 15, no. 3: 219–34.

Maddock, Kenneth. 1983. *Your land is our land: Aboriginal land rights.* Ringwood, Victoria: Penguin Books Australia Ltd.

Rocamora, Joel. 1979. The political uses of PANAMIN. *Southeast Asia Chronicle* 67:11–21.

Salazar, Ernesto. 1977. An Indian federation in lowland Ecuador. Document No. 28. Copenhagen: International Work Group for Indigenous Affairs.

PART VIII
PARKS, CONSERVATION, AND TRIBALS

Alcorn, Janis B. 1984. Development policy, forests, and peasant farms: Reflections on Huastec-managed forests' contributions to commercial production and resource conservation. *Economic Botany* 38, no. 4: 389–406.

Arvelo-Jimenez, Nelly. 1984. La reserva de biosfera Yanomami: Una autentica estrategia para el ecodesarrollo nacional. Caracas: Instituto Venezolano de Investigaciones Cientificas.

Stiles, Daniel N. 1983. Desertification and pastoral development in northern Kenya. *Nomadic Peoples* 13:1–14.

PART IX
POLICY ALTERNATIVES

Aronson, Dan. 1980. Must nomads settle: Some notes towards policy on the future of pastoralism. In *When Nomads Settle,* ed. P. Salzman. New York: Praeger.

Bijlmer, H.J.T. 1953b. Protection of native societies. *Proceedings of the Seventh Pacific Science Congress* 7(1949):131–34, 138–49.

Bodley, John H. 1977. Alternatives to ethnocide: Human zoos, living museums, and real people. In *Western Expansion and Indigenous Culture,* ed. Elias Sevilla-Casas, 31–50. The Hague: Mouton.

———. 1982. *Victims of progress.* Palo Alto, Calif.: Mayfield.

Elkin, A.P. 1934. Anthropology and the future of the Australian Aborigines. *Oceania* 5 no. 1: 1–18.

Goodland, Robert. 1982. *Tribal peoples and economic development: Human ecologic considerations.* Washington D.C.: World Bank.

Haddon, Alfred C. 1903. The saving of vanishing data. *Popular Science Monthly* 62:222–29.

Hanbury-Tenison, A.R., and P.J.K. Burton. 1973. Should the Darien Gap be closed? *Geographical Journal* 139, no. 1: 43–52.

McNeely, Jeffrey A. 1980. The people of Siberut: Indonesia's original inhabitants. In *Saving Siberut: A conservation master plan.* World Wildlife Fund Indonesia Programme. Also in *Work in Progress* 13, no. 3. Gland, Switz.: IUCN/CEP.

Mead, Margaret. 1943. The role of small South Sea cultures in the postwar world. *American Anthropologist* 45:193–97.

———. 1967. The rights of primitive peoples. *Foreign Affairs* 45:304–18.

Oswalt, Wendell H., and James W. VanStone. 1960. The future of the Caribou Eskimos. *Anthropologica* 2, no. 2: 154–76.

Smith, Richard Chase. 1977. The Amuesha-Yanachago project, Peru. Document 3. London: Survival International.

Van Arkadie, B. 1978. The future of vulnerable societies. *Development and Change* 9:161–74.

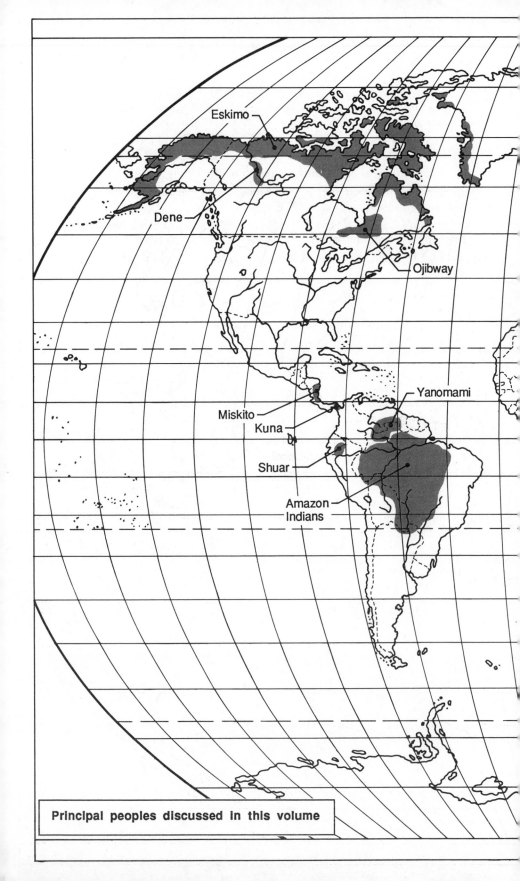

Principal peoples discussed in this volume